The Political Economy of Media and Power

PETER LANG
New York • Washington, D.C./Baltimore • Bern
Frankfurt • Berlin • Brussels • Vienna • Oxford

The Political Economy of Media and Power

EDITED BY JEFFERY KLAEHN

PETER LANG
New York • Washington, D.C./Baltimore • Bern
Frankfurt • Berlin • Brussels • Vienna • Oxford

Library of Congress Cataloging-in-Publication Data

The political economy of media and power /
edited by Jeffery Klaehn.
p. cm.
Includes bibliographical references and index.
1. Mass media—Political aspects. 2. Mass media—Social aspects.
3. Mass media—Influence. 4. Communication in politics.
I. Klaehn, Jeffery.
P95.8.P6436 302.23—dc22 2010002622
ISBN 978-1-4331-0774-0 (hardcover)
ISBN 978-1-4331-0773-3

Bibliographic information published by **Die Deutsche Nationalbibliothek.**
Die Deutsche Nationalbibliothek lists this publication in the "Deutsche Nationalbibliografie"; detailed bibliographic data is available on the Internet at http://dnb.d-nb.de/.

The paper in this book meets the guidelines for permanence and durability of the Committee on Production Guidelines for Book Longevity of the Council of Library Resources.

29 Broadway, 18th floor, New York, NY 10006
www.peterlang.com

Printed in the United States of America

Contents

Preface

With the almost daily avalanche of new books and periodicals in the communications field, selecting your reading becomes a matter of survival. One needs to make careful choices and by implication much of what our learned colleagues write remains unread. Every once in a while a publication ends up on your desk that for various reasons you seriously read. I would like to share with you an argument that should persuade you to read this collection also. It would seem that power is somewhat in disrepute these days as a crucial social scientific concept. In the field of communication research and media studies, there seem to be few, if any, younger generation scholars who follow up the critical political economy approach to the analysis of relations of power that is or was characteristic of the work of such colleagues as Graham Murdock, Peter Golding, Vincent Mosco, the late Dallas Smythe or the late Herbert Schiller. This book is put together by Jeffery Klaehn and advances an analysis of power in relation to media, exploring permanent education and cultural politics as instruments of countervailing power, the promotion of democracy as a tool of power, the manufacturing of news in support of belligerent powers, the propaganda model and its neglect, race and gender hierarchies in TV series, media criticism and resistance to media power, and public versus private broadcasting. As I am not given to underestimating the intellectual qualities of those who buy or loan this book, I will leave judgements about the individual contributions to the reader. I am rather inclined to use this opportunity to argue why the dialectic between media and power is relevant as an object of academic investigation.

Much of the influence that media have upon people's perceptions of the world and of their position in this world is determined by those who hold societal power in the sense of the capability of coercing people to do and/or believe what they otherwise would not do or believe. These are society's political and economic elites that own and/or engineer media contents. They create the political and economic frameworks within which views of the world and opinions about the world are presented to global audiences daily.

Those who hold power are in permanent need of legitimizing their actions and securing the consent of citizens or consumers. The public consent to wage war, for example, needs propaganda channels for persuasive and deceptive rhetoric. Angry power-holders are in need of platforms for their incitement to aggression. The media provide such public stages. Power needs an audience. And media in turn also need the powerful in society, as sources of news and entertainment. Media are fond of stories about strong leaders and about failing leaders. Power in glory and downfall entertains endlessly.

By and large, the world's mainstream commercial media do too little to unveil and demystify power. There is worldwide a paucity of serious investigative reporting. A special issue for investigation would be the relationship between secrecy and power. Too often the mainstream media fail to make public what power-holders prefer to keep behind closed doors. As Joseph Stiglitz argues in *Globalization and Its Discontents,* 'secrecy undermines democracy'. In democratic states, the news media have the task to take the instrument of secrecy away from power-holders so that all concerned can share responsibility for a society's future.

Media are also a potential danger to those in power as they provide discursive spaces for people's self-empowerment. Media may disempower, by censoring and limiting access to information and knowledge, by misleading and/or by educating children to want to know more about consumer practices than about democratic participation. Advertising in media teaches children more about 'pester power' than about citizen's power. However, media may also support people's self-empowerment by providing channels for expression, sharing of experiences and access to knowledge about the decisions others make that impact their lives and information relating to what they might do about such decisions.

In conclusion I would like to express my hope that this book inspires us as researchers to a new wave of critical investigations that help us as citizens to keep the exercise of power within democratic limits.

Cees J. Hamelink
Professor Emeritus, University of Amsterdam

Notes on Contributors

Stuart Allan is Professor of Journalism at Bournemouth University, UK. He is the author of *News Culture* (1999, second edition, 2004), *Media, Risk and Society* (2002) and *Online News: Journalism and the Internet* (2006). His edited collections include *Journalism after September 11* (2002) and *Reporting War: Journalism in Wartime* (2004), both co-edited with Barbie Zelizer, and *Journalism: Critical Issues* (2005). His current work focuses on the online reporting of war and conflict, with a special interest in blogging and citizen journalism.

Robin Andersen teaches Communication and Media Studies at Fordham University and is the Director of the Peace and Justice Studies Program. She has written numerous journal articles and book chapters on media issues and the influence of TV and Advertising on American society. She is the author of *Consumer Culture and TV Programming* (1995) and *A Century of Media, A Century of War* (2006), editor of *Critical Studies in Media Commercialism* (2000) and co-editor, with Jonathan Gray, of *Battleground: The Media* (2007). She is frequently interviewed as an expert source on media issues for radio, television and newspaper reporting. She is also featured in numerous educational documentaries.

Joel Bakan writes and researches in the areas of Constitutional Law, sociolegal studies, legal theory and economic law. He studied at Oxford University as a Rhodes Scholar and served as Law Clerk in 1985 for Chief Justice Brian

Dickson of the Supreme Court of Canada. He joined the Law Faculty in 1990 as Associate Professor after a year's visit from Osgoode Hall Law School, where he had been Assistant Professor since 1987. Professor Bakan teaches Constitutional Law, Contracts, sociolegal courses and the graduate seminar. He has won the Faculty of Law's Teaching Excellence Award twice and a UBC Killam Research Prize. He is also the author of *The Corporation: The Pathological Pursuit of Profit and Power* (2004).

David Berry is Senior Lecturer in Journalism and Media Communication at Southampton Solent University, England. His books include *Ethics and Media Culture: Practices and Representations* (2000) (ed.), *The Romanian Mass Media and Cultural Development* (2004), *Radical Mass Media Criticism: A Cultural Genealogy* (2006) (co-ed.) and *Journalism, Ethics and Society* (2008). David is also founding member and editor of *Fifth-Estate-Online:* The *International Journal of Radical Mass Media Criticism* (www.fifth-estate-online.co.uk).

Roger Clark is former Secretary General of Amnesty International.

Mélanie Claude is a PhD student at the department of sociology and anthropology of the University of Ottawa. She has collaborated with Nicole LaViolette and Richard Poulin the collective book, *Prostitution et traite des êtres humains, enjeux nationaux et internationaux*, Ottawa, L'Interligne(forthcoming) and collaborated to Richard Poulin's essay, *Les jeunes, la pornographie, l'hypersexualisation. Enfances dévastées, tome II,* Ottawa, L'Interligne, 2008.

David Cromwell is an oceanographer and writer from Glasgow, co-founder (with David Edwards) of MediaLens, author of *Private Planet* and co-author, with David Edwards, of *Guardians of Power* (2006).

William Dinan is Lecturer in Sociology at the University of Strathclyde in Glasgow, Scotland. He is a co-founder of Spinwatch.org, a website publishing public interest reporting on spin, deception and lobbying and he is on the steering committee of the Alliance for Lobbying Transparency and Ethics Regulation in Europe (ALTER EU). Recent publications include: *A Century of Spin: How Public Relations Became the Cutting Edge of Corporate Power* (2008) and *Thinker, Faker, Spinner, Spy: Corporate PR and the Assault on Democracy* (2007), both co-edited with David Miller.

Daniel Fischlin and **Martha Nandorfy** are co-authors of the groundbreaking book *Eduardo Galeano: Through the Looking Glass.* Fischlin is also co-author with Ajay Heble of *Rebel Music: Human Rights, Resistant Sounds, and the Politics of Making Music*, in which Nandorfy is a contributor. Both teach at the University of Guelph (Ontario, Canada).

Henry Giroux holds the Global TV Network Chair in English and Cultural Studies at McMaster University in Canada. He is on the editorial and advisory boards of numerous national and international scholarly journals. His most recent books include *America on the Edge* (2006), *Beyond the Spectacle of Terrorism* (2006), Stormy *Weather: Katrina and the Politics of Disposability* (2006), *The University in Chains: Confronting the Military-Industrial-Academic Complex* (2007), *Against the Terror of Neo-liberalism: Politics Beyond the Age of Greed* (2008).

Sylvia Hale is Professor and Chair of the Department of Sociology at St. Thomas University. Her major publications include the widely influential *Controversies in Sociology* textbook (Copp Clark, 1995) as well as *The Elusive Promise: The Struggle of Women Development Workers in Rural North India (McGill University, 1987). She is also an award-winning educator. Her research interests include the family, development, and political economy.*

Cees J. Hamelink is Professor Emeritus of International Communication at the University of Amsterdam (UvA) and editor-in-chief of *International Communication Gazette.* Professor Hamelink is Honorary President of the International Association for Media and Communication Research (IAMCR) and founder of trhe People's Communication Charter. He holds offices in several international organizations and has lectured about media, communication and human rights at universities in more than 45 countries. Among the 21 books he has authored are *Cultural Autonomy in Global Communications* (1983), *Finance and Information* (1983), *The Technology Gamble* (1988), *The Politics of World Communication* (1994), *World Communication* (1995), and *The Ethics of Cyberspace* (2000). He is one of Europe's most well-respected scholors of international communication and human rights.

Robert Jensen is an Associate Professor in the School of Journalism at the University of Texas at Austin and a board member of the Third Coast Activist Resource Center in Austin. He is the author of *Getting Off: Pornography and the End of Masculinity* (South End Press, 2007); *The Heart of Whiteness: Confronting Race, Racism and White Privilege* (City Lights, 2005); *Citizens of the Empire: The Struggle to Claim Our Humanity* (City Lights, 2004); and *Writing Dissent: Taking Radical Ideas from the Margins to the Mainstream* (Peter Lang, 2002).

Yasmin Jiwani is an Associate Professor in the Department of Communication Studies at Concordia University, Montreal. Her doctorate in Communication Studies, from Simon Fraser University, examined issues of race and representation in Canadian television news. Prior to her move to Montreal, she was the Executive Coordinator and principal researcher at the BC/Yukon FREDA Centre for Research on Violence against Women and Children. Her recent publications include *Discourses of Denial: Mediations of Race, Gender and Violence* (2006) and *Girlhood, Redefining the Limits* (2006), co-edited with Candice Steenbergen and Claudia Mitchell. Her work has appeared in *Social Justice, Violence Against Women*, the *Canadian Journal of Communication*, the *Journal of Popular Film & Television, Topia*, and in the *International Journal of Media and Cultural Politics*. She serves on the editorial board of the *Canadian Journal of Women and the Law*, the *Canadian Journal of Communication*, and *Simile*, and is a board member for the Überculture Collective and steering committee member of RACE (Researchers and Academics of Colour for Equality).

Richard Lance Keeble has been Professor of Journalism at the University of Lincoln since 2003. Before that, he lectured at City University in London for 19 years. His publications include *Secret State, Silent Press: New Militarism, the Gulf and the Modern Image of Warfare* (1997), *The Newspapers Handbook* (2005, fourth edition), *Ethics for Journalists* (2008, second edition), *The Journalistic Imagination: Literary Journalists from Defoe to Capote and Carter* (with Sharon Wheeler) (2007) and *Communicating War: Memory, Media and Military* (with Sarah Maltby) (2007). He is also co-editor of *Ethical Space: The International Journal of Communication Ethics*.

Jeffery Klaehn holds a PhD (2007) from the University of Amsterdam (UvA) and is currently completing a second PhD at the University of Strathclyde. He has published in a range of international peer-reviewed journals and has compiled, edited and contributed to several books that have been centrally concerned to explore the dialectic between media, power and social inequality, including *Filtering the News: Essays on Herman and Chomsky's Propaganda Model* (2005), *Bound by Power: Intended Consequences* (2006) and *Roadblocks to Equality: Women Challenging Boundaries* (2008). Jeffery's research interests include pop culture, media, discourse, political economy, power, social inequality, education, and human rights. Jeffery serves as an editorial board member with the *Journal of Global Mass Communication, ImageTexT: Interdisciplinary Comics Studies* and *Fifth-Estate-Online: The International Journal of Radical Mass Media Criticism*.

Justin Lewis is Professor of Communication and Head of the School of Journalism, Media and Cultural Studies at Cardiff University. He joined Cardiff in 2000, having worked for 12 years in the United States at the University of Massachusetts. He has written/edited 10 books about media and politics, his most recent being *Constructing Public Opinion* (2001), *Citizens or Consumers: What the Media Tell Us About Political Participation* (2005) and *Shoot First and Ask Questions Later: Media Coverage of the 2003 Iraq War* (2006).

Donald Matheson is Senior Lecturer in Mass Communication at the University of Canterbury, New Zealand. He is the author of *Media Discourses* (2005) and co-editor of the journal *Ethical Space*. He writes on journalism practices, with a particular emphasis on news language and the communicative ethics of the news, interests which have led him to study weblogs and other digital media. He has previously worked at Cardiff and Strathclyde universities in the UK and as a journalist in New Zealand.

Brian Martin is Associate Professor of Science, Technology and Society at the University of Wollongong (Australia). He has published widely in the areas of dissent, power, human rights and politics.

David Miller is Professor of Sociology in the Department of Geography and Sociology at the University of Strathclyde in Glasgow, Scotland. He is also a co-founder of Spinwatch.org, a website publishing public interest reporting on spin deception and lobbying, and the editor of spinfiles.org, an associated wiki database. David also chairs the 'Teaching about Terrorism' Special Interest Group of Higher Education Academy's Centre for Sociology, Anthropology and Politics. Recent publications include: *A Century of Spin: How Public Relations Became the Cutting Edge of Corporate Power* (2008) and *Thinker, Faker, Spinner, Spy: Corporate PR and the Assault on Democracy* (2007), both co-edited with William Dinan.

Dr. Andrew Mullen is a senior lecturer in politics in the Department of Social Science at Northumbria University in Newcastle-upon-Tyne (Britain). His research interests include the history and politics of European integration, the history and politics of the British Left, international political economy, Western foreign policy, and the media and propaganda. His publications include *The British Left's 'Great Debate' on Europe* (Continuum, 2007), *The 1975 Referendum on Europe* (Imprint Academic, 2007), *Anti- and Pro-European Propaganda in Britain* (Continuum, forthcoming) and *The Political Economy of the European Social Model* (Routledge, forthcoming). He has his own website (www.andymullen.com) and can be contacted at andrew.mullen@northumbria.ac.uk.

Richard Poulin is Professor of Sociology at the University of Ottawa and an expert on globalization and the sex industries. He has worked for more than twenty years on pornography and prostitution, subjects on which he has published several books, chapters of books and articles.

Gerald Sussman is Professor of Urban Studies and Planning and Communications at Portland State University. His teaching areas include Third World development, political economy of urbanization, international communication, critical theories in mass communication and political communication. His research focuses on political economic development, information cities and the political economy of media and information technologies. Dr. Sussman's teaching and research focus on a relatively new concern of urban studies, both in Western and Third World settings: the restructuring of cities as a result of the new international division of labour and the presence of digital communication and information infrastructure.

James Winter is a Professor in the Department of Communication and Social Justice at the University of Windsor, Ontario, Canada, where he teaches courses in media literacy and the political economy of media. He is the author of *Lies the Media Tell Us* (2007); *MediaThink* (2002); *Democracy's Oxygen: How Corporations Control the News* (1997); and *Common Cents: Media Portrayal of the Gulf War and Other Events* (1992).

Editor's Note

My central intent with *The Political Economy of Media and Power* is to reenage, conceptually and analytically, with classical debates concerning the intersections between media and power and to reassert the centrality of the concept of power within the fields of Cultural Studies, Communication Studies and the Sociology of Mass Communication. I wish to explore the intersections between media, cultural politics, public pedagogy and social class interests, and to demonstrate that the range of possibilities for research that may be undertaken relating to these areas is far-reaching. I have chosen to bring together topically diverse subjects for precisely this reason. I wish to give prominence to the importance of power as a force that interfaces with media, communication circuits and public culture in a multiplicity of ways. Another aim I have for the book is to revive the tradition of empirical, political-economic critical inquiry in relation to the scholarly study of communicative power. *The Political Economy of Media and Power* is organized into six main parts: culture and politics, media and government relations, foreign policy and hegemony, media and academia, popular media and culture, and the political economy of media and culture. Chapters included within the book consider media in relation to war, intelligence communities, the state, foreign policy and the cultural politics of militarization. Other chapters explore the ascendancy of power in relation to media, education and public pedagogy, with respect to academic discourses and debates, the pharmaceutical industry, and the sexist saturation of the public sphere. In conclusion, the book turns to the history and theory of radical mass media criticism and explores important questions relating to the role and function of advertising in relation to power, politics, and audiences. It is my hope that the topics covered, arguments made and taken up, and ideas presented within this book will inspire renewed debate and critical engagement concerning the relationship between media and power.

Jeffery Klaehn
Kitchener, Ontario
January 1, 2010

Introduction

DAVID MILLER AND WILLIAM DINAN

The relation between media and power remains the key reason for examining the media of communication and their role in society. Too much of the work currently ongoing in the discipline appears to have lost sight of this, but this collection is a welcome sign of the re-emergence of the classic and most important issues. The question of the media and power is not, however, straightforward. It is not simply a question of media performance or bias. It is not simply a question of whether we can understand the media in terms of the "propaganda model" as outlined by Herman and Chomsky. This is because it is a model of media performance and not a model of the role of the media in the power structure or in the reproduction of capitalist social relations. It is this latter question which is at the heart of concerns about the media and power, but it is a question which has not routinely been treated in its fullest sense.

To understand the multiple and complex roles of even the news media (as opposed to entertainment media including comics, film, TV drama, etc.) requires the analysis of a series of steps in the communication process from the advertising, PR and propaganda strategies adopted by social interests, through media production processes, the content of the output of the media, the use made of media information and its formative impacts on public opinion, belief and action, its direct role in relation to power structures and, lastly, how this feeds back into outcomes, and then communication strategy planning and public relations.

All of this "circuit" of communication needs to be understood and studied. And the circuit has any number of feedback loops which can evade elements of the circuit described above. This is why the propaganda model – a model predicting media performance – needs to be supplemented by other sorts of theories and models examining other elements of the circuits of communication and power.

Staying with the model for a second, we can state that because the model is one of media performance it does arguably neglect the importance of PR and propaganda, though these are incorporated as part of the five filters. In this respect Ed Herman acknowledges that more could be written about the role of the PR industry. But in terms of the wider questions about the role of propaganda and PR in legitimation, some of this would go beyond the question of media performance.

In addition, strictly speaking the model does not have anything to say about the impact of the media. Herman and Chomsky have noted that they would be surprised to find that the overwhelming dominance of official views in the mainstream media had no or little effect. However, it is also clear that this is one of the most penetrating critiques of the model, which is that Herman and Chomsky suggest that this is only a model of media performance and yet use phrases like "manufacturing consent", "opinion control" etc. If we follow the model strictly this is unwarranted, but given the rest of the writings of both authors we can see that there is a context for some of these assumptions in their understanding of the wider process of the manufacture of consent.

Seeing communication in a wider frame than just in relation to mainstream media suggests that propaganda is not just about the manipulation of the media but has other functions too such as ruling-class unity and intra-elite communications. Strategic communications are undertaken in order to manipulate the media with the intention of managing public opinion, as well as to communicate via the media with other elites (e.g. shareholders, political elites, other business groups etc.) and to manage and influence political and business decision making by direct communication (i.e. by lobbying, policy planning groups etc.).

The propaganda model does not predict media impacts on public belief and opinion, though it clearly implies system-sustaining effects. The empirical evidence on the effectiveness of media and propaganda show that the media can significantly affect public opinion. The media do influence opinions and views, sometimes in ways that benefit the powerful and are against the interests of citizens. However, misinformation is no guarantee. A recent PIPA study shows that 14% of those who believed three key misperceptions about the conflict in Iraq did not support the war. So even if propaganda is successful in managing perceptions, people do not necessarily draw the conclusions favoured by the liars who invented the lies.[1] In addition, opinion polls continue to show that in the US and UK (and more so in less neoliberal nations) opinion on most issues of domestic policy is far to the left of the mainstream pro-corporate parties. On private profit versus public services, on healthcare, on education, significant differences remain between public preferences and policy.[2]

This suggests that we need a model which understands that propaganda may be effective in the sense of managing perceptions but not necessarily in outcomes. In addition we might pay attention to the implication that public opinion is not necessarily the dominant power in the land in the era of neoliberalism. In other words we need to think a little more about how power is exercised in society.

This takes us to concepts like power and hegemony. The assumption in much writing on hegemony is that advanced capitalist democracies have moved from rule by coercion to rule by consent. However, the decisive break between consent and coercion outlined by many writers on hegemony is misleading. The notion of hegemony as consent misses the meaning of leadership attached to the term (i.e. including coercion). We can consider the extent to which lies, manipulation and propaganda are in fact coercive forms of communication which problematise the easy coupling of force = coercion and communication = consent.

The third dimension of power, in the famous thesis of Steven Lukes, implies that power can be exercised via ideas. Thick and thin notions of hegemony imply ruling-class propaganda accepted or complied with. But the notion that hegemony (in the sense of consent rather than leadership) is all there is to dominance is mistaken. The easy contrast between coercion and consent is a simplification. Bourdieu understood this, writing that "the only way to understand" some forms of domination "is to move beyond the forced choice between constraint (by forces) and consent (to reasons), between mechanical coercion and voluntary, free, deliberate, even calculated, submission".[3] Moreover, the "power to mislead" must be central to any proper account of propaganda and media.[4]

As a result we are in a position to advance a wider model of the manufacture of consent – or as it should probably be called – the manufacture of compliance. Four key dimensions of this phenomenon can be suggested:

1. *Ruling class unity (ruling class circuits of communication, policy planning groups, lobbying).* In the argument outlined here the manufacture of compliance also involves coercion and the power to mislead. But it crucially also requires relative unity amongst the ruling class. Leadership of allied class fractions is essential and perhaps one of the greatest effects of ideological warfare. Ruling class unity results not just in "ruling ideas" but ruling practices and this in turn implies that these are able to constrain or minimize oppositional ideas and practice.
2. *Fear and resignation (threats or coercion e.g. police and military, hierarchical institutions, dull compulsion of the economic).* People reject the lies, but out

of fear, lack of confidence, threats, strong socialization of hierarchical institutions or exhaustion they do not act. For example, it is perfectly plain that public opinion in the US, in Canada and in the UK is far to the left of the mainstream parties on most issues of domestic and foreign policy.

3. *Manipulation and misinformation (propaganda, lies, censorship, misinformation).* Propaganda misleads about the nature of contemporary problems and their solutions. Information needed for adequate decision making does not reach people.
4. *Persuasion (rational argument, spin and presentation, self interest, ideology).* Persuasion is used in alliance with the other techniques. As Thomas Friedman famously put it,

> For globalization to work, America can't be afraid to act like the almighty superpower that it is. The hidden hand of the market will never work without a hidden fist. McDonald's cannot flourish without McDonnell Douglas, the designer of the F-15, and the hidden fist that keeps the world safe for Silicon Valley's technology is called the U.S. Army, Air Force, Navy and Marine Corps.[5]

This collection then is pitched at the intersection of politics and power, centred on the role of the media in public culture and critical public pedagogy. It is a very timely book as the global financial crisis deepens: this crisis has profoundly disrupted the neoliberal free trade narrative and many of the truths and common-sense assumptions that have dominated public discourse in Western liberal democracies over the past 30 years. The nostrums and policies of the free trade social movement are under threat. But this moment also highlights the need for a coherent critique in, and of, our public culture. This volume is predicated on the assumption that social solidarity and a progressive politics require a reformed media system and critical public communication. Jeffery Klaehn has assembled a fascinating collection of essays and arguments that engage with these issues, addressing access to, and the exercise of, communicative power.

This book represents a welcome return to centre stage of debates about ideology and social interests, after a period of distraction across media and cultural studies with the displacement of power on to individualised consumption promoted by the cultural turn. The collected discussion of power in the opening chapter neatly sets the scene for a wide-ranging exploration of the centrality and complexity of analysing the interrelationships between power and the media. A theme that unifies the approach of many of the scholars contributing to this volume is the urgent necessity of critical scrutiny of power and how to make the exercise of power, first, more transparent and, second, more accountable.

The range of studies and arguments in this book usefully delineate some priorities for those interested in critical public pedagogy: an overarching theme is the intellectual and educational effort to denaturalise the exercise of power by political and corporate elites. The media are a key site for this kind of project in public education. Klaehn and his contributors argue forcefully for an empirical and engaged media studies, reviving the political economy tradition (for example the chapters by Jensen and Mullen reappraising the propaganda model and reflecting on its reception in academic circles) and extending critical inquiry into the roles and activities of powerful actors and institutions (the source studies by Winter and Keeble are but two examples of this approach.).

A unifying feature of the contributions to this volume is their focus on connecting ideas and action, a positioning that can often be seen as problematic in academic circles, where a rigid isolation of values and avoidance of commitment is often mistaken as a proper form of objectivity. These authors show that the best of academic work can and does combine critical analysis with a commitment to a vision of a more participative, transparent and empowered democratic system. Such an orientation has rarely been more urgently required: what follows is a road map to such work in media and communication studies.

NOTES

1. "*Misperceptions, the Media and the Iraq War: Study Finds Widespread Misperceptions on Iraq Highly Related to Support for War*" http://www.worldpublicopinion.org/pipa/articles/international_security_bt/102.php?nid=&id=&pnt=102&lb=brusc
2. Justin Lewis, *Constructing Public Opinion*, New York: Columbia University Press, 2001.
3. Bourdieu, *The Logic of Practice*. Trans. R. Nice. Stanford, CA: Stanford University Press. p. 70 cited in S.Lukes, *Power: A Radical View*. Second edition. Basingstoke: Palgrave Macmillan, 2005. p. 138.
4. Lukes is correct to argue that the power to mislead "takes many forms": "from straightforward censorship and disinformation to the various institutionalised and personal ways there are of infantilizing judgement, and the promotion and sustenance of all kinds of failures of rationality and illusory thinking, among them the "naturalizaton" of what could be otherwise and the misrecognition of the sources of desire and belief", (*Power*, 149).
5. Thomas Friedman in March 28, 1998, *New York Times* magazine cited in Paul D'Amato "Imperialism and the State: Why McDonald's Needs McDonnell Douglas" *International Socialist Review*, 17, April–May 2001. http://www.isreview.org/issues/17/state_and_imperialism.shtml

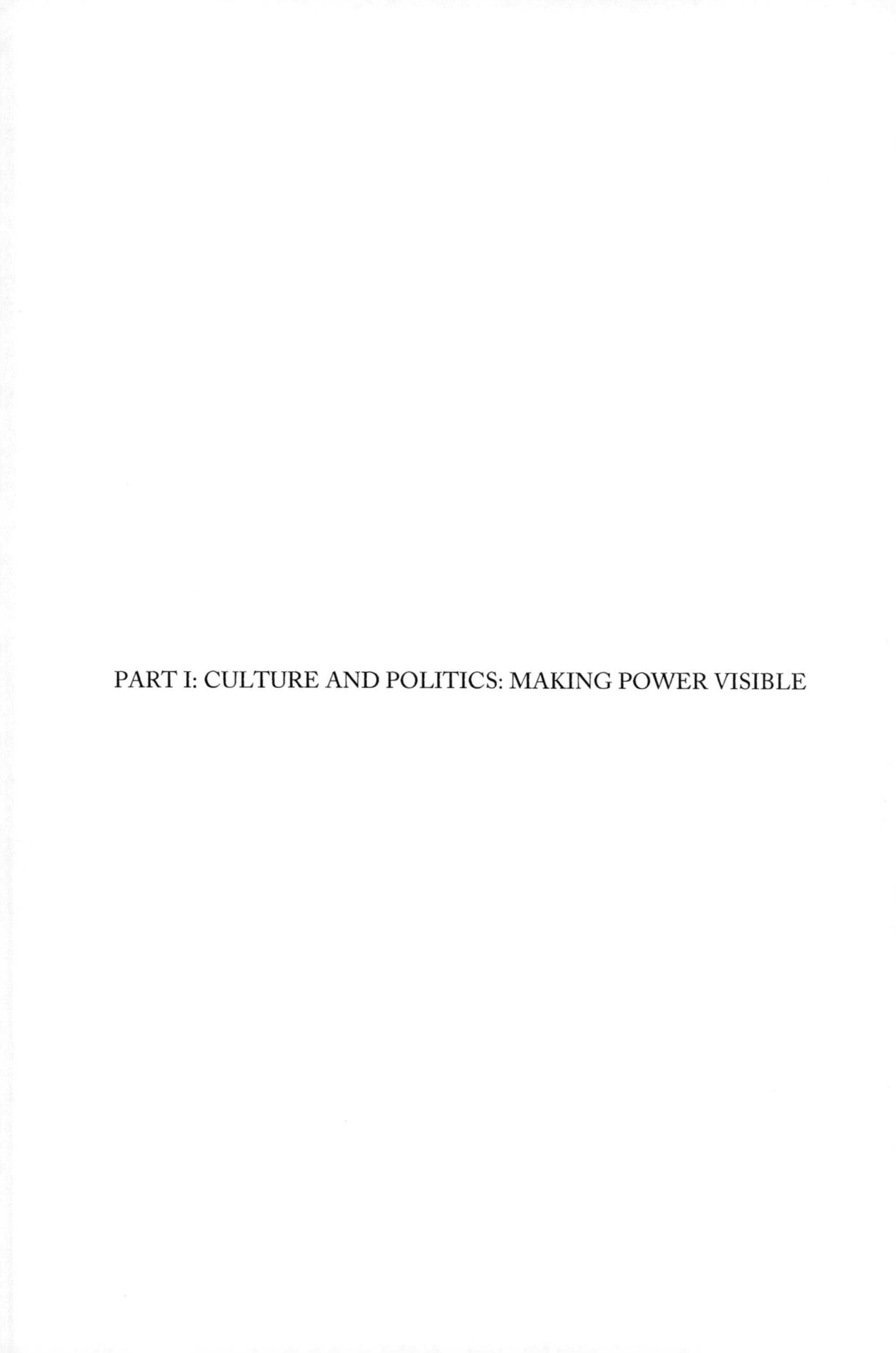

PART I: CULTURE AND POLITICS: MAKING POWER VISIBLE

CHAPTER ONE

Discourses on Power

JEFFERY KLAEHN

My goals for this book are to provide a contemporary state of the art discourse on the concept of power and to explore how power connects with media and public education within the contemporary social world. I wanted to begin the book with an interdisciplinary and politically nuanced discussion exploring these issues, so I invited several of the book's contributors and a range of international discussants to address several timely questions that thematically contextualize the individual chapters which follow. Discussants include scholars from Canada, the United States, the United Kingdom, and Australia. What follows is a unique and groundbreaking treatise that spotlights the dialectic between media, power and cultural politics. It seems to me a uniquely perfect way to begin a book such as this one.

Jeffery Klaehn: How would you define the concept of power? What images and/or metaphors does it evoke for you?

James Winter: A very important aspect of power, which is of course multidimensional, is the ability to control what other people think. To me, this trumps the ability to set wages and impose working conditions, etc. So, imagine a psychic who is telling you what you are thinking at the moment, literally. But he is not *reading* your mind, he is putting *his* thoughts into *your* head, he is *writing* your mind.

Roger Clark: Power is the ability to make things happen. I make two principal assumptions: the first that power is an inert or simply a "potential" energy and that most of its judgments describe its capacity or its application. This may be as simple as turning on a light or as complicated as enforcing the rule of law. Conversely, we often measure power by its absence ("power outage" or "powerlessness"). My second assumption is that power is above all a reflection of the relationship between its source and its application.

In the world of physics, the "horse power" of an engine describes what happens when the full force of energy is applied. By contrast, power in its social context is generally described in terms of end results. Thus we talk of the abuse (or misuse) of power when we measure its negative consequences. Qualifying outcomes is complex, frequently divisive, and generally based on subjective and personal opinion. This in itself leads to confusion, dispute, and ultimately to social disruption.

The relationship between power and its legitimacy (or otherwise) is determined by social contract and political architecture. It could also be argued that the legitimacy of power is established by tradition, inheritance, or even apathy. One of the curious characteristics of power in the social context is its invisibility and its lack of substance until it is used ("turned on"). Nevertheless, the mere suspicion that power exists and *may* be used is often sufficient for it to become real and effective. To properly understand the psychology of our relationships with power (whether real or imagined) is to open the doors to a more effective and more responsible social and political engagement.

The assumption that power will produce positive outcomes underlies much social optimism and underpins the notion of progress. In today's world such optimism is increasingly rare and even harder to justify. One of the great challenges of the twenty-first century may be to overcome the growing conviction that we are increasingly powerless to halt the decline of our civilizations and the destruction of the physical environment that sustains them.

Martha Nandorfy: The very concept of power for me is tainted because I associate it with existing political structures and with structural violence, and how that works systematically around the globe and back through the ages. Power for me suggests domination, subjection of one individual or group's power over another. But that said, there is also this great thing called being or feeling empowered.

Despite the growing prevalence of this positive use of the word, I don't think in terms of power when I'm feeling in control, motivated, and able to express myself to fulfill my desires, and to work toward my goals. Instead, I feel grounded and connected to others, a state that I associate more with well-being than with power; this holistic well-being is also a kind of positive energy that cannot be co-opted by those in power. I guess my reluctance to re-appropriate the concept of power might be directly linked to that well-known insight: "Power tends to corrupt, and absolute power corrupts absolutely." Lord Acton who is credited with this quotation adds, "Great men are almost always bad men."

This brings us to the issue of gender, which you asked me to consider in relation to your questions on power. Positive meanings of power and empowerment grow out of feminist thinking and thinking about the collective struggles of oppressed peoples. Are great women also almost always bad women? This doesn't seem nearly as certain as Acton's assertion of how most powerful men represent their own interests and those of elites with which they are aligned. In terms of images, the most obvious one for me is the image of tanks advancing against unarmed or disproportionately under-armed civilians. This might be somewhat autobiographical on my part; my parents were Hungarian refugees and therefore the image of those tanks acquires a kind of expansive significance for me connected to authoritarian and arbitrary actions. On the other hand, I love the image of indigenous women energetically shaking their fists in the faces of sheepish-looking riot police.

Robert Jensen: The distinction between "power-over" and "power-with" is helpful for me when I think about the gap between the world-as-it-is and the world-as-it-might-be. Those who run this world seek power-over, defined as the ability to make people do what they otherwise would not do. This is the power of the fist and the gun, the power of propaganda and mind control. The quest for power-over is at the heart of hierarchical systems based on a dynamic of domination/subordination, the kinds of systems (patriarchy, white supremacy, imperialism, and corporate capitalism) that we live in today.

Power-with is a very different way of thinking about our relationships, one that sees our individual success depending not on a system that gives us the ability to force others to do what we demand but one that unleashes the creative energy of people to make collaborative success possible. Such a system wouldn't depend on naive notions of human perfection or noble intentions, but instead would seek ways to manage the inevitable disagreements and conflict between people within meaningful guarantees of equality. A simple question is at the heart of this:

What practices, systems, and fundamental conceptions of what it means to be human are consistent with a sustainable human presence on the earth, in societies that provide the necessary resources for all to live a decent life, within cultures that foster individual flourishing alongside a meaningful sense of collective identity, helping us to take seriously our obligations to each other and to the nonhuman world?

OK, that's not so simple. But the struggle to find an answer to that question, rooted in a conception of power-with that reduces the rewards for people to pursue power-over, should be at the core of any project for social and ecological justice.

Joel Bakan: Power is not a thing that people or organizations possess, but rather a consequence and reflection of the social relations that exist between and among them. It can take the form of *coercion*, one actor exerting direct control over another—A gets B, against B's wishes, to do something, or refrain from doing something, or to give something to A, or to somebody else. Coercion is the most obvious and visible form of power. A torturer inflicting pain on his or her victim illustrates its evil potential, but coercion can be used toward positive ends too, as when the state collects taxes to pay for the hospital and the doctor who save the torture victim's life.

Power can also take the form of *influence*, which differs from coercion because the threat of direct detrimental consequences, imposed by A on B, may be absent, yet B still yields to A's demands. A's influence is usually dependent on B believing that A has special knowledge or authority on some issue, or that A has the capacity to reward or sanction B in some direct or indirect way. For example, a politician may vote against restrictive vehicle emissions standards because she believes automobile industry lobbyists are a credible source of information, and she fears losing (or not getting) industry support in financing her campaigns.

A final, and elusive, dimension of power may overlap with coercion and influence, but it is also analytically distinct. Here the question is whether individuals and organizations are *enabled*, or not, by social relations and circumstances—both material and ideological—to fulfill their needs, desires, and aspirations, in economic, social, cultural, and political terms. Paraphrasing Marx, we make choices but not in conditions of our own choosing. To the extent we have more than fewer choices, or the conditions of our choosing are favorable, and to the extent we have some say in determining what those conditions are, we can be said to have more or less of this enabling power. Individuals gain such power through, among other things, material wealth and social status. States, governments, and organizations (including corporations) gain it through, again among other things, ideological conditions that encourage people to believe in their legitimacy and acquiesce to their authority.

So power can be understood in terms of these different, though related, dimensions—coercion, influence, and enabling power. In each instance, the actual constitution of power is as complicated as social relations themselves, and is determined by a combination of law, social structure, and ideology.

Andrew Mullen: The notion of "discourses on power" is useful in two senses. First, it reminds us that there is a dissensus on what is meant by power; its meaning is contested, hence discourses rather than discourse. Ludwig Wittgenstein argued that each theory possesses its own "language game," where words such as power serve as conceptual tools.

The use of the concept of power in different contexts and "language games" changes its meaning; there is therefore no single definition. Nevertheless, there are some common characteristics prompting Wittgenstein to think of it as a "family resemblance" concept.[1] We can identify "power over"— the ability of A to get B to do something which B would not otherwise do— which implies agency and intended effects. Such a meaning was advanced by Robert Dahl.[2] There is "power to"—the ability of A to set the agenda so that an issue of importance to B is deliberately excluded from consideration—which implies agency and manipulation through agenda setting. Such a meaning was explored by Peter Bachrach and Morton Baratz.[3]

There is a third dimension which complements the first and second dimensions, discussed by Dahl, and Bachrach and Baratz respectively. The third dimension—where A affects B in a manner that is contrary to the interests of B—reflects differential interests in the social structure and implies domination. This type of power, identified by Steven Lukes, suggests that bias is not just limited to individual action or agenda setting, it can also take the form of structured and culturally patterned behavior.[4] In other words, individuals are subject to the power relations that are embedded in the social structure into which they are born; individuals are also shaped by the effective deployment of ideology by the powerful in that society. Second, the notion of "discourses on power" also reminds us that power is not just conflictual—concerned with coercion and violence—it is also consensual. In the latter sense, power is internalized, normalized, and reproduced in the discourses of our everyday lives.

In the real world, the use of coercion and violence as a form of power is all too familiar to the peoples of the South—in Africa, Asia, Central and Latin America, and the Middle East—who have been systematically exploited by Northern elites and by elites in their own countries. Such power, which is endured and/or feared on a daily basis, takes the form of arbitrary arrest, detention and torture, B-52 bombers, *coups*, death squads, economic sanctions, invading armies, land evictions, etc.

These methods, used to defend the unequal power relations that benefit aristocratic and/or corporate interests, constitute an effective means of population control. However, this is only true of the South, where the power resources needed for self-defence are scarce, where resistance can be easily overcome and where the peoples of the North, in whose name such actions are taken, are all too often indifferent and/or ignorant.

In the North, people are not normally subjected to such methods of population control. Instead, they have been co-opted into the capitalist system—through consumerism, education, the media and political parties, the creation of a "middle class," propaganda campaigns, etc.,—such that power is exercised in a consensual rather than conflictual manner, in a process that involves the manufacture of consent. What is often forgotten, because people have been systematically denied access to their own histories, is that at one time, the elites in the North also pursued the conflictual power strategy. However, the successful struggle for democracy and similar rights by the working class, in alliance with other progressive forces, required a rethink on the part of the elites as to how to maintain and exercise their power. Their solution, which was to prove much more sophisticated and effective, was the consensual power strategy.

A powerful image that often comes to mind when I think about power is the "ants and bear" recruitment campaign developed by Unison—the main public sector trade union in Britain.[5] The campaign included a television advert featuring a solitary ant going about its business whose way is blocked by a huge bear. In an attempt to get the bear to move out of the way, the ant calls out, "excuse me, excuse me," but it is too small to be noticed. The ant retreats and returns with a fellow ant, but the pair fail to capture the attention of the bear. The pair retreat and return with an army of ants who shout "get out of the way." The bear, clearly startled, does indeed get out of the way and the ants march on. The advert closes with the exhortation, "if you want to be heard, speak in unison."

To my mind, this advert demonstrates that, alone, a working class individual (the ant) is too small to be heard by the managers and owners who constitute the capitalist class (the bear). Working together, on the other hand, the working class (the army of ants) can not only be heard but can also successfully determine its direction and future (and maybe chase the bear away). However, I am also reminded that it is difficult to get the ants to form an army. Some ants are prejudiced against other ants and will have nothing to do with them. Some ants just want to satisfy their own needs and pleasures and give no thought to the bear. Other ants believe that they are leaders with all the answers, in terms of strategy and tactics against the bear. Unfortunately, they too are often prejudiced against other ants that claim to be leaders and will have nothing to do with them. Consequently, small groups of ants are led off in different directions and their paths remain blocked by the bear. This metaphor suggests that power constitutes both a problem *and* a potential means to a better life.

Daniel Fischlin: This may seem paradoxical, but for me power works most efficiently via strategies of hiding, dissimulation, and disguising its actual operations. It works by stealth and by the consensual hallucination that invests "x" person or "y" institution with the agency to execute power in disproportion to other people(s) or institutions. The history of power is actually distinct from the history of power's effects—there is a stunning disregard for this distinction. The lack of transparency round where power is situated is precisely what makes power more effective. Power, in its most corrupt and most dehumanized forms, is profoundly anti-civilization, anticommunity, and anticreative. And yet its effects are material. So, for me, power is defined by the armature of dislocation, indirection, and the difficulty in locating its precise locus and operations—think the silent history of all those meetings behind closed doors that generate major effects in the world such as the decision to go to war in Iraq, or here in Canada, the decision to enter into a state of war with Afghanistan, a country that has never attacked Canada and one of the poorest countries in the world to boot. At the same time, power is all about the overt use of resources and who has his/her finger on the trigger to access those resources. There is no comparison between the obscene amounts of money spent on war globally and the obscenely small amounts spent on true development or true human rights programs or education programs, the latter three better markers of true civil responsibility than the number of missiles you have stacked in silos around the world. And power, in the sense of how I'm using it, is clever—it optimizes the "appearance" of access and responsiveness, as in so-called rights to vote and the appearance of democratic process at the same time as it makes these quasi-obsolete by allowing for lobbyists who are unelected to supersede the rights of citizens to access their representatives. And as a function of economies of both stealth and wealth, power is about the contradiction of classes that it makes manifest: think of the relative wealth of those who have power as opposed to those who wield it in their name: the Senator and the foot soldier; the CEO and the chimney sweep. Power is about class and the dream of class elites to exercise fantasies of infinite progress and consumption. Now what I'm describing is very much a skewed version of abusive powers vested in interlinked military, corporate, and state elites. The other side of all this are other forms of social organization that oppose this dominant disposition—whether in terms of indigenous movements to reclaim land rights or worker/campesino movements aimed at rearticulating the ways in which the means of production are allocated. And we've reached a tipping point in how the dominant narrative of power continues to operate in the face of an overwhelming understanding that this mode has produced a pathological form of civilization: one that is out of balance with planetary, ecological needs; one that promotes extraordinary violence as a means to problem-solve complex global issues; one that overrides basic human rights with narrow economic rights and ancillary military actions associated with the exercise of so-called economic rights; and one that dehumanizes and alienates great masses of people in the name of very specialized economic interests.

David Cromwell: Power comes in many guises, of course. It can be a largely benign phenomenon, as in the care and authority that parents exert over a young child; or it can be malign, as when a strong group or nation subjugates another. This includes the suppression by a state of its own population. Political leaders and state planners have traditionally feared and resisted, often with massive force, popular demands for equity, justice, and functioning democracy. As Chomsky has noted, "Remember, any state, *any* state, has a primary enemy: its own population."[6]

There are countless historical examples, some extending to the present day. Malign power is often cloaked in a mantle of supposed benevolence. Some historians, notably Niall Ferguson, have attempted to rehabilitate the legacy of the British Empire which, in fact, comprised centuries of almost indescribably brutal colonialism soaked in the blood of millions around the globe.[7]

Images and metaphors? It could be the strong protective arms of a mother or father looking after a child. Or it could be a jackboot pressed down on the throat of a supine victim. It could even be a B-52 plane raining down bombs on a city or a rural community. In this latter, violent meaning of power, it is clearly built on military and economic might and driven by a rapacious greed to maintain, strengthen, and expand dominance. Such power will protect itself at almost any cost, any level of suffering. We only have to recall Hiroshima and Nagasaki to see this; the Nazi Holocaust; the suffering of the Chinese people under Chairman Mao; the bloodshed in Latin America under US-sponsored client regimes; the terror in southeast Asia under US attack, with millions killed and many others left maimed and deformed; the slaughter of over a million Iraqis, including half a million young children, in the 1990s under UN sanctions; and the probable death of a similar number of people since the 2003 invasion of Iraq.

But power, too, can be built upon positive qualities: cooperation, altruism, wisdom, love, compassion—the power that arises from people working together to help each other; to build communities, promote human rights, and protect the natural world; the power that comes from educating, emboldening, and inspiring each other. All of that brings to mind images of building homes or bridges or a network of links, akin to a spider's web; something tangible that connects people and resists threats from elsewhere. This benign aspect also reminds me of the energy, enthusiasm, and feel-good aspects of being at the best kind of concert; especially, for me, a rock gig where the band is performing really well and the audience is wholly enthused: there's a strong synergy, then, between the musicians and the audience, to the point where they seem to feed off each other.

Brian Martin: I'm going to start with an example and then relate it to power. Slobodan Milosevic, president of Serbia and head of the Socialist Party, fostered Serbian nationalism to cement his power. In response to Serbian operations in Kosovo, in 1999, NATO forces initiated a massive bombing campaign. Milosevic withdrew troops from Kosovo, but the bombing actually solidified his rule by uniting the Serbian population against the foreign attackers.

In 2000, the grassroots movement Otpor, not linked to any political party, campaigned against Milosevic using leaflets, slogans, music, and humorous stunts. When the police responded with arrests and beatings, Otpor used these to publicize the regime's brutality. Milosevic called an early election; opposition parties created a unified platform. When Milosevic tried to steal the election through voting fraud, the population responded to an opposition call to march on Belgrade. This nonviolent campaign undermined police loyalty and caused Milosevic to capitulate.

Power for oppressive purposes is sometimes called "power over." This is the power of Serbian troops in Kosovo and the power of NATO bombing. In contrast is "power to." This is the power to resist oppression, the power of the Serbian people to oppose Milosevic's regime without harming its functionaries. "Power to" is sometimes called empowerment.

Power can be displayed in actions, such as the NATO bombing, but just as important is the power inherent in social arrangements, such as the economic power of NATO countries to fund military forces and the political power of Milosevic's Socialist Party. Capacities built into social structures enable the exercise of power in action. Milosevic ruled Serbia not through his own physical strength but through his role as party leader.

Social power is a relationship: it exists only through other people's participation or acquiescence. Milosevic's power evaporated when the Serbian people—including many of the regime's troops—stopped obeying and transferred their loyalty elsewhere.

Justin Lewis: Power is the stuff of politics. It can be distributed widely or confined to the few. It can be benign—in the style of Scandinavian Welfare States—or it can have the violence or cruelty of totalitarianism or unrestrained capitalism. It can be used for altruistic endeavors—to promote equality and fulfillment—or used merely for the single-minded pursuit of thoughtless self-interest. If modern politics seems only to span various shades of gray, the great battle remains between those who favor equality, kindness, and altruism and those whose actions lead to elitism, cruelty, and their own advancement at the expense of others.

Perhaps the best demonstration of the misuse of power is the amount of resources we spend on weaponry rather than the relief of human misery. So, for example, we could achieve *all* the Millennium Development Goals —including ending global hunger and providing universal education—with a modest cut in the US military budget—one that would still leave the US as the biggest military power on the planet many times over. And the media have a role too in this power-play.[8]

Jeffery Klaehn: What about the power of corporations and the media?

Joel Bakan: I presume you mean large publicly traded corporations and major mainstream media outlets, and I will answer the question on that basis. As a starting point, I want to consider the three modes of power—coercion, influence, and enabling—in terms of relationships between and among several actors—the corporate sector (as a whole), media corporations, corporations that use the media to advertise their products and services, governments and politicians, nongovernmental activist organizations (trade unions, environmental groups, industry front groups, think tanks, public relations firms, lobbyists, and so on), communities, and individuals.

With respect to power as coercion, several relationships are noteworthy.

First, the laws that create and constitute for-profit publicly-traded corporations, including media corporations, require—coerce—managers and directors always to act in the best interests of shareholders. Every decision they make, every action they initiate must be aimed at creating wealth for shareholders. So, the executives of media corporations have no authority to pursue public interests—such as truth, balance, democracy, or whatever else—as ends in themselves. Corporate law requires that they justify everything they do in terms of serving shareholders' interests. All values and goals are thus subordinate to profit.

Outside of corporate law, however, governments have the authority to regulate—coerce—media corporations to carry, or not, certain kinds of program content, to avoid mergers, takeovers, and acquisitions that lead to undue media concentration, to license or not, and generally, to ensure certain public policies are realized and public interests protected. Regulation is especially pronounced in broadcasting where, because the radio spectrum is understood as public property, media corporations are expected to meet an array of public interest standards, set and enforced by agencies (the CRTC in Canada, or the FCC in the United States), if they wish to get and keep licenses to operate.

So, while corporate law creates entities compelled to pursue profit over all other values and goals, regulatory law can be, and is, used to modify that compulsion by requiring corporations to serve other competing values and interests. To that end, laws have been passed in Canada that, among other things, limit certain kinds of advertising, such as tobacco and direct advertising to children, and require certain proportions of Canadian content on radio and television.

Another kind of coercive relationship is that between corporations (some of which are media corporations) that use media to advertise their products and services and media corporations. The primary source of revenue for most media corporations is the sale of advertising space and time. Their business is to sell audiences to advertisers. Advertisers thus have considerable power over content.

They can punish media corporations by pulling, or threatening to pull, advertising if they do not like general or particular content. This gives them a kind of coercive power over media corporations.

The Corporation, a documentary film I made with Mark Achbar and Jennifer Abbott, provides a vivid example of how a company, Monsanto, used this power when it threatened to pull advertising from the Fox Network if a Fox News affiliate ran a story on the ill effects (for cows and humans) of a hormonal compound, manufactured by Monsanto, that increased milk production in cows. The threats were successful. Fox succumbed and killed the story, demonstrating the coercive power of Monsanto over it.

The way Fox killed the story illustrates a fourth kind of coercive relationship—that between media corporations and their employees. The milk story was created by two Fox reporters, Steve Wilson and Jane Akre, who, after insisting that their story be aired, were fired for insubordination, dramatically illustrating a dynamic that affects journalists across the industry today. As advertisers demand content environments that serve their interests and are conducive to selling their wares, media corporations pass that demand down the line with subtle and sometimes not-so-subtle—indeed coercive—pressures to ensure that journalists fall in line

Power as *influence*, as distinct from coercive power, is also at play in the power of media and corporations, and, again, in different but overlapping ways. To begin with, media corporations, and the advertisers that support them, enjoy the same channels of influence over government as all major corporations—they devote substantial resources to lobbying, litigating, and financing election campaigns, and their top officials circulate in the same elite circles as, and have the ear and respect of, top bureaucrats and politicians. They use this influence in much the same way that other corporations do, primarily to fight against the creation, existence, and enforcement of government regulations that interfere with their profit-making, such as restrictions on content, licensing, and mergers and acquisitions.

Media corporations are also targets of influence for other corporations and the think tanks, industry groups, and public relations firms they support and hire, all of whom, along with sympathetic politicians, aim to secure media content that is favorable to corporations and supportive of pro-business governmental policies. Countervailing influences do exist—trade unions, environmental, and other advocacy groups—but they have fewer opportunities and resources to access media corporations, and their messages are presumptively suspect within the ideological framework in which media corporations operate.

Perhaps the most obvious instance of power as influence, when talking about the corporate media, is the power that media corporations wield over society and governments. Most citizens, and governments too, get their information, analyses, and opinions from mainstream media. What we know about the world, how we find meaning, truth, and beauty, are profoundly shaped by decisions that are made within media corporations, as are our beliefs and actions as citizens—our political orientations, our senses of what is right and wrong, what needs support and what needs to be changed, whether and what movements or causes we become involved with, and how we vote.

In this way, corporate media outlets quite literally constitute public opinion, shape what we are and what we do as citizens, and, in turn, propel political decision-making and action. And none of this happens in a random or pluralistic way. Because the various pressures and influences of, and upon, media corporations push in the same direction—supporting the perspectives and missions of corporations and industry, promoting consumerism and superficial diversions, encouraging skepticism of unions, social and environmental advocacy groups, and activist government, championing pro-corporate economic policies, such as free trade, deregulation, and privatization, and so on—the overall impact of corporate media is to help create and sustain a dominant ideology—a broad public sense of what we can take for granted, what is true and beyond question, what is common sense—that comports with the needs and interests of corporations.

Now I want to turn to the final kind of power, *enabling* power, in the context of media and corporations. In liberal democratic societies, freedom of expression is considered a fundamental right, necessary for the flourishing of individuals and the proper functioning of democratic institutions. In Canada, as in the United States, it is formally protected by law as a constitutional right. The notion that all individuals are equally free to express themselves, even where their ideas are oppositional or their aesthetics unconventional, is a common, and effective, rhetorical riff in defenses of democratic systems over authoritarian and totalitarian ones. And while that notion is appealing, it can mask the fact that the ideal it expresses does not necessarily mirror reality.

Formally it is true—everybody has the right to freedom of expression, just as everybody has the right to own property. In real terms, however, as with the right to own property, the capacity of individuals to exercise their freedom of expression rights effectively is radically unequal. Those who run and own media corporations—newspapers, magazines, and television and radio stations—have massive resources to communicate their messages and perspectives, as do corporations in general because of their capacity to influence media, and to dictate content with their advertising dollars; others, outside the corporate world, have relatively fewer resources to exercise their rights to freedom of expression.

But it is not just a matter of material resources.

As I already mentioned, the corporate media plays a substantial role in constituting a dominant ideology that legitimates and supports the needs and interests of corporations. Ideas and policies that are, in fact, partisan and controversial—such as deregulation and free trade—are systematically presented as beyond question and true to the point where in public opinion, they come to appear that way. In contrast, ideas that oppose these dominant ideologies necessarily appear as partisan and controversial, ones that warrant skepticism and suspicion. The discursive environment, in other words, is not a level playing field. Media corporations produce knowledge that, for the most part, supports and leaves unchallenged the actions, presumptions, and beliefs of the corporate world—and they produce that knowledge in sufficient quantity to constitute dominant ideologies and squeeze out alternative viewpoints. Thus, in addition to their greater material resources, corporations can count on their ideas having more influence, and their challengers' less, because of how those ideas relate to the dominant ideological discourses that media corporations help create.

Robert Jensen: One of the most important tasks in education today is to denaturalize the corporation. Most of the students I teach at the University of Texas at Austin have never considered—and may never have been asked by a teacher to consider—a simple fact: The corporation is not a naturally occurring object, and not an obviously natural way to organize institutions in an economy. They have lived in a world defined by corporations, in which the corporate form is not a topic for investigation, and so it appears to be a natural institution. But, of course, the corporation is a creation of people, at least of a certain elite stratum of people, and like any human institution—especially those institutions with enormous power—it should be the subject of relentless scrutiny.

Corporations are essentially fascistic in design. They concentrate power at the top in a rigid hierarchy, with orders transmitted down. People at the bottom may have "input" in decision-making, but they have no real power within that structure (their power comes from a willingness to resist the structure). Beyond that, workers in a corporation are encouraged to see their sense of self as flowing from the corporation; one's identity is to be found through taking one's place in the corporate hierarchy (expressed in the quintessential phrase "an IBM man").

The corporation is relevant to an analysis of media in two obvious ways. Most news and entertainment media in the United States are corporately owned, and the bulk of the revenue for many of those corporations is selling advertising to other corporations. Such a media system is likely to produce stories about the world that are consistent with, and supportive of, corporate power. Such a media system doesn't bode well for justice, either for people or the nonhuman world.

Daniel Fischlin: It's a cliché to say that the media and the corporations exercise disproportionate or inverse power to their sense of social and global responsibility.

Self-interest rules and drives the nature of this kind of power—and confronting and changing this reality in ways that recognize the importance of good corporate citizenship as well as the reality that economies do matter is a huge problem. Celebrity, which the media manufactures and sells as an anesthetic to a dispossessed citizenry, is a great example of the power to confuse, to ignore, and to manufacture nodes of perceived importance for certain kinds of information that are largely irrelevant. The amount of mind pollution out there is staggering—and it serves political, ideological, and corporate purposes. The "mediascape" must be thought of as its own form of ecology and currently its ecology parallels that of the corporate mentalities that are so implicated in other forms of pollution. The idea that corporations should serve only their shareholders is one of the most perverse articulations of power that has taken root over the past century and a half. And of course that is itself largely a myth because shareholders' views, when they are not in line with the perceived self-interest of a given corporation, will also largely be ignored—same principle as in democracies where large groups of voters can be ignored by power elites who don't see a need for consensus building or sensitivity to concerns other than their own. In Canada, for instance, banks and media operate as a function of the will of the people (through charters and the allocation of publicly owned airwaves to give two instances). And the state gives them the right to quasi-monopolies. The problem is when they divest themselves of their true origins in and responsibilities to the various communities that share the social world with them, and move toward shareholder-defined interests, which are uniquely governed by profit. This is seen to be of economic benefit. A much wider concept of profit would involve sustainable communities, healthy eco-systems, social values that extend beyond narrow economic self-interest (like meaningful and affordable education), and other progressive measures. Think of companies such as Nestlé or Syncrude freely gobbling huge amounts of water in unsustainable ways that in the first case led to the production of more plastic (in bottled water—a horrendous concept) and in the second more oil (from the tar sands) and more of the massive carbon imprint humans are making on the planet. Or think of what happened to the electric car and why GM had no interest in its production and actually played a role in killing the concept. These are only the tip of the iceberg when it comes to citing monumental corporate failures to consider anything more than their own bottom line. Why most large corporations have such a hard time thinking about themselves in terms of a broader network of outcomes and social responsibilities is a measure of how much has to change in baseline philosophies that govern them. The scandalous ways in which nonenvironmental design considerations underlie so much of what actually gets made by corporations is a case in point. And the fatuous argument that environmentally sound design is bad for business is nonsense. In fact, reconstructing business to deliver inputs and outputs that have been reconceived in terms of their total environmental footprint is the *only* way of a future that is survivable—and of course it too will be a business, no doubt very profitable. The lack of this sort of concentrated investigative and critical pressure in the media merely underlines the ways in which corporate and media values are interimplicated and interdependent.

James Winter: Corporations and the ruling class exercise tremendous power in society. Through the parties and candidates they put in office, the elites ensure continuing hegemony, and policies and laws that are in their favor. An example would be the Desmarais family, of Power Corporation, and their influence on prime ministers stretching from Lester Pearson and Pierre Trudeau, to Brian Mulroney, Jean Chretien, and Paul Martin. And guess who backed Bob Rae in the 2006 Liberal leadership race? Paul Desmarais. As for the media, well, Desmarais owns news media, as do about seven of the ten wealthiest Canadian families: the Thomsons, the Rogers, the Pattisons, etc. News media corporations are no longer distinct from other corporations: they have become synonymous. What this means is that the news media have become the ideological branch of the ruling class, manufacturing the public's consent for elite policies.

Brian Martin: The automobile is part of many overlapping systems of power. To build cars requires the mobilization of human and material resources: engineers design cars, companies build them, contractors supply parts, and transportation systems deliver them. Then sellers exchange cars for money and owners drive them.

Cars on their own make no sense without roads: governments build and regulate transportation systems. The legal system is involved to license drivers and deal with disputes over ownership and accidents. The health system copes with deaths and injuries from accidents. Cars affect the environment through air pollution and greenhouse gases. Maintaining reliable sources of oil helps drive international trade, diplomacy, and sometimes war.

The car is the center of a system of transport—sometimes called automobility—that, to most people, seems entirely natural, just the way things are. Few people spend time imagining a world without cars, or even a neighborhood without cars. In a sense, several systems of power have coalesced to create a perception that there is no alternative. Even those who question the car culture usually address limited matters, pushing for safety features, fuel efficiency, car pooling, or better public transport.

The car system is no accident: powerful groups have devoted vast efforts to create and maintain it. Economic power is deployed by the automobile industry, the oil industry, and others. Political power is deployed by car-sympathetic politicians and agencies. Social power is manifest in expectations of family and friends about car ownership and use: young people want to drive as soon as possible. The reality of cars and the inducements of advertisers shape people's thinking, making cars seem necessary, even inevitable, something that can be called ideological power.

Andrew Mullen: Corporations, in the past and the present, have adopted both conflictual and consensual power strategies. In terms of the conflictual power strategy, inspired by the success of the British East India Company in the eighteenth century, private military companies have been formed to protect corporate interests. There has been a proliferation of such companies in the past decade and they now operate in over 50 countries across every continent.[9] The priorities of these private military companies, and the wider corporate sector that they serve, are two-fold: access to strategic resources and the maintenance of an open-door policy in investment and trade. These corporate interests also inform the foreign policies of countries such as Britain, the US, and other imperial states, as revealed in the declassified record.[10] In terms of access, US state planners[11] argued that it was

> important to maintain in friendly hands areas which contain or protect sources of metals, oil and other national resources, which contain strategic objectives, or areas strategically located, which contain a substantial industrial potential, which possess manpower and organized military forces in important quantities.[12]

In terms of the open-door policy, US state planners declared that they were opposed to "barriers or onerous restrictions imposed by governments on the investment and withdrawal of foreign capital."[13] Furthermore,

> American enterprises in other countries should be assured the same right of access to raw materials and markets and to the labour supply of the host country on the same terms as business enterprises operated therein by its citizens or by citizens of third countries.[14]

The US, the dominant state in the postwar world order, insisted upon an open-door policy on the basis that US-based corporations could, in any competition, exploit their size and utilize a variety of economic mechanisms to outmatch their rivals and thus dominate foreign markets. Britain also adopted a free trade policy during its hegemonic period in the nineteenth century.

The principal threats to corporate interests and the foreign policy objectives of Britain, the US, and other imperial states are economic nationalism[15] (independent development) and ultranationalism (delinking from the capitalist global economy). This was true during the Cold War and it remains the case in the New World Order. As noted by state planners,

> Nationalist regimes are responsive to popular pressure for immediate improvements in the low living standards of the masses. This tendency conflicts with the need to protect our resources and provide a climate conducive to private investment and, in the case of foreign capital, to repatriate a reasonable return.[16]

Furthermore, economic nationalism and ultranationalism are perceived as contagious, in the sense that they threaten to set an example to other countries—the so-called "domino effect." When such threats emerge, Britain, the US, and other imperial states launch covert and military interventions in an attempt to destroy these experiments. Unfortunately, these interventions are all too often successful.[17]

Another dimension of the conflictual power strategy is the use of legislation and litigation to criminalize dissent and deter legitimate protest against corporations and their state allies. Two journalists in particular, George Monbiot and Henry Porter, have documented how antiterror and public order legislation passed by the British governments over the past three decades has been used in this way.[18] Corporations and governments around the world have engaged in similar practices,[19] most recently under the guise of the "war on terror."

In terms of the consensual power strategy, corporations have attempted to conflate their *specific* interests with the *general* interests of society, using a variety of ideological mechanisms. First, corporations pursue their interests through advertising and the promotion of a consumerist society.[20]

Second, corporate values are normalized by the education system.[21] Consider, for example, how many millions of people conduct entrepreneurial projects while at school and/or undertake business studies at college or university, where they learn about industrial relations, management techniques, marketing strategies, how to maximize profit and market share, etc. They are taught business, i.e., capitalist values and they are generally encouraged not to challenge the status quo or to criticize these values. However, given that most of these people are going to spend their lives as wage slaves rather than capitalists or entrepreneurs, who constitute only a small percentage of the total population, would it not be more rational and sensible for these people to study trade unionism—the principle of solidarity, how to organize strikes effectively, etc? The power of the capitalist ideology is such that most people will find this argument absurd, subversive even, but it is surely a logical one.

Third, corporations have concentrated their ownership of, and therefore control over, the mass media. The output of the press, radio, and television, generally speaking, serves corporate interests. Edward Herman and Noam Chomsky argued that where there is consensus among economic and political elites on particular issues, media tend to reflect this, to the exclusion of rival perspectives. Furthermore, criticisms of capitalism and discussions of alternatives are usually marginalized. These processes are referred to as agenda setting. In short, the media fixes the boundaries of "thinkable thought" in a way that serves corporate and state interests.[22] Corporations have also "bought off" political parties using donations and other forms of patronage; Thomas Ferguson argued that where the major investors in political parties agree on an issue, the parties will not compete on that issue, no matter how strongly the public might want an alternative.[23]

Fourth, corporate interests have encouraged the creation of a "middle class" which is more likely to align with, and therefore defend, the status quo. Furthermore, they have also denigrated class identity and/or encouraged people to identify as "middle class"—even though they remain wage slaves.

Fifth, corporations have deployed a series of propaganda campaigns to "sell" the capitalist system to the working class in order to undermine their attraction to and interest in anarchism, communism, liberalism, socialism, etc.[24] The need for such campaigns is still expressed today; in a speech to the Confederation of British Industry in 2005, the leader of the Conservative Party, David Cameron, argued that

> one of the threats to Britain's prosperity is the growing cultural hostility to capitalism. In 1970, the MORI polling organization asked the public whether the "profits of large companies help make things better for everyone who buys their products and services." The public agreed—by a majority of two-to-one. Three decades later, when asked the same question, the public—by two-to-one—disagreed; for too many people, profit and free trade are dirty words.

Cameron pledged that a future Conservative government would tackle this situation: "promoting wealth creation means changing the climate of opinion so that politicians and bureaucrats who argue for measures that damage competitiveness are less likely to succeed. In short, we need to campaign for capitalism."[25] In pursuing these strategies, corporations are becoming enormously powerful and wealthy to the point where they dominate the global economy and the world's political systems.[26]

Brian Martin: Ralph Nader first became famous as a whistleblower. In 1966, his book *Unsafe at Any Speed* was published, exposing the car industry. General Motors instigated a covert investigation of Nader which, when exposed, discredited the company. Few whistleblowers have such a good outcome. Sociologist Deena Weinstein argues that bureaucracies, including corporations, are similar to authoritarian states: there is no internal democracy, no permitted opposition movements, no free speech, no free assembly. Anyone who speaks out against a boss, or is critical of the company, is subject to reprisals: harassment, ostracism, reprimands, demotion, transfer, dismissal, and blacklisting.

The power of corporate elites is like the power of rulers of repressive regimes, with one major exception: corporate elites seldom exercise violence against opponents. Their power comes from a widespread acceptance of the legitimacy of hierarchy. If the entire workforce started doing things differently, perhaps producing alternative products, corporate elites would have no way to stop it, except by calling for support from government and other corporations. Internal corporate power thus meshes with state and market power.

Externally, corporations exert power through buying, selling, and manipulating. The key characteristic here is that a few people—corporate elites— have far more power than workers or community members. Bucking the system as an individual is a prescription for disaster. The way to bring about change is through collective action, for example through unions or consumer movements.

The mass media are run by governments or corporations, in both cases run as hierarchical systems. They play a special role in information and communication, but as power systems are not too different from other bureaucracies.

David Cromwell: Well, clearly the media are tied up with power: *Guardians of Power* as the title of the first Media Lens book has it.[27] But this should come as no surprise. For example, the owners of newspapers tend to be rich capitalists with extensive business interests. Even the *Independent*, which many regard as quite progressive (its editorial line was against the Iraq war and it often carries arresting front-cover stories on climate), is owned by a billionaire, Sir Anthony O'Reilly, who uses the paper to buy himself stature and influence, and who sees his paper as part of a business empire. Recently, as he moved to buy out an Australian company, he said the transaction would "yield additional resources for the continued expansion of the INM [Independent News & Media] Group, which we believe will further enhance shareholder returns." This is the language of rampant capitalism.

INM, which owns the *Independent*, proudly proclaims on its website

> The Group has grown consistently over the last 15 years by building a geographically unique and diverse portfolio of market-leading brands, and today manages gross assets of 4.0 billion euros, turnover of over 1.8 billion euros and employs over 10,400 people worldwide.[28]

The group's primary focus is not on high news values and critical reporting, of course, but on growing a diverse portfolio of market-leading brands generating gross assets of billions of euros. O'Reilly is candid about attracting advertisers;

after all, advertising revenues typically make up around 75 percent of the revenues of the so-called quality press in the UK:

> For the advertiser, the newspaper remains the most effective mechanism to convey to the potential consumer the virtue, value, colour and style of any new product, service or offering that he has.[29]

Open the *Independent* any day of the week and you will see that it is crammed full of the usual inducements from big business to buy consumer products, boost the services industry (insurance, banking, and so on), and jet around the world to exotic destinations.

Consider, too, the *Guardian* newspaper, regarded by many as challenging of power and as a kind of in-house paper of the environment movement. The paper is owned by the not-for-profit Scott Trust. But the Trust board members are pillars of the establishment and the Trust itself owns the Guardian Media Group (GMG), a major business enterprise:

> Guardian Media Group has a wide portfolio of media interests. The flagship titles—the *Guardian*, the *Observer*, the *Manchester Evening News*, and *Auto Trader*—are strengthened and supplemented by a range of successful businesses which together from [*sic*] one of the most vibrant media organisations in the UK. Our investments in the Internet, electronic publishing and radio give us a broad and successful commercial base. Guardian Media Group is owned by the Scott Trust.[30]

In March 2007, GMG announced it was planning to sell its minority stake in the Trader Media Group, valued at £1.35 billion. The accompanying press release read like any other puff issued by a huge corporate enterprise on the make. Carolyn McCall, Chief Executive of GMG, said of the forthcoming sale:

> This is good news for GMG and Trader Media Group. We have been able to take advantage of the strong appetite for quality media assets and retain a majority stake in this superb company, from which we expect continued growth.
>
> Apax shares our commitment to the long-term development of Trader Media Group, and is an excellent partner for us in the business. We look forward to working closely with Apax as we build on the success of TMG together.[31]

The *Guardian*, then, is very much part of the corporate business world and the establishment generally.

Similar considerations apply to the BBC (British Broadcasting Corporation). Although it is publicly funded and is ad-free (apart from when plugging BBC products and services), it operates in a cut-throat commercial world, with all the usual corporate media concerns about capturing audiences and maximizing ratings. Moreover, the BBC's senior managers are appointed by the government, and the corporation's operations are overseen by the BBC Trust, mostly consisting of important establishment figures.

The media, then, are not simply owned by corporations; they *are* corporations—with all the implicit attendant consequences.

Justin Lewis: I think we should take a step back and ask what the point of a media system is. The media are the main source of information and culture for most people. That carries a huge burden of social responsibility—one far too important to be left in the hands of lightly regulated, market-driven corporations catering to the needs of advertisers. The early broadcast regulators realized that—but, bullied by the power of big commercial media to focus on profit—we seem to have forgotten it. We have given big media enormous power but relieved them of any responsibility to enhance our democratic or cultural lives.

We should also remember that even if a market broadcast system did cater to audiences (rather than to advertisers), the outcome of that is not necessarily good for us or for society. To put it bluntly, it's not at all clear that the huge amount of time we spend watching TV makes us happy or fulfilled, or, indeed, has positive social consequences overall.

Much as commercial media would prefer to deny it, the media system *is* part of our education system. We should treat it accordingly, which means having a thriving public sector in a carefully regulated system. And that means taking on the big media corporations.

Jeffery Klaehn: In what ways does power manifest itself, ideologically, economically, socially? Whatever you may like to touch upon...

Robert Jensen: The domination/subordination dynamic of systems of power-over plays out from the most intimate levels of our personal lives to the global, in ways that are both conscious and unconscious. We see it in men's use and abuse of women in prostitution, pornography, and other sexual-exploitation industries. We see it in the casual ways some white people sometimes treat non-white people as lesser beings. We see it in the wars of empire fought by the United States to maintain its domination in the world. And, perhaps most profoundly, we see it in the modern human belief that the nonhuman world exists as our candy store and dumping ground—that we have a right to extract from the nonhuman world whatever we like in whatever fashion we like, and then dump the toxic waste we create back into that nonhuman world. This contempt that modern systems have for the nonhuman world is perhaps the most striking manifestation of this pathological conception of power, and the exercise of that kind of power may prove to be the ultimate undoing of the human species. Obviously we are part of that larger world and can't protect ourselves from the consequences of our own pathology.

James Winter: The manifestation of power in our society is reflected in the way the public has accepted the role of spectatorship, the sense that there's really nothing we can do to change the status quo, no matter how terrible. People feel that "the system" is unchangeable. So, wars abroad are deplorable, but others make these decisions and we can't change them. Jobs are disappearing due to free trade agreements, and corporate globalization generally, but these are global initiatives which even whole countries could not resist if they wanted to. We wind up with service sector jobs flipping burgers, but it's far worse in the majority world where people are literally starving or barely surviving—and these are the lucky ones, because they are alive. Look at Haiti, for example. Canada, the US, and France arranged for a coup d'état which removed an elected president, Jean-Bertrand Aristide, in 2004. They replaced him with a Miami talk show host, Gerard LaTortue, and proceeded to slaughter Lavalas's party supporters in the thousands, to teach the people of Haiti that they have no right to run their own country. In the midst of all of this, the then-prime minister Paul Martin flew down to Haiti and bestowed his blessing and hundreds of millions of dollars in Canadian aid money on the illegal, murderous regime of Gerard LaTortue. And there wasn't one comment in the media to this effect. And anyone raising these issues in Canada is either ignored or treated as a conspiracy theorist. Well, that's real power in action. And then there's a news item in the paper: Gildan Apparel Industries of Montreal is closing its Canadian and US factories and "concentrating" its manufacturing in the Caribbean, especially Haiti. What the story doesn't say is that these brutalized people will now accept any wage to work in a sweat shop, because the alternative is death. Well, that's not just ideological control or economic control, it is life and death.

Martha Nandorfy: I'll focus on gender in my response, but I find it hard or not always necessary to separate gender from other forms of marginalization based on class, racialized, and ethnic identity. I associate the abuse of power with imperialistic structures, yet when I wonder about the origins of abuse against oppressed genders: women, gay, lesbian, bisexual, and transgender people, I think patriarchal power can be traced back to indigenous tribal societies as well. Maybe in this sense, imperialism starts internally against a community's own members. Power structures manifest themselves in language and patriarchal power can be traced very far back in most languages though studies have focused on Indo-European languages while much work still needs to be done on other languages, and urgently, because 90% of the world's languages are heading for extinction. This is alarming, not just because we are losing diversity, but because indigenous languages hold keys to other ways of seeing reality and living our lives. In her book *Woman, Native, Other,* Trinh T. Minh-ha asks: "What can such a word as 'human' mean when its collaboration with 'man' and 'men' throughout history of *man*kind has become obvious?" What she draws our attention to is a masculinist (in a supremacist sense) concept of "human" according to which "'*he*,' as an unqualified generic pronoun, can be used correctly to include '*she*'... Imagine a world of *yang* and *yang* instead of *yin* (the female principle) and *yang* (the male principle)—a concept which in China never offers two absolute oppositions—and you will have the inhuman (hu)man-constructed world of Frankenstein" (66–67). I think that the global hegemony of patriarchy is just such a world and that inequality within each society most affects those whose interests are not aligned with masculinist-supremacist power.

David Cromwell: A brief insight into just one damaging impact of power on democracy is the way that the corporate media report on these very issues. In February 2006, front-page headlines greeted the publication of a study called the Power Report on the "meltdown" of British democracy. Plummeting participation in elections, and a growing chasm between the public and mainstream party politics, had prompted a study to be undertaken by a panel led by Helena Kennedy, a Labour member of the House of Lords. The report, titled "Power to the People," was based on a year of surveys and hearings, including online public consultation which generated 1,500 responses.

The *Independent* newspaper in London greeted the report's publication:

> Democracy faces meltdown in Britain as the public rejects an outdated political system which has centralised more authority than ever in a tiny ruling elite, the Power inquiry warns today.

The article continued:

> The inquiry says that there is a "very widespread sense that citizens feel their views and interests are not taken sufficiently into account."[32]

An *Independent* editorial the same day was titled, "The urgent need to return politics to the people." Meanwhile, the *Guardian*'s editors announced grandly, "A cause whose time has come."[33] *Guardian* star columnist Jonathan Freedland suggested ludicrously that a "reforming [Gordon] Brown," then the Chancellor of the Exchequer, and thus the main person responsible for funding the British contributions to the invasion-occupations of Iraq and Afghanistan, might prove "to be the solution."[34]

The above quotes give the briefest of flavors of how restricted, how establishment-friendly and corrupt are the media's limits on any debate about power and democracy. The public arena has been strangled into virtual submission to profit-led, short-term interests. Tellingly, news coverage of the report, as it related to the media itself, included no more than the briefest and most anodyne statements on the recommendation to "reform the rules on media ownership." That was about the extent of the discussion of corporate media dominance. The media's role as defenders of destructive state-corporate power, indeed, of being an integral part of a dangerous system of centralized power, was ignored. Once again, the corporate media had overlooked their own deep complicity in the undermining of democracy.

Justin Lewis: We have increasingly allowed the ubiquitous logic of the advertising industry to rule our lives. So many social, political, and economic activities are based on the shallow notion that happiness and fulfillment will be found in consumption. Our whole idea of progress is now based on that idea— progress is not about creating a *better* society, but about consuming more and better stuff. And the tragedy is that even advertisers know that isn't true— which is why their sales pitch is about ideals, images, and emotions rather than the objects they want you to buy.

Any idea that goes against the logic of a market system based on the increasing production of consumer goods tends to be marginalized. Even when faced with the profound threat of global warming—which will increase death, disease, and human misery on a staggering scale—we can only summon up the feeblest of responses while we carry on consuming. That's ideology for you.

Jeffery Klaehn: In what ways does power manifest itself in international law and within various international bodies, such as the G-20?

Brian Martin: In 2002, President George Bush and senior US government figures began planning to conquer Iraq, culminating in the invasion in March the following year. If such an invasion had occurred a century earlier, no legal issues would have been involved: there was no accepted international law against unprovoked aggression or conquest. But after the two world wars, governments set up international organizations to regulate war, and international law has developed increasing recognition.

The raw exercise of military power has become less acceptable: critics can cite law against it. The power associated with the law derives from people and governments subscribing to the principles involved. Invading Iraq appeared to be a blatant violation of international law, so Bush and company decided to seek an endorsement from the United Nations. But other governments on the UN Security Council—bolstered by massive public protest—were not receptive, despite US government threats and inducements behind the scenes. (The US government, using its enormous economic and political power, threatened trade reprisals and offering money.)

Rather than take the matter to a Security Council vote and suffer the humiliation of a defeat, the US government withdrew its motion and proceeded with the invasion. The violation of international law contributed to an enormous backlash: opinion polls in numerous countries showed decreased respect for the US.

Daniel Fischlin: One of my concerns about how power manifests itself in these structures is as a narrative predicated largely on non-elected elites who make decisions on behalf of global majorities. International law is exceedingly complicated and loophole-ridden—and the proliferation of instruments to exercise international law is part of a massive legal structure that, in my view, tends to obscure basic principles that need reinforcing. In human rights law, for instance, there has been such a plethora of instruments created, with different degrees of commitment (legal or otherwise) by multiple states that one has to wonder about the effectiveness of the overall superstructure. Sure, there's the appearance of concern and action but in terms of the material actuation of the rights of the most disenfranchised and dispossessed one really has to wonder—especially given that the past century has seen a rise of these rights instruments at the same time as the planet has never been as militarized. This disjunction is a manifestation of the true disposition of power at an international level—one that can be measured not in terms of the number of meaningful rights instruments that exist but rather in the total number of bullets and missiles that we've collectively fired in the name of civilization. This latter manifestation of power is where the actual resources are truly being allocated. And if we're to have any hope for a better future, we are collectively going to have to transform this manifestation of power vested in the richest countries and in the forms of international law that tacitly condone this disposition. I find it incredibly ironic as the rhetoric round climate change heats up that we still don't have, in what many would say is the defining creation of international law, the Universal Declaration of Human Rights (1948), a clause that clearly spells out the links between the environment and human rights, with the former being an absolute, irrevocable precondition for the latter.

Jeffery Klaehn: What about intellectuals, and their relationship to power?

Robert Jensen: In the context of this question, I take "intellectual" to mean those people who are given support to pursue intellectual work, understood as the project of (a) collecting data about the world (research); (b) trying to understand how the world works (analysis); and (c) conveying all this to others (teaching, speaking, writing, and media production). I have spent my adult life working either as a journalist or as a professor, jobs in which I have been given considerable resources to pursue these activities, which frees me of the need to do other kinds of productive work, such as producing food or shelter.

Not surprisingly, intellectuals tend to serve the needs of the system that gives them the resources to do this work. For example, the vast majority of journalists and professors with whom I have worked are careful not to challenge the fundamental structure of power-over in the state/corporate system. When they do their work within that framework with even marginal competency, intellectuals are rewarded. Those who challenge that system of power will face obstacles. But it should be noted that the systems in which I have worked in contemporary US society are relatively tolerant of a limited number of intellectuals who challenge those fundamentals. That's due in part to (a) the social movements that helped carve out space for honest, independent, critical inquiry during the 1960s and 1970s; (b) the limited number of decision-makers in the system who retain values of intellectual honesty and, within limits, support the exercise of freedom of inquiry; and (c) the fact that at this moment in our political history, elites are likely not to see the need to repress all critical inquiry, given that the system seems able to co-opt and absorb the current level of dissent. When the system of rewards and punishments is adequate to guide most intellectuals to accept subservience to power, a few outliers can be allowed, especially when those outliers can be cited as evidence of the openness of the system.

James Winter: Just as the news media are now corporate, so too are educational institutions. As public funding declines, corporate money fills the gap, and what's lost is independent research, teaching, and thinking. The most obvious example is medical education, where Big Pharma is, in some cases, virtually providing the lectures to medical students. Also as Chomsky points out, most educators are thoroughly indoctrinated because we've excelled in the education system, and now it's our job to indoctrinate others. Occasionally there are critics of the status quo who appear in academia, but these people largely have been marginalized by mainstream academia. Chomsky himself is lauded for his work in linguistics, but almost completely ignored or treated as a mad man when he talks about these issues. Other things such as the way young academics are required to publish gobbledygook in peer-reviewed academic journals means we are largely sidelined in important debates, which works in favor of the status quo. Mainstream academia is as bad as mainstream media when it comes to censoring critical material. Academics who are critical of power relations are obviously going to be critical of their own universities and administrators, and so they'll be marginalized for this. It's a system of rewards and punishment: conformity is rewarded and independent thinking is punished. The news media help to promote academics who support corporate perspectives, such as Michael Ignatieff, who in turn write books supporting the corporate media view, and the circle of life is complete.

Andrew Mullen: Intellectuals face a clear choice: they can serve the centers of power, the corporations, and the state, or they can challenge these. I agree with Noam Chomsky that "it is the responsibility of intellectuals to speak the truth and to expose lies." I also concur that

> for a privileged minority, Western democracy provides the leisure, the facilities and the training to seek the truth lying hidden behind the veil of distortion and misrepresentation, ideology and class interests through which the events of current history are presented to us.[35]

Pursuing these objectives, however, in terms of research and teaching, is not always easy. Individually, many intellectuals are seduced by power and status,[36] while others find themselves disciplined or ostracized for their critical stance.[37] Institutionally, the guild structure of the university is "one of the mechanisms for containing thought and promoting conformism." Such a structure

> has often served as a marvellous device for protecting [universities] from insight and understanding, for filtering out people who raise unacceptable questions, for limiting research—not by force, but by all sorts of more subtle means—to questions that are not threatening.[38]

Furthermore, the organization of the social sciences can also present problems:

> The economics department is interested only in abstract models of a pure free enterprise economy; the political science department is concentrating on voting patterns and electoral statistics; the anthropologists are studying hill tribesmen in New Guinea; and the sociologists are studying crime in the ghetto.... This is a subtle form of design to prevent inquiry into power; the disciplines are constructed so that certain questions cannot be posed.[39]

Moreover, these individual and institutional barriers to critical inquiry are being exacerbated by the neoliberal project and the marketization of further and higher education.[40]

David Cromwell: Well, first of all—and this has been said before many times by others—never trust anyone who regards himself/herself as an "intellectual!" Is that not rather a pretentious, aggrandizing term to bestow upon anyone? Next, let's recognize that if we're talking about those who work in universities and research institutes, there is immense pressure to conform to an increasingly rigid, authoritarian, corporate-led agenda in both research and teaching. Bids for funding are extremely competitive, and there are certainly disincentives for straying outside accepted, often unstated, norms in academic life.

Howard Zinn notes that the centralization of political power and corporate wealth ensures that the universities "produce people who will fit into existing niches in the social structure rather than try to change the structure... These larger interests [established power] are internalized in the motivations of the scholar: promotion, tenure, higher salaries, prestige—all of which are best secured by innovating in prescribed directions." This occurs not as the result of any grand conspiracy, "but through the mechanism of a well-oiled system, just as the irrationality of the economic system operates not through any devilish plot but through the profit motive and the market ..."[41]

It is difficult to put one's head above the parapet for fear of contravening terms and conditions of employment, or out of simple fear of approbation or ridicule. To take just one very minor example from my own experience: a couple of years ago I sent around an email at work (a research and teaching establishment) asking for volunteers to monitor a military exercise that would be taking place in and around the docks of Southampton, which houses our center. I was reprimanded, politely but firmly, by the center's director because, by the terms of my employment, this constituted unacceptable political activity while at work.

Another example: in 2002, Mark Levene, a friend and historian at the University of Southampton, and I set up the Forum for The Study of Crisis in the 21st Century, or "Crisis Forum" for short.[42] This brings together activists and academics to analyze the nature of the crisis facing humanity— the threats of climate change and nuclear annihilation being two very visible signs of this crisis—in a genuinely holistic way; and to empower "ordinary" people to surmount this crisis. By its very nature, the Crisis Forum is interdisciplinary, and also challenging of the status quo, bringing people together with numerous overlapping skills and interests. But obtaining funds from any of the UK's research councils (or anywhere else for that matter) for such an initiative—in particular, to enable researchers to spend time on projects, and to bring in people with administrative skills on a reasonable salary—has proved a frustrating affair. This is a familiar story, of course, which has seen countless initiatives run to corporate sources for grant money, struggle on a shoestring budget, or simply fold. So, there are real constraints on deviating from accepted ways of doing things in academia.

Jeff Schmidt, a former editor at *Physics Today*, goes into this whole intriguing phenomenon of conformity and obedience to power in an excellent book called *Disciplined Minds*. The "qualifying attitude" of a disciplined professional is, he writes, "an uncritical, subordinate one, which allows professionals to take their ideological lead from their employers and appropriately fine-tune the outlook that they bring to their work. The resulting professional is an obedient thinker, an intellectual property whom employers can trust to experiment, theorize, innovate, and create safely within the confines of an assigned ideology.

The political and intellectual timidity of today's most highly educated employees is no accident."[43]

This applies very much to academics, a highly privileged class of professionals, who

> generally avoid the risk inherent in real critical thinking and cannot properly be called critical thinkers. They are simply ideologically disciplined thinkers. Real critical thinking means uncovering and questioning social, political and moral assumptions; applying and refining a personally developed worldview; and calling for action that advances a personally created agenda... Ideologically disciplined thinkers, especially the more gung-ho ones, often give the *appearance* of being critical thinkers as they go around deftly applying the official ideology and confidently reporting their judgments.[44]

We can see this in the op-ed pages of the *Guardian*, for instance, almost every day of the week where all too many academics have lined up to hail Blair's "Gladstonian" policy of "humanitarian intervention[ism]" (to quote Oxford don Timothy Garton Ash[45]) or, since the utter disaster inflicted upon Iraq, to bewail the reduced likelihood of such a "benign" foreign policy ever being pursued again. This is the refrain shared by many obedient experts and journalists alike. For example, Julian Borger of the *Guardian* reported, in his usual role of stenographer to power:

> Tony Blair's idea of persuading the UN to enforce a no-fly zone over Darfur is likely to be a hard sell. As one aid official put it: "British and American bombing to advance humanitarian goals is a damaged brand on the world stage."
>
> The television pictures from Iraq have cut the public appetite for humanitarian intervention.[46]

But the bigger obstacle to peace and justice is the silence of academics. This fits a grand narrative where the essentially benign motives of governments are taken for granted, and where radical measures are frowned upon in academia. Historian Mark Curtis notes:

> It still amazes me how many people in NGO [nongovernmental organisation] circles, where I have often worked, retain essentially liberal outlooks— prepared to accept that reform within the existing system is the only required, or possible, strategy and often barely aware of the ideological role of the mainstream media. Governments are often still viewed in good faith and their public claims accepted, rather than being automatically dismissed or even questioned, as I think should be the default position. This outlook is based partly on knowledge, which is not surprising given the silence of academics and mainstream media reporting. It may be partly due to fears of the consequences at the workplace of adopting a more "radical" perspective.[47]

But these fears, while partly understandable, have significant repercussions for those on the receiving end of brutal state power. As Edward Herman rightly noted in the aftermath of the first Gulf War, "it is the function of experts and the mainstream media to normalise the unthinkable for the general public."[48]

Perhaps if academics—and "intellectuals" generally—took a stronger, more critical stance on state and corporate policies, we would take one small step closer to a world based on peace, wisdom, and compassion.

Justin Lewis: I suppose academics in more prosperous societies have the luxury to think about the broader social consequences of things, but they also operate in a world in which certain ideas are more valuable (in its crude, monetary sense) than others. What the academy does provide is a space for questioning some of our prevailing assumptions.

Jeffery Klaehn: Why is the concept of power important in relation to the study of human rights?

Martha Nandorfy: In the context of increased hegemonic globalization advanced by "free" (unfair) trade and communication technologies, issues of human rights and dignity cannot be understood without examining global networks of power. More and more, state power is intertwined with corporate power even if in certain instances governments and multinational business interests conflict. Western thinking on human rights from a purely individualistic perspective is clearly inadequate in a world where the majority is oppressed and has been divested of their land, which in turn is being destroyed together with air and water quality. The very basis of Western philosophy, Christianity, capitalism, and colonialism must be challenged in order to envision a human rights movement that places human beings back in communities with collective interests informed by an ecology of knowledge[s]. Understanding structural violence and how it is rooted in white supremacy and individualistic desire for power and wealth is crucial for envisioning a more equitable and sustainable future. How does élite power coalesce in institutions with global mandates like the WTO, the WB, and the IMF? Western tradition conceives of human power against nature, while feminist and indigenous thinking roots humans in nature, land being the source of life and knowledge. The concept of power lines connecting concentrated capital defended by increasingly totalitarian militarization is important for understanding the web of interests that systematically privileges profit over human and environmental rights.

Roger Clark: I would rephrase the question as follows: why is an understanding of power important in human rights work? Both assumptions described above are helpful in knowing how power "plays out" and how power relates to human rights. The legitimacy of power within society is the foundation of human rights and provides the ground for their definition and the justification for their defence. The concepts of natural law and social contract lie at the basis of this analysis. Any justification for a universal approach to human rights work is possible only if there is an agreement that the rights themselves are universal. The struggles and tribulations of the UN system are a consequence of failure by the international community to reach consensus on the nature of social and political power.

Many of today's challenges to human rights come from a return to a relativism that says that some rights are appropriate at some times and in some places. Unfortunately, this also implies that violations of rights may be appropriate at some times and in some places. The events of 9/11 continue to drive this accelerating agenda, leaving human rights considerably more precarious than they have been for some time. This proclaims that the means (including, for example, torture) may justify the ends or that human rights violations may be permissible "for the greater good." It is when faced with the tangible abuse of power that we most readily react and demand the protection of "our" rights. The real problem is two-fold: the abuse of power may not be widely acknowledged or even sensed, and the need to respond may not be felt as sufficiently worthwhile. It is one of the key responsibilities of the human rights NGOs to find ways of addressing these challenges.

There remains the fundamental question of how to begin addressing and remedying the abuses of power that do occur. For those who work in the human rights field, a sophisticated understanding of social, economic, and political levers opens up potentially effective ways to deal with human rights violations that are a denial of legitimate social and political power relationships. These are crucial avenues for bringing influence to bear, for challenging the abuses and misuses of power, and for achieving positive change. By harnessing the collective energies of social, economic, and political power it becomes feasible to reaffirm human rights and the rule of law and to work effectively for their realization. On such a basis, it may also be possible to recover some optimism for a renewal of human sustainability.

Brian Martin: Torture is the exercise of physical power against individuals to cause pain, for purposes of extracting information or causing fear. Torture of an individual involves a power relation between the torturer and the victim, but there is a wider dimension. Most torture is carried out by governments—dozens of them around the world—and these governments use their economic and political power to protect torture and torturers from scrutiny, through secrecy, police powers, bureaucratic arrangements, and international diplomacy.

Human rights discourse can be an effective rhetorical tool to oppose torture and other assaults on human rights. But human rights declarations do not by themselves lead to observance. State power frequently trumps human rights.

Most people are familiar with the arms trade; fewer are aware of the massive trade in the technology of repression: electroshock weapons, leg irons, stun grenades and computer surveillance systems. The biggest producers of this technology are Western companies; Western governments have regulations about export but loopholes allow a vigorous trade. Opponents of the trade in torture technology are confronting a powerful system. They use the language of human rights; to be successful, they need to mobilize public opinion. In 2004, images of abuse and torture at Abu Ghraib prison in Iraq by US prison guards were published in the mass media. Most torture is carried out in secret, because so many people are outraged by it. The Abu Ghraib photos broke through this secrecy barrier. Few torturers are ever brought to justice, but US military investigators pursued the perpetrators at Abu Ghraib.

However, senior US officials responsible for policy at Abu Ghraib and other prisons worldwide were not prosecuted, though they were named (at least by some commentators) and thereby shamed. In most countries where torture is carried out, there are no consequences for perpetrators and officials. Torture will continue as long as the power systems that sustain it.

Jeffery Klaehn: What are your thoughts on engagement and resistance?

Joel Bakan: It's an excellent idea—engagement and resistance. That's my basic thought. Even a quite conservative conception of democracy, it seems to me, includes—indeed requires—engagement and resistance. That is the duty of citizens in democracies, to be engaged in the governance of society, and to resist power and institutions that are hostile to the public interest, arbitrary, and undermining of freedom, equality, and social justice. Corporations, though recently re-branding themselves as socially responsible and benevolent, remain what they have always been—unaccountable to anybody but themselves, and legally programmed to do whatever they must to advance their own and their owners' financial interests. They have great power over our lives and the capacity to do much harm. They should be engaged and resisted, subject to democratic controls and public interest standards.

Yet, we, as a society, are doing the opposite. We are, through policies like deregulation and privatization, releasing corporations from democratic controls and granting them ever more freedom and power over our lives. Even activism is being privatized, as NGOs, often funded by private wealth, and in alliance with major corporations, are increasingly relied upon to solve the world's public problems.

Sometimes it seems as though we are giving up on the democratic institutions that constitute the public sphere. We are falling into the trap, perhaps unwittingly, of privatization ideology, believing that only private, voluntaristic, non-state institutions can deliver what needs to be delivered— that they are more efficient, less prone to corruption, and more benevolent than their counterparts in the governmental sphere.

While it is naive to believe that extant governments are exemplars of ideals of democracy and social justice, it is worse than naive to believe that we will be better off if we shift our political commitments to an alliance of corporate and activist nongovernmental institutions. For me, the solution lies with reinvigorating, rebuilding, and re-forming democratic and public governmental institutions, at both domestic and international levels. These, at least in theory if not currently in practice, are designed to manifest the ideals of democracy and social justice. It is certainly a challenge to make them actually serve the ideals that legitimate them, but it is in that direction—not the further privatization of politics and everything else—that we should be moving.

James Winter: It's an uphill battle, of course, but tremendous strides have been made by relatively few people, such as Chomsky or Michael Moore, or Michael Albert and Lydia Sargent of *Z Magazine* and Zmag.org. I sense a tremendous growth in resistance, as the injustices and absurdities become increasingly apparent. Young people involved in the anticorporate globalization movement learned valuable lessons about the nature of our police state, and they have been radicalized. Getting your head beaten in for carrying a protest sign will do that to you. The illegal invasions of Afghanistan and Iraq and the oil motive are transparent. People are heavily brainwashed, but they are not stupid.

I'm very optimistic, because ultimately, power is in the hands of the people, no matter how brutal the state, no matter how much weaponry it has. And even Western ideological hegemony has its limits. The ruling class is scared stiff of democracy and people power. Critical documentaries questioning power relations have exploded in number, and young people are soaking these up. What we saw in Seattle and Quebec City was just the beginning. We're in a brief hiatus right now because of 9/11, homeland security, and the terrorist-under-the-bed mentality. But as people realize that the so-called terrorists are really our allies in challenging the oppressors and global hegemony, this will change. The world will change.

Martha Nandorfy: I recently saw a documentary film about feminism entitled *Landscaping* (Homem, D'Aguiar, and Collet) in which a feminist view of the world is conceived of as a landscape that welcomes anyone committed to justice. In this way, feminism is not constrained within the woman's body (though many experiences, and thus outlooks and knowledge are rooted in the body).

If only women are able to think and act according to feminist principles and values, it becomes a bit like that bad joke about experimenting with reversing the traffic lanes. (This is a joke designed to make fun of certain regions or countries, which I'll skip here because it doesn't really serve any purpose). As the joke goes, in such and such a place they will implement this experiment by having trucks drive in the opposite lanes for a month, and if that works out well, then cars and other vehicles will also make the lane change.

Engagement and resistance varies enormously according to different regions, economic systems, social structures, etc. In affluent countries buying power must be replaced with doing power. Think how women in rich countries are reduced (and often happily accept being reduced) to shopaholics. An important step toward democratization will be to dismantle mass media as we know it, and to create alternative media to open up discussions on how we can live in harmony with the earth and each other, and what the implications of our daily actions are across the globe.

Women are disempowered in very different ways in different parts of the world, from the shopaholic who might even think that feminism is no longer an issue because individual wealth equals freedom, to the living nightmare of rape camps in war-torn regions where women suffer the brunt of the violence and humiliation of their flesh. Despite these vast experiential differences, we can all inform ourselves about the whole gamut of injustices and work actively to construct equitable social and political arrangements based on environmental rights and sustainability in all areas of human activity.

Daniel Fischlin: I can't separate engagement and resistance from education thought of in the broadest and most integrated sense—as something that occurs throughout the trajectory of any one life in all situations and circumstances. For me, the engagement that nourishes meaningful acts of resistance—locally or globally, individually or collectively—arises from meaningful forms of viral education that teach us to think of otherness and difference as an opportunity to learn more about ourselves and our place in the larger web of interconnectedness that we must address responsibly and creatively. The ancient Indian notion of *so-hum*—"you are therefore I am"—powerfully sums up this root form of engagement and resistance located in an ability to think beyond one's own narrow interests. Resist the urge to think of yourself as an independent entity without concern for your dependence on a complex interweaving of othernesses. Engage with others beyond your own spheres of interest and influence. Reach out. Civil responsibility and the ability to see far beyond the local implications of actions begin in a basic relationship of empathy and an awareness of the interconnectedness of all things and all beings. This is the bottom line for any real education that is truly informed—that globalizes this basic awareness of the sophisticated, beautiful inter-relatedness of all things. Whether in ancient Indian philosophy or in First Nations wisdom that teaches respect for the Earth that is our only possible home, engagement and resistance are only meaningful when they emerge from genuine affection and understanding about the baseline realities that make us part of a complex ecosystem of living, breathing, social beings. This is the root of it all, but how engagement and resistance get manifested are a whole other matter: whether in terms of the different forms of social organization that take place to articulate resistance; whether in terms of the ways in which people decide to allocate their own resources in support of resistance. For me, resistance at this late stage of things—with ecological disaster close at hand and the outrageous amount of resources wasted on military expenditures in a climate of infinite war pursued in the name of illusory securities—will increasingly be meaningful only insofar as direct, material pressure is brought to bear on how our collective social resources are allocated by small, self-interested elites.

David Cromwell: The title of Howard Zinn's recent collection of essays, *A Power Governments Cannot Suppress* makes the crucial point. When people join together in a common endeavor to protect and promote grassroot concerns, state power really does tremble. The government knows it is at the mercy of its population and that real, substantive change *can* be pushed through. Zinn has pointed out time and again the historical examples of progress brought about by "an aroused citizenry": the abolition of slavery in the United States, the women's suffragette movement, the civil rights and environmental activism of the 1960s, the ending of the state policy of apartheid in South Africa, and so on. As Zinn says,

> There is a basic weakness in governments, however massive their armies, however vast their wealth, however they control images and information, because their power rests on the obedience of citizens, of soldiers, of civil servants, of journalists and writers and teachers and artists. When the citizens begin to suspect they have been deceived and withdraw their support, government loses its legitimacy and its power.[49]

My feeling, shared with my Media Lens co-editor David Edwards, is that the left and grassroots activism generally has been grievously harmed and hampered by a wrong-headed belief that anger, and even hatred, fuels successful resistance. On the contrary, anger and hatred lead to dead hearts, burnout, and ultimate failure. As Victor Hugo once aptly said, "Hatred is the winter of the heart."

In *The Compassionate Revolution*, Edwards argues that the global capitalist system is dependent on the promotion of the three "poisons" of greed, hatred, and ignorance: greed for profit at any cost in terms of human and animal suffering; hatred of obstacles to profit; and ignorance of the cosy link between Western corporations and Third World dictators, helping to protect Western profits.[50] Activists could learn from the truly revolutionary potential contained in the conviction that "compassion is the basis and cause of all happiness," rather than anger and rage at "the enemy": business and political leaders. The antidote to exploitative social systems, argues Edwards, is rational awareness rooted in unconditional kindness and compassion for all. To the extent that we hate the architects of exploitation, we promote the very forces on which exploitation depends. By marrying the political arguments of Noam Chomsky and Edward Herman with the compassionate awareness of Buddhist writers such as Aryasura, Geshe Kelsang Gyatso, and Stephen Batchelor, Edwards shows how we can instigate a compassionate revolution in which the only enemies and casualties are poisonous greed, hatred, and ignorance.

Andrew Mullen: History instructs us that corporations, states, and other centers of power are not unassailable—a fact that holds true today. Ordinary people possess the ability and, if they act collectively, the power, to effectively challenge these institutions and shape their own destinies. There are many examples of ordinary people starting to organize in new ways to these ends: the anticapitalist/globalization movement, the antiwar movement, the World Social Forum, political campaigning using the Internet, alternative media sources (e.g. *Indymedia* and Media Lens), etc. However, while these progressive forces often know what they are up against, they are all too often vague about what should replace the status quo. These forces, building upon the anarchist and Marxist traditions, need to further develop and promote a coherent analysis of the world and engage in a serious debate about tactics and strategy. Exhortations that "another world is possible" are not enough.

Brian Martin: East Timor was invaded and illegally occupied by the Indonesian military in 1975, leading to massive loss of life over the course of the following two decades. By the 1990s, the East Timorese resistance movement (Fretilin) shifted its emphasis from armed struggle in the countryside to civilian protest in the cities. On December 12, 1991, there was a peaceful pro-independence protest as part of a funeral march in Dili, the capital city of East Timor. Indonesian troops opened fire on the marchers as they entered Santa Cruz cemetery.

This massacre might have remained hidden except that Western journalists were present, recording the events. Testimony, photos, and video footage caused outrage internationally and triggered a massive expansion of international support for East Timor's independence.

In this instance the Indonesian military seemed to have an overwhelming advantage. But killing hundreds of peaceful protesters backfired on the Indonesian government, because it was widely seen as a gross abuse of power and because vivid, credible information was made available to receptive audiences.

Perpetrators of injustice commonly use five methods to reduce outrage about their actions. They cover up the actions, devalue the target, reinterpret the events to be something less objectionable or to blame others, use official channels to give an appearance of justice, and intimidate or bribe targets, witnesses, and supporters. All these methods were used by the Indonesian government in relation to the Dili massacre, but in this case these efforts did not succeed. Those trying to mobilize against injustice need to counter each of these five methods. They need to expose what happened, validate the target, interpret the events as unjust, avoid official channels, and resist or expose intimidation and bribery.

The injustice at Dili was obvious and dramatic: troops were shooting peaceful protesters without provocation. Earlier, when Fretilin had used armed struggle, Indonesian atrocities and human rights violations had not caused nearly the same outrage, because the situation was perceived and cast as a war, in which both sides were perpetrators of violence, and also because the Indonesian aggression against East Timor received minimal media coverage in the U.S. and most other Western media. Apparent weakness—for example a commitment to nonviolence—can sometimes be a great source of strength in terms of resisting power and responding to abuses of power

The key goal in resistance is mobilization: encouraging more people to understand what is happening and to support or take action. This is a long-term process. What seems to be a defeat can be the foundation of success. The Dili massacre was a terrible tragedy but, on the morning after, many East Timorese were smiling because they knew, due to the presence of Western observers, that this time their suffering would be noticed. They were right.

Robert Jensen: We all are searching for an understanding of what it means to be human, what a meaningful life in the modern world might look like. Many of us believe that simply enriching oneself and retreating into some kind of isolation from the world in an attempt to protect our possessions is not a meaningful life. Yet that's exactly what the dominant culture encourages, which is why there are so many affluent people living materially comfortable lives in gated communities who are spiritually dead.. What is the antidote to it? The only one I know is engagement in the political life of the culture and resistance to those illegitimate structures of authority that create such a profoundly unjust world. For those of us living in relatively privileged positions, maintaining such engagement and resistance is often difficult (though never as difficult, of course, as living on the other side of that privilege). It can be hard to imagine strategies that will transform those institutions and produce a more just world. It's easy to become discouraged and give up. But the key is realizing that there is no meaningful life in this society if one abandons engagement and resistance. One can retreat from that, but it comes at the price of spiritual death.

Justin Lewis: For me, it's all about education—so that we are aware of what really is on offer—refusing to accept our own powerlessness, and accepting that doing something small is better than doing nothing at all.

NOTES

1. Ludwig Wittgenstein, *Philosophical Investigations*, Oxford: Oxford University Press, 1967.
2. Robert Dahl, "Power," in David Shills, *International Encyclopedia of the Social Sciences*, Volume 12, New York: Macmillan, 1968.
3. Peter Bachrach and Morton Baratz, "Two Faces of Power," *American Political Science Review*, Vol. 56, No.4, 1962, pp. 947–952.
4. Steven Lukes, *Power: A Radical View*, London: Macmillan, 1974.
5. See www.unison.org.uk
6. Quoted in *Understanding Power: The Indispensable Chomsky*, edited by Peter R. Mitchell and John Schoeffel, New York: The New Press, 2002, p. 70.
7. See, for example, John Newsinger, *The Blood Never Dried*, Bookmarks: London, 2006.
8. See J. Lewis, "The Role of the Media in Boosting Military Spending" in *Media, War and Conflict,* Vol. 1, No. 1., 2008, 108–117.
9. See P. Singer, *Corporate Warriors: The Rise of the Privatized Military Industry*, London: Cornell University Press, 2003; Burma Campaign UK, *Totalitarian Oil – Total Oil: Fuelling the Oppression in Burma*, London: Burma Campaign UK; Campaign Against the Arms Trade, *Corporate Mercenaries: The Threat of Private Military and Security Companies*, London: CAAT, 2006; Garry Leech, *Crude Interventions: The US, Oil and the New World (Dis)order*, London: Zed, 2006.
10. For a critical account of British foreign policy, see Mark Curtis, *The Ambiguities of Power: British Foreign Policy since 1945*, London: Zed, 1995; Mark Curtis, *The Great Deception: Anglo-American Power and World Order*, London: Pluto, 1998; Mark Curtis, *Web of Deceit: Britain's Real Role in the World*, London: Vintage, 2003; Mark Curtis, *Unpeople: Britain's Secret Human Rights Abuses*, London: Vintage, 2004. For a critical account of US foreign policy, see Noam Chomsky, *Year 501: The Conquest Continues*, Boston: South End Press, 1993; Noam Chomsky, *World Orders, Old and New*, London: Pluto, 1994.
11. State planners are tasked with developing and maintaining the economic and political power of the state, both domestically and on the international stage, in the "national interest" The liberal/pluralist view is that the state governs in the interests of everyone; the "national interest" therefore equates to the "common good." However, the critical/Marxist view is that, generally speaking, the state governs in the interests of the ruling elite and its corporate allies. Thus understood, the work of state planners— employed in the British Foreign Office, the Russian Kremlin, the US State Department, etc.—is primarily concerned with foreign policy formulation and safeguarding the position of the state *vis-à-vis* others within

the global capitalist economy. Their work is augmented by policy analysts working within civil society (think tanks for example) and the private sector (public relations companies for example).

12. Special Ad Hoc Committee of the State-War-Navy Coordinating Committee, Report of Committee Meeting, April 21, *Foreign Relations of the United States*, Vol.III, pp.164–165, 1947.
13. State Department (Executive Committee on Economic Foreign Policy), "Statement of United States credit and investment policy," August 11, *Foreign Relations of the United States*, Vol.I, Part 2, p.947, 1948.
14. State Department, Memorandum to the Secretary of State, February 8, *Foreign Relations of the United States*, Vol.I, p.632, 1949.
15. Economic nationalism tends to reflect the needs and wishes of the general population rather than corporations. It often results in a functioning democracy and policies such as capital controls, nationalization, progressive taxation, regulation, state intervention, etc. As such, it interferes with the prerogatives of elite management and the interests of the ruling elite, corporations, and capitalism more generally.
16. National Security Council, NSC-5432: "US policy towards Latin America," *Foreign Relations, 1952–1954*, Vol.IV, p.83, 1954.
17. See William Blum, *Rogue State: A Guide to the World's Only Superpower*, London: Zed Books, 2000; William Blum *Killing Hope: US Military and CIA Interventions Since World War II*, London: Zed Books, 2003.
18. See www.monbiot.com and www.guardian.co.uk for articles.
19. See www.hrw.org and www.amnesty.org for reports.
20. See Paul Baran, *The Longer View*, New York: Monthly Review Press, 1970; Naomi Klein, *No Logo*, Toronto: Knopf Canada, 1999.
21. See Ralph Miliband, *The State in Capitalist Society*, London: Quartet, 1973.
22. Edward Herman and Noam Chomsky, *Manufacturing Consent: The Political Economy of the Mass Media*, New York: Pantheon, 1988.
23. Thomas Ferguson, *Golden Rule*, Chicago: University of Chicago Press, 1995.
24. See Elizabeth Fones-Wolf, *Selling Free Enterprise: The Business Assault on Labor and Liberalism, 1945–1960*, Chicago: University of Illinois Press, 1994; Mike Hughes, *Spies at Work*, London: 1 in 12 Publications, 1994; Alex Carey, *Taking the Risk Out of Democracy*, Sydney: University of New South Wales Press, 1995.
25. See www.cbi.org.uk for a transcript of the speech.
26. See Joel Bakan, *The Corporation: The Pathological Pursuit of Profit and Power*, London: Constable, 2004.
27. David Edwards and David Cromwell, *Guardians of Power: The Myth of the Liberal Media*. Pluto Press: London, 2006 (AQ: Please confirm change).
28. Independent News & Media website, www.inmplc.com/main.php?menu=menu2&mb=cp, accessed April 29, 2007.
29. Anthony O'Reilly, quoted, Independent News & Media Plc Annual Report 2004, p.3.
30. Guardian Media Group website, www.gmgplc.co.uk/gmgplc/businesses/businessesintro, accessed April 10, 2007.
31. "Guardian Media Group Announces Sale Of Stake In Trader Media Group," March 23, 2007; www.gmgplc.co.uk/gmgplc/media/news/article/article114.html

32. Nigel Morris, "Bleak view of the gulf between people and government", the *Independent*, February 27, 2006.
33. Editorial, the *Guardian*, February 28, 2006.
34. Jonathan Freedland, "Without power of our own, we wait on the whims of politicians," *Guardian*, March 1, 2006.
35. Noam Chomsky, *American Power and the New Mandarins*, Harmondsworth: Penguin, 1969, pp.256–257.
36. See Christopher Simpson, *Science of Coercion: Communication Research and Psychological Warfare, 1945–1960*, Oxford: Oxford University Press, 1994; Noam Chomsky et al., *The Cold War and the University*, New York: New Press, 1997; Christopher Simpson (Ed.) *Universities and Empire*, New York: New Press, 1998.
37. See Jeff Schmidt, *Disciplined Minds: A Critical Look at Salaried Professionals and the Soul-Battering System that Shapes their Lives*, Oxford: Rowman and Littlefield, 2000.
38. Milan Rai, *Chomsky's Politics*, London: Verso, 1995, pp.138–139.
39. Ibid.
40. See Alex Callinicos, *Universities in a Neo-liberal World*, London: Bookmarks, 2006.
41. Howard Zinn, *The Politics Of History*, University of Illinois Press, Urbana, 1990, p. 9.
42. Crisis Forum website, www.crisis-forum.org.uk.
43. Schmidt, *Disciplined Minds*, p. 16.
44. Ibid., p. 41.
45. Timothy Garton Ash, "Blair's bridge: A strategic choice to stay close to the United States led us to Iraq. Was it worth it?," *Guardian*, September 4, 2003.
46. Julian Borger, "Blair's no-fly zone plan likely to be grounded despite growing crisis: Death toll continues to grow but hopes of relieving Darfur tragedy diminished by intervention in Iraq," *Guardian*, March 28, 2007.
47. Curtis, "Unpeople," p. 322.
48. Quoted, John Pilger, "The Truths they never tell us," *New Statesman*, November 26, 2001.
49. Howard Zinn, *A Power Governments Cannot Suppress*, City Lights, 2007, p. 13.
50. David Edwards, *The Compassionate Revolution*, Green Books, Totnes, 1998.
51. (James Daley, "*Independent News & Media* close to APN deal," *The Independent*, February 13, 2007).

PART II: MEDIA AND GOVERNMENT RELATIONS

CHAPTER TWO

Promoting War: The Power Politics of Manufacturing News

SYLVIA HALE

This chapter explores how ruling relations, or active practices of power, work to shape mass media coverage of war, and thus to manage public consent to war. Winning consent to war is never easy. Wars are always exceptions to normal governance. They entail sanctioned mass killing of people defined as "enemies" and destruction of their properties on a massive scale – activities that under normal times are considered criminally deviant. Wars also consume enormous economic resources, entail the virtual certainty of loss of life of members of one's own society, and the risk of violent retaliation.

International law, forged through the United Nations Conventions at the end of the Second World War defines military actions across internationally recognized state boundaries as illegal, and subject to sanction by the United Nations as a whole. Henceforth, only defensive war would be considered legitimate, war to defend one's own state against immanent attack from another. National boundaries were considered fixed by 1945, regardless of how they may have been changed by earlier conflict, and no territories gained through war would henceforth be internationally recognized. Furthermore, neither the United Nations nor its member states has the right to intervene in military conflicts or civil wars within national boundaries, with the one important exception of preventing "genocide." The Geneva Convention defines "genocide" as acts committed with intent to destroy, in whole or in part, an ethnic, racial, or religious group. These conventions have not been sufficient in themselves to prevent war, but they do pressure the governments of states that engage in war to justify such engagement on the international stage as legitimate self-defence against a criminal external aggressor, or as morally defensible humanitarian intervention in another "rogue" state to prevent such state from practicing genocide. Without such justification, states at war risk global opposition, punitive sanctions, and "rogue" status.[1]

States that become engaged in war also require the consent or at least acquiescence from their own populations, especially in democracies, in order to sustain the immense human and material costs of war in the long term. Such consent is always contested, and never completely achieved; it has to be continually renewed. Waging war has to appear as meaningful, reasonable, and morally justifiable policy to influential leaders and followers across different sectors of the population. Supportive mass media coverage of policies and practices surrounding war is a critical element in sustaining mass consent to war. Consequently, strategies to manage the media's coverage of war have become an important part of state and military strategy for waging war.

In totalitarian states, control of the media can be a straightforward matter of dictating content and suppressing dissent. The notion of "propaganda state" was first applied to the early years of Soviet Communist rule where the government employed newspapers, cinema, radio, posters, school books, plays, and art as arms of the state to purvey the communist message. In Nazi Germany Joseph Goebbels similarly commanded mass media to promote the state's message and to stigmatize enemies. Overt dissent was silenced.[2] In contemporary western democracies efforts by the state and military leaders to promote the supportive media coverage of war have to be subtler. Freedom of the press is a principle entrenched in the constitutions of all democratic states. Journalists do not simply function as mouthpieces for the state. To the extent, therefore, that media coverage of war does conform to state and military policies, that conformity itself has to be explained.

Mass media, and especially television, constitute the primary source of factual knowledge for the large majority of the population about the purposes and conduct of war. How media frame that knowledge to convey a sense of meaning and significance to events profoundly impacts on public opinion, and thus support for or opposition to war. Opinions are distinct from facts in the analytical sense that facts are in principle verifiable whereas opinions, as personal judgements, are not. However, they are inextricably connected, in that people, including journalists, draw on what they believe to be factual accounts to formulate opinions.[3] The "facts" that journalists themselves have access to what journalists think they know and how they come to know about "events" that constitute war frame how they in turn represent war for mass audiences.

The central focus of this chapter is thus not on media content as such, but on research into the active strategies employed by governments and military elites to construct knowledge of war for media outlets. It considers two very different wars, the US-led NATO intervention in the civil wars in Yugoslavia between 1990 and 1999, and the US-led invasion of Iraq in 2003. The first theatre of war was justified as humanitarian intervention in a sovereign state to prevent ethnic cleansing and potential genocide; the second as legitimate, if preemptive, invasion of a sovereign state to protect the free world from the threat of a rogue state with weapons of mass destruction.

NATO INTERVENTION IN YUGOSLAVIA: THE CASE FOR HUMANITARIAN WAR

The dominant representation in all forms of Western mass media of the civil wars in Yugoslavia cast aggressive Serbian ethnic nationalism as the main driving force in the conflicts. Majority ethnic Serbs, under the leadership of Slobodan Milosevic, fomented civil war with the objective of establishing a "Greater Serbia" and cleansing the region of ethnic minorities. Croatians, along with Muslims in Bosnia-Herzegovina and Kosovo fought defensive wars to protect their territories from Serbian expansionism. The United States and NATO forces were called to intervene militarily in a humanitarian operation to prevent the ethnic cleansing and mass death that would have occurred without such intervention.

Immediately after the war even left-leaning journalists described the intervention as "illegal but legitimate,"[4] illegal in that it contravened the UN Charter prohibiting involvement in internal conflicts within the former sovereign state of Yugoslavia, but legitimate because Milosevic's genocidal ambitions had to be stopped. Three American journalistic reports supporting this general view of the conflicts were deemed worthy of Pulitzer prizes for their quality of international reporting.[5]

The question of how this standard representation came to dominate Western media, both mainstream and left-leaning sources, is particularly pressing in the light of critical post-war scholarship that casts grave doubt on the accuracy of this representation.[6] These critics charge not simply that factual details are incorrect or omitted, but that the entire narrative is fraudulent. Their counterclaim is that villains and victims were in fact reversed: the Serbian leaders were not the instigators of ethnic cleansing, but rather were the victims, and further that the NATO bombing raids did not constitute "humanitarian intervention" to save Bosnian and Kosovar Muslims from slaughter, but unjustified bombing of Serbian residents who were themselves the victims of targeted terrorism. The objective of this chapter is not to judge the claims and counterclaims, but to make visible some of the active practices of political and military leaders that helped to manufacture the prevailing media representation, and the practices that contributed to media acquiescence in this representation.

WAR PROPAGANDA IN YUGOSLAVIA

In his analysis of "Balkan Holocausts" Macdonald[7] describes each of the major political leaders that emerged in the first post-Communist elections in Yugoslavia – Serb leader Milosevic, Croat leader Tudjman, and Bosnian-Muslim leader Izetbegovic – as engaging in mass propaganda to promote ethnic-based identities and fears for political gain. Typically they employed practices like drawing selectively from more than five centuries of checkered history of the Balkans to represent their own group as historically victimized by others, embellished with inflated numbers of people killed in different atrocities, and invocations of "genocide." They staged mass rallies as huge media propaganda events to commemorate anniversaries of famous battles and tragedies – Milosevic staging the 600-year anniversary of the Battle of Kosovo, and Tudjman the 52nd anniversary of the World War II slaughter of Croatian "patriots" by Serbian militias. They used such political narratives to promote patriotism among their electoral supporters and to generate and justify claims to territory in turbulent post-Soviet politics. Academics, writers, and artists joined in the mass ethnicization, producing a flood of publications promoting images of distinctive Serbian and Croatian religions and cultures, and highlighting small differences in dialect and script in Serbo-Croatian language.

Each of the political leaders tried to control mass media to promote their messages and to stifle criticism. However, it is the Croatian leader that Macdonald describes as bringing to bear the full oppressive power of the state over mass media to enforce compliance.[8] One of the first acts of the Croatian government was to enshrine articles into the constitution that granted sweeping presidential prerogatives to restrict constitutional rights in times of war or threat to the independence and unity of the republic. Tudjman used these rights to replace media editors and managers, to punish journalists, and to impose very strict rules for reporting military affairs. His government also completely took over the running of radio and television, turning it into a mouthpiece for the regime. Tudjman also specifically purged all journalists with mixed Serb/Croatian parentage from the state news agency, framing them as "enemies of Croatia." He also took over formerly independent papers, purging any media editors, managers, and journalists who challenged him. When he further purged

Serbs from the police force, universities, and most government bureaucracies, he faced no criticism from mass media.

These extreme measures might have sent warning signals to Western media that information coming out of Croatia might not be trustworthy. The dominant perspective in Western political discourse and media, however, remained that Serbian expansionism, not extremist Croatian ethnic secessionism, caused the conflict. Political leaders inside Yugoslavia all lobbied for international support for their causes of separation from, or preservation of Yugoslavia. International recognition for the independence of states that broke away from the Federation was a critical first stage in gaining legitimacy at home. Then, as the civil wars progressed, leaders sought money and weapons from foreign supporters. The biggest goal, which was ultimately decisive in the division of Yugoslavia into ethnically defined mini-states, was direct military intervention from the United States and NATO allies on the side of Croatian and Muslim secessionist forces, to bomb the Federal Yugoslav forces, referred to in Western media as "Serb" forces. This military intervention contravened international law and so it had to be carefully crafted and legitimated.

That crafting was accomplished in large part by the public relations firm of *Ruder Finn Global Public Affairs*, working under contract with the Croatian and Bosnian-Muslim governments. According to Diana Johnstone,[9] the Croatian government hired Ruder Finn in August 1991 to develop strategies to communicate with the US Congress and Senate, the State Department, and other relevant agencies, with the goal of bolstering Western military support. The Bosnian-Muslim leader Izetbegovic signed a contract with the same firm in June 1992 to promote a stronger leadership role for the United States in the Balkans. What followed was a massive and highly successful manufacturing of war narratives on a global scale, designed to mobilize and to legitimate US-NATO military involvement on the side of Croatian and Bosnian Muslims against the Yugoslav Federation and the Serbs.

Ruder Finn organized trips to Croatia for US Congressmen, combining selective onsite visits with video clips of death and destruction. The firm also set up a "Bosnian Crisis Communication Centre" designed to put local leaders in contact with American, British, and French government officials and mass media. It coached and assisted the Bosnian foreign minister in the preparation of press releases, and letters to world leaders and officials. It organized press conferences, and arranged personal contacts with key members of foreign governments like British Prime Minister Margaret Thatcher, American Vice-president Al Gore, and 17 other members of Congress. The Crisis Centre also prepared a regular stream of articles and war narratives for American media outlets, including the *New York Times*, the *Washington Post, USA Today,* and the *Wall Street*

Journal. Ruder Finn bragged that its greatest public relations success was getting Jewish opinion on side, despite the fact that Croats and Bosnians had persecuted Jews during the Second World War. It managed to turn this around by a story of the horrendous conditions in Serb internment camps in Zagreb, to convey the impression that Croats and Bosnians had endured persecution similar to Jews.

The most decisive public relations coup in promoting support within America for military intervention on humanitarian grounds, in the view of American journalist Samantha Power, was access to "Serb concentration camps."[10] By the summer of 1992, Serb, Muslim and Croatian forces had all set up prison camps for people considered threatening to their respective territorial control.[11] The Red Cross counted 2,692 prisoners in 25 detention centres – 1,203 held by Bosnian Serbs in 8 camps, 1,061 by Muslims in 12 camps, and 428 by Croats in 5 camps. Johnstone records that Ruder Finn focussed only on Serb camps. The Serbs invited Western media representatives to their camps, while Muslims and Croats did not. Ruder Finn arranged the publication of an iconic image of "a thin man behind barbed wire" in hundreds of Western media outlets, with captions like "Belsen 92" and "Ethnic cleansing means camps, rapes, murders, execution and mass deportations of non-Serb populations … a murderous ideology." The photograph and caption conveyed direct parallels between the death camps for Jews in Nazi Germany and the camps in Serbia. The photograph, however, was a simulacrum – a false representation of a "reality" that did not exist.[12] The emaciated man was actually suffering a long-term illness and not at all representative of the prisoners around him; he was in a transit camp, not a "concentration" camp, and the barbed wire in the picture was actually in front of the cameraman, not the prisoners. From this time on, Herman and Peterson argue, Western mass media began filtering almost all information about the conflicts in Yugoslavia through the prism of the Holocaust, with Serbs in the role of Nazis.[13]

Vastly inflating numbers of casualties was another tactic in the mass media propaganda war. A press release managed by Ruder Finn embellished a story of one girl who was sexually assaulted by three Serb prison guards into "maybe tens of thousands of assaults against Muslim and Croat women in Serb prison camps in northern Bosnia." [14] The State Commission for War Crimes in Sarajevo claimed 20,000 "well documented cases" of rapes intended to force Muslim women to conceive Serb children as part of a campaign of ethnic cleansing and genocide against Muslims. Bosnian Muslim President Izetbegovic topped this in January 1993 while attending talks in Geneva and later Washington, claiming 200,000 Muslim women in Bosnia had been victimized in the "most massive raping in human history."[15] Johnstone comments that there was no evidence even for the 20,000 rapes, let alone the 200,000. Izetbegovic also echoed reports that more than 200,000 people had thus far been killed in Bosnia-Herzegovina, or approximately 1,000 a day. These claims were reported as fact in an array of mass media, including the *Washington Post,* National Public Radio, Associated Press, the London *Independent* and the *New York Times*. The dubious credibility of the source was not questioned. The reports of violence and carnage in the media promoted public outcry in favour of humanitarian intervention. The figure of 200,000 became a baseline figure below which estimates rarely dropped. Two forensic research reports issued after the war ended, however, concluded that no more than a total of about 100,000 were killed on all sides of the Yugoslav conflict.[16]

Other tactics to discredit Serbian forces and promote US-NATO military intervention were more sinister. They involved instigating and provoking staged mass violence that could be used to vilify Serbs in foreign media. During the four-year siege of the Bosnian city of Sarajevo, Serbs were held responsible for three explosions in 1992, 1994, and 1995 that killed Muslim civilians, including people standing in a breadline and in a marketplace. Later, British and French investigators concluded that these explosions had been deliberately set by Muslims, killing civilians on their own side to blacken the reputation of Serb "aggressors."[17] Islamic fundamentalists recruited from Iran, allegedly with the support of the Clinton administration, may have been ultimately responsible for these bombings. They may have felt culturally far removed from the secular wine-drinking, pork-eating Bosnian Muslims.

The most serious allegation of atrocities raised against Serb forces concerns the Serb attack on the town of Srebrenica in July 1995, established by the United Nations as a safe haven for Muslim civilians in a Serb-dominated area of Bosnia. Serbs were charged with slaughtering as many as 8,000 civilians when they found it undefended by UN peacekeeper forces. This massacre was reported extensively in the Western media as "the worse atrocity in Europe since the Second World War."[18] Bosnian Serbs acknowledge that atrocities happened, for which the Srpska Serb government issued an official apology in June 2005. However, they contest the circumstances that led up to the attack on Srebrenica and the numbers allegedly killed.[19] The United Nations peacekeepers failed to demilitarize Srebrenica, as a supposed "safe haven," with the result that armed forces in the town were able to use weapons smuggled in regularly with food supplies to carry out a series of murderous raids on nearby Serb villages. Serbs claim that they attacked the town to stop these raids, and they further claim that the number of people killed was only a fraction of the reported 8,000 dead. The Red Cross estimated that about 5,000 residents had already fled from the enclave before Serb forces arrived, and about 3,000 were arrested by Bosnian Serbs. Serb forces separated out women and children and bussed them from the town as they routed the men. Six years of forensic research in the region found a total of 2,028 bodies.[20] Western media reports narrated the Srebrenica story as the mass murder of up to 8,000 people in a safe haven as "genocide," without qualification, and without discussion of the violent attacks on Serb villages that preceded it.

Johnstone argues that the entire Srebrenica episode was staged by Bosnian Muslims with their American backers, using civilians as pawns. The plan was to attack Serb villages around Srebrenica in order to goad the Serbs into launching an offensive against the town, while arranging for UN-protectors to be absent. This was part of a broader plan to let Bosnian Serbs keep the area around Srebrenica in return for leaving more extensive Serb-inhabited territory in western Bosnia. The genocide charge provided justification for the US-led NATO bombing campaign against Serb forces in Bosnia between 30 August and 20 September 1995 to pressure Yugoslav Serbs into a peace agreement that recognized Bosnia's independence on terms favourable to the Muslim faction.

Within a month of the Srebrenica conflict, as the NATO bombing commenced, Croat forces launched Operation Storm to drive over 250,000 Croatian-Serb residents out of the newly independent state, killing more than 1,000 of them, and with another 2,000 or more missing. This is now recognized as the most extensive ethnic cleansing of the entire decade of war in Yugoslavia. Yet this forced removal of people did not receive widespread coverage in Western media, nor was it referred to as "genocide" or even as "ethnic cleansing," but rather as "driving out foreigners." Journalists were far more interested in following up a story of aerial photographs of graves around Srebrenica than the forced exodus of Serbs from Croatia.[21]

Stories of the massacre by Serb forces of 45 Kosovar Albanians in the village of Racak in Kosovo on 15 January 1999 provided the impetus and justification for the 78-day NATO bombing of Serb positions and infrastructure between 24 March and 10 June 1999. Western verifiers who were invited to the village reported seeing scores of bodies in a gully, and reported the scene as a mass execution. Subsequent forensic research concluded that the victims had not died through execution-style killing and neither had they been killed in the village location, since there was no blood on the ground in the vicinity. The more likely explanation is that members of the Kosovo Liberation Army had trucked in the bodies to stage the scene for the investigators – a plan that Johnstone suggests was known to the CIA.[22] The KLA was well known as a terrorist organization, responsible for killing Serb police officers, as well as Albanian Muslims working in the Yugoslav federal public service jobs in police, forestry, postal service, and public utilities. On the day of the alleged Racak massacre, the KLA had killed five Serb police officers and two Albanians, and then fled into the village, with Serb police in pursuit. This staged violence set the scene for charging the Serbs with massacre. Reports of the massacre flooded Western media but subsequent research that challenged its veracity was not reported.

In summary, these active strategies used by secessionist forces in Yugoslavia to manage not just local, but global mass media, were extremely successful in projecting a one-sided account of war as the dominant representation in Western media. Journalists who published such reports of Serb concentration camps, the mass rapes of Muslim women, and the Srebrenica massacre won Pulitzer prizes for their works.[23] Their accounts helped to win mass public support and international legitimation for NATO military intervention on the side of secessionist republics against the federal Yugoslav state. In 2006, Serbian leader Slobodan Milosevic died in custody in The Hague where he was being tried for war crimes in an ad hoc tribunal –The International Criminal Tribunal for the Former Yugoslavia, set up, staffed, and funded by the United States. None of the media challenged the American bias built into the tribunal. Media coverage still pervasively characterized Milosevic as the central villain responsible for the wars in Yugoslavia, and overwhelmingly continued to cite the exaggerated numbers of over 200,000 dead rather than subsequent research supporting half that number dead for all sides combined.[24] Western political leaders, including Clinton, Tony Blair, and Vaclav Havel, and UN Secretary General Kofi Annan all praised NATO's humanitarian intervention in Yugoslavia as a war that placed the principle of human rights above the rule of states.[25]

The puzzling question that remains is why the secessionist war narratives prevailed rather than more even-handed war coverage, or narratives favouring Yugoslav federal forces or challenging military intervention. Even left-leaning liberal papers that are routinely critical of US militarism represented the intervention in Yugoslavia as legitimate. A partial explanation lies in the powerful international political interests in the United States and Europe in favour of military intervention. The United States and its NATO allies welcomed the opportunity to demonstrate the continued relevance of NATO as a military alliance in the post–Cold War era, and to flex their military muscle independent of United Nations controls. Milosevic was a particularly important target because his commitment to a socialist economy in Yugoslavia stood in the way of Western capitalist expansion into former Soviet markets. All pronouncements about the war from the American government and the Pentagon elites supported the secessionist version of events. Another part of the explanation, that will be explored further below, concerns why the mass media acquiesced so readily in purveying the dominant war narratives.

WAR PROPAGANDA FOR THE IRAQ INVASION

Strategies for the management of media coverage within America of the US-led invasion of Iraq in 2003 show important parallels to those employed within

Yugoslavia although the contexts and the framing of the war narratives differ. The principle audience for American war narratives was the American population itself rather than foreign media, but the American government is not a "propaganda state." The authoritarian methods of media centralization and purging of unpatriotic and dissenting voices from media jobs instituted by the Croatian government were not possible in America. What the government and Pentagon military elites orchestrated instead was a massive and multifaceted campaign to manufacture war narratives, to constantly monitor and manage public opinion, to circumvent journalists whenever possible from communicating directly with mass audiences, to manage journalists in carefully monitored situations, and to train cadres of analysts with vested interests in promoting official war narratives to serve as war commentators for mass media outlets.

The decision by the Bush administration to invade Iraq in March 2003 followed years of deliberation since the previous Gulf War against Saddam Hussein's government in 1991, and it came 18 months after the 11 September 2001 terrorist attacks (often referred to simply as 9/11) on the World Trade Centre in New York, and the Pentagon. Public mood in America was still very much in favour of military retaliation against terrorist organizations, but the connection between 9/11 and the Iraq government was not obvious, and fears that America might sink into another military quagmire like Vietnam were being expressed. Military elites within the Pentagon, the heart of the US military command, believed strongly that the US military had failed in Vietnam principally because of mass public opposition to the war at home, that had culminated in Congress voting to cut off war funding. Pentagon elites were determined that Congressional interference and public opposition would not be allowed to undermine the planned invasion of Iraq. Nothing was to be left to chance in the management of the new war narrative.

The Pentagon hired consultants from the public relations firm of *Hill and Knowlton* to assist in managing its public information campaigns.[26] This was the same firm that managed Pentagon information campaigns for the 1991 Gulf War, and that constructed the war story of Iraqi soldiers invading a Kuwaiti hospital and throwing premature infants from incubators to die on the floor. The story later turned out to have no basis in fact. One of the tasks assigned to consultants in 2001 was to sell American cultural values to Arabs through a radio station that mixed rock and pop music with testimonials to the happiness of Muslims living in multicultural America.[27]

By 2002 as it was preparing to invade Iraq, the Bush administration raised public opinion polling to the status of science, commissioning almost continuous polling to determine prevailing attitudes and concerns among the American public, on which to craft new speeches and messages for mass consumption, followed by more polls to test the effectiveness of the messages and to craft new ones. Polls revealed a wide range of concerns and motives that might be harnessed for war narratives but that risked developing into antiwar movements if not carefully managed. Hundreds of carefully crafted speeches prepared by and for spokespersons in multiple layers of government and military bureaucracies addressed these hopes and concerns.

In the weeks and months following the 9/11 attacks, mass public opinion in America was strongly in favour of military action to avenge the terrorism and to protect America from the threat of future attacks. Military force against Afghanistan, the home-base of the terrorist network "al-Qaeda" and its leader Osama bin Laden, the alleged mastermind behind the attacks, was readily justified as retaliation for the attacks and defence against planned future attacks. Linking the planned invasion of Iraq as a revenge for 9/11 attacks was more difficult, as there was no direct evidence that Saddam Hussein's secular Ba'athist government had any links to al-Qaeda or to 9/11, or to religious fundamentalism. In place of facts, the subjective impression or sense in the minds of masses of people that there were some connections was carefully constructed in multiple public speeches by President Bush and other senior government personnel who elided references to "al-Qaeda," "terrorist attacks," and "Saddam Hussein" in linked sentences. Such sentences did not literally state that Hussein was involved with 9/11 attacks, in ways that could be challenged or falsified, but were sufficient to promote the suspicion in mass audiences that he was. These impressions were compounded with constant repetition of the claim that Saddam Hussein might have, was known to have had, almost certainly did have, and certainly was prepared to develop, an arsenal of weapons of mass destruction that could or might find their way into the hands of terrorist organizations. In multiple speeches, government spokespersons mentioned that the Iraqi regime "had a history of reckless aggression in the Middle East," that it boasted "a deep hatred of America," that "it harboured terrorists," it "continued to possess and conceal some of the most lethal weapons ever devised," and the like.[28]

This kind of impression management through innuendo to generate public opinion in favour of war with Iraq is a powerful example of common-sense reasoning described by Justin Lewis [29] in which people form opinions on the basis of what they think they know, and how they come to know it. These propaganda messages were so successful that public opinion polls carried out months after the invasion of Iraq showed that the majority of Americans believed that Saddam Hussein was responsible for the 9/11 attacks and that American soldiers had found weapons of mass destruction in Iraq.[30]

Public opinion polls in the months before the invasion indicated a growing acceptance among American people that war with Iraq was likely, but that they preferred it to be part of a coordinated international military force sanctioned by the United Nations, as the 1991 Gulf War had been, rather than a unilateral American invasion. The State Department played to these audience concerns through multiple references to UN sanctions against Iraq and UN resolutions requiring Iraq to destroy in verifiable ways any stockpiles of weapons of mass destruction, and through the highly publicized and lengthy speech prepared for Secretary of State Colin Powell to deliver to the UN Security Council on 6 February 2003. In the speech Powell insisted that the State Department had verifiable evidence that the Iraqi regime did indeed have such weapons, had not destroyed them, was evading UN inspectors, had contacts with known al-Qaeda terrorists, and was conspiring to buy components for developing nuclear weapons technology. When the U.N. still balked at armed invasion of Iraq, American government speeches turned to representing the UN Security Council as sharing America's assessment of the Iraqi regime, but lacking the resolve or will to take decisive action. Hence, the U.N. required American leadership to coordinate a "broad coalition" of like-minded countries, a "coalition of the willing" to take action to protect the free world. Once the invasion began, the centralized Office of Global Communications, managed by public relations consultants, mandated the use of the term "Coalition Forces" to refer to American–British forces, to sustain the impression of global free-world involvement in the invasion.

Public opinion polls revealed far higher support for "humanitarian" war like the intervention in Yugoslavia to protect victims of targeted ethnic cleansing than for a war of aggression. These sentiments were harnessed to the invasions of Afghanistan and Iraq through multiple references in public speeches to America's goal of spreading freedom and democracy to the Middle East, liberating the citizens of Afghanistan and Iraq from brutal dictatorships, and from arbitrary imprisonment and torture, thus spreading a new era of human rights to these beleaguered countries, and above all, liberating women in these societies from tyranny. Videos of Afghan women shrouded in burqas filled the airwaves, along with narratives describing them as forbidden to leave their homes unescorted, or to take jobs, being flogged for revealing any part of their bodies in public, and of girls forbidden to attend school. Hussein was described as a tyrant who tortured and gassed his own citizens. Americans were assured that masses of people would welcome American soldiers as liberators.

These war narratives represented the United States on the side of Good against unmitigated Evil in the world. President Bush's first address to the American nation after the terrorist attacks carefully avoided any reference to America's military, political, and economic policies in the Middle East. He addressed the question of "why do they hate us" as an issue of antimodernism and religious fanaticism. "They hate our freedoms," he declared. He invoked classic themes of good against evil, civilization against barbarism, democracy against fascism and totalitarianism, and prosperous pluralist democracies against feudal tribalism. America's messianic mission in the world would be to spread freedom and democracy in the world. Frequent invocation of God's blessing on America in President Bush's speeches and of hearing a calling from God to rid the world of evil-doers, helped to confirm the image of humanitarian intervention.

The last fear expressed by the American public, that the new wars would drag America again into a protracted Vietnam-style war with hundreds of thousands of civilians slaughtered and massive loss of American soldiers, was countered by military experts extolling the newest "smart" weapons capable of precision targeting of military installations, with minimal "collateral damage" of civilian injuries.

In summary, almost all the important concerns and talking points identified in opinion polls were carefully addressed and built into public speeches preceding the Iraq invasion: terrorism and weapons of mass destruction, international coalition support, humanitarian goals, a messianic struggle for Good against Evil, and the promise of easy military victory with soldiers welcomed as liberators. The term "almost" is critical for what these carefully orchestrated public speeches omitted. The speeches prepared for President Bush to deliver omitted any reference to the long history of America's military, political, and economic policies in Middle East, including support for Israel's militaristic policies, America's military bases in Saudi Arabia that Osama bin Laden noted as justifying the 9/11 terrorist attacks, and strategic interests in controlling Iraqi oil fields. The 9/11 attacks were referenced as "ground zero," the beginning of a new world order of global war on terror, as if the attacks themselves had no history. Bush rejected as irresponsible, partisan, and defeatist those critics who tried to blame America for all the wrongs in the Middle East. He asserted that anyone who implied that America "acted in Iraq because of oil or because of Israel, or because we misled the American people," was guilty of siding with the enemy who attacked America.[31]

Coinciding with the narratives justifying invasion of Iraq, the Bush administration instituted a massive public campaign to promote the need for enhanced homeland security embodied in the new Department of Homeland Security and the PATRIOT Act signed into law on 26 October 2001. This massive 342-page Act circumscribed many rights and freedoms from American citizens, giving officials extraordinary powers of surveillance to execute nationwide search warrants, to tap emails, electronic address books, and computers, to view bank records, to conduct roving wiretaps on phones anywhere, and to designate any group, foreign or domestic, as "terrorist."[32] The inauguration of homeland security measures was accompanied with continuous emphasis by government officials and spokespersons on levels of threat and vulnerability to future terrorist attacks. Conjectures about levels of risk of terrorist attack were communicated through colour-coded warning signals as "severe" (red), "high" (orange), "elevated" (yellow), or "guarded" (blue) but never nonexistent, and these levels were routinely referenced in news broadcasts and community events. The pervasive climate of fear following the 9/11 attacks, heightened further by this heavy emphasis on homeland security measures, formed the context in which public narratives promoting war were heard.

Constant repetition of war narratives in a constantly stirred-up atmosphere of fear were central strategies in the management of public opinion. Audiences were bombarded with a staggering array of texts including official speeches, media interviews, press releases, radio and television programs, and articles by leading figures in administration, representing official thinking on the "war on terror." Jackson counts over 6,000 public speeches on the topic of homeland security and counter-terrorism in the first two years after the 9/11 attacks.[33]

BUILDING IN SINCERITY

For public speeches to be effective, they have to come across to audiences as sincere, and this requires the right mix of facial expression, demeanour, and intonation in speech delivery, especially for speeches that are clearly scripted in advance. There is no guarantee that audiences will accept or even pay attention to public speeches. The Bush administration hired experienced communications staff from television networks with expertise in lighting, camera angles, story line, and backdrops, to stage-manage the President's public appearances and speeches.[34] According to Gallagher, this emphasis on "deploying the spectacle" began even during Bush's election bid in 2000, when Bush arranged to have a ranch constructed at Crawford, Texas, as a backdrop for homespun articles and pictures of himself as "at home on the ranch," and as "just another sun-hardened ranch hand," ready to step forward and do his duty for America.[35] Later, for a speech delivered at Mount Rushmore, media handlers positioned the platform so that Bush's profile would be exactly in line with the four carved stone heads of former presidents.

Such extreme care in crafting the President's public appearances, especially for major speeches and addresses to the nation, were designed to hold audience attention and convey an air of trustworthiness. Rutherford describes Bush's speech to the nation on 17 March 2003, to announce the start of war with Iraq as "a command performance" – he was dressed in black, with the American flag in the background, and with cameras in close-up mode to establish eye contact with the audience. The image that his media handlers created was of "a moral father figure who would always speak the truth to young colleagues."[36] President Bush and his staff of media experts accomplished another command performance of epic proportions on 1 May 2003, barely one month after the invasion of Iraq began. In the morning Bush appeared in black suit to lead the nation on the World Day of Prayer. In the afternoon, he was displayed as "commander-in-chief," landing in a fighter jet on the flight deck of the *USS Abraham Lincoln* and wearing a flight suit and carrying a pilot's helmet. White House staff arranged for the navy to fly a banner reading "Mission Accomplished" as a backdrop to the scene in which Bush informed the nation that American troops had secured Baghdad and toppled the regime of Saddam Hussein, and that active combat was over. This image, and especially the banner, would come back to haunt the President and be the butt of many internet jokes as the years of military occupation dragged on. As a piece of stagecraft, however, it worked exceptionally well to keep audiences tuned in to the news.

WAR AS MANAGED INFOTAINMENT

Once the invasion of Iraq began in March 2003, the management of war narratives went into high gear. The American government could not take over mass media entirely for the duration of the war, as had the Croatian government, but it nonetheless tried to manage and control war narratives, especially the interpretive frames within which audiences came to believe they "knew" what was happening. The most direct method of control was daily broadcasts by military elites, timed to hit the airwaves early each morning. Pentagon communication experts spent a quarter of a million dollars to design the set from which General Tommy Franks gave his morning reports from Qatar on the progress of the invasion, complete with before–after photos of successful missile strikes from the previous day. The special power of such broadcasts is that they bypassed civilian journalists entirely. They framed the agenda to which media commentators responded.

The second closely related communication strategy developed by the Pentagon was to promote a select group of expert military analysts and administrators who could be relied upon to deliver themes and messages about the war that would echo the Pentagon line. Even before the 9/11 attacks, Pentagon communications strategists had recruited some 75 "key influentials" who could be counted on to support Rumsfeld's priorities. Most of them were decorated war heroes and retired generals and senior officers, and they conveyed the image of being authoritative and informed experts who were independent of the current administration. They were soon in high demand by media networks to provide informed commentary on the war, and they commanded stipends of $500 to $100 for each appearance. They acted as "message force multipliers" for the Pentagon.[37] What the networks mostly did not know, or did not care to ask about before 2008, was that most of these supposed independent analysts were part of the military–industrial complex, operating private businesses that were seeking contracts with the military. Barstow notes that these critical details became public knowledge only on 20 April 2008, when the *New York Times* successfully sued the Defense Department to get 8,000 pages of email messages between the Pentagon and the consultants.

A close symbiotic relationship developed between consultants, the Pentagon, and the media networks. The consultants were able to forewarn the Pentagon of planned media stories; the Pentagon gave them privileged access to military briefings that enhanced their status as informed consultants, and ensured that their media commentaries supported the Pentagon line. In return the consultants earned status as informed consultants, and had privileged access to push their business interests with key figures like Rumsfeld and Cheney at the top of Defense Department.

The Pentagon coached these military analysts to see themselves as part of a team, training them in how to incorporate ideas from the briefings into talking points as media consultants, but representing the points as their own ideas. Records of email correspondence revealed how they were encouraged to slip in references to al-Qaeda in comments about Iraq, to give as their considered opinion that Iraq had weapons of mass destruction, and was developing nuclear weapons technology, and to opine that the invasion would be quick and inexpensive, and be viewed as a "war of liberation" by average Iraqi people.

The Pentagon also arranged for key analysts from CNN and ABC networks and research group columnists to visit selected sites in Iraq and report on their visits to model schools, refurbished government buildings, and the like. The columnists role was to promote a positive narrative for Iraq as bursting with political and economic energies. The Pentagon used these consultants to counter instances of "bad-news" bias of mainstream journalists, to marginalize war critics, and to promote public support for the war. The first trip was so successful from the Pentagon's standpoint of news management, that several more trips were organized. These included a special trip for ten analysts to the Guantanamo Bay Prison after a damning report was issued by Amnesty International. Consultants were coached to counter the report by commenting on how they found the prison to be "professionally run" and to use "humane treatment."

The Pentagon closely monitored these media consultants, hiring the private contractor *Omnitec Solutions* to use "corporate branding expert tools" to track every media appearance by all the analysts. Any that strayed from the Pentagon line, as in suggesting that the war was not going as well as expected, risked being cut out of select group. They would lose access to the Pentagon briefings that sustained their image as well-informed media consultants. More importantly, they jeopardized their privileged access to Pentagon elites who controlled the allocation of lucrative business contracts. As just one example, William Cowan, a favoured consultant on the Pentagon-sponsored trip to Iraq, was chief executive of a new firm, WVC3 Group, that was seeking contracts from the coalition to deliver counterintelligence services in Iraq. Cowan kept quiet on major discrepancies between what he saw in Iraq and Pentagon media statements so as not to jeopardize these contracts. When he finally broke with the Pentagon line on 3 August 2005, to comment that the US was "not on a good glide path right now" in Iraq, he was precipitously fired from the analysts group.

The administration was not able to prevent all negative news from hitting the media, but Pentagon communications staff were able to send emails out to their cadre of media consultants to prime them on how to lead media discussions and write columns consistent with the preferred Pentagon interpretations. Images of carnage in Baghdad and other major cities in Iraq were available for those who knew where to look, posted on the internet by the Arab media network Al Jazeera broadcasting from Qatar, with correspondents stationed in Baghdad, and by dissident individuals and reporters. However, Pentagon spokespersons and media consultants were largely able to conceptualize them for audiences as enemy propaganda, or as minor setbacks. One instance when information control did seriously break down was when graphic pictures of American soldiers torturing Iraqi prisoners at Abu Ghraib prison were posted on the internet. Scenes that gripped the mass media included prison guards jeering at naked male prisoners piled in a heap, and threatening naked prisoners with attack dogs. One picture of a female prison guard, Private Lynndie England, smiling as she dragged a naked prisoner by a leash around his neck, became ubiquitous in the media.[38] Such pictures prompted calls for Secretary of Defense Donald Rumsfeld to resign. They also prompted swift damage control by the Defense Department to defame England as sexually depraved and sadistic, and in no way typical of US military conduct.[39] Such talk suppressed debate of wider questions about how Rumsfeld's policy of supporting torture as a legitimate means to extract information from prisoners contributed to the behaviour of prison guards.

Rumsfeld himself came under direct attack in the media on Friday, 14 April 2007, when several of Rumsfeld's former generals, none of them network military analysts, went public with a critique of how Rumsfeld had managed the war, and especially of his policy of outsourcing military tasks to the private sector while cutting back on career soldiers. Email records showed that Rumsfeld called 17 loyal military analysts to a secret meeting at the Pentagon to strategize on how to "crush these people" who were representing the war as a lost cause, and press the message that the war strategy had been brilliant, very successful, with low casualties, and how America had advanced militarily, got control over oil, sovereignty, access to the geographic heartland of the Middle East, and focus discussion on the next milestone in the global war on terror, the confrontation with Iran.[40] Barstow notes that even General Petraeus met with these military analysts at the time when he was testifying before Congress about Iraq. In short, these consultants functioned very effectively as support systems for government and Pentagon war policies. Military leaders provided selected daily information bites for the media on the conduct of the war, and consultants provided approved commentary to put a positive spin on the information.

CO-OPTING COOPERATIVE JOURNALISTS

An innovative third strategy developed by the Pentagon was designed to manage the war narratives of civilian journalists. It was virtually impossible for the administration to block the access of journalists to the front lines once the war began, especially in an era when even amateurs can send instantaneous internet transmissions using cell-phone cameras. But it was imperative to ensure that most of the coverage would be sympathetic to the military's view of the war as "humanitarian intervention," and as using "precision smart bombs" that cause minimal "collateral damage." The strategy the Pentagon adopted was to embed journalists with American forces. Some 600 carefully selected reporters were given a condensed course in basic military training and then placed with American troops in the field.[41] The result was that reporters developed close relations of comradeship and loyalty with the soldiers. They felt their fears and exhaustion, and their elation with successes. Embedded reporters often used the term "we" when talking about the troops, indicating how closely they came to identify with the soldiers whose everyday lives they shared.[42]

Audiences of 24/7 news coverage of the war during the critical first month of the invasion and push towards Baghdad gained the impression of seeing the war through the eyes of American soldiers. Reporters bounced along in tanks, shooting real-time videos of rockets being fired and silhouettes of distant buildings crumbling. People described themselves as becoming addicted to the news, glued especially to the nonstop CNN coverage of events. By agreement with the Pentagon, American mass media agreed not to show images of American casualties or Americans being taken prisoners. What audiences also did not see was the destruction and carnage on the streets of Iraqi towns crushed by "coalition forces." By one estimate, Gallagher comments,[43] over 10,000 Iraqi soldiers died in the fighting as coalition forces pressed on to Baghdad, but the heaps of dead bodies and body parts stacked high beside the road leading towards Baghdad were not in the focus of CNN war coverage. The footage that was replayed hundreds of times on American television was of the giant statue of Saddam Hussein being toppled with the help of a US tank.

A related strategy consistent with the image of "humanitarian war" was to personalize war narratives around individual soldiers represented as moms and dads with their families back home. In effect, the war image was feminized.[44] Official speeches routinely made a point of stressing "our courageous men and women in uniform." The media featured stories that focussed on images of moms who combined military courage and femininity, sleeping in barracks with photos of their children under their pillows; stories of soldiers sending goodwill messages home, and of children missing their moms and dads, wishing they would come home. Such stories of families coping with the stress of parents being in the armed forces in a conflict zone worked both to personalize and to depoliticize war. The focus is on individual lives, not the big picture. Advice to parents on how to tell children about war encouraged telling stories about our courageous heroes, and how lucky we are to have such heroes to protect us.

Media images of troops as occupation forces favoured scenes of troops throwing candy at Iraqi children, and poignant stories of an American soldier cradling a child whose parents had been killed in cross-fire; of troops setting up a charity to pay the school fees of an Afghan child whose father was dead; and of school children in America contributing to a charity to help Afghan children.[45] The focus on children also promoted the theme of "restoring lost childhood" for children in Afghanistan whose lives had been ruined by the Taliban's extremist rules that prohibited playing music, and even banning kite-flying. Happy children in occupied Kabul were filmed buying DVD players. What American media did not dwell on were images of terrified children, smashed houses, and war-ravaged towns. Major network news channels admitted later that they had concerns that war coverage would cost them advertising dollars as advertisers did not want their products associated with negative images of war. In reality, war coverage was sufficiently humanized and comfortable that advertisers soon returned.

A further strategy that the military tried at least once was a Hollywood-style simulation of a human-interest war movie for television. Commandos filmed their colleagues carrying out a daring raid to rescue an injured American soldier, female supply clerk Private Jessica Lynch, held captive in an Iraqi hospital. The footage of Special Forces rushing Jessica Lynch on a stretcher to a waiting helicopter, while comrades held off sniper fire from the roof of the hospital, was replayed hundreds of times on American television. Newscasts embellished the images with stories from "unnamed government sources" of how she had "fought fiercely and shot several enemy soldiers" after Iraqi soldiers ambushed her supply convoy, and "emptied her weapon before being stabbed and finally taken prisoner."[46] Jessica was greeted back home in Virginia with a hero's welcome.

A few days later, however, the story came apart, when journalists from the British BBC and Associated Press visited the hospital where Lynch was held. It became apparent that the footage was a fraud, or rather a simulacrum of a reality that did not exist, much like the iconic thin man behind barbed wire in the Balkan conflicts. By the time Jessica was being "rescued" Iraqi soldiers had long since left the area, so there was no sniper fire. Moreover the hospital staff had twice tried to get Jessica back to American forces but had been turned back. The film of American forces rushing the hospital, shooting guns, and breaking the door to shouts of "Go, go, go!" was all a show. Moreover, Private Lynch did not "fight fiercely" or get stabbed. She got knocked out when she accidentally rolled her vehicle. When ABC News subsequently tried to cover more objectively how the "rescue" looked to Iraqi hospital staff, the network apparently received hundreds of letters from audience members complaining that they were undermining the troops.

Potential stories of military bravery, injuries and death of American female soldiers that were not served up for American television underscore how deliberately the military contrived this movie event of Jessica Lynch's rescue for its appeal to white American mass audiences. An African American woman, Shoshana Johnson, was captured during the same ambush of Lynch's convoy.[47] She was shot in the legs and held captive in the Iraqi hospital for 22 days, but no movie was made of her ordeal. A Native American female soldier, Private Lori Piestewa, died during the Iraq mission – the first ever Native woman soldier to be killed, but her story did not make headlines. Only a young, blond, white woman soldier was selected for the military's Hollywood-style movie.

In summary, through these many strategies the Pentagon communications staff managed to maintain a carefully edited, upbeat message on the Iraq war for mass media consumption. Audiences who watched the almost nonstop war coverage on American television were led to think they knew that the war was going well, and that "collateral damage" limited. Their soldiers were courageous heros and heroines, carrying out a humanitarian mission to protect the world from terrorists bent on mass destruction, and to bring democracy and freedom to Iraq. Most Iraqis welcomed the American liberators. Problems were due mostly to "death squads," "insurgents," and "extremists" bent on fomenting civil war, never to the American invasion itself.

Management of media discussion still continued in 2008 with spokespersons from the Bush administration representing the next stage of the war on terror as confrontation with Iran, citing its alleged "weapons of mass destruction," its rogue status, the fact that it is within five to ten years of developing nuclear weapons technology, and thus that Iran poses an immense terrorist threat. This Pentagon perspective meets with widespread support across mass media with the usual media consultants. The counter message that virtually all the Middle Eastern states have the technical capacity to develop nuclear weapons within a time span of 5–10 years as a projection from knowing how to run nuclear power stations, there is no direct evidence that Iran is actually developing such weapons. Iran in any case is no threat to the US and is very unlikely to attack Israel because it would mean national suicide, and is mostly afraid of a rogue Pakistan, a fact that received little consideration.[48] The Obama administration first tried to change the tone of the rhetoric, offering to begin direct talks with the Iranian government. However, with the disputed elections in Iran in 2009 that returned Ahmadinejad to power, much of the old tone of dangerous rogue state has returned, along with the discourse of supporting the ordinary people of Iran against their oppressive government.

MEDIA WARS

This last section explores war coverage from the perspective of mass media – the reporters, journalists, and commentators whose daily work it is to collect available information about war and convert it into news. These strategies vary from active endorsement and support of war narratives and interpretive frames provided by government and Pentagon, to passive acquiescence by acting merely as a conduit for messages from government sources, and much more rarely to critical questioning and resistance to the government line. As noted above, Western democratic governments, including American, are not propaganda states. Governments cannot take over and run mass media as their own mouthpieces. To the extent that the mass media did echo the war narratives of the Pentagon and governing elites, this has to be explained.

There are significant structural reasons why everyday journalism reflects governing perspectives, many of them spelled out in the early critical study by Chomsky and Herman *Manufacturing Consent* (1988).[49] Mass media outlets in America are mostly subunits of giant corporate capitalist enterprises. They depend on advertising revenues and subscriptions to generate profits. Hence the news, reporting, commentaries, and infotainment generated around wars are circumscribed by concerns with how such coverage will affect audience ratings and corporate clients that buy advertising space. When heads of media corporations met with Attorney General John Ashcroft in November 2001 to discuss war coverage and patriotism, none of them opposed Ashcroft's call to voluntarily limit free speech and freedom of the press to support the war effort. For the most part they shared the view that loose talk and excessive criticism of the war effort might undermine troop morale and thus aid the enemy and support terrorism. They also recognized that the appearance of patriotism was important for their "bottom-line" concern with pleasing audiences and thus advertisers. News channels like

CNN were concerned in the run-up to the Iraq war that advertisers were unwilling to buy advertising time that would link their products to negative and emotionally stressful war images. Optimistic and upbeat war coverage thus meshed with the interests of the media elites as closely as it did with the Pentagon.[50]

Heads of media corporations also largely shared the worldview of the government and the Pentagon that the expansion of corporate capitalist development into the formerly communist economies of Yugoslavia and the breakup of feudal and fundamentalist political regimes in the oil-rich Middle East were consistent with values of humanitarian intervention and liberation of oppressed peoples that Pentagon military analysts associated with American military incursions. The Pentagon had little need to employ force to control mass media outlets when the owners of these outlets were predisposed to be supportive.

Financial interests as well as cultural ties linked media to Pentagon. Some of the corporate owners of mass media are themselves directly involved in the military–industrial complex as beneficiaries of Pentagon contracts. General Electric which owns the media network NBC ranked as the 14th largest defense contractor in the United States in 2008.[51] Also on the Pentagon payroll is Time-Warner, part owner of CNN. More generally, the large majority of corporate advertisers, selling an immense variety of consumer goods, became recipients of Department of Defense contracts under Rumsfeld's policy of outsourcing the military to private enterprise. Nick Turse[52] counts some 47,000 prime contractors and over 100,000 subcontractors, selling everything from cheesecake, coffee, sneakers, boots, underwear, eye-glasses, mattresses and pillows, to computers, video games, vehicles, aircraft, and weapons. Turse describes it as a "new military-industrial-technological-entertainment-academic-scientific-media-intelligence-homeland security-surveillance-national security-corporate complex."[53]. All of these 150,000-plus companies buy advertising time from media outlets and are likely to avoid programmes and channels that appear to be too overtly critical of the Defense Department at a time when they are trying to sell their products to the Defense Department. This predisposition not to be too critical of the war effort fostered the general pattern of shallow and noncritical war coverage.

Audiences were themselves complicit in supporting media outlets that promoted optimistic and patriotic views of war, and in turning against programmes that implied criticism of the troops. The footage of the rescue of Private Jessica Lynch, described above, proved immensely popular with Fox News audiences, while ABC's attempt to denounce the footage as fraud prompted hundreds of letters from the public criticizing them for not supporting the troops. Once a country goes to war, even people who are strongly committed to the antiwar movement tend to silence themselves for fear of undermining the morale and thus endangering the lives of soldiers at the front.[54] Mass media share in and play to these powerful emotions.

GETTING THE JOB DONE: WAR REPORTING AS EVERYDAY WORK

Media workers who share the responsibilities of producing regular and sustained news coverage of war on a 24-hour, 7-days-a-week basis in the case of major television news channels, and daily and weekly newspaper and magazine coverage, must have reliable sources. These sources must be readily available, capable of supplying continuous and variable information, stories and pictures, be cheap and quick to access, and be credible. Official government and military sources are by far the most important. Journalists depend on them for regular briefings, insider information, breaking news about events as they unfold, and special scoops about planned operations.

Mundane practical considerations involved in publishing a continuous stream of material for tight, daily deadlines thus virtually ensure that the bulk of mainstream media coverage of war will reproduce the official government/ military accounts. Time pressures also ensure that most of this coverage takes the form of a fragmented reporting of events as they happen. A content analysis of American mass media coverage of the Iraq war showed that half of all coverage fitted the frame of descriptive reporting of events, without any deeper analysis of underlying conditions or political contexts, or competing interpretations of what such events might mean.[55] A further quarter of all war coverage consisted of statements from people in authority. In total, then, three quarters of all media coverage presented the official government/Pentagon view of the war without any critical comment.

Journalists do have some leeway to raise questions about information received and attach their own interpretations and analysis, but there are limits to the extent of critical opposition they can raise without jeopardizing their access to future material. Military analysts who questioned the effectiveness of troops in Iraq found themselves excluded from the inner circle invited to Pentagon briefings. CNN correspondents long enjoyed privileged access to Israeli military sources with insider knowledge of Middle-East political and military policies, but they learned the hard way that this privilege came with the price of continued loyalty to the Israeli side of the conflicts.[56] When CNN correspondents sought out Arab and Palestinian sources for alternative coverage of the 2002 Israeli invasion of the West Bank, the Israeli military responded by excluding them from future briefings and coverage of Israeli military actions. The more overtly pro-Israeli Fox News Channel began to overshadow CNN as the more-informed news source on regional satellite television. CNN made amends to the Israeli military by promising to air a series of large interviews with families of Israeli victims of terrorist attacks, and by promising to avoid their pro-Palestinian "bias."

THE LIMITS OF CREDIBLE KNOWLEDGE

Journalists who rely on official sources like the Central Intelligence Agency (CIA) and the Federal Bureau of Investigation (FBI) generally know that these agencies have their own agendas and will slant information accordingly. They generally also know that these agencies will sometimes use journalists to plant distorted information and analysis in the mass media to manipulate public opinion, or as a ploy in foreign policy diplomacy. Continued access to highly informed and privileged sources is worth the cost of cooperating in such ploys. One such instance, Jenkins suggests,[57] is the sudden shift in blame for the bombing of Pan Am flight 103 over Lockerbie, Scotland, in December 1988 that killed 270 people. The original version supported by British and American intelligence agencies was that agents for the governments of Iran and Syria were responsible. This version was "confirmed" by Iranian defectors and dramatized in movies. However, in August 1990 the same intelligence agencies suddenly switched their analysis to assert that Libya and Libya alone was responsible for the terrorist attack, citing as evidence the finding of fragments of clothing with residue of the plastic explosive Semtex and a label linked to a Maltese store owner who claimed to remember selling the explosive to a Libyan agent. The political context for the sudden switch was that Iraq under Saddam Hussein invaded Kuwait in August 1990 and the US government wanted political support from Syria and Iran for a coalition attack on Iraq. It was thus expedient to absolve these former enemies of charges of mass murder of Americans over Lockerbie. Mass media news sources in Britain and America reported official accounts of changed intelligence largely without further comment.

A central argument in Jenkins' study of terrorism is that there will always be inherent limits to what journalists or anyone else can know for sure about the murky realities of global terrorism, and limits on what they can say. Journalists are necessarily dependent on the goodwill of government intelligence agencies for background information, tips, and briefings that they can use to construct credible reports. After the 9/11, attacks both the FBI and the CIA planted leaks and counter-leaks through the media to imply that intelligence blunders that might account for the colossal failure to predict and disrupt the attacks were blamable on the rival organization.

Conspiracy theories were pervasive, but most of them were bogus and any journalist who backs a conspiracy claim that gets discredited risks a damaged reputation. Deception is a potent weapon in any war, with accusations of terrorist activity being one tactic to support or discredit enemies. Long after the American invasion of Iraq failed to turn up weapons of mass destruction, the claim that the American government deliberately fabricated the charge to legitimate the invasion has gained widespread credibility. Before the invasion, however, few journalists could have risked speculating publicly about fraudulent charges.

Jenkins suggests that there actually was much damning evidence of Iraqi involvement in terrorism during the 1980s, but the American government underplayed the evidence because it feared Iran and Syria more than Iraq, and the media followed the government line. After Iraq's invasion of Kuwait in 1990 triggered the Gulf War, intelligence reports continued to link Saddam Hussein's government with terrorist activities, including the 1993 attack on the World Trade Center, a plan to hijack a commercial airliner and crash it into the CIA headquarters in Virginia, plans to bomb a dozen jumbo jets over the Pacific, and possible links to anthrax attacks inside America. Again the American government had reasons to downplay the information out of fear that a new war would poison US–Arab relations.[58] How much of such "intelligence reports" are based on strong or corroborated evidence, vague speculation, a highly selective cobbling together of disconnected fragments, wild imaginings of terror suspects extracted under torture, or officially sponsored, fabricated leaks that could be resurrected as needed to help justify a long-preplanned invasion of Iraq, will likely always remain matters of speculation, with credibility heavily dependent upon political context. Journalists who had access to insider intelligence tips may, not unreasonably, have felt safer reporting the interpretations backed by communications officials in the intelligence agency, rather than putting their own ill-informed spin on such material.

CHALLENGES FOR RESPONSIBLE JOURNALISM: REPORTING THE YUGOSLAV WARS

The account so far represents journalists as passive conduits of information from communications officers with the government, Pentagon, and intelligence services, without the skill or the will to critically question their sources. The question that remains to be explored is the scope for professional journalism to provide critical and informed reporting, commentary, and analyses that go beyond reproducing official versions. The principle of freedom of the press at the heart of political democracy calls on the media to provide some level of oppositional voice to governments. Audiences also expect more of journalism. Most viewers hope and even expect to learn the truth from mainstream media outlets about stories like the rescue of Private Jessica Lynch, not just from obscure internet sites. Journalists in their own professional code of ethics expect this of themselves.

This next section explores what Western journalists could have known or ought reasonably to have questioned in their reporting that might have provided a more balanced and truthful account of the Yugoslav civil wars and US-led NATO bombing of Serbian forces. Herman and Peterson[59] are scathing in the criticism of what they term the "remarkable gullibility," the "very high gullibility quotient," the laziness of Western reporters, in not bothering to carry out even cursory credibility checks on sources of blatantly partisan and extremist claims, and the highly simplified Good/Evil characterization of the conflicts that journalists themselves promoted by searching out and reporting on evidence that fitted this predefined labelling, while ignoring what should have been obvious contrary evidence. This retrospective examination of accounts of the Yugoslav wars explores what might be learned from these failures in responsible journalism.

An important qualification for any retrospective accounting is that it is far easier to see patterns a decade after the events than as they are actually happening. Herman and Peterson characterize the USA and NATO intervention in Yugoslavia as one of foreign powers cynically harvesting a civil war to boost NATO's relevance in the post–Cold War era after the disintegration of the Soviet Union; to humiliate the European Union relative to NATO forces; to overthrow the UN Charter's commitment to noninterference in conflicts within a sovereign state – which paved the way for future US interventions in Afghanistan and Iraq; and to dismantle the last socialist holdout on the European continent.[60]

In fairness to journalists, much of this retrospective reading of the Yugoslav wars was not visible in the mid-1990s. Scholarly research took five to ten years to begin to unravel the complicity of Western governments in the breakup of Yugoslavia, to call into question the assumed role of specifically Serbian nationalism in the wars, and the charges of genocide levelled against Serbian leader Milosevic. The meticulous forensic research needed to make visible evidence countering some of the charges of massacres also had to wait until the conflict ended. It is still a challenge to accept the claim that American and NATO leaders were capable of such a colossal manufacturing of reality as to orchestrate the breakup of Yugoslavia and to accomplish the reversal of aggressors and victims in global media. Any mainstream journalist who put forward such claims in the mid-1990s might expect to be castigated, and to have his or her reputation for respectable journalism destroyed. Nonetheless, there is much that Western journalists could reasonably have known and have investigated, and should have made known to Western audiences as the conflicts were unfolding. Had more journalists held themselves to these higher standards of journalism, Herman and

Peterson maintain, mainstream Western understanding of what was unfolding in Yugoslavia might have been markedly different.

Western journalists ought reasonably to have known about the Croat leader Tudjman's dictatorial takeover of Croatian mass media soon after he came to power in 1990, and his deliberate purging of journalists with Serb and Serb–Croat parentage, before active conflict erupted.[61] A sense of solidarity with displaced journalists might reasonably have alerted Western journalists to question the quality of subsequent war narratives coming out of Croatia. It should also have alerted them to be more sceptical and more ready to check partisan press releases crafted by employees of the American-based Ruder Finn public relations team hired by Croatian and Bosnian governments. Reasonable scepticism towards a muzzled national press and a hired public relations firm should have led more Western journalists to follow up on the iconic "thin man behind barbed wire" image, much as BBC and Associated Press reporters checked out the setting of the rescue of Private Lynch in Iraq.

Western journalists also might reasonably have followed up the extreme claims by Bosnian Muslim leader Izetbegovic in January 1993 that "the most massive rape in human history" had occurred in Bosnia, with Serbs raping and attempting to impregnate upwards of 200,000 Bosnian women. One might expect a wealth of "human interest" stories about the plight of tens of thousands of illegitimate babies and distraught mothers or pregnant women seeking abortions. The telling absence of supporting evidence, early in the war years, for such claims should have given journalists good reason to demand more supporting evidence before reproducing other extremist claims in the future.

Herman and Peterson also focus critical attention on the closeness in time between the story of the massacre by Serb militias of Bosnian Muslims in the safe haven of Srebrenica in July 1995, and the massive expulsion of an estimated 250,000-plus Croatian-born Serbs from Croatia in August. Western journalists could well not have been able to verify at the time whether there were 2,000 or 8,000 victims in Srebrenica but they could easily have documented the displacement of 250,000 or more Serbs from Croatia and thus opened the question whether Croats rather than Serbs were more guilty of "ethnic cleansing." It is understandable that journalists would extrapolate from a video that claimed to show Serb militiamen executing six Bosnian Muslim men from Srebrenica to boost their narrative of 8,000 dead in the Srebrenica massacre. However, it is less understandable that Western journalists would not extrapolate from a video of Croatian military commander Naser Oric boasting that he had killed 114 Serbs during the expulsion of Serbs from Croatia, and of another commander ordering that Serb villages be torched. Herman and Peterson recount the story of a room full of journalists assembled at a press conference organized by United Nations

Military Observers in Zagreb in August 1995 to discuss human rights violations by Bosnian Croats during this massive ethnic cleansing operation. These journalists got up and left the UN press conference before it started, to follow an official from the US Embassy in Zagreb who promised to show photographs of possible mass graves at Srebrenica.[62]

Western journalists can be faulted for giving such extensive and unquestioned coverage to stories that fitted the official version of Serb-Evil versus Croat/Muslim-Good while downplaying stories that reversed this polarity. The two stories of Srebrenica massacre and Croat ethnic cleansing were never given equivalent coverage by Western media. A decade later, on the 10th anniversary of the two events, Western media carried hundreds of accounts of Srebrenica as "the worst atrocity in Europe since the Second World War" compared with only 15 mentions of "the greatest expulsion ... or ethnic cleansing in Europe since the Second World War."

Journalists can be forgiven for citing estimates given by government officials of up to 8,000 at Srebrenica and 200,000 dead in Bosnia at the time when events were still unfolding. There is less excuse for continuing to cite these exaggerated figures long after credible forensic research had set these figures at 2,028 and about 100,000 for all of Yugoslavia combined. Herman and Peterson's database search of Western journalists writing their opinion pieces following Milosevic's death in custody in 2006, found that of 202 reports, 187 continued to cite the exaggerated figures.[63] Herman and Peterson also castigate Western journalists for their pervasive failure to question the credibility of Milosevic's four-year trial by the International Criminal Tribunal for the Former Yugoslavia (ICTY) despite the readily available evidence that the Tribunal was set up, funded, and staffed by agents of the American government, and that it accepted hearsay evidence, and evidence gained under torture.

Western media can also be faulted for failing to question information generated by agents of the Kosovo Liberation Army, even though it was common knowledge in the region that the organization was involved in terrorist activities and drug trafficking. Western journalists could not be expected to know that the "massacre" at the village of Racak was staged, although observers invited to the scene by KLA fighters might have been more vigilant in checking for evidence of the alleged execution-style killing. However, they could reasonably have questioned more closely why the US and NATO forces sided with the extremist KLA militia faction rather than the moderate Democratic League that was elected to power under the leadership of Ibrahim Rugova. They could also have paid attention to the testimony by British Defence Secretary George Robertson in the House of Commons that the KLA had killed more people in Kosovo during the previous year than the Serbs had. This testimony was given on 24 March 1999, the same day that NATO began its 78-day bombing of Serb positions. Yet mainstream journalists did not factor this information into their coverage of NATO's "humanitarian intervention" on the side of Kosovars against Serb violence.

In summary, Herman and Peterson characterize much of Western media coverage of the Yugoslav wars as wilfully negligent journalism. Western journalists accepted from the start the American government's simplistic characterization of Serbs as villains and maintained this line of interpretation throughout the ten years of conflict. In so doing, they failed to maintain basic standards of objective journalism. Journalists showed "remarkable gullibility" in accepting extremist partisan statements by officials who had obvious vested interests in pressuring their own cause, and repeatedly failing to follow up obvious evidence that contradicted their Good/Evil dichotomy.

Herman and Peterson are especially critical of shoddy journalism that they find even in Pulitzer-prize-winning reports.[64] One such report focussed on confessions by Boris Herak, a Bosnian Serb who admitted to a large number of killings and rapes of Bosnian Muslim women. The report omitted further testimony by Boris Herak alleging that UN General Lewis Mackenzie was also guilty of rapes and murders at a local brothel – testimony that casts doubt on the credibility of Herak's other confessions. Another prize-winning report detailed lurid "death-camp" stories of Serbs slaughtering thousands of Muslim prisoners, slitting their throats, and cutting off their noses and genitals – basing these "facts" on second- and third-order hearsay from an enemy source. Yet another prize-winning report covered the story of thousands of Bosnian Muslims massacred at Srebrenica – based on reports from unnamed American officials, and a spy-satellite photograph showing empty ammunition boxes and "a decomposing human leg protruding from the freshly turned dirt."

In conclusion, Western mass media coverage of the Yugoslav war pervasively presented only one side of the war narrative, thus helping to sustain the US-NATO view of the war as humanitarian intervention, a war that even reporters in left-leaning publications like *The Nation* could characterize as illegal but legitimate. Parallels can be drawn between how CNN reporters became embedded with the Israeli side of the Israel–Palestinian conflict – privy to rich details of Israeli military activities, but at the cost of not talking with Palestinians – and how Western reporters became embedded with the NATO side of the Yugoslav conflict. They obtained rich details of NATO and allied activities but at the cost of not talking with Serbs.

Reporter Lawrence Martin of *The Globe and Mail*[65] summed up war coverage of the Kosovo war in 1999 as "one of the most shameful exercises in one-sided reporting." The mix of how NATO orchestrated media coverage, combined with structural dynamics of how war reporting gets done, resulted in the

Albanian–Kosovar side of the conflict prevailing to the near exclusion of the Serb side. One might add further that it was the KLA view that prevailed, rather than that of moderate Kosovo Muslim politicians who were willing to compromise with the Serb–Yugoslav side and keep Kosovo in the federation. Martin describes war as a journalists' trap, in which media can easily get inside their own war lines but are blocked from the enemy lines. War correspondents thus, often unavoidably, violate their own first rule of journalism – the need for balance. The result, from the Vietnam war to the war in Iraq, is that the media are complicit in feeding the "blissful blindness" of political leaders who feast on their own stereotypes and propaganda.

LESSONS LEARNED? TALKING WITH THE TALIBAN IN AFGHANISTAN

Mass media coverage of Canadian involvement in the conflict in Afghanistan in 2008, specifically in such mainstream outlets as *The Globe and Mail* and the CBC have shown qualities of reporting and analysis well above the partisan and shallow journalism criticized above. The bulk of everyday coverage still consists of speeches and press releases by military leaders and politicians extolling Canadians to "stay the course" because we are making "significant progress" towards the avowed public goals of rebuilding Afghanistan and training their security services to take over in 2009 or 2011. Typical television images provided by embedded reporters show soldiers readying their tanks for battle, and moms and dads coping with life in Afghan barracks, braving the roadside bombs and the all-too-frequent deaths. But alongside such routine coverage have been innovative and sometimes fiercely critical war narratives that challenge the propaganda.

In March 2008, *The Globe and Mail* ran a week-long series of articles titled "Talking to the Taliban" based on interviews with 42 Taliban fighters in five different districts in Kandahar province, carried out between August and November 2007. Interviews, along with multimedia coverage, were conducted by an Afghan researcher with strong connections to the insurgency, in cooperation with reporter Graeme Smith (Stephen Northfield *The Globe and Mail* 22 March 2008,A17). The interviews challenged the official view of the Taliban as ruthless terrorists threatening the West through their ties to al-Qaeda and global jihad. These "men with the guns" saw themselves as fighting to defend their villages from air strikes by foreign troops and to avenge family members killed. Most were from tribes disenfranchised by the current Karzai government, their means of livelihood destroyed by the poppy eradication program. They were hostile to deeply corrupt Afghan police who routinely demand bribes from villagers even to move about. Most were not concerned whether Taliban leader Mullah Mohammed Omar returned to power, and knew little or nothing about al-Qaeda leaders. They were unable even to guess where Canada is on the map. The central goals they articulated were to get foreign troops out of Afghanistan and to return to a Muslim state. A smattering of letters to the editor commenting on the series expressed the view that such journalism risks undermining troop morale and should be avoided. Martin's response[66] is that we have to reach outside our own patriot tent and get beyond stereotypes of heroes and enemies – or "scumbags" to quote Canada's then top general Rick Hillier.

Also in March 2008 the CBC ran a series focussing on progress, or lack of it, in the war in Afghanistan. The central message was an uncompromising view of failure of Canadian forces to reach their objectives of stability and development in Afghanistan. Soldiers win control of a region, insurgents withdraw, soldiers move on, and insurgents return. Funds to train Afghan soldiers and police disappear into an impenetrable fog of corruption, incompetence, and "ghost" personnel, and the new government in Kabul is so weak that President Hamid Karzai is sometimes called the "Major of Kabul." Readily available reports on the mainstream CBC website provide informative coverage of the political history of Afghanistan. These reports provide mainstream media viewers with extensive evidence to suggest that Canadian involvement in Afghanistan is in serious trouble and far from achieving even the modest political goals set out by political leaders. The announcement in July 2008 of an agreement between the Karzai government and an American consortium to build a pipeline from Central Asia across Kandahar region prompted open discussion both of the role of oil interests in the Iraq and the Afghanistan invasions, and whether Canadian soldiers would be involved in guarding the pipe.[67]

An important part of the explanation for the different quality of coverage of the Yugoslav wars and the wars in Iraq and Afghanistan is the difference in political climates. Cottle [68] estimates that about 19% of all mass media news coverage on the war on terror takes the form of either "contest"(9%), presenting conflict as a fundamental opposition between two opposing interests, or "contention" (10%), an array of voices with differing interests that are not necessarily in opposition. The problem with media coverage of NATO bombing in Yugoslavia is that essentially there was no contest. Elites in all political parties, along with cultural elites in churches and academia, were pervasively in favour of NATO's "humanitarian intervention." Even politicians on the left supported intervention to prevent violent ethnic cleansing. Similarly, with the 2003 American invasion of Iraq, the Republicans and Democrats in Congress overwhelmingly voted in favour, and stood up strongly behind Commander-in-Chief George W. Bush. There was contention around which of a range of motives were the more pressing or credible, but no contest about the rightness of war for the media to take up.

This changed significantly only with the run-up to the 2008 presidential elections when candidates McCain, Obama, and Clinton took openly opposing stands on whether America should ever have invaded Iraq and how fast American troops should be pulled out.

In contrast, Canada's participation in the invasion and occupation of Afghanistan was always contentious and contested. Mass media could readily fill their airwaves with credible and respected political and cultural elites debating the pros and cons of Canada's role in Afghanistan. In 2007 when the research on "Talking to the Taliban" and other documentaries were being prepared, the Canadian government was locked in debate over whether or not to extend the mission beyond 2009. This political-cultural context in which airing contentious views on a war in progress is politically acceptable, provided Canadian journalists and media outlets with a more supportive atmosphere in which to research and highlight material with negative and critical content.

These processes may be self-supporting in both cases. Consensus around the Iraq war among elites in the US limited easy media access to respected-but-contentious views, created an atmosphere hostile to critical coverage, and thus promoted consensus media coverage that stifled critical thinking among media audiences. Dissent around the Afghanistan war and the Iraq war in Canada facilitated contentious media coverage and more balanced and critical journalism that in turn sustained informed media audiences that expected and rewarded better reporting. Exposé and investigative reporting in television coverage of conflicts is statistically rare, estimated in Cottle's study [69] as only 0.3% of all coverage. But in the era of 24/7 news channels, this can still be important. Critical television documentaries, radio commentaries, and newspaper columns, even if they only appear once a month or a few times a year, can contribute significantly to nuanced understanding of conflicts that drag on over years. Journalism as a discipline requires special skills. At their best, journalists draw on theoretical frameworks from the social sciences – political science, history, economics, sociology, psychology – apply them to the analysis of world events as they are actually unfolding, and then produce reports instantly in forms readily understandable to average audiences. Individuals with these skills have the power to contribute in significant ways to public understanding of events. Some Canadian journalists have made and are making outstanding contributions to understanding war.

Gwynne Dyer, a Canadian journalist currently based in London, England, has contributed a wealth of investigative reporting over many years with highly critical and historically informed commentaries on global conflicts. His columns are carried monthly in over 175 papers in 45 countries. In 1997, Conrad Black, then owner of Hollinger International newspaper chain, pulled Dyer's columns from the *Jerusalem Post* and major Canadian newspapers, including the *National*

Post, because of Dyer's critique of Zionist politics in Israel. Asper, the owner of *CanWest Global*, who bought most of Conrad Black's newspaper holdings in 2000, continued the ban. Dyer's columns are still carried in smaller Canadian regional papers, including Irving-owned papers in New Brunswick. Dyer published four books between 2003 and 2007 all taking a strongly critical approach to the Bush administration's "war on terror."

Naomi Klein is another Canadian journalist who has produced prolific and critical articles, commentaries, documentaries, and books on corporate globalization and the corporate economic roots of the war and occupation of Iraq. One important practical reason why such investigative reporting will always be a statistically small proportion of all mass media war coverage is that investigative reporting takes time. It takes years to pull together the material for books like Klein's *The Shock Doctrine* (2007) or Dyer's *The Mess They Made* (2007) or journalist Linda McQuaig's *Holding the Bully's Coat: Canada and the U.S. Empire* (2007), but these books contribute widely to mass media war coverage by providing the critical interpretive frames on which others can draw.

The challenge for Canadian audiences is to pressurize all corporate media owners and their corporate advertisers to support and feature more investigative reporting through the attention and importance we accord to it.

NOTES

1. Dyer, Gwynne. 2004. *Future: Tense. The Coming World Order.* Toronto: McClelland and Stewart, pp. 205–215.
2. Rutherford, Paul. 2004. *Weapons of Mass Persuasion: Marketing the War Against Iraq.* Toronto: University of Toronto Press, pp.185–186.
3. Lewis, Justin. 2001. *Constructing Public Opinion: How Political Elites Do What They Like and Why We Seem To Go Along With It.* New York: Columbia University Press.
4. Bricmont, Jean. 2007. *Humanitarian Imperialism: Using Human Rights to Sell War.* Delhi: Monthly Review Press, 8. Herman, Edward S., and Peterson, David. 2007. "The Dismantling of Yugoslavia: A Study in Inhumanitarian Intervention (and a Western Liberal Left Intellectual and Moral Collapse)." *Monthly Review* October: 1–57. p. 45.
5. Herman and Peterson. "The Dismantling of Yugoslavia" pp. 35–39.
6. Brock, Peter. 2005. *Media Cleansing.* Los Angeles: GM Books; Hudson, Kate. 2003. *Breaking the South Slav Dream: The Rise and Fall of Yugoslavia.* London: Pluto Press; Johnstone, Diana. 2002. *Fool's Crusade.* New York: Monthly Review Press; Laughland, John. 2007. *Travesty.* Ann Arbor, MI: Pluto Press; Mandel, Michael. 2004. *How America Gets Away with Murder.* Ann Arbor, MI: Pluto Press.
7. MacDonald, David Bruce. 2002. *Balkan holocausts? Serbian and Croatian victim-centred Propaganda and the War in Yugoslavia.* Manchester and New York: Manchester University Press.

8. Ibid. pp. 101–103.
9. Johnstone. *Fool's Crusade.* pp. 66–69.
10. Power, Samantha. 2002. *A Problem from Hell: America and the Age of Genocide.* New York: Basic Books, pp. 268–269.
11. Johnstone. *Fool's Crusade.* p. 71.
12. Herman and Peterson. "The Dismantling of Yugoslavia." p. 36.
13. Ibid.
14. Johnstone. *Fool's Crusade.* p. 79.
15. Herman and Peterson. "The Dismantling of Yugoslavia," p. 23.
16. Ibid. p. 24.
17. Hudson. *Breaking the South Slav Dream.* p. 116; Johnstone. *Fool's Crusade.* pp. 66–67.
18. Herman and Peterson. "The Dismantling of Yugoslavia," p. 19.
19. Ibid. ; Hudson. *Breaking the South Slav Dream*, p. 117; Johnstone, . *Fool's Crusade.* p.110.
20. Herman and Peterson. "The Dismantling of Yugoslavia," p. 19.
21. Ibid. p. 20.
22. Hudson. *Breaking the South Slav Dream.* p. 167; Johnstone. *Fool's Crusade.* p. 234.
23. Herman and Peterson. "The Dismantling of Yugoslavia.'
24. Ibid. p. 26.
25. Ibid. p. 47.
26. Rutherford. *Weapons of Mass Persuasion.* p. 60.
27. Ibid. pp. 28–31.
28. Ibid. p.36.
29. Lewis, Justin. 2001. *Constructing Public Opinion.* New York: Columbia University Press.
30. Rutherford. *Weapons of Mass Persuasion.* p. 33; Hunt, Krista, and Kim Rygiel. 2006. "(En)Gendering the War on Terror: War Stories and Camouflaged" in Krista Hunt and Kim Rygiel (Eds.) *(En)Gendering the War on Terror: War Stories and Camouflaged Politics.* Burlington: Ashgate Publishing House. pp. 1–24, 8.
31. Bricmont. *Humanitarian Imperialism.* p. 32.
32. Jackson, Richard. 2005. *Writing the War on Terrorism: Language, Politics and Counter-Terrorism.* Manchester and New York: Manchester University Press, p. 14.
33. Ibid. p.16.
34. Gallagher, Stephen. 2008. "Jessica Lynch, Simulacrum" *Peace Review: A Journal of Social Justice* 19: pp.119–128.
35. Ibid. p.121.
36. Rutherford. *Weapons of Mass Persuasion*, p. 34.
37. Barstow, David. 2008. "Behind TV Analysts: Pentagon's Hidden Hand." *The New York Times* 20 April.
38. Jeffreys, Sheila. 2007. "Double Jeopardy: Women, the US Military and the War in Iraq." *Women's Studies International Forum* 30: pp.16–25.
39. Brittain, Melissa. 2006. "Benevolent Invaders, Heroic Victims and Depraved Villains: White Feminists in Media Coverage of the Invasion of Iraq" in Krista Hunt and Kim Rygiel (Eds.) *(En)Gendering the War on Terror.* pp 73–96, 86.
40. Barstow. "Behind TV Analysts: Pentagon's Hidden Hand."
41. Rutherford. *Weapons of Mass Persuasion.* p. 71.
42. Gallagher. "Jessica Lynch, Simulacrum." p.123.

43. Ibid. p. 128.
44. Scott, Catherine V. 2006. "Rescue in the Age of Empire: Children, Masculinity, and the War on Terror," in *(En)Gendering the War on Terror.* pp. 97–117.
45. Ibid.
46. Gallagher. "Jessica Lynch, Simulacrum." pp. 124–125.
47. Brittain. "Benevolent Invaders, Heroic Victims and Depraved Villains." pp. 82–83.
48. Dyer, Gwynne. 2007. *The Mess They Made: The Middle East After Iraq.* Toronto: McClelland and Stewart, pp. 143–169.
49. Chomsky, Noam and Herman, Edward S. 1988. *Manufacturing Consent: The Political Economy of the Mass Media.* New York: Pantheon.
50. Rutherford. *Weapons of Mass Persuasion.* pp.102–103.
51. Shah, Anup. 2008. "Illusion: The Mainstream Media Gives us Balanced Reporting." In Paul Buchheit, (ed.) *American Wars: Illusions and Realities.* Atlanta: Clarity Press, pp. 47–54.
52. Turse, Nick. 2008a.*The Complex: How the Military Invades Our Everyday Lives.* New York: Metropolitan Books. Turse, Nick. 2008b. "The Real Matrix: The Pentagon Invades Your Life." *Tomdispatch.com* 25 April.
53. Turse. "The Real Matrix." p. 7.
54. Mazali, Rela. 1998. "Parenting Troops: The Summons to Acquiescence." In Lois Ann Lorentzen and Jennifer Turpin (Eds.) *The Women & War Reader.* New York and London: New York University Press. pp. 272–286.
55. Cottle, Simon. 2006. "Mediatizing the Global War on Terror: Television's Public Eye." in Anandam P. Kavoori, and Todd Fraley. (Eds). *Media, Terrorism, and Theory: A Reader.* Lanham, MD: Rowman & Littlefield Publishers Inc. pp. 19–48.
56. Jenkins, Philip. 2003. *Images of Terror: What We Can and Can't Know About Terrorism.* New York: Aldine de Gruyter, p. 143.
57. Ibid. pp. 11–12.
58. Ibid. chapter 9.
59. Herman and Peterson. "The Dismantling of Yugoslavia."
60. Ibid. p. 1.
61. MacDonald. 2002. *Balkan Holocausts?* pp. 102–103.
62. Herman and Peterson. "The Dismantling of Yugoslavia." p. 21.
63. Ibid. p. 26.
64. Ibid. pp. 36–39.
65. Martin, Lawrence. 2008. "When it comes to war reporting, we need to talk to the other side." *The Globe and Mail* 31 March, 2008. p. A.13.
66. Ibid.
67. Ibid. p. A13.
68. Cottle. "Mediatizing the Global War on Terror: Television's Public Eye.'
69. Ibid.

CHAPTER THREE

Hacks and spooks – Close Encounters of a Strange Kind: A Critical History of the Links between Mainstream Journalists and the Intelligence Services in the UK

RICHARD LANCE KEEBLE

THE MEDIA AND THE SECRET STATE

Alongside the "democratic" state in Britain there exists a secret and highly centralized state occupied by the massively over-resourced intelligence and security services (MI5, MI6, GCHQ, the Cheltenham-based signals spying centre, and the armed forces' special intelligence sections), secret armies and undercover police units.[1] As Anthony Sampson highlights, MI5 and MI6 are only part of a much wider intelligence community: "This includes private companies, often employing ex-MI6 officers, which have their own interests in cultivating mystery and which rapidly expanded in the 1980s and 1990s, benefitting from the global marketplace."[2] For Richard Aldrich, historians have been slow to acknowledge the influence and power of the secret state: "Unlike France, where secret service has always remained a less than respectable activity, consigned to the fringes of government, in post-war Britain it was at the very centre."[3] Paul Todd and Jonathan Bloch in their detailed analysis of global intelligence conclude that "Britain remains the most secretive state in the Western hemisphere."[4]

The radical historian E.P. Thompson in an early, seminal paper on the emergence of the "secret, unaccountable state within the state"[5] argued that it had been, paradoxically, "aided by the unpopularity of security and policing agencies." "Forced by this into the lowest possible visibility, they learned to develop techniques of invisible influence and control. It was also aided by the British tradition of Civil Service neutrality; this sheltered senior civil servants from replacement or investigation when administrations changed, and afforded to their policies the legitimation of 'impartial, non-political intent.'"

Significantly, in their analysis of the contemporary secret state, Stephen Dorril and Robin Ramsay gave the media a crucial role. They identified the heart of the secret state as the security services, the cabinet office and upper echelons of the Home and Commonwealth Offices, the armed forces and Ministry of Defence, the nuclear power industry and its satellite ministries together with a network of senior civil servants. As "satellites" of the secret state, their list included "agents of influence in the media, ranging from actual agents of the security services, conduits of official leaks, to senior journalists merely lusting after official praise and, perhaps, a knighthood at the end of their career."[6,7]

Yet examining the links between Fleet Street journalists and the intelligence services is incredibly difficult. Only a few researchers and journalists (significantly all male) – such as Stephen Dorril, author of a seminal history of MI6,[8] David Leigh and Richard Norton-Taylor of the *Guardian*, Martin Bright of the *Observer*, freelance journalist Paul Lashmar, investigative reporters Nick Davies, Mark Hollingsworth, Phillip Knightley, John Pilger and Robin Ramsay, editor of the alternative journal, *Lobster* – have managed to penetrate, but only slightly, the fog that envelops the work of the spooks.

THE LEGAL FOUNDATIONS OF THE SECRET STATE: BEYOND THE GLARE OF THE PROBING MEDIA

Significantly, from the 1980s onwards, a raft of legislation has both reinforced the secret state's growing powers and protected it from probing media. The 1989 Security Services Act (actually drafted by MI5 lawyers) placed the service on a statutory basis for the first time and provided it with legal powers to tap phones, bug and burgle houses and intercept mail.[9] The *UK Press Gazette* commented (6 September 1993): "The greatest invasion of privacy is carried out every day by the security services, with no control, no democratic authorisation and the most horrifying consequences for people's employment and lives. By comparison with them the press is a poodle."[10]

The 1989 Official Secrets Act (OSA) replaced the 1911 OSA, which had proved notoriously cumbersome, particularly after civil servant Sarah Tisdall was jailed in 1983 for leaking to the *Guardian* government plans for the timing of the arrival of cruise missiles in England. Then followed the acquittal of top civil servant Clive Ponting charged under Section 2 (1) of the OSA after he leaked information showing the government had misled the House of Commons over the sinking of the Argentinean ship, the *Belgrano*, during the Falklands conflict of 1982. The 1989 Act covered five main areas: law enforcement, information supplied in confidence by foreign governments, international relations, defence, and security and intelligence. The publishing of Ponting-style leaks on any of these subjects was banned. Journalists were also denied a public interest defence. Nor could they claim in defence that no harm had resulted to national security through their disclosures.

The Intelligence Services Act of 1993 created the Intelligence and Security Committee which meets in secret to overview services' activities, reporting to the prime minister and not parliament. Following the 1996 Security Service Act, MI5's functions were extended to "act in support of the prevention and detection of crime." The incoming Labour government then moved to extend the powers allowing the intelligence services and other government agencies to conduct covert surveillance.

The system of Defence Advisory Notices (better known as D Notices) also serves to restrain the media in their coverage of sensitive security issues.[11] Once a notice is issued by the secretary of the Defence, Press and Broadcasting Advisory Committee, editors are asked to censor reporting. The system, introduced in 1912 to prevent breaches in security by German spies, is entirely voluntary.[12] There are five notices in all: covering the operations, plans and capabilities of the UK armed forces, the nuclear industry, emergency underground oil reserves, and so on.[13] Around 800 media professionals have a copy of the official list (though it is available on the web at www.btinternet.com/~d.a.notices). In July 2000, the new D Notices secretary, Rear Admiral Nick Wilkinson, said the system was "not allowed to stifle debate about politically sensitive matters." And in November 2007, Simon Bucks, associate editor of Sky News Online and vice-chair of the Defence, Press and Broadcasting Advisory Committee, commented:

> Some people, mainly from civil liberty groups, have been critical of the system in the past – accusing it of indulging in cosy self-censorship. But the media members of the current committee are no pussycats and demand firm evidence that national security is threatened before agreeing to government requests...The current secretary, Air Vice-Marshal Andrew Valliance (whose contact details are also on the website), takes an independent line sometimes to the chagrin of the MoD.[14]

Some critics argued in 1999 that the harassment of former *Sunday Times* defence correspondent Tony Geraghty after he refused to submit his book, *The Irish War*, for clearance exposed the myth of the "voluntary" system. Geraghty became the first journalist charged under the new OSA after he revealed the extent of the army's surveillance operations and MI5's dirty tricks in Northern Ireland. In the sections the army particularly did not like, *The Irish War* mentioned the army's Caister/Crucible computers, which contain intelligence data on most people living in Northern Ireland; the Vengeful computer, which tracks vehicle movements around the province; and the Glutton TV camera system, which scans and automatically reads number plates of vehicles at locations as far apart as Derry, Dover and Gretna Green.[15] The charges against Geraghty were eventually dropped – and later, in November 2000, so were those against Col. Nigel Wyld, one of his alleged contacts.

The *Sunday Times* Northern Ireland editor, Liam Clarke, was also summoned by the police special squad after his newspaper was prevented by an injunction from publishing allegations of further dirty tricks by the army's Force Research Unit – a clandestine cell set up to handle informants in the IRA (Irish Republican Army) and Loyalist paramilitary groups.[16] According to Robin Ramsay, Clarke fell victim to the rivalries between the RUC (Royal Ulster Constabulary) Special Branch and the army, with the RUC leaking to the *Sunday Times* details of the series of assassinations in Northern Ireland by the army's Force Research Unit. "A barrow-load of official secrets have been exposed by this one. We have the extraordinary situation in which one arm of the British secret state is trying to bust the journalist concerned, Liam Clarke, for leaking information given to him by another of the state's secret arms."[17]

NEWSPAPERS "PLAYTHINGS OF MI5"

While it might then be difficult to identify precisely the impact of the spooks (variously represented in the press as "intelligence," "security," "Whitehall" or "Home Office" sources) on mainstream politics and media, from the limited evidence it looks to be enormous. As Roy Greenslade, media blogger at the *Guardian* and editor of the *Mirror* at the time of the Gulf crisis in 1991, commented: "Most tabloid newspapers – or even newspapers in general – are playthings of MI5."[18] Journalist, former MI6 officer and Soviet spy Kim Philby once said that MI6 had penetrated the "English mass media on a wide scale," running agents in the *Daily Telegraph*, *Sunday Times*, *Daily Mirror*, *Financial Times* and the *Observer*.[19] Spy novelist John le Carré, who worked for MI6 between 1960 and 1964, has even claimed that the British secret service then controlled large parts of the press – just as they may do today.[20]

Investigative journalist David Leigh [21] has recorded a series of instances in which the secret services manipulated prominent journalists. He mentions reporters are routinely approached by intelligence agents: "I think the cause of honest journalism is best served by candour. We all ought to come clean about these approaches and devise some ethics to deal with them. In our vanity, we imagine that we control these sources. But the truth is that they are very deliberately seeking to control us." Leigh identifies three ways in which the secret intelligence service (SIS) manipulates journalists:

- They attempt to recruit journalists to spy on other people or attempt to themselves go under journalistic "cover."
- They allow intelligence officers to pose as journalists "to write tendentious articles under false names."
- And "the most malicious form": they plant intelligence agency propaganda stories on willing journalists who disguise their origin from readers.

John Simpson, BBC world affairs editor,[22] describes in his autobiography how he was once approached by a "man from MI5." "At some point they might make me broadcast something favourable to them. Or they might just ask me to carry a message to someone. You never knew," he said. But Simpson adds: "It doesn't do journalists any good to play footsie with MI5 or the Secret Intelligence Service; they get a bad reputation." *Observer* foreign correspondent Mark Frankland talks in his autobiography of his time in SIS in the late 1950s:[23] "Journalists working abroad were natural candidates for agents and particularly useful in places such as Africa where British intelligence was hurrying to establish itself."

Bill Norris, former Africa correspondent of the *Times* and associate director of the media ethics campaigning body PressWise, says: "I will not wear a uniform, carry a gun or act as a spy for my own government or any other. Yet I have known reporters who will do any or all of these things and regard them as perfectly ethical."[24] He tells of the time when working for the *Times* in the 1960s, he was asked to spy for his country by the military attaché at the British High Commission in Lagos. He turned down the offer, much to the surprise of the colonel. "I later learned that his offer had been taken up by one of my colleagues on a rival paper."

Jonathan Bloch and Patrick Fitzgerald, in their examination of covert UK warfare, report the editor of "one of Britain's most distinguished journals" as believing that more than half its foreign correspondents were on the MI6 payroll.[25] And in 1991, Richard Norton-Taylor revealed in the *Guardian* that 500 prominent Britons paid by the CIA and the now-defunct Bank of Credit and Commerce International included 90 journalists.[26] Many journalists have admitted wanting actually to become spies: Taki, the *Spectator*'s "High Life" correspondent, has confessed he tried to become a CIA agent after he found out that his father had been one. The BBC *Newsnight* presenter Jeremy Paxman admitted that he had approached an SIS recruiter at university but was turned down.[27]

MI5 certainly kept a close eye on all BBC staff between 1948 and 1985 through a vigorous system of vetting.[28] From Room 105 on the first floor of Broadcasting House, in London, the BBC employed a security liaison officer, known as "Special Assistant to the Director of Personnel" who sent the names of all successful job applicants to MI5's C Branch that checked these against the records. Not even the Home Secretary knew of this vetting. Thus Lord Rees was shocked when it was revealed in the *Observer* in 1985. Hollingsworth and Fielding report, "The practice was abolished soon after its public disclosure. Today only the director general and two senior executives are vetted by MI5 as they are considered key personnel in the event of a national emergency."[29] Currently MI5 has 33,000 dossiers on individuals and groups considered "security risks," and 95,000 files on people and organizations that have received "protective security advice." But on top of these official figures, the security services have hundreds of thousands of other closed files on microfiche.[30]

ORWELL AND THE SPOOKS

Going as far back as 1945, George Orwell, no less, became a war correspondent for the *Observer* and *Manchester Evening News* – probably as a cover for intelligence work. Significantly most of the men he met in Paris on his assignment were working for intelligences services of one kind or another. One of them was Malcolm Muggeridge who introduced him to P.G. Wodehouse.[31] Muggeridge had been assigned to keep watch on the comic novelist who was suspected of having Nazi sympathies following his broadcasts in the summer of 1941 from Berlin for the American CBS network.[32] Orwell had written an article in defence of Wodehouse in February just before leaving on his assignment (though it was not published until July in the *Windmill* magazine) and may simply have wanted to express his admiration to the creator of Jeeves and Bertie Wooster.[33]

Malcolm Muggeridge (1903–1990) began his journalistic career as Moscow correspondent for the *Manchester Guardian* and during the Second World War served in the British Secret Intelligence Services in Brussels, Lourenco Marques in Portuguese, East Africa and Paris where he was assigned to watch the comic novelist P.G. Wodehouse. Later he worked closely with the Information Research Department (IRD) and the CIA-funded Congress for Cultural Freedom and *Encounter* magazine.[34] During the late 1940s he was the *Daily Telegraph*'s Washington correspondent and became its deputy editor before a four-year stint (1953–1957) as editor of the satirical journal *Punch*.

Orwell also met the philosopher (and fellow old Etonian) A.J. "Freddie" Ayer, who was in Paris for the Secret Intelligence Service (MI6) since they were particularly concerned about the danger of a Communist coup.[35] Another writer Orwell saw was Ernest Hemingway whom he had previously met in Barcelona during the Spanish Civil War. The American novelist, who was serving as a war correspondent and staying at the Paris Ritz, had close links with members of the Office of Strategic Services (OSS, the forerunner of the CIA) and his son, Jack, was member of the OSS.[36] Carlos Baker's account of the meeting in his biography of Hemingway,[37] based on a letter he wrote to the critic Hervey Breit on 16 April 1952, only adds to the mystery: "Orwell looked nervous and worried. He said he feared that the Communists were out to kill him and asked Hemingway for the loan of a pistol. Ernest lent him the .32 Colt that Paul Willerts had given him in June. Orwell departed like a pale ghost."

Orwell's possible links with MI5 have been explored in detail by West.[38] West reports a "retired CIA officer in Washington" asserting that Orwell worked for MI5 and suggests that he could have developed contacts with Maxwell Knight, head of MI5's Department B5(b) counter-subversion unit and a former pupil of Orwell's prep school, St Cyprian's in Eastbourne. Yet Anthony Masters[39] makes no reference to Orwell in his biography of Knight. Speculation about Orwell's links with the secret services intensified after Sheldon reported in his biography of Orwell[40] that he had drawn up a "little list" of 35 people, briefly (and somewhat crudely) identifying their political leanings, religious affiliations, sexual preferences and possible Communist sympathies.[41] According to Lashmar and James,[42] Orwell supplied the list to his friend and the sister-in-law of the author Arthur Koestler, Celia Kirwan (née Paget) in 1949 when she was working for the secret state's propaganda unit, the IRD, recently established by the Labour government. However, Newsinger notes,[43] "It is most unlikely that Orwell realized the real nature of IRD at the time." Kirwan denied that the list ever reached the Foreign Office.[44]

WAS ORWELL'S 1945 WAR ASSIGNMENT AN INTELLIGENCE MISSION?

Perhaps the closest clues to Orwell's possible intelligence links lie in his extremely close friendship with David Astor, the millionaire *Observer* journalist whose father owned the newspaper and who was to be its celebrated editor from 1948 to 1975. Astor served with the covert Special Operation Executive (SOE) and thereafter maintained close links with intelligence. Both Cockett[45] and Crick[46] report that Astor had been determined to meet Orwell after reading his *Lion and the Unicorn* (1941) and finally secured an introduction to him through Cyril Connolly, an old Etonian friend of Orwell, who was then editing the influential journal *Horizon* and filling in for the *Observer*'s literary editor. They met in a café near the BBC off Portland Place where Orwell was working on broadcasts to India. "They quickly became friends, recognizing each other's directness and simplicity and David seeing him as an intellectual guide and companion." After leaving the BBC in November 1943, Orwell planned to report for the *Observer* from Algiers and Sicily following the Allied landings, but the authorities turned him down on health grounds. Orwell then quickly acquired the post of literary editor at the leftist weekly *Tribune*, which he held until February 1945 when he resigned to take on the war reporting assignment.

Was it a cover for an intelligence mission? Dorril[47] reports that in 1944 Astor was transferred to a unit liaising between SOE and the resistance in France, helping the French underground in London spread the word to groups throughout Europe. Most significantly, while in Paris, perhaps inspired by Astor, Orwell attended the first conference of the Committee for European Federation, bringing together resistance groups from around Europe. The French novelist and editor of *Combat*, Albert Camus was among those present. Bernard Crick, in his seminal biography of Orwell (1980), comments interestingly that there was a "curious lack of letters to any of his friends while in France and Germany and none of them can remember him talking about the time."[48] So Orwell was, indeed, strangely secretive about the assignment. Astor, however, was later adamant that Orwell had no intelligence links[49] and Peter Davison, editor of Orwell's twenty-volume collected works, commented: "I doubt if Orwell would be involved with intelligence – but that by no means says he wasn't."[50]

JAMES BOND TO THE RESCUE?

Some of the most important research into the links between hacks and spooks has been conducted by Phillip Knightley, author of *The First Casualty* (2000), a seminal history of war correspondents, and *The Second Oldest Profession* (1987), a history of the intelligence services. He has even claimed that at least one intelligence agent is working on every Fleet Street newspaper.[51] In particular Knightley has highlighted the activities, immediately after the Second World War, of the Kemsley Imperial and Foreign Service, better known by its cable address, Mercury. It was part of the Kemsley and then the Thomson chain of newspapers, which provided foreign news and features to papers such as the *Sunday Times* and the *Empire News*.

The head of Mercury was Ian Fleming, celebrated author of the James Bond spy novels. Fleming, who had served in British naval intelligence during the war, controlled a worldwide network of journalists many of whom had wartime intelligence backgrounds. Cedric Salter, formerly of the SOE, was sent to

Barcelona; Ian Colvin (who had close SIS links) to Berlin and Henry Brandon, an "SIS asset," to Washington. Donald McCormick, formerly in Naval Intelligence became Mercury's correspondent in Tangier and later foreign manager at the *Sunday Times*. Anthony Terry, the *Sunday Times* man in Bonn, also worked as a Mercury correspondent and as an officer of British intelligence in Berlin and Vienna. Fleming required his correspondents to write regular "situation reports," or "Sitreps" providing background information – not for publication – about activities in their parts of the world. Fleming's biographer Andrew Lycett records McCormick saying that material from these Sitreps was "passed on to branches of Intelligence as and when this seemed justified."[52] Anthony Cavendish, a former SIS officer, writes, "At the end of the war a number of MI6 agents were sent abroad under the cover of newspapermen. Indeed, the Kemsley press allowed many of their correspondents to co-operate with MI6 and even took on MI6 operatives as foreign correspondents."[53]

Eric Downton, a legendary Canadian war correspondent, who worked with Reuters and spent 24 years on the *Daily Telegraph*'s foreign staff, told Knightley,[54]

> During my time with Reuters and the *Telegraph* I was appalled by the extent to which the British news media co-operated with MI5 and MI6 and the widespread use made of British foreign correspondents by Six. Roy Pawley, foreign editor and later managing editor of the *Telegraph*, was a servile lackey of Five and Six. *Telegraph* foreign correspondents were given direct orders to work with Six. When I went to Moscow for the *Telegraph* shortly after Stalin's death, I was ordered by Pawley – who said Lord Camrose and Michael Berry were aware of these activities – to work for the Six man in the embassy who had the usual cover of press attaché. Before I left London for Moscow I was briefed by Six officials on what they wanted me to do. *The Times* and the *Telegraph*, as I observed it, were particularly close to the intelligence services but all the major British newspapers, and the BBC apparently, had degrees of symbiosis. Presumably this sort of thing still goes on.

According to Richard Norton-Taylor, *Guardian* security specialist, there is a category of people who are particularly attractive to intelligence agencies: "They may be informers, arms dealers, businessmen, even journalists. Their common value is their special access to groups or targets which the agencies have in their sights but cannot reach on their own. And if anything goes wrong, the agencies can always resort to the well-worn defence of 'plausible deniability'."[55] Thus during the later 1950s, MI6 began recruiting on a massive scale anyone (journalists, businessmen, academics) who might be useful on their travels to the Soviet bloc to gather intelligence – and perhaps even help with introductions to Soviet officials who might be "turned."[56]

IRD: PROPAGANDA ARM OF THE EMPIRE

The release of Public Record Office documents in 1995 about some of the operations of the MI6-financed propaganda unit, the Information Research Department of the Foreign Office, threw light on this secret body – which even Orwell, we saw, had aided by sending them a list of "crypto-communists." Set up by the Labour government in 1948, it "ran" dozens of Fleet Street journalists and a vast array of news agencies across the globe until it was closed down by Foreign Secretary David Owen in 1977. It was funded, like MI6, by the "secret vote" and was thus beyond parliamentary scrutiny. John Rennie, its second head between 1953 and 1958, was later appointed head of MI6.

IRD distributed across the globe "white" (true), "grey" (partially true) and "black" (false) propaganda, planting smears, lies, false rumours and forged official reports about the Soviet threat in the media. As Phillip Deery commented, "IRD worked hard to ensure that its propagandists—speechwriters, broadcasters, journalists and politicians—used the most effective words and phrases in their articles and speeches."[57] And according to John Pilger, [58]

> In the anti-colonial struggles in Kenya, Malaya and Cyprus, IRD was so successful that the journalism served up as a record of those episodes was a cocktail of the distorted and false, in which the real aims and often atrocious behaviour of the British was suppressed. Thus the bloodshed in Malaya was and still is misrepresented as a "model" of counter-insurgency; the anti-imperial uprising in Kenya was and still is distorted as a Mau Mau terror campaign against whites; and the struggle for basic human rights in Northern Ireland became and remains a noble defence of order and stability against IRA terror.

By 1960, IRD was the largest and fastest-growing department of the post-war Foreign Office though the official *Diplomatic List* for the year would have given no such indication.[59] But under Harold Wilson, the Labour Party cut funding to IRD when it took office in 1964, again in 1968 and "slashed" funding in 1970.[60] The CIA's expansion in 1965 of the London-based propaganda unit, Forum World Features, with the knowledge and cooperation of British intelligence, was probably a response to the political and financial pressures on IRD.

IRD also targeted a number of domestic organisations: its Psychological Warfare Consultations Committee carried out "psychological operations against any peace movements" and planned "intelligence service operations against progressive organisations in England."[61] Mark Curtis reports on one IRD operation which, with the support of the British ambassador in Jakarta, aided the overthrow of President Sukarno in Indonesia in 1965. "This was part of a wider

British-backed campaign to replace the regime: the result was up to a million deaths in a bloodbath by the Indonesian army and its allies."[62]

CIA RECRUITS BRITISH JOURNALISTS

In 1975, following Senate hearings on the CIA, the reports of the Senate's Church Committee and the House of Representatives' Pike Committee highlighted the extent of agency recruitment of both British and US journalists. In the States, newspapers such as the *New York Times* had a secret agreement with the CIA to employ at least 10 agents as reporters or clerks in its foreign bureaus.[63] Feminist writer and journalist Gloria Steinem was revealed to be a CIA member but never apologized. She said: "In my experience, the agency was completely different from its image; it was liberal, non-violent and honourable."[64]

The Pike Committee found that 29 per cent of the CIA's covert operations was directed at "media and propaganda," meaning that in 1978 the agency had spent in this area as much as the combined budgets of the world's biggest news agencies (AP, Reuters and UPI) put together.[65] Nick Davies, in his remarkable study of MI6 and CIA propaganda arts, notes, "The CIA kept no agents in Reuters, simply because it was British owned, and the CIA recognised that it was MI6 territory. However, when the need arose, the CIA used the MI6 agents in Reuters to place its own stories and Pike concluded that the agency had done this frequently."[66]

LEAKER KING AND THE PLOT TO OUST PRIME MINISTER WILSON

The most famous whistleblower of all, Peter (*Spycatcher*) Wright, revealed that MI5 had in newspapers and publishing companies agents whose main role was to warn them of any forthcoming "embarrassing publications."[67] Wright also disclosed that the *Daily Mirror* tycoon, Cecil King, "was a longstanding agent of ours" who "made it clear he would publish anything MI5 might care to leak in his direction." [68] Selective details about Wilson and his secretary, Marcia Falkender, were leaked by the intelligence services to sympathetic Fleet Street journalists. Further false stories claimed Wilson was involved in corrupt land deals and had links with the KGB. Edward Short, deputy leader of the Labour Party and leader of the House of Commons, was also smeared: it was suggested he was involved in tax evasion, channelling secret funds via a Swiss bank account to offshore locations.[69] Wright commented: "No wonder Wilson was later to claim that he was the victim of a plot."[70]

King was also closely involved in an extraordinary scheme in 1968 to oust Prime Minister Harold Wilson and replace him with a coalition headed by

Lord Mountbatten.[71] Peter Wright later confessed that just before the 1974 general election he had planned to leak a secret MI5 file on the Prime Minister (codenamed "Henry Worthington") to the press. "The plan was simple. MI5 would arrange for selective details of intelligence about leading Labour Party figures, but especially Wilson, to be leaked to sympathetic pressmen."[72]

In 1994, Stella Rimington, then MI5's director general, denied the existence of any anti-Wilson plot. But two years later, Lord Hunt, cabinet secretary throughout the 1974–1979 Labour government, told Channel 4's *Secret History* programme, "There is absolutely no doubt at all that a few malcontents in MI5 who were right-wing, malicious and had serious personal grudges were giving vent to this and spreading damaging and malicious stories about some members of the Labour government."[73] Moreover, according to Peter Wright, MI5 always had about twenty senior journalists working for it in the national press. "'They were not employed directly by us, but we regarded them as agents because they were happy to be associated with us."[74] David Leigh, in *The Wilson Plot* (1989), his seminal study of the smearing of Harold Wilson before his sudden resignation in 1976, quotes an MI5 officers, "We have somebody in every office in Fleet Street."

Hugh Cudlipp, editorial director of the *Mirror* from 1952 to 1974, was closely linked to intelligence, according to Chris Horrie, in his book about the history of the newspaper.[75] And Cudlipp played a significant role in the plot to oust Prime Minister Wilson.[76] Wright also referred to a "senior executive" at the *Mirror* who was controlled by an MI5 Section D4 agent runner. Seamus Milne[77] reports that Cyril Morten, the *Mirror*'s managing editor, worked closely with MI6 and happily employed an MI6 agent as a *Mirror* photographer. David Walker, the *Mirror*'s foreign correspondent in the 1950s, was named as an MI6 agent following a security scandal while Stanley Bonnett, editor of the Campaign for Nuclear Disarmament's journal, *Sanity*, in the early 1980s was exposed as an intelligence agent by whistleblower and former MI5 officer Cathy Massiter in a *20/20 Vision* programme on Channel 4.[78]

THATCHER: THE SPOOKS AND THE MEDIA

Urban reports that during Margaret Thatcher's years at Number 10 (1979–1990), spending on the intelligence services doubled and MI5 became a key player in the government machinery. Milne comments,[79] "The cosy relationship between elements of the intelligence service and the right wing of the Tory Party proved to be a vital lubricant in smoothing Margaret Thatcher's rise to power." Yet rivalries between the various branches of intelligence could often spill out into the pages of newspapers. For instance, soon after Thatcher became PM in 1979 she sent Sir Maurice Oldfield, head of MI6, to Belfast to coordinate intelligence. MI5 reacted furiously, considering the appointment of an MI6 chief to oversee their officers in Northern Ireland as a public criticism of their work. As Hollingsworth and Fielding report, "Suddenly, journalists in Belfast were receiving calls from RUC Special Branch alleging that Oldfield was a closet homosexual who combed the towns of Ulster looking to seduce young men. These malicious stories were traced back to MI5."[80]

Significantly, following his appointment as MI5 director general in 1985, Sir Anthony Duff and Bernard Sheldon, his legal advisor, made special efforts to cultivate close links with the press. Urban reports, "Duff and Sheldon focused their early efforts on the editors of quality newspapers, meeting them for lunch with the aim of convincing them that the service was modern, forward-looking organisation which did not conspire against the Labour Party and was not stuffed with KGB agents." [81]

PROPAGANDA AND THE POPISH PLOT

One of the most controversial attempts at media manipulation by the CIA occurred following the attack on Pope John Paul II in Rome in May 1981. In September 1982, an article appeared in *Reader's Digest* by Claire Sterling, a conservative journalist, and Paul Henze, former CIA station chief in Turkey, claiming that the would-be assassin was a Turk, Mehmet Ali Agca, who, they said, was working for Bulgarian intelligence, and thus ultimately for the Soviet Union. In the context of Cold War rivalries, this was an explosive story. For two years, the allegations were picked and recycled in Britain and across the global media. Later, the story was revealed to have been fabricated.[82]

MAXWELL AND MOSSAD — AND FURTHER REVELATIONS

According to Stephen Dorril, intelligence gathering during the miners' strike of 1984–1985 was helped by the fact that during the 1970s MI5's F Branch had made a special effort to recruit industrial correspondents – with great success.[83] *Guardian* journalist Seumas Milne claimed that three-quarters of Fleet Street's industrial correspondents were at that time agents for MI5 or for Scotland Yard's Special Branch.[84] MI5 was also suspected of leaking smears to the Robert Maxwell-owned *Daily Mirror* as part of an elaborate disinformation campaign against the miners' leaders Arthur Scargill and Peter Heathfield in 1990. Both were accused of using Libyan funds to pay the mortgages on their homes during the earlier strike.[85] There was one major problem with the story: neither Scargill nor Heathfield had mortgages!

In 1991, just before his mysterious death, *Mirror* proprietor Robert Maxwell (born Abraham Lajbi Hoch in Czechoslovakia in June 1923) was accused by the US investigative journalist Seymour Hersh in his book, *The Sampson Option*,[86] of acting for Mossad, the Israeli secret service, though Dorril suggests his links with MI6 were equally strong.[87] In particular, Maxwell was suspected of orchestrating the discrediting and exposure of Mordechai Vanunu after he revealed the existence of Israel's nuclear programme in the *Sunday Times* of 5 October 1986.[88]

Further evidence of journalists' links with intelligence emerged in investigations by British Customs after the collapse of the Bank of Credit and Commerce International (BCCI) amidst allegations of massive fraud and money laundering. The CIA, for instance, relied on the Saudi Arabian government to fund anti-Communist groups such as the Contras in Nicaragua and Unita in Angola through secret BCCI accounts.[89]

Following the resignation of Richard Gott from the *Guardian*, as its literary editor in December 1994 in the wake of allegations that he was a paid agent of the KGB, the role of journalists as spies suddenly came under the media spotlight – and many of the leaks were fascinating. For instance, according to the *Times* editorial of 16 December 1994, "Many British journalists benefited from CIA or MI6 largesse during the Cold War."

The intimate links between journalists and the secret services were highlighted in the autobiography of the eminent newscaster Sandy Gall.[90] He reports without any qualms how, after returning from one of his reporting assignments to Afghanistan, he was asked to lunch by the head of MI6. "It was very informal, the cook was off so we had cold meat and salad with plenty of wine. He wanted to hear what I had to say about the war in Afghanistan. I was flattered, of course, and anxious to pass on what I could in terms of first-hand knowledge."[91]

BAZOFT AMBIVALENCES

Another major controversy erupted in March 1990 following the hanging of *Observer* journalist Farzad Bazoft in Iraq on charges of spying.[92] An explosion had destroyed the Al-Iskandrai weapons complex 30 miles south of Baghdad on 17 August 1989 and Bazoft had travelled there with an English nurse, Daphne Parish,[93] taking photographs and even soil samples. After being arrested by Iraq security police, he had "confessed" (allegedly under torture) to being an Israeli spy.[94] Immediately following the hanging, British intelligence leaked information that Bazoft had stolen £500 from a building society ten years earlier. According to John Pilger, MI5, acting on behalf of the Thatcher government, was "desperate for any excuse not to suspend its lucrative arms deals with Saddam Hussein."[95]

The *Sun*'s "exclusive" headline went, "Hanged man was a robber"; the *Daily Mail*'s "Bazoft a perfect spy for Israel"; *Today*'s, "Bazoft was an Israeli agent"; and a *Sunday Telegraph* editorial condemned Bazoft as a spy, likening investigative journalism as an offence against the state. The investigative journalist Simon Henderson also argued that Bazoft was a spy for British intelligence. He had been provided with special containers for soil samples by a contact at the British embassy in Baghdad who later sent the samples to London by diplomatic bag for chemical analysis.[96] Henderson concluded, "At no time did the British admit that Bazoft had been spying, nor did Iraq flesh out its allegations. The reason was clear: if Britain admitted to spying the two countries would have had to break off diplomatic relations." Neither country wanted this. "So the Bazoft incident was left to die down." [97] But the veteran BBC foreign correspondent John Simpson argues strongly that Bazoft "was precisely what he claimed to be – a journalist looking for a good story".[98] A few months after the execution, in August 1990, Iraqi forces invaded neighbouring Kuwait thus provoking the international crisis that ultimately led to the Gulf conflict of 1991.

Yet the Bazoft mystery continues. In 2003, the *Observer* tracked down Kadem Askar, the colonel in the Iraqi intelligence service who conducted the first interrogation of Bazoft. He claimed he knew the journalist was innocent – but could not stop Saddam Hussein, the Iraqi President, who was determined to have Bazoft executed.[99]

A RENEGADE SPOOK REVEALS ALL

In December 1998, Labour MP Brian Sedgemore named Dominic Lawson, editor of the *Sunday Telegraph*, in parliament as an MI6 agent after receiving information from former MI6 officer Richard Tomlinson.[100] The *Guardian* also reported that Lawson had published articles in the *Spectator* while he was editor by a "Ken Roberts," who was actually an MI6 officer, and by Alan Judd aka Alan Petty, another MI6 officer. Machon adds, "Although Lawson has denied the claims that he was a paid agent of MI6, we do know that he regularly and uncritically reproduces stories from MI6 sources in the *Sunday Telegraph*."[101]

Another major controversy erupted in 2001 after Tomlinson published *Russia, Big Breach: From Top Secret to Maximum Security*, in which he claimed spies posed as journalists on four out of every ten missions.[102] Tomlinson, who was assigned to Yugoslavia during the height of the Bosnian conflict, used a forged card of the

National Union of Journalists to gain access to top Serbian sources. Tomlinson also confirmed that MI6 still set up news agency "fronts" to provide cover for its operations. For instance, in 1992, the Truefax agency was set up in central London by Tomlinson and a KGB defector with the aim of recruiting Russian journalists to spy for Britain.

In the reporting of Northern Ireland, there have been longstanding concerns over security service disinformation. Susan McKay, editor of the Dublin-based *Sunday Tribune*, has criticized the reckless reporting of material from "dodgy security services." She told a conference in Belfast in January 2003 organized by the National Union of Journalists and the Northern Ireland Human Rights Commission "We need to be suspicious when people are so ready to provide information and that we are, in fact, not being used."[103]

GROWING POWER OF SECRET STATE

Thus from this evidence alone it is clear that there has been a long history of links between hacks and spooks in both the UK and US. But as the secret state grows in power, through massive resourcing, through a whole raft of legislation – such as the Official Secrets Act, the anti-terrorism legislation, the Regulation of Investigatory Powers Act 2000 and so on – and as intelligence moves into the heart of Blair and Brown's ruling clique, so these links are even more significant.[104]

Mark Almond, lecturer in modern history, commented: "More than any predecessor, Blair has relied on a kitchen cabinet in Downing Street but one made up of a cabal of diplomats and intelligence officials rather than ambitious, if unelected party apparatchiks. Blair has liberated British politics from the influence of politicians."[105] Professor David Beetham has similarly highlighted the "secret, warfare" state which has totally undermined the democratic system.[106]

Since 11 September 2001 all of Fleet Street has been awash in warnings by anonymous intelligence sources of terrorist threats. The former UN arms inspector, Scott Ritter, revealed in his book, *Iraq Confidential*, the existence of an MI6-run psychological warfare effort, known as Operation Mass Appeal. According to Ritter, "Mass Appeal served as a focal point for passing MI6 intelligence on Iraq to the media, both in the UK and around the world. The goal was to help shape public opinion about Iraq and the threat posed by WMD."[107] MI6 propaganda specialists, at the time, claimed they could spread the misinformation through "editors and writers who work with us from time to time." Thus there have been constant attempts to scare people – and justify still greater powers for the national security apparatus.

To take just one example, Michael Evans, the *Times* defence correspondent, reported on 29 November 2002, "Saddam Hussein has ordered hundreds of his officials to conceal weapons of mass destruction components in their homes to evade the prying eyes of the United Nations inspectors." The source of these "revelations" was said to be "intelligence picked up from within Iraq." Early in 2004, as the battle for control of Iraq continued with mounting casualties on both sides, it was revealed that many of the lies about Saddam Hussein's supposed WMD had been fed to sympathetic journalists in the US, Britain and Australia by the exile group, the Iraqi National Congress.

In his evidence to a Special Immigration Appeal Commission in July 2002, the *Observer* reporter and intelligence expert Martin Bright highlighted the way in which journalists were constantly fed unverifiable information by the intelligence services about alleged Al Qaeda threats to the UK. To illustrate his point he referred to an article in the *Independent* of 16 September 2002 headlined "MI5 searches for terror cells based in Britain" by two journalists with "impeccable reputations," Paul Lashmar and Chris Blackhurst:

> They report that at least three terrorist cells linked to Bin Laden are at large in Britain and that the UK has been a major base for Bin Laden's operations. They add that there are believed to be dozens of terrorists in Britain associated with Bin Laden. One "intelligence source" is then quoted as saying: "There is no reason why what happened in America couldn't happen in Britain or any European country. The terrorists are in place, and there is very little to stop them." A source, this time from "Whitehall" adds: "The problem is, these groups are amorphous and hard to identify until the they commit a terrorist act." This is terrifying stuff.[108]

Stephen Dorril reports on how journalists would be given secret briefings or access to Iraqi defectors and would take them at their word, even though defectors are the most unreliable of all sources.[109] He lists a series of manufactured stories carried in the lead-up to the Iraq invasion – the three giant cargo ships said to be carrying Iraqi weapons of mass destruction (*Independent*, 19 February 2003); "Saddam "killed missile chief" to thwart UN team" (*Sunday Telegraph*, 2 March 2003) and "Saddam's Thai gen spree hints at getaway plan" (*Sunday Times*, 9 March 2003).

SEXED UP — AND MISSED OUT

During the controversy that erupted following the end of the "war" and the death of the arms inspector Dr David Kelly (and the ensuing Hutton inquiry), the spotlight fell on BBC reporter Andrew Gilligan and the claim by one of his sources that the government (in collusion with the intelligence services) had "sexed up" a dossier justifying an attack on Iraq. The Hutton inquiry, its every twist and turn massively covered in the mainstream media, was the archetypal media spectacle that drew attention from the broader and more significant issue of mainstream journalists' links with the intelligence services.

On 26 May 2004, the *New York Times* carried a 1,200-word editorial admitting it had been duped in its coverage of WMD in the lead-up to the invasion by dubious Iraqi defectors, informants and exiles. Chief among the *Times*' dodgy informants was Ahmad Chalabi, leader of the Iraqi National Congress and a Pentagon favourite before his Baghdad house was raided by US forces on 20 May 2004. Then, in the *Observer* of 30 May 2004, David Rose admitted he had been the victim of "calculated set-up" devised to foster the propaganda case for war. "In the 18 months before the invasion of March 2003, I dealt regularly with Chalabi and the INC and published stories based on interviews with men they said were defectors from Saddam's regime." And he concluded, "The information fog is thicker than in any previous war, as I know now from bitter personal experience. To any journalist being offered apparently sensational disclosures, especially from an anonymous intelligence source, I offer two words of advice: *caveat emptor*." [110] No British newspaper has followed the example of the *New York Times* and apologized for being so easily duped by the intelligence services in the run-up to the illegal invasion of Iraq.

Rose, in a later article in the *New Statesman*, reported in detail on how the "spooks" had fed a series of lies to their media cronies: in one instance, an official insisted the preachers Abu Hamza and Abu Qatada – now said by the same agency to have been Britain's most dangerous men throughout the 1990s – were "harmless rent-a-gobs" who might have a high public profile but had no hard links with jihadist terrorism.[111] MI5 sources also originally claimed there was "no connection" between the 7/7 cell behind the London bombings and the failed 21/7 cell. "Only two years later, thanks to evidence given in criminal trials, did it become clear that both claims were false. In fact, the two leaders of the 7/7 gang, Mohammad Sidique Khan and Shahzad Tanweer, had been observed by MI5 surveillance officers at least four times, and were known to be connected to another, now convicted, terrorist cell." Rose asks why the media have been duped by the intelligence services for so long.

> One reason, aside from the lunches and the limos, is that editors are extremely reluctant to lose the access they have: the spooks' stories may be unreliable, but they often make good copy, and if everyone is peddling the same errors, it doesn't much matter if they turn out to be untrue. Another, as a seasoned BBC correspondent put it to me, may be a judgment that if MI5 and MI6 sometimes peddle disinformation, many viewers and readers may not very much care as "we're all on the same side."

Significantly in 2007, a new research, information and communication unit (modelled on the IRD) was set up by Home Secretary John Reid to target the BBC and other media outlets as part of a counter-offensive against Al Qaeda.[112]

CONCLUSION: HOW CONSPIRACY THEORY CAN BE USEFUL

One of the main problems with intelligence is that anyone attempting to highlight its significance is accused of lacking academic rigour and promoting "conspiracy theory." [113] Jeffrey M. Bale commented that, "serious research into genuine conspiratorial networks has at worst been suppressed, as a rule been discouraged and at best looked upon with condescension by the academic community. An entire dimension of political history and contemporary politics has thus been consistently neglected."[114] But given the close links between politicians, journalists and the intelligence services some conspiratorial elements have to be acknowledged to be behind the mainstream media's reporting.

With the emphasis on intelligence, the focus of journalism shifts from objective, verifiable "facts" to myth: in effect, there is a crucial epistemological shift. As general Richard Myers, Chairman of the Joint Chiefs of Staff, admitted in the lead-up to the Iraq invasion of 2003, "Intelligence doesn't mean something is true. You know, it's your best estimate of the situation. It doesn't mean it's a fact. I mean, that's not what intelligence is." [115] And Stephen Dorril commented, "The reality is that intelligence is the area in which ministers, and the MI6 info ops staff behind them can say anything they like and get away with it. Intelligence with its psychological invite to a secret world and with its unique avoidance of verification is the ideal means for flattering and deceiving journalists."[116]

Similarly, the historian Timothy Garton Ash stressed, "The trend in journalism as in politics, and probably now in the political use of intelligence, is away from the facts and towards a neo-Orwellian world of manufacturing reality."[117] With the reporting of the "war on terror" being dominated by intelligence sources, separating the manufactured myths and the misinformation from the truth becomes all the more difficult. But it's a challenge both journalists and media consumers have to take up.

NOTES

1. Precise figures on funding of the intelligence services are difficult to identify. Mark Hollingsworth and Nick Fielding, *Defending the Realm: MI5 and the Shayler Affair* (London: André Deutsch, 1990), 48, say that with the election of the Labour Party in May 1997 they found "new friends." "They persuaded the new government to increase their

aggregate budget to £743.2 million for 1999–2000, £745 million for 2000–2001 and £746.9 million for 2002–2003. The amount for MI5 alone was not published until 1998 when it was announced as £140 million a year." However, Paul Todd and Jonathan Bloch, *Global Intelligence: The World's Secret Services Today* (London: Zed Books, 2003), 106, calculate that, following leaks from the National Audit Office about overspends – from £140 to £250 million (MI6) and £85 to £227 million (MI5) – on high-profile city offices and a range of other scandals involving IT contract overruns, an unofficial estimate of £2.5 billion to be closer to the mark. Todd and Bloch suggest that the cost of the intelligence services is Britain's "greatest secret." An earlier, excellent study of the intelligence services and their manipulation of the media appeared in David Leigh, *The Frontiers of Secrecy: Closed Government in Britain* (London: Junction Books, 1980).

2. Anthony Sampson, *Who Runs This Place? The Anatomy of Britain in the 21st Century* (London: John Murray, 2004), 151.
3. Richard Aldrich, *Espionage, Security and Intelligence in Britain 1945–1970* (Manchester and New York: Manchester University Press, 1998), 3.
4. Todd and Bloch, *Global Intelligence*, 102.
5. E.P.Thompson, *Writing by Candlelight* (London: Merlin Press, 1980), 156–157.
6. Stephen Dorril and Robin Ramsay, *Smear! Wilson and the Secret State* (London: Fourth Estate, 1991), x–xi.
7. Hollingsworth and Fielding (*Defending the Realm*, 49) report that officers of MI5's H Branch ("Corporate Affairs") interact with GCHQ, the police, customs, ports and immigration services and are responsible for liaising with the media.
8. Stephen Dorril, *MI6: Fifty Years of Special Operations* (London: Fourth Estate, 2000).
9. See Todd and Bloch, *Global Intelligence,* 102. The foreign intelligence service, SIS, was first officially acknowledged in the House of Commons on 6 May 1992 and put on a statutory footing with the Intelligence Services Act of 1994.
10. Mark Urban, *UK Eyes Alpha: The Inside Story of British Intelligence* (London: Faber, 1996), 53. Urban, of BBC's *Newsnight*, is a former military intelligence officer (see Hollingsworth and Fielding, *Defending the Realm*, 43).
11. Liberty and Article Article 19, *Secrets, Spies and Whistleblowers: Freedom of Expression and National Security in the United Kingdom* (London: Liberty and Article 19, 2000), 22–24.
12. See its website at www.dnotice.org.uk.
13. Ed Sheldon, "Public Exposure," *Press Gazette*, 5 May 1999.
14. Simon Bucks, "DA-Notice Voluntary Code under Threat from the Net," *Press Gazette*, 16 November 2007. http://www.pressgazette.co.uk/story.asp?sectioncode=1&storycode=39465 (accessed 1 January 2008).
15. See Duncan Campbell, "Led by the Nose," *Guardian*, 2 November 2000. http://www.guardian.co.uk/politics/2000/nov/02/freedomofinformation.uk (accessed 7 March 2008).
16. Richard Norton-Taylor, "Secrets and Spies," *Guardian*, 18 May 2000.
17. Robin Ramsay, *Politics and Paranoia* (Hove: Picnic Publishing, 2008), 253.
18. Seamus Milne, *The Enemy Within: The Secret War Against the Miners* (London: Pan Books, 1994), 262.
19. Nick Davies, *Flat Earth News* (London: Chatto and Windus, 2008), 235.
20. Stephen Dorril, *The Silent Conspiracy: Inside the Intelligence Services in the 1990s* (London: Heinemann, 1993), 281.

21. David Leigh, "Britain's Security Services and Journalists – The Secret Story," *British Journalism Review*, vol. 11, no. 2 (2000): 21–26. www.bjr.org.uk/data/2000/no2_leigh.htm (accessed on 14 October 2006). It also appeared in the *Guardian* of 12 June 2000 under the title "Tinker, Tailor, Soldier, Journalist."
22. John Simpson, *Strange Places, Questionable People* (London: Pan Books, 1998), 296–297.
23. Mark Frankland, *Child of My Time* (London: Chatto and Windus, 1999), 92.
24. Bill Norris "Media Ethics at the Sharp End," *Ethics and Media Culture: Practice and Representations* (edited by David Berry) (Oxford: Focal Press, 2000), 329.
25. Jonathan Bloch and Patrick Fitzgerald, *British Intelligence and Covert Action* (London: Junction Books, 1983), 134–141.
26. John Pilger, *Heroes* (London: Pan Books, second edition, 1983), 496.
27. Phillip Knightley, "Journalists and Spies: An Unhealthy Relationship," *Ethical Space: The International Journal of Communication Ethics*, vol. 3, nos. 2 and 3 (2006): 7–11.
28. Alan Protheroe, former Assistant Director General of the BBC, was also a Territorial Army intelligence officer specializing in army-media relations. See Ramsay, *Politics and Paranoia*, 188.
29. Hollingsworth and Fielding, *Defending the Realm*, 105.
30. Ibid., 114.
31. Gregory Wolfe, *Malcolm Muggeridge: A Biography* (London: Hodder and Stoughton, 1995). See also Muggeridge's autobiography *Chronicles of Wasted Time Vol 2: The Infernal Grove* (London: Fontana, 1975), 256–257.
32. Frances Donaldson, *P.G.Wodehouse: A Biography* (London: Carlton Publishing Group, 1982/2005).
33. Richard Keeble, "Orwell as War Correspondent: A Reassessment," *Journalism Studies*, vol 2, no. 3 (2001): 393–406.
34. See Frances Stonor Saunders, *Who Paid the Piper? The CIA and the Cultural Cold War* (London: Granta Books, 1999).
35. A.J. "Freddie" Ayer, *Part of My Life* (London: Oxford University Press, 1978). Ben Rogers, *A Life: A.J. Ayer* (London: Chatto and Windus, 1999), 192.
36. Charles Whiting, *Hemingway Goes to War* (Stroud: Sutton, 1999), 104.
37. Carlos Baker, *Ernest Hemingway: A Life Story* (Harmondsworth: Penguin, 1972), 672–673.
38. W.J. West, *The Larger Evils: Nineteen Eight-Four: The Truth behind the Satire* (Edinburgh: Canongate, 1992), 162–166.
39. Anthony Masters, *The Man Who Was M: The Life of Maxwell Knight* (Oxford: Blackwell, 1984).
40. Michael Shelden, *Orwell: The Authorised Biography* (London: Heinemann, 1991), 467–469.
41. Saunders, *Who Paid the Piper?*, 298–301.
42. Paul Lashmar and Oliver James, *Britain's Secret Propaganda War 1948–1977* (Stroud: Sutton, 1998), 97. This is the most detailed study of the activities of IRD to date.
43. John Newsinger, "The American connection: George Orwell, "Literary Trotsykism" and the New York Intellectuals," *Labour History Review*, vol. 64, no. 1 (1999): 23–43.
44. In a letter to the author from Peter Davison dated 24 February 1999.
45. Richard Cockett, *David Astor and the* Observer (London: Deutsch, 1991), 94.
46. Bernard Crick, *George Orwell: A Life* (Harmondsworth: Penguin, 1982), 425–426.
47. Dorril, *MI6: Fifty Years of Special Operations*, 457.

48. Crick, *George Orwell,* 481. See also Gordon Bowker, *George Orwell* (London: Little, Brown, 2004), 324–326. Bowker's is probably the best biography of Orwell.
49. In an interview with the author, London, November 1999.
50. In a letter to the author dated 7 December 1999.
51. Richard Keeble, "Spooks Are Represented on Every Newspaper," *Press Gazette*, 9 October 2003.
52. Andrew Lycett, *Ian Fleming* (London: Weidenfeld and Nicolson, 1996), 170.
53. Knightley, "Journalists and Spies," 8.
54. Ibid.
55. Dorril, *The Silent Conspiracy,* 274.
56. Ibid., 275.
57. Phillip Deery, "The Terminology of Terrorism: Malaya 1948–52," *Journal of South East Asian Studies* (June 2003). http://www.accessmylibrary.com/coms2/summary_0286–4205179_ITM (accessed 11 June 2008).
58. John Pilger, *Hidden Agendas* (London: Verso, 1998), 495–496.
59. Aldrich, *Espionage, Security and Intelligence in Britain,* 2–3.
60. Dorril and Ramsay, *Smear! Wilson and the Secret State*, 110.
61. Mark Curtis, *Unpeople: Britain's Secret Human Rights Abuses* (London: Vintage, 2004), 107.
62. Ibid.
63. Peter Preston, "The Spooks Who Ruled the States," *Observer*, 3 February 2008.
64. Ibid.
65. Davies, *Flat Earth News*, 226.
66. Ibid. For further details on the CIA's penetration of the mainstream media in the US see Greg Bish, "The Covert News Network" in *You Are Being Lied to: The Disinformation Guide to Media Distortion, Historical Whitewashes and Cultural Myths* (edited by Russ Kick) (New York: The Disinformation Company, 2001), 40–43. For instance, a leaked internal CIA memo, dated 20 December 1991, boasted that the agency had "contacts with every major wire service, newspaper, news weekly and television network in the nation."
67. Peter Wright (with Paul Greengrass), *Spycatcher: The Candid Autobiography of a Senior Intelligence Officer* (London: Viking, 1987).
68. Ibid., 369.
69. Hollingsworth and Fielding, *Defending the Realm,* 22.
70. Wright, *Spycatcher*, 370.
71. Andrew Marr, *A History of Modern Britain* (London: Pan Macmillan, 2007), 305–308. See also Scott Newton, "Harold Wilson, the Bank of England and the Cecil King 'coup' of May 1968," *Lobster* (Winter 2008–2009): 3–8.
72. Hollingsworth and Fielding, *Defending the Realm,* 23.
73. Ibid.
74. See British intelligence and the covert propaganda front. http://nelsonmandela2.blogspot.com/ (accessed on 14 June 2008).
75. Chris Horrie, *Tabloid Nation: From the Birth of the Daily Mirror to the Death of the Tabloid* (London: Deutsch, 2004), 237.
76. Newton, "Harold Wilson, the Bank of England and the Cecil King 'coup' of May 1968," 7.
77. Milne, *The Enemy Within*, 263.
78. Urban, *UK Eyes Alpha*, 46–47. Dorril, *The Silent Conspiracy,* 25–28.

79. Milne, *The Enemy Within*, 341.
80. Hollingsworth and Fielding, *Defending the Realm*, 123.
81. Urban, *UK Eyes Alpha*, 54–55.
82. Davies, *UK Eyes Alpha*, 229.
83. Dorril, *The Silent Conspiracy*.
84. Milne, *The Enemy Within*.
85. Robin Ramsay, "The Miners and the Secret State," in *Shafted: The Media, the Miners' Strike and the Aftermath* (edited by Granville Williams) (London: Campaign for Press and Broadcasting Freedom, 2009), 73–80. Roy Greenslade, then editor of the *Daily Mirror*, later apologized for his role in the Scargill smear affair. http://www.guardian.co.uk/media/2002/may/27/mondaymediasection.politicsandthemedia (accessed on 6 April 2009).
86. Seymour Hersh, *The Sampson Option* (London: Faber and Faber, 1991).
87. Dorril, *The Silent Conspiracy*, 276. Russell Davies, in *Foreign Body: The Secret Life of Robert Maxwell* (London: Bloomsbury, 1995), 21–25, records how Maxwell's publishing ventures had begun in collaboration with the German company, Springer-Verlag, and bankrolled by the Secret Intelligence Service. Funding was organized through Hambro's bank – and Charles Hambro had been a member of the Secret Operation Executive, the covert military organization set-up by Churchill during the Second World War. George Kennedy Young, the future Deputy Chief of MI6, was responsible for "running" Maxwell while based in Vienna. Desmond Bristow, a former SIS officer, says of Maxwell, "I know he was kept on very sort of – how would we put it? – *discreetly* by MI6 for quite a long time. Probably, in fact, till the end of his days." Davies also records (p. 213) the *Guardian* reporting that communications from Maxwell's yacht "were intercepted by GCHQ, with the help of British submarines, after a tip-off from the CIA in the late eighties that he was suspected of being involved in arms deals. His conversations were sent by low frequency transmission to GCHQ's outstation at Edzell on Tayside, Scotland."
88. Maxwell's *Sunday Mirror* had run a "spoiler" on Vanunu a week before the *Sunday Times*' exclusive, presenting him as a con man pushing false stories about Israel's nuclear secrets. See Roy Greenslade, *Maxwell's Fall: The Appalling Legacy of a Corrupt Man* (London and New York: Simon and Schuster, 1992), 329. But Greenslade argues that Maxwell was not a Mossad agent and that Hersh had been misled by his source, Ari Ben Manashe, a former Mossad agent and arms dealer.
89. Ibid., 300.
90. Sandy Gall, *News from the Frontline: A Television Reporter's Life* (London: Heinemann, 1994).
91. Ibid., 158.
92. Richard Keeble, *Secret State, Silent Press: New Militarism, the Gulf and the Modern Image of Warfare* (Luton: John Libbey, 1997), 62.
93. Daphne Parish gives her version of events in *Prisoner in Baghdad* (London: Chapman Publishers, 1992). She was sentenced to 15 years in prison but released on 16 July 1990 following the intervention by the Zambian President Kenneth Kaunda at the request of the *Observer*'s owner "Tiny" Rowland.
94. See Kenneth R. Timmerman, *The Death Lobby: How the West Armed Iraq* (London: Fourth Estate, 1992), 357–358.

95. John Pilger, "Shedding Crocodile Tears," *New Statesman*, 20 March 1992.
96. See also Dilip Hiro, *Desert Shield to Desert Storm: The Second Gulf War* (London: Paladin/HarperCollins, 1992), 67–68.
97. Simon Henderson, *Instant Empire: Saddam Hussein's Ambition for Iraq* (San Francisco: Mercury House, 1991), 214–216. Rupert Allason, the former Conservative MP, who writes on espionage as Nigel West, also commented: "It is highly likely Bazoft will have tried to capitalize on his knowledge and background by offering information to the Israelis. Mossad [the Israeli secret service] almost certainly snapped him up, and might well have been unaware of his criminal background." (see Hiro, *Desert Shield to Desert Storm,* 69).
98. John Simpson, *From the House of War* (London: Arrow Books, 1991), 54–65.
99. See http://en.wikipedia.org/wiki/Farzad_Bazoft (accessed on 11 July 2008).
100. Annie Machon, *Spies, Lies and Whistleblowers* (Lewes, East Sussex: The Book Guild, 2005), 135.
101. Ibid., 136. See Ramsay, *Politics and Paranoia,* 253–254 for more on the *Telegraph*'s links with the spooks.
102. Paul Lashmar, "My Name's James Bond: Here's My NUJ Card. British Spies Posing as Journalists Make Genuine Foreign Reporters' Jobs Much More Difficult," *Independent*, 30 January 2001.
103. See http://www.nuj.org.uk/inner.php?docid=635 (accessed on 14 October 2006).
104. See Richard Keeble, *Ethics for Journalists* (London: Routledge, second edition 2008), 254–255 on the implications of the Blair government's anti-terrorism legislation for investigative journalism in the UK.
105. Mark Almond, "So How Will He Be Judged," *Guardian*, 15 May 2003. Ramsay (*Politics and Paranoia*, 250) comments on the intelligence links of the Blair clique: "Within his inner group, we have Peter Mandelson, who has been around MI6 since his early 20s, and Jonathan Powell, ex-FCO [Foreign and Commonwealth Office] in Washington…Four of the Blair cabinet are alumni of the Anglo-American Project; three of the Blair cabinet have passed muster at Bilderberg meetings; and the entire defence team in Blair's cabinet in 1997 were members or associates of the Trade Union Committee for European and Transatlantic Unity, created by the Americans in the 1970s – probably, though not yet probably created by the CIA – and currently funded by NATO."
106. David Beetham, "The Warfare State," *Red Pepper*, June 2003.
107. Davies, *Foreign Body,* 231. See also Michael Meacher, "The Very Secret Service," *Guardian*, 11 November 2003. The government later admitted the existence of Mass Appeal. See "Revealed: How MI6 Sold the Iraq War," Nicholas Rufford, *Sunday Times*, 28 December 2003. See: http://www.timesonline.co.uk/tol/news/uk/article839897.ece (accessed on 14 October 2006).
108. Martin Bright, "Terror, Security and the Media," *Observer,* 21 July 2002. http://www.guardian.co.uk/world/2002/jul/21/humanrights.comment (accessed on 14 October 2003).
109. Stephen Dorril, "Spies and Lies," in *Tell Me Lies: Propaganda and Media Distortion in the Attack on Iraq* (edited by David Miller) (London: Pluto Press 2004), 112.
110. David Rose, "Iraqi Defectors Tricked Us with WMD Lies, but We Must Not Be Fooled Again," 30 May 2004, *Observer*. http://www.guardian.co.uk/media/2004/may/30/Iraqandthemedia.iraq (accessed on 14 October 2006).

111. David Rose, "Spies and Their Lies," *New Statesman*, 27 September 2007.
112. See Alan Travis, "Revealed: Britain's Secret Propaganda War against Al-Qaida," *Guardian*, 26 August 2008. http://www.guardian.co.uk/world/2008/aug/26/alqaida.uksecurity (accessed on 6 April 2009).
113. Robin Ramsay, *Conspiracy Theories* (Harpenden, Herts: Pocket Essentials, 2000).
114. Jeffrey Bale, "Conspiracy Theories and Clandestine Politics," *Lobster* (Hull 1995): 16–22.
115. Andrew Stephen, "America," *New Statesman*, 4 August 2003.
116. Dorril, "Spies and Lies," *Free Press*, April, 4 2003.
117. Timothy Garton Ash, "Fight the Matrix," *Guardian*, 5 June 2003.

CHAPTER FOUR

A Regime of Propaganda: The Systemic Bases of Promotional Political Culture

GERALD SUSSMAN

> I am not particularly concerned whether either gunpowder or propaganda have benefited or harmed mankind. I merely emphasize, at this point, that propaganda on an immense scale is here to stay
>
> – GEORGE V. ALLEN, ASSISTANT SECRETARY OF STATE FOR PUBLIC AFFAIRS, 1948–1949.[1,2]

THE ICT MODE OF DEVELOPMENT

The demise of Keynesianism, succeeded by neoliberalism in the 1970s, has been central to a worldwide economic and political restructuring, with profound cultural impacts as well. Select semi-peripheral countries that have been integrated into the new international division of labour have drawn the major share of overseas manufacturing investment, as the First World shifted to what Castells[3] has described as an informational economy. With countries such as China, Vietnam, Mexico, Turkey, and India taking on more of the production of material commodities, the United States, Britain, and other leading OECD economies have concentrated more on the production of immaterial goods and promotional services.[4] What is required of a promotional economy is a perfection of the circulation of product to target demographic and final consumption through intensified marketing, sales promotion, advertising, public relations, and related image and consumer management fields. "Today, the ideology of consumerism functions to conflate the concepts of consumption and citizenship and capitalism and democracy, as if consumption offered a resolution to social and political struggles".[5] Indeed, the only way a services-focused transnational economy can be sustained, as observed by J. K. Galbraith in *The Affluent Society* (1958) and *The New Industrial State* (1967), is through intensification of consumerism, which requires maximum exposure to commercial and political propaganda.

Commodification now filters into every pore of society, breaking down, with Schumpeterian aggression, the moral and social barriers of society, including what was once the relative sequestration of children from its imperial clutch. The nominally public airwaves are now more extensively produced for profit by corporate media in a more competitive multimedia environment that makes them more desperate for the advertising dollar, pound, euro, and sister currencies. One of the manifestations of this commodification is the intensification of product placement and plugola (marketing the network or parent company's assets in news and public affairs programming). To cite one recent example, Cisco Systems retains a long list of media outlets in which the company covertly weaves in paid product appearances and even pays for script adaptations to feature its line of goods. Its media clients include *CSI: NY* (CBS), *24* (Fox), *Heroes* (NBC), *You, Me and Dupree* (Vivendi Universal), and *I am Legend* (Time Warner/Warner Bros.). In an episode of the popular television drama, *24*, "the words 'Cisco Telepresence' [videoconferencing system] appear in a close-up that fills the screen".[6] Coke makes a regular appearance in front of transatlantic media impresario Simon Cowell on the hit show, *American Idol.*

Unbeknownst to most viewers, American news stations routinely insert video news releases offered to them by industry and government agencies. This behaviour reflects a larger trend of commercialisation and political indoctrination in the news through various forms of propaganda that continues to undermine professional journalism. A study by a group of media unions found that almost 80% of 400 journalists surveyed believed that journalism standards have declined, and 69% said that corporate owners exercise too much influence over news reporting.[7]One credible measure of the centrality of commercial propaganda is the money spent on promoting goods and services. The total advertising expenditure in the United States, reaching $271 billion in 2005, was greater than the GDP of all but 31 other countries in the world (and all but 3 of what became 27 independent states from the former Soviet Union and socialist Central and Eastern Europe). According to the U.S. Department of Labor, in 2006 there were approximately 583,000 people in advertising, marketing, promotions, public relations, and sales management.[8] This is a small fraction of the actual employment involved in promotional work, which, apart from the usual selling occupations in mass media, would also count telemarketers, lobbyists, speech writers, graphic designers, commercial illustrators, window display designers, and a myriad of other jobs in which at least part of the work involves pitching commodities, images, services, private or government interests, or public policies. One 2003 study cites a U.S. Bureau of Labor Statistics calculation of over 15 million Americans in sales positions alone.[9]

In an information and communication technology (ICT)-intensive economy, such as it is, the general mode of persuasion becomes a more central factor in production and requires higher-order propaganda functions. Indeed, the new capacities for surveillance and storing, processing, merging, and massaging data on citizens has outpaced consumption and thereby given greater importance to the stimulation of public taste and management of "public opinion".[10] The infrastructure of surveillance and propaganda is more densely networked than in the past, both in the commercial–cultural and political–diplomatic spheres of influence. As one specialist on propaganda has noted,

> Through the use of modern instruments and techniques of communications it is possible today to reach large or influential segments of national populations – to inform them, to influence their attitudes, and at times perhaps even to motivate them to a particular course of action... [and] by appealing over the heads of governments directly to public opinion, effective propaganda and other measures would encourage popular opinion to support U.S. policies, which would in turn exert pressure on government policymakers.[11]

Building on the traditional understanding of propaganda, i.e., the various instrumental forms of representation serving specific broad objectives of organised and powerful and would be powerful interests, my analysis draws on a more *systemic* understanding of promotional practices in (nominally) democratic states rooted in a digital communications mode of development.[12] That is to say, propaganda is more than symbolic expression summoned up for freestanding organisational projects of public persuasion. Propaganda has become intrinsic to and pervasive throughout the services and informational economy underpinning the "symbolic state".[13] It is intrinsic to a political economy whose corporate and state agents have relocated large segments of manufacturing industry offshore and government tasks to the private sector and turned to a wage and salary workforce made up of information processors (so-called "knowledge workers"). America increasingly is a nation of sellers.

Apart from the work of skilled professional propagandists, the normal routines of "knowledge work" commonly include promotional assignments. Repetitive scripted greetings, salutations and solicitations are part of the value-added repertoire of restaurant, fast food, and other retail service employees as means of encouraging consumption. The pitch of telemarketers and responses from technical support staff are so monotonously standardised that they often sound prerecorded. Workers in auto repair, oil change, and car wash facilities walk through a rapid sequence of time–motion choreography and promotional palaver that reduces them to industrial cyborgs. The Taylorist regimen that one associates with factory production has (d)evolved not towards "post-industrialism", as giddy technological determinists such as futurologist Alvin Toffler or the more respectable Harvard sociologist Daniel Bell anticipated, but rather to *hyperindustrialism* – the extension of Fordist factory practice, discipline, and regimentation to the flexible Fordism of the computer-aided services sector, which imposes a more penetrating system of regulation and surveillance of informational labour coupled with declining union rates and greater alienation from the control of production.

Information is now constituted as a factor of production, and propaganda is its fetishised expression that draws on the labour (i.e., that which produces exchange value) of both the formal (waged and salaried) and the informal sector, i.e., audiences as producers and consumers[14] – the latter generally unremunerated. Propaganda is no longer incidental in the new political economy; it resides at its core. Information designed for propaganda is massaged within a network of "superpanoptic" surveillance[15] from which copious data are extracted from consumers.[16] In the networked informational economy, the distinction between formal (paid) and informal (unpaid) labour, as well as the division of mental/manual labour, disintegrates, as the immaterial "knowledge" of consumptive habits and preferences is fed into the circuit of extraction/production/promotion/consumption.

The valorisation (and self-commodification) of personal values, attitudes, life styles, demographics, and opinions renders consumer identity as an input that converges with formal informational labour in producing exchange value. "Viral marketing" (inverting the invasive meaning of computer virus) is a recent industry term for marketers relying on either stealth or the consent of individuals and their social networks on the Internet to pass along product information and images. The marxist autonomista Maurizio Lazzarato refers to the informal immaterial labour contribution as "informational and cultural consent",[17] although *consent* to how their labour is ultimately used is rarely if ever solicited. This form of labour extraction constitutes not simply exploitation, i.e., undercompensation for delivered value, but *superexploitation*, operating within a ubiquitous "social factory". Harry Braverman (1974)[18] made a parallel point about capitalism's historical and relentless knowledge and skill transfers from worker to machine and the consequent degradation of labour through automation, although he confined his analysis to a traditional spatial and social conception of workplace.

The technological means for effecting a spatially and socially networked division of labour have enabled a reorganisation of production into more globally specialised and hierarchical segments. As the leading trilateralist economies, led by the United States, move to the tertiary stage of production, offshore manufacturing has retrograded to state-supported sweatshop relations of production in countries such as China, Pakistan, and Bangladesh, where international labour standards are largely unenforced. Delinking symbolic from material production, "[b]rand names, product definition and design, and marketing are being kept in-house, while manufacturing, logistics, distribution, and most support functions are being outsourced".[19] The circuit of production–consumption relies on repression of out-of-sight Third World workers and democratic social movements, a brutal division of labour, reminiscent of early capitalism, that subsidises "higher end" in-house functions in the transnational headquarter states.

Within the core ICT-based economies, grounded in selling and the employment of symbolic goods (graphic images, data, electronic games, media, and other immaterial commodities), repression has a softer character. As mass-produced manufactured consumer goods (clothing, footwear, toys, computers, phones, television sets, hardware, and the like) are produced offshore, domestic industries have moved to advertising and marketing activities and other producer services. In the last 50 years of the twentieth century, manufacturing jobs in the United States were downsized from more than one-third of the total to just over one-tenth, while service employment rose to about 80%.[20] This has led the United States and other leading capitalist economies to become marketing cultures rooted in the "culture-ideology of consumerism",[21] consecrating consumption (cf. George W. Bush's early post-9/11 exhortations to consume) as the single most important act of citizenship. The mass media now regularly invite audiences (as labour) to "vote" on performances, products, and news spin.

THE REGIME OF PROPAGANDA

In the early postwar era, Jacques Ellul[22] provided the most extensive analytical treatment of propaganda in modern society, though he refused to define the term. A conventional view of propaganda might define it as a form of speech, text, or other audio or visual message designed not to inform but to enjoin the receiver in a subordinate relationship of uncritical belief. Propaganda may be based on false or misleading information, or it may contain accurate information or both. The point of propaganda is not necessarily to deceive but rather to internalise or reinforce in the audience deference to the authoritative status of a particular advocacy bearing a clear or implicit rationale or policy prescription that on some level requires the audience's participation or consent. To such an understanding, I would add that propaganda implies a relationship of asymmetrical power between the interest that the propagandist represents and the audience to whom the message is addressed. Propaganda has become not simply occasional in its use but rather part of a larger programme of social regimentation.

Ellul observed that the purpose of propaganda is not only to agitate people to action but also to reinforce their societal roles,[23] thereby wielding a totalising influence by inducing social assimilation to elite norms and claims about progress. And, with Marcuse, he drew connections between modern propaganda and technological society, but his failure to ground an explanation of technology and technique within the logic of market forces rendered his notion a limited and somewhat technological-determinist view of social change. Ellul's arguments were lodged not as much in political analysis as in his deep-seeded Christian sense of morality. He tended to see technology and the propaganda of technique as dark, antidemocratic, autonomous forces rather than artifacts of an aggressive but socially contested system of power and left readers with few tools for collective intellectual self-defence.

In any event, the current foundations of propaganda are more systemically embedded than in Ellul's time. Transnational enterprises, with the active support of the neoliberal state, have turned their attention in their "home" markets to newer "creative" industries and producer services, including advertising, marketing, public relations, polling, focus group analysis, and other information management activities. Given their global reach, these technologies and whole industries of persuasion now form part of a world propaganda apparatus, whose clientele are found throughout the commercial and political spheres – and which is growing most rapidly in the emerging integrated market economies, such as in Central and Eastern Europe.

The purpose in this chapter is to discuss how promotional activities within the ICT mode of development have expanded not only in the service of consumer ideology but also in the production of political consensus – what the journalist-intellectual Walter Lippmann described as the elites" historic role in the "manufacture of consent".[24] In the reorganised technological and institutional settings of this new political economy, commercial and political characteristics in the production of consensus have converged. Propaganda is no longer simply an aspect of statecraft; it has become the centre of discourse in American politics. Propaganda is the prevailing discursive practice of hegemonic power and, as I discuss, of everyday life.

Whereas the generation of propaganda under the notorious Nazi regime was largely confined to a distinct public sector, its American variant was never constrained in this way and has proved to be more enduring. America's public sector has been incrementally absorbed and transformed by a predominant corporate culture, and in the process the notion of "public" itself has been privatised wholesale, creating a broad consensus within U.S. party politics on the corporatist and imperial objectives of the state. The principal function of propaganda, regardless of which party (or faction more accurately) is in power, is to internalise business values and symbolic actions as the natural, inevitable, and progressive (even revolutionary)[25] norms of society. Indeed, the now routine, private subcontracting of public affairs – from welfare programmes, prison management, charter schools, and Big Three "pouring rights" at public high schools to the majority of armed forces occupying Iraq, and even CIA duties[26] – and the casualness with which American business leaders and lobbyists traverse the "revolving door" of government and corporate offices reveal the relentless commoditisation of politics and public life. So committed is the U.S. government, particularly under neoconservatives, to eliminate "nonessential" functions of the state, that it subcontracts the practice of kidnapping, incarceration, and torture of suspected "terrorists" to third countries, a practice known in bureaucratic parlance as "extraordinary rendition".

The origins of professional U.S. state propaganda go back to the First World War, when Woodrow Wilson issued an executive order for the creation of a Committee on Public Information to marshal a national consensus for war on the side of Britain and France.[27] Headed by a journalist, George Creel, its membership included Wilson advisers Lippmann and Edward Bernays, who became a founder of the public relations industry. Both Lippmann and Bernays held the view that elites had an obligation to manage the attitudes of the "herd" of ordinary people:

> "The public must be put in its place", Walter Lippmann declared.... That goal could be achieved in part through "the manufacture of consent", a "self-conscious art and regular organ of popular government". This "revolution" in the practice of democracy should enable a "specialized class" to manage the "common interests" that "very largely elude public opinion entirely".[28]

Bernays shared a similar outlook about the necessity of social engineering. In his book, *Propaganda,* originally published in 1928, Bernays begins with the proposition, "The conscious and intelligent manipulation of the organised habits and opinions of the masses is an important element in democratic society. Those who manipulate this unseen mechanism of society constitute an invisible government which is the true ruling power of our country".[29] Bernays' writing enjoyed the admiration of a fellow master manipulator, the Nazi head of the German Ministry of Public Enlightenment and Propaganda, Joseph Goebbels.[30]

The Second World War provided another laboratory for the development of propaganda and psychological warfare in the service of U.S. political–military objectives. Among the academics and communication specialists engaged in the U.S. wartime propaganda effort were Wilbur Schramm, Paul Lazarsfeld, Hadley Cantril, and George Gallup (all in the Office of War Information), Morris Janowitz, W. Phillips Davison, Saul Padover (all in the intelligence organisation, Office of Strategic Services, the predecessor of the CIA), and Daniel Lerner,

William S. Paley (later CEO of CBS), and Edward Shils (all in the Army's Psychological Warfare Division).[31] The postwar development of the academic field of communication studies in the United States was very much directed or influenced by their instrumental conceptions of communicative practice. To this day, the study of mass communication favours a focus on audience reception.

Alex Carey described how business propaganda throughout the twentieth century was designed for "taking the risk out of democracy". By this he meant that democracy has been enclosed by a corporate-dominated political order to prevent independent public expression from interfering with its privileged agenda-setting position. This requires the control of key instruments of informational dissemination, including mass media, government, universities, and other institutions of public persuasion. By the 1950s, propaganda was not simply a tool of industry but an industry in and of itself.[32]

It is not only corporations that have reduced risk in the project of power concentration; it is also government. The use of advanced instruments of data collection on citizens (and as consumers) enables the corporate state to assure that regulation of policy in support of steady business profits and market management will meet with little resistance. The dividends of enormous state investment in advanced informational technology (telecommunications, launching devices, digital computers, Internet, and other communicative infrastructure), rationalised through a legitimating discourse of "national defence", have been largely conferred upon the business sector. Together with hundreds of billions of dollars in other forms of state subsidy, this effectively has established a kind of socialist welfare system for risk-averse plutocrats, with bailouts for failed corporations – and capitalist, risk-intense "free markets" for the poor. The main risks of membership in the society (stable work options, housing, education, safe food, air, and water, healthcare, and military service) are borne precariously by working people. The Enron and subprime mortgage lending scandals, the corporate theft of worker pension funds, and military service on behalf of ExxonMobil and other "disaster capitalism" industries are just a few examples of class-based risk shifting. Such contradictory realities require a steady stream of perception management.

PROPAGANDA FOR POLITICAL AND COMMERCIAL MANAGEMENT

One way that the state reduces the risks of democracy is by marginalising public participation in political representation. In supporting a system in which corporate consultants and lobbyists manage the electoral process, corporate elites ensure that political candidates will be beholden to those who finance the political sphere and the best elections that money can buy. Thomas Ferguson (1995)[33] calls this the investment theory of politics. Another is by tranquilising alienated workers with highly produced escapist entertainment media to rest and replenish the work ethic, emotionally seduce workers to put wages into consumption, and induce fear and anxiety about the state of the community and the world to reinforce loyalty to established authority.

The pervasive multimedia diffuse the impulse to consume in ever-greater degrees,[34] a feature of contemporary capitalism that harvests vast quantities of serviceable information for production and distribution. What Castells calls the informational mode of development can be observed in electioneering practices, wherein advanced communication media and techniques employed by organised interests for propaganda are now central to the electoral process. Jean Baudrillard noted that "Propaganda becomes the marketing and merchandising of idea-forces of political men [sic] and parties with their "trade-mark image"....This convergence defines a society – ours – in which there is no longer any difference between the economic and the political, because the same language reigns in both, from one end to the other".[35]

Communications technology is the machinery and information is the petroleum of political–commercial convergence. The surveillance of consumer demographics and habits, supported by information collecting and sorting technology, enables a hyperactive system of selling. The technologies of surveillance and persuasion form the centre of an informational and propaganda economy in capitalist as well as former socialist and Third-World political economies. This industrialisation of commodity consumption and the professionals who work in it have migrated to the formal political sphere. Augmented by polling, focus group analysis, citizen databases, and other information surveillance/management software/hardware, communication professionals have become the artisans of popular political discourse. Mark Poster argues, along the lines of Baudrillard, that the notion of "public" has slid into "publicity" and that "character" has been replaced by "image".[36]

On a broader political canvas, the state solicits public compliance through media-aided persuasive appeals. Political propaganda not only depends on new technologies and techniques of marketing politics and politicians, but also relies on a culture of consumerism in which the general populace has become conditioned to be sold as audiences to industries. Government reluctance to protect citizens from commercial list-sharing enterprises or intrusions into their web use – not to mention the government's own covert surveillance of phone and email communication – has given corporations carte blanche to market people as commodities, with little concern or accountability for the consequences. Direct-to-consumer advertising of blockbuster drugs is one laissez faire practice by which citizens are targeted by weakly regulated pharmaceutical companies that spend more on product promotion and campaign financing than on research. The patent medicine industry and highly profitable private insurance companies, not physicians, call the shots on how medicine is researched and how health care is and is not delivered in America. One physician wrote that "even the most respected medical journals seemed more like infomercials whose purpose was to promote their sponsors" products rather than to search for the best ways to improve people's health'.[37] Pharmaceutical companies are among the most active users of video news releases, which are forms of stealth advertising produced to look like news items and given free to willing television news outlets that fail to disclose the clients that pay for such stories. The pharmaceutical industry is also Washington's top lobbyist.

The government has followed the lead of business in the production of fake news. Public relations firms were hired by the Bush administration to produce and distribute policy propaganda and government "success stories" packaged as standard television news items, with actors posing as journalists, to make them appear as if they were station or network produced. In some cases, syndicated journalists were secretly put on the government payroll to cheerlead for administration policy initiatives. At least 20 different government agencies under the Bush administration were involved in producing hundreds of fake television news segments.[38] The White House even permitted a fake journalist to participate in official media briefings as if he were part of the credentialed press corps.

Under the Smith–Mundt Act of 1948 (Public Law 402), the government is forbidden from using taxpayer money to disseminate propaganda within the United States. The federal Government Accountability Office determined that several of the Bush administration's covert attempts to use the media to influence public opinion were improper. (The White House instructed government agencies to ignore the GAO finding.) Under the Act, it is also illegal to distribute to American audiences transmissions of overseas U.S. propaganda, a rule rendered largely meaningless, however, in the era of the Internet. According to Patricia Kushlis, a former 28-year Foreign Service officer in the U.S. Information Agency (USIA), which was in charge of much of the government's foreign propaganda, a large proportion of its overseas transmissions is in fact received by Americans.[39]

Although not original to their administration, Bush and Cheney routinely employed spin as another form of propaganda. For this, they relied in particular on conservative spin masters Karl Rove and Frank Luntz, a specialist in taking Orwellian liberties with language to manipulate public opinion on policy issues. In the manner of Lysenkoism, Environmental Protection Agency science reports on climate change were edited to reflect the administration's policy preferences. *New York Times* journalist Judith Miller was fed false information by the administration about Iraq's "weapons of mass destruction", which she then dutifully reported in her paper so that the White House, citing her "findings", could claim independent confirmation of their existence. Government–press coordination of these sorts is redolent of Goebbel's style of state propaganda.

PROFESSIONALISATION OF POLITICAL PROPAGANDA

Contrary to the claims of political consultants, the ideological management of elections and public policy within their professional circle shows no evidence of improving the participatory character of electoral politics. On the contrary, it has tended to consolidate the control of politics by big moneyed interests, which expands disproportionately with each election cycle, by interlinking the corporate rolodex – through consultants who work with industry in polling, PR, advertising, marketing, media consulting, spin doctoring, and lobbying – with political parties and candidates.[40] New technologies provide private consulting groups with the means for steering politics from citizens to professionals and redirecting public attention from issue debates to simplistic representations of "character" and other visceral matters.[41] This is evident in the ways in which promotionalism has become the dominant form of political communication: the wider presence of "news" reporting by political pundits and "experts", many of whom have no formal journalistic training; greater access to voters via highly crafted direct mail; the rapid growth of political advertising through media purchases (inducing higher campaign expenditures, more compressed sound bite news coverage, and lower overall coverage and voter turnouts); the constant attention to photo opportunities; speed dial political telemarketing; the entry of highly produced websites and blogging sites; politicians' telecommunication-assisted "satellite tours" serving as local news election coverage; computer-mediated opposition research; reliance by mainstream media and speechwriters on professional polling, focus group, and "perception analyser" (dial metre) data; and still other means of mass-produced and customised communications.

Using digital means of producing propaganda, corporate PR advisers carry over to modern propaganda-ready electioneering practices their skills in image making. Political organisations presume that if they are good at selling commodities and corporate brands, they are likely to be successful at selling candidates and policies. The acceleration of propaganda use is thus tied "to the harnessing of the revolution in communications"[42] and the breakdown of boundaries that previously restricted its colonisation of physical and social space. PR has long been part of American politics, well before it was regarded as a profession, but the advent of mass media, broadcasting, and narrow band digital technologies has accelerated the pace of PR in politics.

Nobody worked harder at perfecting his political image than Richard Nixon, a politician, many have said, defeated by his own television persona in 1960 and by the considerably more telegenic figure of Kennedy. In 1968, as Joe McGinnis reported, that changed. Nixon had Roger Ailes (currently president of Fox News) as his media adviser. But Nixon never came to accept the rigours of popular politics (he referred to audiences as "applause machines"), a disposition that led him to turn to secret war in Southeast Asia and the attempted destruction of the opposition party at Watergate.[43] By the time Hollywood celebrity Ronald Reagan came to the White House in 1981, an entourage of media, new technology, and professional expertise were brought along to cultivate a positive image of the president and other high-level officials in his administration.

Since then, the professionalisation and stylisation of politics, discussed at length elsewhere,[44] has rapidly accelerated. In congressional campaigns, the hiring of pollsters, media consultants, and fundraisers, in that order, reflecting the symbiosis and coordination among image makers, corporate patrons, and politicians, is *de rigueur*. Among consultants themselves, the polled opinion is that the most important route to campaign success is "getting the message right" (i.e., having an effective propaganda strategy). Political advertising, particularly via television, is the first line of battle in the management of public attitudes.[45] In 2004, political campaigns spent $2.74 billion in political advertising and marketing, an amount expected to double in 2008.[46]

The professionalisation of politics is premised on propaganda claims about "modernisation" and the apolitical assumption that political stability requires management of its processes by experts, which is assumed to represent an advance over citizen ('amateur') supervision. Since the Reagan era, political propaganda has been more fully wedded to private enterprise. Currently, many of the PR functions of government are outsourced to private strategic communications firms, such as the Lincoln Group and the Rendon Group.[47] They are among the 30,000 political consultants in the United States who enjoyed an estimated turnover of $7 billion in 2008.[48] The overwhelming majority of political consultants believe that they have rightly transcended the power of political parties. One extensive study on the subject found a direct correlation between the degree of professionalisation and the diminishing importance of party organisations.[49] With professional management, elections are less about democratic engagement and the quality of citizenship and more essentially about "winning", the political consultant's most important credential. Indeed, professional consultants tend to prefer lower election turnouts, because smaller numbers lend themselves to easier surveillance and data crunching, less cost, and greater predictability. Citizens are activated only in the last instance, the act of casting ballots (i.e., delivering themselves as endorsers of the corporate political agenda); the rest is taken care of by the professionals. As the most fundamental form of propaganda in corporate-dominated societies, the resonant expression of "democracy" establishes the ideological underpinning of elite control.

Professional electioneers insist on the command of all communicative aspects of the political or electoral process – from polling, to photo opportunities, to spin doctoring – which makes politicians highly dependent on their propaganda skills. Consultants are creatures of a neoliberal regime that privileges markets, not citizens, in determining the country's priorities. As flacks to organised power, they serve to legitimise the corporate ownership of public affairs, especially in the U.S. context where money is "the mother's milk of politics". By driving up the costs of elections in a pay-to-play system, opening the door to lobbyists who regard politics as a cost of doing business, political consultants, together with the mainstream media, help to normalise sound bite political communication and a narrow spectrum of corporate-friendly policy options over most of the important aspects of law making and public administration.

Without reference to the political economic or ideological foundations of electioneering, professionalisation is a totalising disquisition on the primacy of process, which is imperiously promoted as the standard for the rest of the world, marginalising issues of political participation. Such a narrative protects elite electoral interests and permits heavily disproportionate influence of financial and industrial executives. Class stratification is thus maintained through apolitical conceptions of professionalisation and practices that draw on the reciprocal interests of professional consultants, mainstream media, business corporations, political parties, candidates and other state functionaries and ideologues.

Class domination, however, is never stable and continually requires social reconditioning through indoctrination. Addressing the "necessary illusions" of an earlier era, Robert Brady, an American economist who studied the centralising characteristics of fascism, discussed how propaganda is employed in the maintenance of power:

> When these ideas and techniques are focused on the "sale of ideas", the net result may be summarised as forceful persuasion, via calculating doctrinal exegesis, of those potentially convertible social layers who are most apt to be won over to the rules of status at the lowest per capita cost, by articulate and ideologically ambidextrous spokesmen for those who have a special vested interest in the maintenance of the status quo.[50]

Propaganda is usually disseminated without ambiguity and based on sweeping unexamined truth claims, reflecting an implicit set of underlying moral and religious beliefs and privileges. One of the more prosaic discussions of the elite's propaganda role is offered by the U.S. President, George W. Bush: "See, in my line of work, you gotta keep repeating things over and over and over again for the truth to sink in – to kinda catapult the propaganda".[51] If this task relied on the president, propaganda would be a far less significant matter, but the reality is that a broad set of interests converge in the construction of propaganda, which include mainstream media; religious and educational institutions; industrial, financial, and trade associations; chambers of commerce; various political, economic, and foreign policy councils; and numerous other elite organisations, together engaged in an overdetermination of core doctrinal beliefs.

FOREIGN POLICY PROPAGANDA

How is the "truth" that Bush and other government agencies attempt to impart constructed for public education? A 2004 Defense Department study drawn from a group of invited representatives from industry, universities, private consulting groups, and government agencies found that "Nothing shapes U.S. policies and global perceptions of U.S. foreign and national security objectives more powerfully than the President's statements and actions, and those of senior officials. *Interests, not public opinion, should drive policies'* (italics added).[52] Apparently, it is not what the public thinks that matters but rather the will of organised interests. As a nation that rhetorically employs "democracy" as the rationale for regime change in the Middle East, Eastern Europe, and elsewhere, this would not be an encouraging message for those people it seeks to set free. In Appendix D to that report,[53] which provides an executive summary of a previous (October 2001), Defense Department study on "managed information dissemination", the meaning of strategic communications is rather clearly summarised in its final conclusion:

> Information is a strategic resource – less understood but no less important to national security than political, military, and economic power. In the information age, influence and power go to those who can disseminate credible information in ways that will mobilize publics to support interests, goals, and objectives. What is required is a coherent approach as to how we think about managed information dissemination and the investments that are required for its more effective use by America's diplomats and military leaders.[54]

Although the word "propaganda" reappears from time to time in State Department missives, the more favoured term for describing the use of instrumental communication is "public diplomacy",[55] an official function handled by the State Department, Department of Defense, White House, U.S. Agency for International Development (USAID), and the Broadcasting Board of Governors, which oversees the state's broadcast propaganda operations. However, the practice of public diplomacy is widespread, reaching beyond these agencies and immediate policy objectives. It includes more benign instruments of persuasion, such as international student, faculty, cultural, artistic, and professional exchanges and fellowships, the Peace Corps, Rotary Club, religious groups, and other overseas programmes into which aggressive U.S. efforts at regime change is often smuggled. If a distinction can be made between some of these exchanges and propaganda, and it is often difficult to determine their precise purposes or effects, it is that the former may be at least partly conceived as expressions of humanitarian development (even when it redounds to the favourable reputation of the donor state), whereas the latter are more direct and explicit instruments operating on behalf of expansive and powerful state interests. It is perfectly clear why the State Department prefers the term "public diplomacy" to describe institutions like Voice of America, Radio Free Europe/Radio Liberty, Radio Marti, Radio Sawa, and some activities of the CIA.[56]

Public diplomacy represents a form of "soft power", which can be seen as the pacification underside of an imperial foreign policy. In January 1983, Reagan signed a secret National Security Decision Directive 77, titled "Management of Public Diplomacy Relative to National Security", under the supervision of CIA director William Casey. This was "America's first peace-time propaganda ministry", designed to keep Congress, the press, and the electorate in tow with the foreign policy line developed by the State Department and National Security Council.[57] Public diplomacy was conceived as "comprised of those actions of the U.S. Government designed to generate support for our national security objectives". As part of this new propaganda apparatus, an International Information Committee was created to administer assistance to foreign governments and private groups "to encourage the growth of democratic political institutions and practices" consistent with U.S. global interests, particularly with respect to the Soviet Union and its allied states. According to the Reagan government's plan,

> This will require close collaboration with other foreign policy efforts – diplomatic, economic, military – as well as a close relationship with those sectors of the American society – labor, business, universities, philanthropy, political parties, press – that are or cold be more engaged in parallel efforts overseas....[in] programs and strategies designed to counter totalitarian ideologies and aggressive political action moves undertaken by the Soviet Union or Soviet surrogates.[58]

Under the Directive, a "public affairs committee" was formed to take over the business of the Project Truth Policy Group (subsequently folded into "Project Democracy'). The committee was run by a former CIA propaganda specialist, Walter Raymond, Jr., inside the National Security Council. According to Robert

Parry, a *Newsweek* and Associated Press correspondent during the Reagan years, "[t]he project's key operatives developed propaganda "themes", selected "hot buttons" to excite the American people, cultivated pliable journalists who would cooperate, and bullied reporters who wouldn't go along".[59] Raymond resigned his CIA post in order to take on this assignment. But clearly his training in CIA "psyops" (psychological operations) was integral to the task at hand.[60]

The purpose was to "achieve a specific intelligence objective, not foster a full-and-open democratic debate", covertly using media outlets to disseminate the propaganda. Raymond coordinated the propaganda effort of the Central American Public Diplomacy Task Force, which included the State Department, USAID, USIA, Defense Department, the NSC, and the CIA.[61] Reagan's illegal efforts to overthrow the Sandinista government in Nicaragua in the 1980s, led by Colonel Oliver North and endorsed by the National Security Council, followed a similar propaganda style. This initiative was labelled the "Democracy Program".[62] Reagan's Office of Public Diplomacy was shut down in 1988, when the Comptroller General found that it had "engaged in prohibited, covert propaganda activities designed to influence the media and public to support Administration Latin American policies".[63] Public diplomacy would soon resurface.

OLD AND NEW COLD WARS

U.S. foreign policy propaganda did not conclude with the collapse of the Soviet Union and its allied communist parties in Central and Eastern Europe (CEE) in the early 1990s and the presumed final triumph of capitalism over socialism. A number of American policy planners, however, see the collapse of communism as only the beginning of American ideological hegemony and imperium. Former U.S. secretary of state, Zbigniew Brzezinski observed, "As the imitation of American ways gradually pervades the world, it creates a more congenial setting for the exercise of the indirect and seemingly consensual American hegemony. And as in the case of the domestic American system, that hegemony involves a complex structure of interlocking institutions and procedures, designed to generate consensus and obscure asymmetries in power and influence'.[64] With a focus on recent Bush era initiatives, this chapter next examines the U.S. "democracy promotion" agenda in the CEE region, which has been a principal focus of propaganda since the onset of the Cold War. I also briefly discuss another, more recent U.S. propaganda front, the Middle East.

The multiple propaganda tactics of the United States and its European allies was a major stimulus to the collapse of the Soviet system. For the United States, it involved a range of Cold War instruments – mainstream media, exchange programmes, volunteer organisations, philanthropic and foundational groups, intelligence and espionage agencies, the deployment of electronic, radar, and sonar surveillance, political defections, disinformation campaigns, and other forms of political subversion. It also involved specific propaganda apparatuses, such as the secretly CIA-run Radio Free Europe and Radio Liberty and other media operations, including "Operation Mockingbird" (a covert project started in the late 1940s to manipulate segments of domestic and foreign media). At one time, some 400 of the American press corps, joined by many foreign journalists, were clandestinely doing propaganda work for or with the CIA,[65] as were several major private foundations, publishers, businesses, financial houses, airlines, PR firms, think tanks, student organisations, scientists, political and religious leaders, and well-known academics, among others. Regular CIA employees engaged in propaganda efforts in the 1950s numbered around 3,000.[66]

With the end of the Soviet/CEE communist bloc, the United States in the name of "democracy promotion" began to exercise a free hand by introducing economic "shock therapy" to convert these "transition" states to neoliberal market economies and support their membership in the regional security organisation NATO. The limited emphasis in the region on civil society building through development of foreign-funded NGOs, financed by USAID and the National Endowment for Democracy (NED),[67] is inscribed with a core assumption that individual citizens and groups are better endowed than government to look after popular social needs. This notion is a public sector corollary to commercial subcontracting in which government functions are largely delegated to interest groups. Such a concept of public is rooted in the idea of "the property-bearing individual who chooses to participate in civil society and forms associations... [whose goals] are driven by a commitment to advancing the condition of the self".[68] Fractious polities fragmented into multiple pro-Western, "free market" elite organisations and NGOs are far easier for Western powers to control than is a centralised and nationalist-oriented government. Propaganda-intense elections featuring Western-supported candidates, such as those that occurred during the "colour revolutions", *infra*, serve the purpose of legitimating this neoliberal ordering of society.[69] In the absence of dense participatory structures and active social movements, elections largely serve as symbolic events to create or maintain a sense of state legitimacy. Political uprisings that force elections tend to be quickly co-opted or marginalised from real power sharing once the electoral spectacle is completed.

Since the 1990s, the CEE region has been the main target of USAID, NED, and other public and private "democracy promotion" groups. Billionaire financier George Soros has dedicated his life to overthrowing communist and nationalist rule in the region and has set up a network of foundations for this purpose.

USAID, which directs U.S. funding priorities in democracy assistance, describes the logic of its involvement in CEE in economic terms:

> In 1989, and again in 1992, the leaders and people of Central and Eastern Europe and Eurasia called out to the Western world for help—to make the transition to market-oriented democracies....Many parts of the U.S. government eagerly joined the effort to show these new independent states how to become market democracies.[70]

If USAID is the principal funding source, NED is the principal agent of "democracy promotion". William Blum, who quit his position at the State Department in 1967 in opposition to the U.S. invasion of Vietnam and has since written authoritative studies on U.S. foreign policy, argues that NED's basic philosophy is that

> working people and other citizens are best served under a system of free enterprise, class cooperation, collective bargaining, minimal government intervention in the economy and opposition to socialism in any shape or form. A free market economy is equated with democracy, reform and growth, and the merits of foreign investment are emphasized.... In short, NED's programs are in sync with the basic needs and objectives of the New World Order's economic globalization, just as the programs have for years been on the same wavelength as US foreign policy.[71]

Two Washington insiders and specialists in democracy assistance analysis do not see a strong commitment on the part of the United States to participatory democracy:

> Since 1989, promoting strong economic and security relationships has been the paramount policy initiative for the United States in the region, while promoting democracy is an ancillary goal. (The approximately $150 million the U.S. government has spent since 1989 on programs aimed at helping the former communist countries of central and eastern Europe carry out democratic transitions represents only 6.5 percent of all U.S. assistance to the region in this period).[72]

Moreover, they assert, "Democracy assistance not only establishes an unequal relationship between donor and recipient but assumes a kind of political intervention by donors that has rarely been undertaken so explicitly by a donor government".[73]

Starting in 2000, the CEE region became the focus of local and globally inspired and foreign-aided "colour revolutions" (a term referring to oppositionist party emblems) – initiatives to overthrow elected but contested heads of state by extra-legal means. The first to come under the crosshairs of U.S. and E.U. regime change monitors was Slobodan Milošević, whom they failed to destroy after a NATO bombing campaign in 1999 but which killed thousands of civilians and created more than a million refugees and displaced persons. Milošević's eventual removal through a foreign-funded and partly managed electoral event instigated other foreign-supported coups in Georgia, Ukraine, and, in a failed effort, in Belarus.[74] Although the oppositionist uprisings in these countries represented the initiatives of social movements at some level, the tactics heavily relied on U.S. training and promotional activities with pre-tested, modular techniques and technologies designed as a template for regime change. The use of the term "revolution" was part of the arsenal of propaganda that Western governments and the mainstream media deployed, along with false references to targeted leaders as "dictators", in order to rationalise foreign intervention and unconstitutional means of deposing heads of state. Indeed, if these were in any way revolutions, as some observers noted, they were failed revolutions.[75] Transitions to stable, rule-of-law, participatory democracies have yet to occur in the region.

BRANDING NATIONS

Perhaps the most enduring impact of U.S. intervention has been to make the targeted regions safe for public relations. Ernst and Young, one of the largest global accounting and auditing firms, conducts "attractiveness surveys" for Central and Eastern Europe to measure how well they appeal to potential transnational corporate investors. Meanwhile, Simon Anholt, a journal editor, international marketing adviser, and former PR specialist for Hill & Knowlton (a firm that has worked closely with pro-Western Middle Eastern regimes) in Budapest and London, provides a service for foreign governments that he calls "nation branding", which he defines as "the business of applying corporate marketing theory to countries".[76] That is to say, countries must take seriously their "brand image" in the transnational corporate community if they intend to remain viable economic entities. "The word brand excites a great deal of contentious discussion", says Wally Olins, chair of London-based Saffron Brand Consultants, who prefers to call the practice "reputation management" – as if that were less contentious.[77]

Discussing nation branding in Central and Eastern Europe, Anholt contends that images of CEE countries are constituted by their capacity to institute neoliberal reforms and thereby attract foreign capital. As he argues, "Having a country brand is necessary to attract investors but not enough; there must be an infrastructure, a skilled workforce, favourable tax policies and returns on investment" and that

> for countries whose image is better than reality (Poland, Czech Republic or Romania), the challenge is to transform their superior image into concrete investment projects while the countries that score higher on reality than image (Hungary, for example) should improve their perception in the market and level of notoriety.

Even better, he suggests, the Czech Republic ought to change the English version of its name to make it an easier vocalisation for foreigners and that Estonia would be well served to adopt the German name Estland (for its association with high-ranking Finland on the attractiveness scale).[78]

Most of the U.S. government's "public diplomacy" initiatives of late have concentrated on the Middle East and not with good results. Shortly after 9/11, as part of the U.S. government's effort to wage psychological warfare against its enemies in the region, the Rumsfeld-led Pentagon created an Office of Strategic Influence (OSI) and to help them hired Victoria Clarke, who previously ran the Washington D.C. Office of Hill & Knowlton, as public affairs officer.[79] Clarke's approach was to achieve "information dominance" and "to recruit "key influentials" – movers and shakers from all walks who with the proper ministrations might be counted on to generate support for Mr. Rumsfeld's priorities'.[80] They also brought in the Rendon Group, a self-styled "perception management" consulting firm involved in numerous secret programmes of the United States in the Middle East and elsewhere.[81]

An unnamed Pentagon official said the Department's propaganda tactics range "from the blackest of black programmes to the whitest of the white".[82] Revelations about its black propaganda intentions forced the Pentagon to abandon the OSI project in February 2002. In October 2006, Rumsfeld revived the idea of creating a "rapid response" propaganda unit in the Pentagon to counter stories in the U.S. and international press that the Department of Defense (DOD) deemed negative. His successor Robert Gates dropped the unit and folded some of its functions into its public affairs office.[83]

The *New York Times* revealed in April 2008, based on DOD internal communications, that starting in 2002, the Pentagon recruited most of the country's top television military news analysts, who concurrently held positions as defence contractors. These hand-picked analysts and former military officials, all without media credentials, were inserted as objective and authoritative experts for major network and cable news channels, dutifully and uncritically reporting stories they were fed *in camera* by Bush administration leaders at the Defense Department, the State Department, the Justice Department, and the White House. Their sources included Dick Cheney, attorney general Alberto Gonzales, and national security adviser, Stephen Hadley. The news analysts also worked with Pentagon officials in writing opinion articles, one of which, a tribute to Rumsfeld, appeared in the *Wall Street Journal*.

This relationship essentially rendered them as DOD and defence industry propaganda surrogates for military policies in the Middle East and elsewhere. It enabled the Bush administration to use the mainstream media as its psychological operations division while skirting federal restrictions on domestic propaganda.[84]

Even if the analysts were not *directly* paid by the government to do its propaganda work, they saw their contacts with the news media as a means of fostering opportunities for lucrative business ties to defence contractors, "either as lobbyists, senior executives, board members or consultants". John C. Garrett, for example, a retired Army colonel and analyst for Fox news, is also a lobbyist at Patton Boggs, a lobbying firm that "helps firms win Pentagon contracts".

The *Time*s found that the Pentagon's "information apparatus" used the analysts "in a campaign to generate favorable news coverage of the administration's wartime performance" and as influential "message force multipliers" to disseminate DOD talking points and counteract critics. Brent Krueger, a senior aide of former Pentagon public affairs spokesperson Victoria Clarke, who ran the propaganda operation, explained that the military analysts were effectively "writing the op-ed" for the invasion and occupation of Iraq.[85] The major television news media that employed the analysts refused to report on the controversy. Clarke now works as a commentator for network news.

PROPAGANDA AND THE NEOLIBERAL STATE

It is not that the imposition of U.S. and E.U. transnational marketing culture will necessarily succeed in regions marked for global integration, but the efforts in transferring the mass consumption model certainly inflict costs, waste, and suffering that will postpone democracy and deter local, organic initiatives towards building secure and socially just societies. The Georgia–Russia conflict in 2008 was certainly encouraged on some level by aggressive Western intervention in the region. Other Western-inspired conflicts undoubtedly will follow. Despite the rhetoric, democracy does not appear to be the central purpose of this intervention.

In the ideal neoliberal world order, "transition" governments do not disappear; rather they are downsized to reduce the social welfare functions of the state (subcontracted to private agencies or NGOs) and facilitate the objectives of transnational capital. For critics of globalisation, "The radical dynamism of global free markets is seen as sandblasting the authenticity of cultures and demolishing traditional authority structures".[86] For neoliberals, government downsizing is cast as responding to the need for democratic opportunity and efficiency. Economic and social historian Eric Hobsbawm, elaborating on this latter discursive strategy, comments that the emphasis on the limits of "state capacity" diverts attention from the transnational community's desire to evade public debate about economic policies. This is achieved, he argues, by turning to the informal mechanisms of NGOs to effect policy change, thereby bypassing a broader consultation and engagement of the populace. Neoliberals view state building not as a participatory as much as a technocratic and administrative exercise.[87]

The public character of government is diminished by its subsumption into the prevailing business culture. In the United States, it is common for ex-politicians and government officials to work as lobbyists or consultants for foreign clients, making a fiction of distinctions between public and private sector activities. Former presidential candidate Robert Dole was a lobbyist for the UAE in the United States. Former secretary of state Madeline Albright served as a lobbyist for the UAE in China. And former secretaries of state, Henry Kissinger and Alexander Haig, both represented US transnational corporations doing business in China. Former New York City mayor and presidential candidate Rudy Giuliani was hired as a consultant for the Mexican government. These are just a few of the hundreds of high-level federal employees and officials who have taken advantage of the "revolving door" to return to or assume second careers as well-paid hired guns for foreign interests in the United States and abroad.

The conduct of overseas "public diplomacy" is now more fully integrated with the commercial, "entrepreneurial", and systemically promotional character of contemporary transnational capitalism. For officials who work abroad, business interests, corporate identity, and propaganda are unified components of "public service". According to a study of the Center on Public Diplomacy at the University of Southern California, its former director finds that the overseas diplomat is now conceived as a servant not of the public sector but as a knowledge professional on behalf of the corporate sphere: "The territory? Cerebral. The currency? Ideas. The marketplace? Global. The diplomat? Part activist, part lobbyist, and part street-smart policy entrepreneur".[88]

Politics has been restructured and submerged within a technological and surveillance-mediated strategy of branding, marketing, and consumerism designed to distract the public from everyday realities of inequality and social injustice. Citizenship is reduced to spectatorship. What Guy Debord described in *The Society of the Spectacle* as a world of illusion is the "reality" contemporary propagandists seek as the dominant social order: "The spectacle in general, as the concrete inversion of life, is the autonomous movement of the non-living".[89]

Framed largely through media, politics has taken on the character of spectacle.[90] Commenting on the September 2002 timing of the propaganda campaign for the invasion of Iraq, Bush's chief of staff, Andrew Card, former lobbyist for the automobile industry, offered a glib promotional rationale: "From a marketing point of view, you don't introduce new products in August".[91]

What lessons can be gleaned from this understanding? The totalising effect of propaganda within an ICT mode of development lays naked for all to see the social construction of knowledge and value. The fetishisation of daily life has nearly reached its practical limits. The entire society is transformed into a factory in which the production of ideas and images converge the former sense of dyadic oppositions: work and leisure, producer and consumer, political and cultural, government and industry, First World and Third World, and on and on. "All that is solid melts into air." The citizen – as labour, as consumer, as audience – produces value in every capacity, rendering the shared knowledge, information, identities, and values of citizens the central factor of production in the Western economy. If one still needed convincing, it makes explicit the reality that in a socially produced economy, there can be no legitimate assignment of private profit. The corresponding form of governance to such an economic order can only be socialism – the social creation of goods and the social ownership of their production. In no other era could socialism have a better defence of its principles.

NOTES

This chapter forms part of my forthcoming book, *Branding Democracy* (Peter Lang).

1. John Brown, "The Anti-Propaganda Tradition in the United States". Bulletin Board for Peace website, no date. Accessed 9 July 2008 at http://www.bulletinboardforpeace.org/articlebrown.htm
2. Manuel Castells, *The Rise of the Network Society*. Hoboken, NJ: Wiley-Blackwell, 2000.
3. The notion of immaterial labour is actually a second degree fetishisation, inasmuch as the immaterial aspects of production are linked to material aspects that take place elsewhere, often in Third-World settings, where superexploitation is typical of working conditions. The repression of Third-World workers subsidises the relative freedom of their Western counterparts engaged in tertiary forms of productive labour.
4. Kaela Jubas. "Conceptual Confusion in Democratic Societies: Understandings and Limitations of Consumer-Citizenship". *Journal of Consumer Culture* , 7 (2), 2007, 251.
5. Stephanie Clifford, "Product Placements Acquire a Life of Their Own on Shows". *New York Times*. 13 July 2008, C1.
6. Carey L. Higgins and Gerald Sussman, "Plugola: News for Profit, Entertainment and Network Consolidation". In T. Gibson and M. Lowes, eds., *Urban Communication and the World-Class City: Production, Text, Context*. Lanham, MD: Rowman & Littlefield, 2006, 156.
7. U.S. Department of Labor, Bureau of Labor Statistics. "Occupational Outlook Handbook", 2007, at http://www.bls.gov/oco/ocoS020.htm#emply
8. Brian W. Lambert, "In the Marketing Mix". Unpublished paper presented at the Professional Sales Symposium of the United Professional Sales Association, Washington, D.C. 24 November 2003, 8, at http://www.brianlambert.biz/docs/New_Role_of_Sales_in_Marketing_Mix.pdf

9. I use the term "public opinion" in a conventional sense here, i.e., from what pollsters claim to be shared symbolic understandings of public representations, although I share Bourdieu's scepticism about whether there is ever such a thing as shared interpretation (opinion) implied by pollster reports.
10. Kenneth A. Osgood, "Propaganda". In Alexander DeConde, Richard Dean Burns, and Fredrik Logevall, eds., *Encyclopedia of American Foreign Policy*. New York: Charles Scribner's Sons, 2001 at http://findarticles.com/p/articles/mi_gx5215/is_2002/ai_n19132468
11. Castells, *The Rise of the Network.*
12. Nicholas J. O'Shaughnessy, *Politics and Propaganda: Weapons of Mass Seduction*. Ann Arbor: University of Michigan, 2004.
13. The audience as consumers produce value in at least three ways. One is through the information that is extracted from them through various forms of surveillance (Nielsen ratings, surveys, and other forms of data gathering); a second is through the labour of watching and listening to commodified media, a task indispensable to the market; and the third is through the publicity that audiences extend to media and advertisers, including solicited online reviews, in helping bring additional audience to entertainment and news (i.e., as secondary propaganda agents).
14. David Lyon, *Surveillance Society: Monitoring Everyday Life*. Milton Keynes, UK: Open University Press, 2001.
15. Aristotle Inc. is said to have a database on 175 million Americans. Many major U.S. campaigns, mostly Republican, including those of George W. Bush, John McCain, and Rudy Guiliani, as well as numerous Senate, House, and gubernatorial candidates have paid for Aristotle's voter data. Ukraine's Viktor Yushchenko availed of its services in the 2004 election. But it does not end there. Aristotle also sells its voter lists to commercial enterprises, including major banks, such as U.S. Bancorp: Discussed in James Verini, "Big Brother Inc". *Vanity Fair*. 13 December 2007. Online edition.
16. Maurizio Lazzarato, "Immaterial Labour". In P. Virno and M. Hardt, eds., *Radical Thought in Italy: A Potential Politics*. Minneapolis: University of Minnesota Press, 1996, 133–147.
17. Harry Braverman, *Labor and Monopoly Capital: The Degradation of Work in the Twentieth Century*. New York: Monthly Review Press, 1974.
18. Timothy J. Sturgeon, "Does Manufacturing Still Matter?: The Organizational Delinking of Production from Innovation", 1997, 14. Unpublished paper available at http://brie.berkeley.edu/publications/WP%2092B.pdf
19. Barbara Hagenbaugh, "U.S. Manufacturing Jobs Fading Away Fast". *USA Today*. 12 December 2002. Online edition.
20. Leslie Sklair, "The Transnational Capitalist Class and the Discourse of Globalisation". *Cambridge Review of International Affairs*, 14 (1), 2000, 67–85.
21. Jacques Ellul, *Propaganda: The Formation of Men's Attitudes*. New York: Alfred A. Knopf, 1965.
22. Konrad Kellen, "Introduction". In Jacques Ellul, *Propaganda: The Formation of Men's Attitudes*. New York: Alfred A. Knopf, 1965, vi.
23. Edward Herman and Noam Chomsky picked up Lippmann's phrasing and employed it ironically in a critical analysis of state and media propaganda. See their book, *The Manufacture of Consent: The Political Economy of the Mass Media*. New York: Pantheon Books, 1988.

24. Jean-Maria Dru argued in his prescriptions for advertising that corporations adopt images of "disruption" in order to appropriate the spirit of youth and represent brand identification as a form of revolutionary action. See his *Disruption: Overturning Conventions and Shaking Up the Marketplace*, New York: Wiley, 1996.
25. 'According to one senior administration official involved in intelligence-budget decisions, half of the CIA's work is now performed by private contractors – people completely unaccountable to Congress. Another senior budget official acknowledges privately that lawmakers have no idea how many rent-a-spies the CIA currently employs – or how much unchecked power they enjoy". See James Bamford, "The Man Who Sold the War", *Rolling Stone*. 17 November 2005, at http://www.rollingstone.com/politics/story/8798997/the_man_who_sold_the_war/print
26. Britain's propaganda techniques employed in the First World War to win over the public to war, including people in its colonies and in America, were also much admired by the likes of Goebbels. Much of its propaganda poster art is on display at the Imperial War Museum in London.
27. Noam Chomsky, *Hegemony or Survival: America's Quest for Global Dominance*. New York: Metropolitan Books, 2003, 6.
28. Bernays, *Propaganda*, 2005, 37.
29. Franklin Roosevelt's New Deal paralleled Goebels' efforts in terms of mobilising the public through propaganda. See Stuart Ewen, *PR!: A Social History of Spin*. New York: Basic Books, 1996, 290–336.
30. Christopher Simpson, *Science of Coercion: Communication Research and Psychological Warfare, 1945–1960*. New York: Oxford University Press, 1996
31. Alex Carey, *Taking the Risk Out of Democracy: Corporate Propaganda Versus Freedom and Liberty*. Chicago: University of Illinois Press, 1995.
32. Thomas Ferguson, *Golden Rule: The Investment Theory of Party Competition and the Logic of Money-Driven Political Systems*. Chicago: University of Chicago Press, 1995.
33. Andrea Migone, "Hedonistic Consumerism: Patterns of Consumption in Contemporary Capitalism". *Review of Radical Political Economics*, 39 (2), Spring 2007, 173–200.
34. Jean Baudrillard, *Simulacra and Simulation*. Ann Arbor: University of Michigan Press, 1994, 88.
35. Mark Poster, *What's the Matter with the Internet?* Minneapolis: University of Minnesota Press, 2001, 78.
36. John Abramson, *Overdosed America: The Broken Promise of American Medicine*. New York: HarperCollins, 2008, xii.
37. David Barstow and Robin Stein, "Under Bush, a New Age of Prepackaged News". *New York Times*. 13 March 2005. Online edition.
38. Patricia Kushlis, "Radio Free What?" 23 April 2008. Online at http://whirledview.typepad.com/whirledview/public_diplomacy/index.html
39. Gerald Sussman, *Global Electioneering: Campaign Consulting, Communications, and Corporate Financing*. Lanham, MD: Rowman & Littlefield, 2005.
40. Dennis Johnson, *No Place for Amateurs: How Political Consultants Are Reshaping American Democracy*. New York: Routledge, 2001.
41. Osgood, *Propaganda*.
42. Joe McGinnis, *The Selling of the President, 1968*. New York: Penguin, 1969.

43. Sussman, *Global Electioneering.*
44. Dennis Kinsey, “Political Consulting: Bridging the Academic and Practical Perspectives”. In Bruce I. Newman, ed., *Handbook of Political Marketing.* Thousand Oaks, CA: Sage, 1999, 116–118.
45. Patrick Quinn and Leo Kivijarv, “U.S. Political Media Buying 2004”. *International Journal of Advertising,* 24 (1), 2005, 131.
46. The Lincoln Group and Rendon Group, once partners, both provide psychological operations services for the U.S. government, especially on behalf of the military in the Middle East. The Lincoln Group was one of three PR organizations to share up to a $300-million five-year contract for the Pentagon in “psychological operations efforts to improve foreign public opinion about the United States, particularly the military”. See Renae Merle, “Pentagon Funds Diplomacy Effort”. *Washington Post.* 11 June 2005. Online edition. One of its objectives was to pay Iraqi news media to place unattributed articles written by the U.S. military, which raised concerns that deceptive reporting “could easily migrate into American news outlets”. See Thom Shanker, “No Breach Seen in Work in Iraq on Propaganda”. *New York Times.* 22 March 2006. The Rendon Group, which has rendered media services for presidential candidates in both U.S parties, received $100,000 per month from the Kuwaiti royal family during Desert Storm and also won a $23-million contract from the CIA to produce anti-Saddam propaganda. See Alexander, Cockburn, and Jeffrey St. Clair, *Imperial Crusaders: Iraq, Afghanistan and Yugoslavia,* London: Verso, 2004, 322.
47. Freke Vuijst, “Zonder Netroots Ben Je Nergens” (Without Netroots You’re Nowhere). *Vrij Nederland.* 19 January 2008. Online edition.
48. Fritz Plasser, “Parties’ Diminishing Relevance for Campaign Professionals,” *Harvard International Journal of Press Politics,* 6 (4), 2001, 46, 52.
49. Robert A. Brady, *Business as a System of Power.* New York: Columbia University Press, 1943, 292.
50. See YouTube, “Catapult the Propaganda”. 24 May 2005. Retrieved: 16 October 2006 from: http://video.google.com/videoplay?docid=6276292210262805511&q=propaganda&total=26069&start=10&num=10&so=0&type=search&plindex=0
51. United States Department of Defense, *The Politics of the World-Economy: The States, the Movements and the Civilizations,* New York: Cambridge University Press, 2004, 3.
52. The title of the October 2001 report is “Appendix D: Executive Summary and Recommendations of the DSB [Defense Science Board] Task Force on Managed Information Dissemination (MID)”. The DSB is an advisory committee of the Secretary of Defense.
53. U.S. Department of Defense, *Politics of the World-Economy,* 99.
54. In a 2006 report of pollsters, politicians, and academics, sponsored by the University of Southern California’s (USC) Center on Public Diplomacy of the Annenberg School of Communication and the Pew Research Center, public diplomacy was defined as image building, designed for the purpose of helping to improve “negative public opinion abroad” towards the United States. Critical to this task is “the importance of identifying elite opinion when conducting polling research”, which is taken “as a barometer of a broader public opinion”. And business leaders are seen as “an under-utilised group of opinion leaders, which could potentially play an important role in public diplomacy initiatives”. See Joshua Fouts, “Executive Summary”. In J. Fouts, ed., *Public Diplomacy, Practitioners,*

Policy Makers, and Public Opinion. Los Angeles: USC Center on Public Diplomacy, 2006, 8, 11. Online at http://uscpublicdiplomacy.org/pdfs/USCCPD_PublicDiplomacy_WPO_2006.pdf

55. Humphrey Taylor, "The Practice of Public Diplomacy". In J. Fouts, ed., *Public Diplomacy, Practitioners, Policy Makers, and Public Opinion*. 48.
56. John Stauber and Sheldon Rampton, *Toxic Sludge Is Good for You: Lies, Damn Lies and the Public Relations Industry*. Monroe, ME: Common Courage Press, 1995, 162.
57. U.S. White House, "Management of Public Diplomacy Relative to National Security". National Security Decision Directive Number 77. 14 January 1983. Online at http://www.fas.org/irp/offdocs/nsdd/23–1966t.gif
58. Robert Parry, "History of Guatemala's Death Squads". 11 January 2005. Online at http://www.thirdworldtraveler.com/Global_Secrets_Lies/HxGuatemala_ DeathSquads.html
59. Robert Parry, *Secrecy and Surveillance: Rise of the Bush Dynasty from Watergate to Iraq*, 2004. Arlington, VA: The Media Consortium, 220, 224.
60. Ibid., 219–221.
61. Hernando Calvo Ospina, "The CIA's Successors and Collaborators". *Le Monde Diplomatique*. August 2007. Online at http://mondediplo.com/2007/08/04ned
62. Stauber and Rampton, *Toxic Sludge Is Good for you*. 167.
63. Zbigniew Brzezinski, *The Grand Chessboard: American Primacy and Its Geostrategic Imperatives*. New York: Basic Books, 1997, 26–27.
64. Carl Bernstein, "The CIA and the Media: How America's Most Powerful News Media Worked Hand in Glove with the Central Intelligence Agency and Why the Church Committee Covered It Up". *Rolling Stone*. 20 October 1977, 55–67.
65. Alex Constantine, "Mockingbird: The Subversion of the Free Press by the CIA', 2000. Online at http://www.spartacus.schoolnet.co.uk/JFKconstantine.htm
66. See Gerald Sussman, "The Myths of 'Democracy Assistance': U.S. Political Intervention in Post-Soviet Eastern Europe". *Monthly Review*, 58 (7), December 2006, 15–29.
67. Thomas Jacobson and Won Yong Jang, cited in Mohan J. Dutta-Bergman, "Civil Society and Public Relations: Not So Civil After All". *Journal of Public Relations Research*, 7 (3), 2005, 272.
68. Sussman, "The Myths…'
69. U.S. Agency for International Development, "A Decade of Change: Profiles of USAID Assistance to Europe and Eurasia", 2000. Online at http://www.usaid.gov/locations/europe_eurasia/ten-year/
70. William Blum, *Rogue State: A Guide to the World's Only Superpower*. Monroe, ME: Common Courage Press, 2000, 180, 181.
71. Paula R. Newberg and Thomas Carothers, "Aiding – and Defining – Democracy". *World Policy Journal*. Spring 1996, 97.
72. Ibid., 99.
73. See Sussman, "The Myths…"
74. Mark R. Beissinger, "Promoting Democracy: Is Exporting Revolution a Constructive Strategy?" *Dissent*, Winter 2006, 18–24.
75. Lee H. Teslik, "Anholt: Countries Must Earn Better Images through Smart Policy" (Interview with Simon Anholt). Council on Foreign Relations. 6 November 2007. Online at http://www.cfr.org/publication/14719/anholt.html?breadcrumb=%2F

76. Wally Olins, "Nation Branding in Europe". 3 December 2005. Online at http://www.sbs.ox.ac.uk/news/archives/EMBA/National+branding+in+Europe.htm
77. Cited in György Szondi, "The Role and Challenges of Country Branding in Transition Countries: The Central and Eastern European Experience". *Place Branding and Public Diplomacy*, 3, 2007, 8–20.
78. Cockburn and St. Clair, *Imperial Crusaders*, 321.
79. David Barstow, "Hidden Hand of Pentagon Help Steer Military Analysts". *New York Times*. 20 April 2008. Online edition.
80. Rendon's projects in the Middle East included the promotion of the Iraqi National Congress (INC) under the controversial leadership of Ahmed Chalabi, the development of the Iraqi Broadcasting Corporation and Radio Hurriah (which during Saddam's time transmitted messages from Kuwait to Iraqi opposition leaders), propaganda work for the Kuwaiti exile government during the Iraq invasion of that country in 1990–1991, along with other projects, by its own claim, in a total of 91 countries. According to *New Yorker* correspondent Seymour Hersh, the CIA paid Rendon close to a hundred million dollars for its services on behalf of the INC. See Liam Kennedy and Scott Lucas, "Enduring Freedom: Public Diplomacy and U.S. Foreign Policy", *American Quarterly* 57 (2), 2005, 309–333; "Rendon Group", updated 28 June 2007, at http://en.wikipedia.org/wiki/Rendon_Group; and Bamford, 2005.
81. Jessica Hodgson, "Pentagon Steps Up Propaganda Efforts". *Guardian*. 19 February 2002. Online edition.
82. Michael Roston, "Pentagon Kills Rumsfeld 'Propaganda' Unit". *The Raw Story*. 13 July 2007. Online at http://rawstory.com/news/2007/Pentagon_kills_Rumsfeld_propaganda_unit_0713.html
83. Such restrictions originate with the U.S. Constitution (Article I, Section 7, clause 7), which forbids the use of federal funds without legal appropriation. Subsequent legislation (5 U.S.C. 3107) in 1913 prohibits federal funding "to pay a publicity expert unless specifically appropriated for that purpose". P.L. 108–447, Div. H. Sec. 624 restricts U.S. agency communications directed at Americans "for publicity or propaganda purposes" (in its words for content that is for "self-aggrandizement", contains "puffery", is "purely partisan in nature", or is engaged in "covert propaganda") unless authorised by Congress. See Kevin R. Kosar, "Public Relations and Propaganda: Restrictions on Executive Agency Activities". *CRS* [Congressional Research Service] *Report for Congress*. 8 February 2005, 5–6.
85. Barstow, "Hidden Hand of Pentagon".
84. O'Shaughnessy, *Politics and Propaganda*. 146–147.
85. Cited in David Chandler, *Empire in Denial: The Politics of State Building*. London: Pluto, 2006, 90.
86. Fouts, *Public Diplomacy*. 22.
87. Guy Debord, *Society of the Spectacle*. 2006 (orig. 1967). Trans. Ken Knabb. Oakland, CA: AK Press, 1
88. Murray Edelman, *Constructing the Political Spectacle*. Chicago: University of Chicago Press, 1988.
89. Jan Nederveen Pieterse, "Neoliberal Empire". *Theory Culture & Society*, 21 (3)2004, 123, 128.

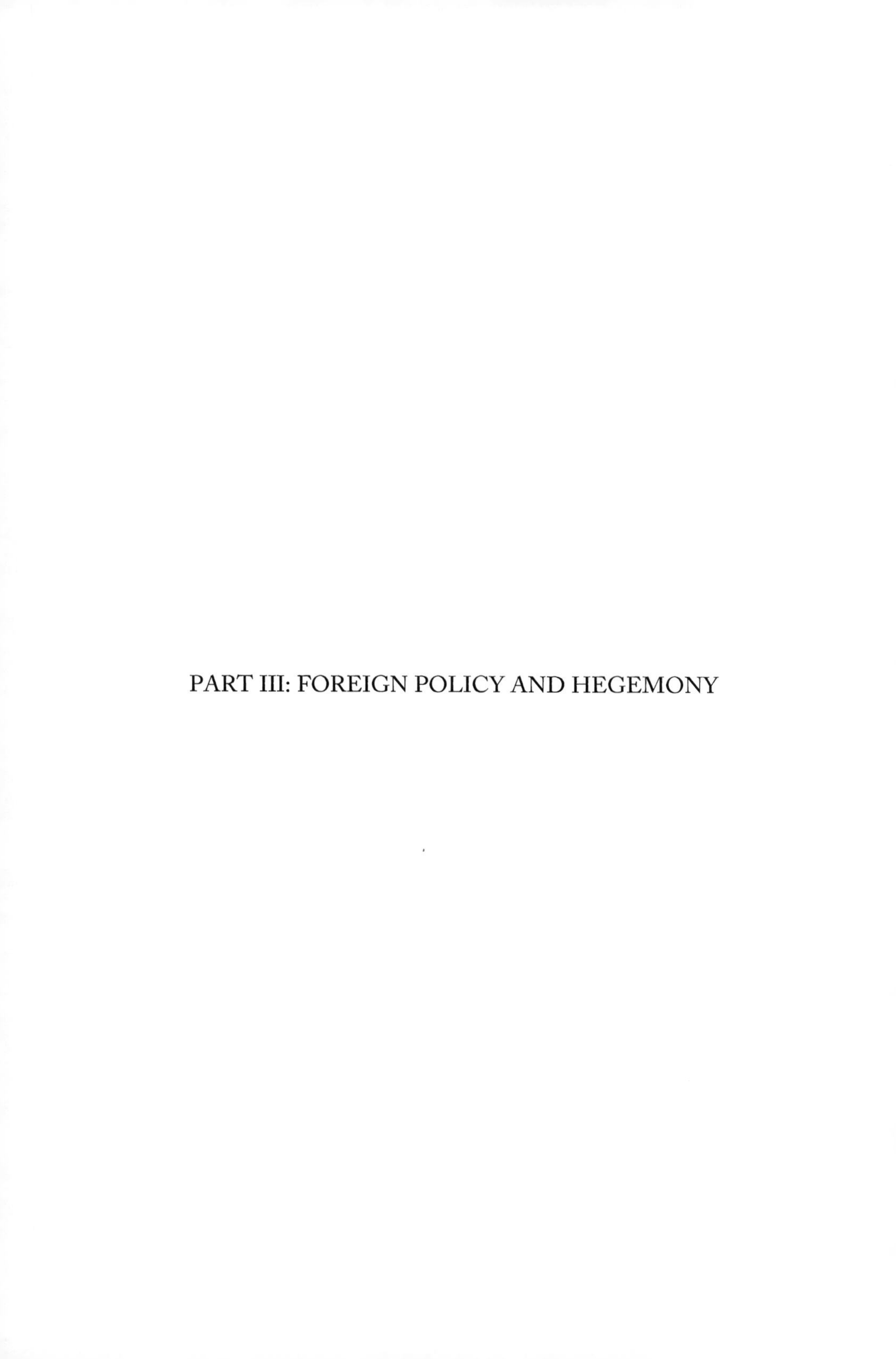

PART III: FOREIGN POLICY AND HEGEMONY

CHAPTER FIVE

Images in Wartime: The Mediation of Power

STUART ALLAN AND DONALD MATHESON

> Newer technology provides a non-stop feed: as many images of disaster and atrocity as we can make time to look at.
>
> SUSAN SONTAG[1]

For the photographer confronted with the challenge of bearing witness to the tragedies of war on our behalf, the effort to *record* human consequences is simultaneously one of *interpretation*, of assigning apposite meaning and relevance. The representation of violence, in other words, is partly constitutive of its reality, which makes this interpretive process acutely political. Important questions thus arise regarding "our camera-mediated knowledge of war", to use Susan Sontag's phrase, which will necessarily highlight the exercise of communicative power. "Look, the photographs say, *this* is what it's like. This is what war *does*. And *that*, that is what it does, too", she observes. "War tears, rends. War rips open, eviscerates. War scorches. War dismembers. War *ruins*,"[2] Such imagery, it follows, invites a shared stance or point of view with the photographer, regardless of its implicit claim of being a "record of the real" faithful to journalistic impartiality. The ways in which a photograph of an atrocity privilege a moment, effectively making "real" events which "we" might otherwise choose to ignore, is as much a question of framing (including but also, by definition, excluding) as it is of objectification. Such photographs "give rise to opposing responses", Sontag points out.

"A call for peace. A cry for revenge. Or simply the bemused awareness, continually restocked by photographic information, that terrible things happen,"[3] In each instance, photography makes possible the means to apprehend – at a distance – other people's pain, with all of the moral implications such a form of spectatorship engenders.

This chapter's discussion is informed by Sontag's engagement with the visual politics of suffering. We begin by recognising that in times of war, the culture of othering ordinarily permeating Western journalism can be thrown into sharp relief. The ideological purchase of certain "us and them" dichotomies, recurrently inflected in news reports which counterpoise the structural interests of "people like us" against the suffering of strangers, may be disrupted and challenged by images produced by diverse constituencies. Such images can range from those shot by photojournalists, to ones taken for entirely different reasons by participants in the violence, or even those captured by ordinary citizens who happen to be in the wrong place at the wrong time, amongst other possibilities. Despite these differences, however, this imagery recurrently exhibits a shared commitment to "making real" the horrors of events in warzones. Accordingly, this chapter aims to offer an evaluative assessment of this capacity, both in theoretical terms and with respect to its practical realisation vis-à-vis specific images – namely, from the prison of Abu Ghraib and the execution of Saddam Hussein – produced by individuals situated outside the realm of professional journalism. It is argued that this form of eyewitness imagery raises important questions about the mediation of discursive power, a process that is shown to be uneven, contingent and frequently the site of resistance from those whose interests are being called into question.

VISUAL TRUTH-TELLING

Since the early 2000s, digital cameras, camcorders and camera phones have become part of the culture of U.S. and other Western militaries, near-ubiquitous in ordinary soldiers" kit bags.[4] The vast majority of the images recorded by these military personnel appear to be innocuous snaps or amateur videos, emailed home or posted on websites to connect with families and friends, or shared within barracks or on military websites. A glance at a site such as Militaryphotos.net shows many thousands of shots of soldiers posing alongside their equipment or in their living quarters. A few, however, display aspects of military life that contrast starkly with the official image of the occupying forces. In particular, "trophy images" – images of dead or injured enemy, sometimes involving posing with the body, in rare cases even cutting off the head or limbs or otherwise abusing the body, that in past wars would seldom have been viewed by more than a handful of people

– can be found amongst the snapshots, celebrating not just victory but the total power of the victor. The meaning of these digital images, it has become apparent, is not just in what they bear witness to, but in the insights they provide into the individuals taking and distributing them.

During the U.S.-led wars in Iraq and Afghanistan, such "kill-zone" imagery has found a wider, though still limited, audience on specialist interest websites, among them amateur pornography websites that allows soldiers to exchange graphic images for access to pornography (one of the most notorious "bodies-for-porn" sites, NTFU, operated for over two years before it was closed for violating Florida felony obscenity laws). To some, the inter-related worlds of violence and pornography revealed in this circulation of digital images exposed basic truths about war, among other possibilities. One critic, writing on the communal weblog (hereafter blog) Metafilter about the porn for trophy image exchange, stated:

> [T]his is the perfect collection of anti-war photos. War is incredibly ugly, and the current administration has done (for their party) a superb job of sanitzing [sic] anything the least bit objectionable or graphic. This solves that. The human costs of war must be told, and the American public being the thick-headed fools that most of them are, told in the most graphic, bread-and-circuses form.[5]

The image of war is suddenly out of the hands of the political marketer or the cautious editor and in the hands of others – among them soldiers, citizens, activists. The circulation of images taken by such people happens in a way that appears at times to cut across a view of war as tidy or morally comfortable.

In one sense, it should be noted, there is nothing new about such imagery. The Spanish–American war of 1898, Susan Moeller points out, "had three or four soldiers who brought their brand-new Kodaks to the front".[6] Professional photographers have also, from the earliest days of the technology, recorded images which have fuelled accusations of atrocity in war. What distinguishes war imagery in a digital culture is the speed with which such images are transmitted. As a result, they become very quickly inserted into different contexts, including into wider public debate about the conflict from which they arise. Soldiers" private snaps may become public documents at any moment; practices usually tightly constrained by military regulation and segregation are exhibited for reinterpretation by others, such as the Metafilter blogger above. In a process which appears anarchic to politicians and to journalists alike, these pictures are trophies of war one moment, entertainment the next, then pornography and finally evidence of the "truth" of war. Moreover, these digital snaps from the warzone appear often to be viewed and interpreted in ways distinct from images that have been purposely taken for public consumption. On a number of occasions during the conflicts in Iraq and Afghanistan, soldiers" images not intended as public documents were treated as more authentic, more credible and ultimately better records of what was "really happening" than the accounts of military or political figures or the images of professional photojournalists. They have become, one journalist wrote, "the unofficial "true" record of the war".[7] As with much citizen journalism, the lure of the soldier's digital image is that it differs in some fundamental way from professional journalism or other "official" genres.

The photoblog of Sean Dustman, a medical corpsman in the U.S. Navy serving in Iraq and a self-confessed "shutterbug", illustrates the phenomenon. Dustman started a photoblog six months before he was sent to Iraq. Once there, his site became, he said later, something of an unofficial record of his unit after repeated requests for copies of his photographs from his fellow Marines. Soon the pages at dustmans.photoblog.com – containing nearly 4,000 images in the first year alone – were attracting soldiers" relatives seeking evidence that their loved ones were safe and some vicarious contact with them.[8] Of particular interest is that Dustman's photoblog – along with the text blog he also kept – seems to have taken on a number of roles at once. It was the place to put the results of his photography; it was a record for his troop of Marines; it was a form of interpersonal communication; and it was also read by some as a form of journalism, particularly after television interviews, blogger awards and the re-publication of some of his entries in a book of military bloggers gave him a high public profile. The way Dustman's blog flitted in and out of the public eye, which was far from unique, brought the personal dimension of those recording their participation in conflict to the forefront of the public consciousness.

The repercussions of this movement between front and back spaces very soon became apparent in Iraq in quite a spectacular way. "Images define wars", as Jerry Lanson points out. "So if war looks like a Fourth of July fireworks display over Baghdad," he writes, members of the public "are a lot more likely to feel an energizing, if uneasy, excitement at the "shock and awe" of US military might than if war looks, for example, like a frightened American captive".[9] Lanson's observation – made in March 2003 when the Al Jazeera network provoked outrage in the West with its decision to broadcast footage of captured American soldiers – proved equally telling a year later when the captives concerned were Iraqi. Digital photographs of terrified Iraqi prisoners being tortured by U.S. soldiers in the notorious Abu Ghraib prison shattered the norms of Pentagon-sanctioned imagery at a stroke.

'THESE UNBELIEVABLE PHOTOGRAPHS'

To date, no so-called amateur imagery has engendered a greater impact on public perceptions of war than the shots of U.S. soldiers abusing their prisoners.

Secretary of State Donald Rumsfeld expressed his exasperation when called to account for their actions before Congress:

> We're functioning with peacetime constraints, with legal requirements, in a wartime situation, in the Information Age, where people are running around with digital cameras and taking these unbelievable photographs and then passing them off, against the law, to the media, to our surprise, when they had not even arrived in the Pentagon.[10]

The story is one of a powerful form of representation outside the knowledge and therefore the control of those in authority. Yet it is also a story of the fragility of that representation in the face of established practices of representing war. Briefly, news about what was happening inside the prison broke when the CBS News programme *60 Minutes II* went to air on 28 April 2004 with several of the horrific images in its possession. In the course of the ensuing furore, CBS was widely heralded for its shocking exclusive. Closer scrutiny of its handling of the story, though, revealed that the programme's producers had provided Pentagon officials with ample opportunity to prepare a "media response" (around 11 pages in length) before the images were broadcast. Specifically, details emerged that eight days before the report was to air, CBS anchor Dan Rather had been contacted by General Richard B. Myers, Chair of the Joint Chiefs of Staff, requesting that the broadcast be delayed, if not suspended altogether. Myers reportedly expressed his concerns about the potential repercussions for U.S. forces in Iraq, fearing that the release of the images might result in further deaths of soldiers.

Few would dispute that it was understandable for Pentagon officials to be making such a request of CBS News, given their interest in "managing" the crisis. Far less comprehensible, in the opinion of critics, was CBS's decision to grant it. Evidently when *60 Minutes II* finally went on air, their primary motivation was to preempt Seymour Hersh's report on the prisoner abuse – complete with photographs – which they had heard was about to be published by *The New Yorker* magazine.[11] Many of those who had been dismayed by CBS's apparent willingness to bow to Pentagon pressure were quick to speculate about what might have happened otherwise. Had CBS not feared being scooped by Hersh, would it have broadcast a less substantive treatment of events, or even elected to hold the story back altogether? Rather himself had explained to viewers why the request was granted in a "postscript" to the story:

> A postscript. Two weeks ago, we received an appeal from the Defense Department, and eventually from the chairman of the military Joint Chiefs of Staff, General Richard Myers, to delay this broadcast given the danger and tension on the ground in Iraq. We decided to honor that request while pressing for the Defense Department to

> add its perspective to the incidents at Abu Ghraib Prison. This week, with the photos beginning to circulate elsewhere and with other journalists about to publish their versions of the story, the Defense Department agreed to cooperate in our report.[12]

Jeff Fager, executive producer of *60 Minutes II*, later insisted that he felt "terrible" about the delay. "News is a delicate thing," he stated. "It's hard to just make those kinds of decisions. It's not natural for us.; the natural thing is to put it on the air. But the circumstances were quite unusual, and I think you have to consider that".[13] Many critics were less than convinced, to put it mildly, arguing that there was no justification for suppressing the story. Some believed that defence officials' agreement to "co-operate" signalled little more than a desire to "spin" the story in a manner that would help contain adverse publicity.

The scandal, according to the official line, revolved around the actions of some "bad apples", and was not indicative of systemic policies and procedures. Evidence to the contrary was readily available elsewhere, of course, not least with respect to the abuses committed in Afghanistan and Guantanamo Bay. Meanwhile there could be no denying the sad reality that two weeks of CBS self-censorship must have had painful consequences for the Iraqi prisoners in question. These snapshots from digital cameras, saved onto CDs and passed around prison staff, showed the physical and sexual abuse of Iraqi prisoners in shocking detail. In one, a guard used an Alsatian to menace a cowering, naked man. In another, naked men were piled on top of each other to simulate group sex while a guard took a photo. In another, a bruised corpse lay wrapped in cellophane, with a smiling guard posing beside it, giving the thumbs-up sign. In perhaps the most infamous of them, a thin, hooded figure stood atop a box, arms outstretched, with electrodes dangling down from his fingers. In *The New Yorker*, investigative journalist Seymour Hersh claimed that some of the prisoners in the images were raped and at least one was tortured until he died. Soon, he and journalists at other publications were able to gather textual evidence showing that the incidents were not exceptional, but examples of routine violent and degrading treatment of prisoners.

It is hard to overstate the importance of these images, not just because of their longer-term symbolic impact on the public memory of the occupation of Iraq, but also because their particular nature as private digital images allowed a hitherto suppressed and denied story of systemic abuse to become public. Human rights organisations had reported severe human rights abuses in prisons in Iraq a year earlier and in Afghanistan and Guantanamo Bay before that, but few Western news outlets, and almost none in the U.S., had picked up on their concerns. The whistleblower who was CBS's initial source for its Abu Ghraib story later said he had been rebuffed by many politicians and journalists before *60 Minutes* took up the story.[14] A number of correspondents in Baghdad admitted later that they had been approached by Iraqis with stories and evidence of torture at the hands of U.S. soldiers, but had done little further research on the claims and rarely published them. Anthony Shadid, the *Washington Post* Islamic affairs correspondent, remembered:

> People would show us the scars of handcuffs on their hands, whatever, the bruised backs, and I don't think we pursued them nearly as rigorously as we should have. I think it's very difficult to prove who's beaten somebody.[15]

Stories of other abuses, including strong evidence that U.S. troops stood by as Afghan forces executed up to 3,000 Taliban prisoners, individual deaths of prisoners at U.S. military prisons, and the "extraordinary rendition" by the U.S. of prisoners to third countries where torture was used, had been similarly "buried, played down or ignored" by editors and reporters in the U.S. These accounts were typically deemed implausible, and most certainly unpalatable in a country where mainstream journalism had become narrowly patriotic in the aftermath of the September 11 attacks.[16]

One of the conditions enabling journalists to finally report the story was that an official paper trail substantiated it. The Pentagon had known of the images from the Baghdad prison since at least January 2004, three months before the *60 Minutes II* and *The New Yorker* stories. Leaked copies of its reports on the abuse added to the impact of both stories, allowing reporters to confirm both the abuse and also its systemic nature. Umansky quotes an Associated Press correspondent, Charles Hanley, whose stories six months earlier of similar military abuse of Iraqis had languished because they lacked such official confirmation.[17] By April 2004, reporters could underpin their evidence with the military's own reports so that the stories became more than mere accusations. But it was clearly the shocking visual evidence of torture – the pictures themselves – that made the story compelling. O'Neill notes that CNN admitted dropping another story on prisoner abuse because "without having the actual photos to hand, 'this was not such a big story'".[18] The Abu Ghraib images allowed these allegations to become facts for Western journalists.

The pictures' status as a particular kind of fact, then, lies at the heart of how this story – when so many others were abandoned or neglected – became powerful. Barbie Zelizer's description of the news image's twin status within journalism's understanding of itself is a useful starting point in exploring this power.[19] She notes that photographs appear to stand not only as a particularly powerful form of evidence for journalists but also as pegs on which larger, more abstract meanings are hung. Thus, on the one hand, they are better able than words to act as eyewitness testimony connecting the viewer with the event and compelling public attention. The Abu Ghraib images indeed stood as incontrovertible evidence, able to refute claims by the U.S. government that it did not use torture. One commentator argued after the scandal broke that "in an era when there is less trust of the media than there has been in the past, where print and audio can leave people unmoved, a photo has tremendous impact, because it's evidence".[20] On the other hand, Zelizer argues that images are more often used by news organisations to support and illustrate written text. Photographs tend to have the status of the typical or the conventional, and so become a "tool for interpreting events in ways consonant with long-standing understandings about the world".[21] A number of commentators argue that the Abu Ghraib images made sense in such ideological terms. They recalled for some the atrocity image genre dating back to the Belgian Congo or Nazi death camps,[22] thereby placing the invasion of Iraq intertextually in quite different ways to official imagery (and claims that the Bush administration and its allies were bringing freedom and civilisation to the country). "It is difficult to imagine a worse propaganda defeat," stated one editorial writer.[23]

However, as important as the ability of these photographs to convey a particular truth about the U.S. invasion of Iraq was their origin as digital snapshots sent by guards to their friends and colleagues. This gave them a two-fold power. First, as Sontag has argued, these were messages as much as objects.[24] The acts of photographing and then sending images to other soldiers by email or on CDs were acts of participation in a shared world. To outsiders, the meanings they trailed as they moved from that private world to the public space of the news page signalled a military culture in which fear, hatred, violence and comradeship were mixed and whose pleasures reflected that mixture. For it was the attitudes that lay behind the acts of taking these photographs, the deliberate posing of victims in order to abuse them further by recording their humiliation, that horrified many commentators on the images. Viewing these images was thus to come much closer to the torture than viewing photographs taken, for example, by a third party such as a human rights organisation or a journalist. It was to hear at first hand a message of sadism and dehumanisation. Indeed, as Malik argues, an element of excitement is mixed in while viewing such illicit images.[25] As large numbers of other pictures and abuse stories were made public in the following year, a military subculture became apparent in which soldiers traded in images of violence against Iraqis, the Taliban and others. As home-made DVDs such as "Ramadi Madness", a compilation of trophy images shot by reservists after a tour in the dangerous city of Ramadi, and image-sharing websites such as NTFU.com, LiveLeak and Under Mars came to public knowledge, a picture of a systemic disrespect for others" lives or cultures among the U.S. military and its allies became clear.

Second, and related to the first point, the images were private. Because they were not intended for public consumption, they appeared separate from the efforts of those seeking to control public debate and were therefore more "authentic" voices from the warzone. Thus we must be cautious in assessing claims that Abu Ghraib images are evidence of a "digital democratization", in which new technologies are

> letting little people make big waves. During World War II, US prison guards didn't have the power to flood their government with bad publicity. And in Saddam Hussein's Iraq, abused prisoners had no chance of seeing their plight vividly brought to the world's attention.[26]

For the images were taken, later reports suggested, for multiple reasons: as personal records of the guards' work, to humiliate the prisoners so as to weaken their resolve to resist interrogation – read torture – efforts and to entertain the guards. It was precisely the fact, then, that they were not motivated by an intention to "make waves" in public that gave the images their power. Knowledge of their provenance, that is, the accompanying knowledge about the secret and sadistic world they were part of and that they had come to public light against their authors' wishes, provided a good deal of their meaning.

Werbach, pointing to the rapidity with which the images circulated among U.S. bloggers, contends that the Abu Ghraib scandal signalled the growing power of this media form. These images, he writes, "weren't first leaked or published by blogs but the fact that blogs got wind of them and pointed to them made the news spread like wildfire". As a result, he adds, "[a]nybody, including the White House and the executive suite, who feels it's important to limit the flow of information is going to have to deal with how blogs are now making that harder".[27] However, others maintain that the Abu Ghraib images did not have an immediate political impact in the U.S. It was in their wider circulation, through Arab news channels, blogs and propagandist collections of horror images on CDs, that they grew into a major challenge to the legitimacy of the U.S. occupation. Umansky notes that an initial lack of interest in concerns about torture from the Republican-dominated Congress and a subdued news media led to "scattered sprinkles" of coverage there.[28] Images which conflicted so utterly with the official scripts which until then had dominated news coverage were perhaps difficult to report on, allowing the Bush administration's framing of the story as one of "a few bad apples", rather than as a widespread policy of abuse, to prevail.[29] In Europe, coverage was more extensive, but it was in the Arab media that the images received heaviest coverage. There the photographs and accompanying news articles reinforced already widespread stories of abuse, but also struck deeply in a culture where sexual degradation is particularly offensive. One blogger, Riverbend, wrote that the images were "like a nightmare come to life":

> Everyone knew this was happening in Abu Ghraib and other places...seeing the pictures simply made it all more real and tangible somehow.[...] People are so angry. There's no way to explain the reactions – even pro-occupation Iraqis find themselves

> silenced by this latest horror. I can't explain how people feel – or even how I personally feel. Somehow, pictures of dead Iraqis are easier to bear than this grotesque show of American military technique. People would rather be dead than sexually abused and degraded by the animals running Abu Ghraib prison.[30]

The widespread horror in Iraq and the wider Arab world at the photographs prompted a damage-limitation exercise from the White House, including personal apologies by President Bush on some Arab news channels. The images therefore came to be read across the world in terms of their impact on Arab audiences. This re-reading continued to echo for a long time. One British journalist, writing five months later, described seeing the images "everywhere in Iraq", in fliers, on CDs, on videos in the markets and on Iraqi websites. He quoted Sheikh Abdul Sattar Abdul Jabar, the head of the Iraqi Islamic Clerics Association, saying, "I have seen a CD show one thousand male and female Iraqis being abused by the Americans. You can watch that CD in the market or you can go to Abu Ghraib and see it with your own eyes".[31]

The story of the Abu Ghraib images is not, then, a simple tale of "digital democratization", but a complex mixture of competition between CBS and *The New Yorker*, of the documentation which surrounded the images, of the particular status of these private digital photographs as insights into the culture within the prison, of the rapid circulation of the images around the world, and much else. It should also not be forgotten that, while slow to react, it was elite news outlets that subsequently uncovered much of the abuse story. *The New Yorker*, CBS, *Newsweek* and the *Washington Post* detailed a deliberate lack of clarity in U.S. official policies around the use of torture. European and U.S. newspapers traced the "extraordinary rendition" of prisoners across Europe and Asia. Indeed, a number of critics have pointed to the role of some blogs in attempts to shut down journalism which exposed prisoner abuse and torture by U.S. forces. When, in December 2004, the Associated Press published images found by its reporter Seth Hettena on the commercial image sharing website Smugmug, showing members of the U.S. Navy's special forces apparently abusing Iraqi prisoners, the backlash in right-wing and military blogs and other websites against the "outrageous reporting" of this "nutbag Islamofascist sympathiser'[32] drowned out questions about prisoner abuse. One newspaper editorial saw the response as typical of a tendency in U.S. public opinion at the time to attack the messenger:

> The Internet echo chamber, predictably, is filled with outrage not at what is depicted in the SEALS photos, but at the reporter who found them and at the newspapers that printed them. Never mind that the photos were apparently available for everyone to see, if they only knew where to look.[33]

Other journalists received death threats online after producing similarly "unpatriotic" coverage. Much more insidious for being all the more subtle, however, was the presumption – recurrently reaffirmed across the Western mediascape – that the terms "abuse" and "mistreatment" were the most appropriate labels to describe the unconscionable cruelty meted out to Abu Ghraib's prisoners. The concerted efforts of officials to discount the validity of the word "torture" proved remarkably successful, revealing once again the power and influence institutional authorities wield as news sources in the mainstream press. "The photos may have driven the story," Bennett et al. point out, "but the White House communication staff ultimately wrote the captions".[34]

Our discussion turns in the next section to consider a further example of how imagery taken by an ordinary citizen can decisively unravel the moral tidiness of war, as presented in official accounts, and thereby cast into dispute the legitimacy of official truth-claims. "Leaked from Cellphone" was how an anonymous user described a short video they posted on the LiveLeak.com website, the raw footage of which rapidly ignited a blaze of controversy around the globe.

'TOO GRAPHIC TO BE SUITABLE'

'Saddam Hussein, the dictator who led Iraq through three decades of brutality, war and bombast before American forces chased him from his capital city and captured him in a filthy pit near his hometown, was hanged just before dawn Saturday during the call to prayer,' With this sentence, the *New York Times* broke the news of Saddam's execution to its readers on 30 December 2006. The front-page news account continues by describing the court process leading up to the hanging, before providing the following details about the actual event:

> His execution at 6:10 a.m. was announced on state-run Iraqiya television. Witnesses said 14 Iraqi officials had attended the hanging, at the former military intelligence building in northern Baghdad, now part of an American base. Those in the room said that Mr. Hussein was dressed entirely in black and carrying a Koran and that he was compliant as the noose was draped around his neck.
>
> "He just gave up", said Mowaffak al-Rubaie, Iraq's national security adviser. "We were astonished. It was strange. He just gave up," [. . .]
>
> Mr. Hussein, in handcuffs, was given to the Iraqis by American troops. The Iraqis led him from his cell to a judge's chamber and then to an execution room, a bare unadorned concrete room, according to a witness. It was only a few short steps up the gallows.
>
> As the rope was placed around his neck, Mr. Hussein turned to Mr. Rubaie.
>
> "He told me, don't be afraid", he recounted. "There was a conversation with him,"

> He did not elaborate. He asked that his Koran be given to someone. Mr. Rubaie took note of the person's name.
>
> Iraqis have Mr. Hussein's body but they have not agreed upon a place for burial.
>
> As Mr. Hussein awaited the hangman, he was apparently unaware that the American military was already making plans to dispose of his personal effects [...].[35]

These details, evidently acquired on a second-hand basis by the newspaper's reporters, appeared to suggest that the Iraqi government's decision had been implemented in a formal, methodical and solemn fashion. The description of Saddam, ostensibly accepting his fate with composure, arguably helped to reaffirm the impression that the execution proceeding had been administered dispassionately.

This perception was reinforced, in turn, following the release within hours of a videotape recording of the execution by Iraqi government officials. News organisations around the world, in anticipation that such a videotape would be made available, had been pondering how best to incorporate it into their coverage. "I think it might be appropriate at some point to see an image of Saddam after he is hanged", Steve Capus, president of NBC News, stated the day before. "I think about that iconic image of Nicolae Ceausescu in Romania, lying literally in the gutter. I want to do this with a measure of taste, but I don't want to stand in the way of history".[36] Questions about matters of taste and propriety, especially in the event that the images proved too graphic to be suitable, were promptly answered by each news organisation in turn shortly after two Arab networks, Alhurra and Al Arabiya, broke the news that Saddam was dead. In the case of BBC News 24, its controller Kevin Bakhurst remarked:

> This morning [30 December, 2006] I was in the building as the pictures actually came in from Iraqi television. We showed them on a time delay first on Breakfast to give us the option of cutting out – which we did on first showing.
>
> We quickly reached the decision on Breakfast (and for the early part of the day and evening on BBC One) not to show the noose being put around Saddam's neck as there could be many children on school holiday watching – possibly passively. Even then, we gave a warning ahead of John Simpson's report.
>
> For News 24 and for the late evening bulletin tonight on BBC One, we decided to show all the pictures of the execution as people are choosing actively to watch a news channel – and the late bulletin is on after the watershed [9 pm].
>
> We have also tried to reflect all the voices and views: Shia and Sunni, Arab world, European and American – although no British government minister wants to comment on camera today, nor does President Bush.
>
> I hope the decisions we have made have allowed us to tell the story properly and well across all the channels whilst respecting the audiences they all have, at this time of year in particular.[37]

In the next day's edition of the *New York Times*, John F. Burns reported that Iraqi citizens had been "crowding around television sets to watch mesmerizing replays" of the videotape.[38] He explained that it "showed the 69-year-old Mr Hussein being led to the gallows at dawn by five masked executioners, and having a noose fashioned from a thick rope of yellow hemp lowered around his neck,' The final portion of the videotape is described as portraying Saddam as appearing "almost unnaturally calm and cooperative" in his demeanour. "The message seemed to be that he had lived his final moments with unflinching dignity and courage," Burns wrote, "reinforcing the legend of himself as the Arab world's strongman that he cultivated while in power,"

Any image of the execution as a duly methodical meting of Iraqi justice would soon be shattered, however, with the startling realisation that the execution had been surreptitiously recorded by an observer using a mobile (or cell) telephone. The two minutes of grainy, shaky footage – which unlike the officially authorised video included an audio tract – was widely presumed to have been shot by one of the guards, although the precise circumstances of its production were not revealed. Where the official version had abruptly halted with the tightening of the noose around Saddam's neck, the unofficial version documented his verbal exchanges with his captors (who were clearly determined to torment him), followed by the moment of his demise as the trapdoor opens and drops out of the gallows platform. The video clip comes to an end with a close-up of Saddam, his neck clearly broken, and the jubilant shouting of several of those gathered in the chamber. In sharp contrast to the "weirdly calm and dignified" silence of the earlier video, to use the words of BBC correspondent John Simpson, this version makes readily apparent the extent to which unseen witnesses sought to mock and deride the dictator.[39] "Altogether, the execution as we now see it is shown to be an ugly, degrading business," Simpson commented, "which is more reminiscent of a public hanging in the 18th Century than a considered act of 21st Century official justice," Moreover, he added, the "most disturbing thing about the new video of Saddam's execution for crimes precisely like this, is that it is all much too reminiscent of what used to happen here". For Richard B. Woodward, writing in the *Wall Street Journal*, "in everything from the partisan chants of Shiite bystanders to the grainy, low-lighted jumpiness of the footage and the horror-movie ski masks of the executioners, the video images of the execution contradict the fragile message that a secure and democratic government is in charge, rendering justice to someone who deserves to die".[40]

The ensuing "Bluetooth frenzy" – as CNN correspondent Arwa Damon labelled it – sparked by the "snuff reality show," a phrase used by the *New York Times*, attracted considerable attention within the press. An *NYT* editorial published on 4 January 2007 observed that the 'graphic cellphone video' made apparent that the "condemned dictator appeared to have been delivered from United States military custody into the hands of a Shiite lynch mob". Amongst widespread expressions of revulsion, a range of commentators insisted that the footage was likely to inflame sectarian tensions in the region, thereby deepening what was already a desperate crisis. Others concurred, pointing out that Saddam's calmly measured response to his tormentors was certain to generate sympathy in the eyes of some, thereby elevating his status to that of a martyr. Regarding the attendant media politic, Edward Helmore, writing in London's *Observer* newspaper, believed the posting of the telephone footage on the internet signalled the end of mainstream news organisations' editorial control over what reaches the public domain.[41] "This is now a familiar story," he remarked, "from the savage beheadings of American hostages in Iraq to Saddam's hanging, debate over what should and should not be shown has been made all-but irrelevant in the age of mobile phones and YouTube". This point was further extended by commentators struck by the ways in which telephone video was evolving into a news tool, one which effectively changed the nature of the news story being reported. "It brought to a fore the sense that wow, this is a ubiquitous technology", maintained Mark Lukasiewicz, NBC News's vice president for digital media. "Cameras are now in places where cameras never used to be. That's transformational,"[42] The implications of this apparent transformation, whereby digital technology enabled anyone to become an instant news reporter, were profoundly unsettling for some. "The Saddam video proves again that no act is too gruesome or intimate that someone won't try to take a picture of it and share it with the wired world", Woodward concluded. "We better get used to living without visual boundaries – and with the curiosity and flexible morality of the viewer as the only limit on what we can see – from now on,"[43]

'OUR DIGITAL HALL OF MIRRORS'

First-person photography, this analysis of the examples above suggests, renders problematic several familiar assumptions about the mediation of power underpinning visual culture. While the news photograph's claim to offer a literal record – a neutral reflection of reality – is inscribed in the photojournalist's commitment to dispassionate reporting, the image generated by the ordinary citizen makes explicit its interested perspective. Ideology, denied a role in shaping professional form and practice, is reaffirmed as inevitable where interpretation displaces translation. Facts and values converge. The citizen's authority is no more than that of the eyewitness, one whose precarious subjectivity undercuts any rhetorical appeal to the certainties of objectivity, regardless of how comforting the latter may be.

The power of photographs, Susan Sontag argues, is "to define, not merely record, the most abominable [of] realities".[44] How she might have assessed the significance of the Saddam Hussein execution video is sadly a matter of speculation, given that she succumbed to leukaemia in December 2004. In her incisive critique of the Abu Ghraib photographs, however, she devoted particular attention to how certain images can "lay down the tracks" with regard to how conflicts will be judged and remembered. "Photographs have an insuperable power to determine what we recall of events", she wrote in an essay titled "Regarding the Torture of Others" published in May 2004.[45] "[It] now seems probable," she added, "that the defining association of people everywhere with the war that the United States launched pre-emptively in Iraq last year will be photographs of the torture of Iraqi prisoners by Americans in the most infamous of Saddam Hussein's prisons, Abu Ghraib". Photography displayed its power via this capacity to reveal what was otherwise being denied: specifically, that members of the U.S. military had tortured their prisoners. The meaning of these pictures, she contends, involves more than the cruelty of the acts performed: "the horror of what is shown in the photographs cannot be separated from the horror that the photographs were taken – with the perpetrators posing, gloating, over their helpless captives". It is this latter dimension which warrants a connection being drawn, in her reading, between these soldiers' casual "idea of fun" and the "increasing acceptance of brutality in American life" in everyday contexts. In other words, it follows, it is not sufficient to simply lay the blame on the Bush administration, even though it needs to be recognised that its policies made such acts likely. Rather, it also needs to be acknowledged that these images are representative of the "fundamental corruptions of any foreign occupation" authorised or condoned by its citizens. "Considered in this light," she surmises, "the photographs are us,"

Sontag's intervention, and the fierce backlash it generated from largely pro-war, right-wing commentators, underscores the importance of photography in defining what counts as reality in wartime. And yet, she cautions, such images can do little more than to invite the viewer "to pay attention, to reflect, to learn, to examine the rationalisations for mass suffering offered by established powers".[46] Such a careful, methodical contemplation of meaning will likely raise more questions than it will answer, but it is in this difficult commitment to interpretation that insights emerge into how the horrors of war are gradually being normalised as part of our visual culture. Photographs, she reminds us, help to make real matters which we may otherwise choose to ignore, as we struggle to keep other people's pain at a safe distance. In "our digital hall of mirrors", moral responsibilities cannot be assuaged by official reassurances or justifications. "The pictures will not go away," Sontag observes. "That is the nature of the digital world in which we live,"[47]

NOTES

Please note that portions of this chapter draw upon material in Donald Matheson and Stuart Allan, *Digital War Reporting* (Cambridge: Polity, 2009).

1 Susan Sontag, *Regarding the Pain of Others* (New York: Farrar, Straus and Giroux, 2003).
2. Ibid., p. 7.
3. Ibid., pp. 11–12.
4. Ellen Simon, "Digital Cameras Change Perception of War", *MSNBC*, 27 September 2004.
5. NucleophilicAttack, "Comment: The True Face of War", Metafilter, 23 September 2005. http://www.metafilter.com/45343/The-true-face-of-war.
6. Susan D. Moeller, *Shooting War: Photography and the American Experience of Combat* (New York: Basic Books, 1989).
7. Devin Friedman, "Postcards from Hell", *The Australian Magazine*, 10 June 2006, p. 21.
8. James Hebert, "The Art of Blogging Attracts a Burgeoning Number of Fans", *San Diego Union-Tribune*, 18 July 2004, pp. 1–3.
9. Jerry Lanson, "War Isn't Pretty, nor Is News of It", *Christian Science Monitor*, 25 March 2003.
10. Cited in "Called to Account: Secretary Rumsfeld", PBS Online NewsHour, 7 May 2004. http://www.pbs.org/newshour/bb/military/jan-june04/rum_05–07.html.
11. Seymour Hersh, "Torture at Abu Ghraib", *The New Yorker*, 10 May 2004.
12. Dan Rather, *60 Minutes II*, CBS TV, 28 April 2004.
13. Cited in Washington Post, "CBS Delayed Abuse Report at the Request of Gen. Myers", *Washington Post*, 4 May 2004, p. A18.
14. James Dao and Eric Lichtblau, "The Struggle for Iraq: The Images; Soldier's Family Set in Motion Chain of Events on Disclosure", *New York Times*, 3 August 2004.
15. Anthony Shadid, quoted in "Into the Abyss: Reporting Iraq 2003–2006: An Oral History", *Columbia Journalism Review*, 45: 4 (2006): pp. 15–76.
16. Eric Umansky, "Failures of Imagination", *Columbia Journalism Review*, 45: 3 (2006): pp. 16–31; see also Barbie Zelizer and Stuart Allan, eds., *Journalism after September 11* (London & New York: Routledge, 2002).
17. Umansky, "Failures of Imagination", p. 21.
18. Brendan O'Neill, "A Shunned Story", *Press Gazette*, 27 May 2004, p. 5.
19. B. Zelizer, "Death in Wartime: Photographs and The "Other War" in Afghanistan", *Harvard International Journal of Press Politics*, 10: 3 (2005): pp. 26–55.
20. Mark Jurkowitz, "A War of Images: The Bombardment of Brutal Pictures from Iraq Is Making the Conflict a Reality for Americans", *Boston Globe*, 15 May 2004, p. C1.
21. Zelizer, "Death in Wartime", p. 28.
22. Sharon Sliwinski, "Camera War, Again", *Journal of Visual Culture*, 5 (2006): pp. 89–93.
23. Paul Kelly, "The Damage Is Done", *Australian*, 8 May 2004, p. 30; see also Pal Ahluwalia, "Delivering Freedom: Australia's Witnessing of Abu Ghraib", *Journal of Visual Culture*, 5 (2006): pp. 93–96.
24. Susan Sontag, "Regarding the Torture of Others", *New York Times*, 23 May 2004.

25. Suhail Malik, "Fucking Straight Death Metal", *Journal of Visual Culture*, 5 (2006): pp. 107–112.
26. Robert Wright, "Technology Changing How We See War: Up Close", *Los Angeles Times*, 23 May 2004.
27. In Dan Hunter and Kevin Werbach, "10 Questions With... Dan Hunter and Kevin Werbach on Blogs and a New Information Center of Gravity", *Journal of Financial Planning*, 18: 9 (2005): pp. 10–18.
28. Umansky, "Failures of Imagination", p. 22.
29. Kari Andén-Papadopoulos, "The Abu Ghraib Torture Photographs", *Journalism*, 9: 1 (2008): pp. 5–30; Mark Danner, "Abu Ghraib: The Hidden Story", *New York Review of Books*, 51: 15 (2004).
30. Riverbend, "Just Go", Baghdad Burning, 7 May 2004. http://riverbendblog.blogspot.com/2004_05_01_riverbendblog_archive.html.
31. Jack Fairweather, "Abuse Propaganda Fuels the Hatred of Westerners", *Daily Telegraph*, 21 September 2004.
32. Matthew Heidt, "Seals Ambush the AP This Time", Froggy Ruminations, 28 December 2004. http://froggyruminations.blogspot.com/2004_12_01_archive.html.
33. Virginian-Pilot, "Blind Loyalty Isn't Patriotism", *Virginian-Pilot*, 2 January 2005, p. J4.
34. W. Lance Bennett, Regina G. Lawrence and Steven Livingston, *When the Press Fails: Political Power and the News Media from Iraq to Katrina* (Chicago: University of Chicago Press, 2007), p. 107.
35. *New York Times*, 30 December 2006.
36. Cited in B. Carter, "How Much Should Be Shown of a Hanging? Network Executives Wonder and Wait", *New York Times*, 30 December 2006.
37. Kevin Bakhurst, "Saddam's Execution", The Editor Blog, *BBC News*, 30 December 2006.
38. John F. Burns, "Hussein Video Grips Iraq; Attacks Go On", *New York Times*, 31 December 2006.
39. John Simpson, "Saddam Hanging Taunts Evoke Ugly Past", BBC News Online, 31 December 2006.
40. Richard B. Woodward, "Subtext Message", *The Wall Street Journal*, 4 January 2007.
41. Edward Helmore, "Saddam's "Snuff Video" Signals the End of Editorial Control", *The Observer*, 7 January 2007.
42. Cited by Associated Press, 7 January 2007.
43. R. B. Woodward, "Subtext Message".
44. Sontag, *Regarding the Pain of Others*, p. 23.
45. Sontag, "Regarding the Torture of Others".
46. Sontag, *Regarding the Pain of Others*, p. 104.
47. Sontag, "Regarding the Torture of Others".

CHAPTER SIX

The Power of Images at Times of War

ROBIN ANDERSEN

We live in a culture that effortlessly confirms the power of the image. Collective assumptions about the significance of visual documentation are arguably most strongly held during times of war. Indeed, in the days leading up to the invasion of Iraq in 2003, the Pentagon promised that through the new practice of "embedding" journalists with U.S. troops, the American pubic would be able to "see war as it really is."[1] War photojournalism is most often associated with what documentarians refer to as war's "human cost." Those who attempt to make sense of the relationship between war and its imagery have no doubt scanned the annals of the photographic record to survey what is now a vast collection of images of horror and suffering. But the twenty-first-century "war on terror" carried out in Iraq, as presented on American television and in the mainstream press, looks notably different from past wars. The documentation of death and suffering has been muted, yet the record is punctuated by some of the most horrific images in modern memory.

War photography has often been witness to the grim business of military belligerence, sometimes as it occurs, and other times in photographs that continue to circulate in the cultural firmament for years to come. Photojournalists continue to risk their lives to snap the images that bring home the consequences of global conflict to publics whose lives are set in sharp contrast to such suffering.

Many have long believed that it is the image that can "tell the truth," witness the conduct, raise the awareness, and create the outcry to end the conflict.[2]

Indeed, the U.S. military also believes in the power of the image. The vast public relations apparatus that packages, promotes, and celebrates the necessities of war revels in the power of imagery. One only need conjure any of the slick advertisements for the Armed Forces to confirm the reliance on the visual message, the handsome, chiseled face, the tall uniformed salute, "the power of one," as the Army ad proclaims. Images of the American president that called for the invasion of Iraq, as will be discussed below, mimicked the stance, attitude, and settings of such promotions, as well as other cultural constructs of war and heroism.

These are the opposite ends of the spectrum of power assigned to the visual field of conflict, the images of glory and strength that celebrate, forever contrasted to those of pain and sorrow that condemn. These divergent sets of renderings are cast in a didactic relationship in an endless dual over the definition of the *real* and the power to define the true meaning of war. Yet the truth of war and the power that visuals confer constitute a cultural space much less clearly defined than those on the far end of this spectrum. More often then not, images occupy a fogged middle ground, a territory defined by complex image histories and media environments where photographs are the contested terrains and battles over interpretation are either won or lost. In addition, the lack of key depictions of the realities of war is as meaningful as those that are ubiquitous, and as events transform the significance of certain captured moments, the once unquestioned power assigned to them vanishes. High-stakes battles over the visual record of conflict are as important for the possibility of war and peace as the ones conducted with guns and bombs. The power of war imagery was confirmed when four months into his presidency, President Obama reversed his decision to release additional torture photos taken at the Abu Ghraib prison outside of Baghdad.[3] With these complexities in mind, this chapter revisits some of the photojournalism of wars, past and present, and reevaluates a few of the most disturbing visuals documents from Abu Ghraib.

Attempting to make some sense of the nature and meaning of war images and the historical and social power conferred upon them leads us first to some observations about the differences between witness and stagecraft, accident and choreography.

THE "ACCIDENTAL" WAR PHOTOGRAPH: BEARING WITNESS

The photojournalists of war are a daring bunch; these are mostly underpaid, often freelance media professionals who have been killed in significant numbers over the years, bearing witness to the numerous conflagrations of modernity.[4] They follow in the footsteps of those who have left a legacy of disturbing war photography. Such pictures can be called accidental because they have not (most of the time) been staged. Certainly conditions for their taking have been prescribed, defined, and set by the theater of conflict, and at times, journalists have been allowed to occupy that same stage. They follow combatants, share the battlefield, and witness the results by clicking the shutter at the exact moment when the inevitable murder, killing, injury, or death occurs. At key historical moments, most notably during the Vietnam War, battlefield imagery has influenced democratic publics to turn away from the support of further aggression.[5] Some of the strongest examples of war photojournalism have depicted the innocent, whose lives are taken though they never agreed to carry a gun, defend a despot, a homeland, or the U.S. constitution.

Another type of "accident" of war is "friendly fire," when soldiers are killed not by enemy combatants, but by their fellow soldiers. One of the most emotive photographs from the Vietnam War, described as "powerful" by Phillip Knightley[6] was taken in 1966 by Larry Burrows, known by the Marines as "the compassionate photographer." The picture depicts a wounded African American soldier, with a white head bandage soaked in blood, reaching out to a fellow soldier who sits on the ground covered in brown dirt. There he sits, his eyes open in a frozen, vacant stare. The first-aid center where wounded Marines were being treated before being evacuated by air had just come under fire from U.S. tanks, and this "sitting" Marine and two others were killed. The chaotic scene is dirty and bewildering, and the expansive, full-color landscape of bleeding men and denuded jungle evokes the senseless destruction of war, including a loss that has reaches across racial barriers. The Vietnam War also took Larry Burrows who went down in a helicopter over Laos in 1971.

THE LOSS OF WITNESS

Documenting American combat casualties, including the graphic visual record of the consequences of friendly fire, has been greatly curtailed in recent conflicts. The case of Patrick Tillman is a useful illustration of the degree to which the military – from the battlefield to the photo shoot – has succeeded in directing and controlling the power of images over the four decades from Vietnam to Afghanistan and Iraq.

Patrick Tillman was a popular football player with a handsome, chiseled face who walked away from a huge contract with the NFL's Arizona Cardinals to enlist in the Army after 9/11. His background and striking appearance made him a recruiter's dream and a walking billboard for the military. So when his fellow

Army Rangers killed him in an ambush in eastern Afghanistan on April 22, 2004, the Army went into "lockdown mode." They burned his uniform and the body armor that had the bullet holes to prove he had been killed by American weapons. They posted armed guards and effectively stopped the survivors from talking to the press. Instead of dignifying Patrick's life with the truth about what happened, the Army fabricated a narrative claiming he was killed by enemy gunfire as he led his team to help another group of ambushed soldiers.[7]

Never pictured in the blood and dirt of war's grim consequences, like Burrow's sitting soldier, no image of Patrick in death exists to challenge the visions of strength and glory. The image of Tillman that endures is a portrait of him, very much alive, in uniform, and framed by the American flag.

THE ABSENCE OF DEATH

During the invasion of Iraq, embedded journalists signed contracts agreeing to censor images of wounded American soldiers in return for access to the desert invasion of 2003. The loss of witness to death would result in a corresponding loss of expressions of public mourning and awareness of those killed in Iraq, as the documentation of suffering continued to be greatly curtailed across the media spectrum. Adding to the attitude that the invasion was to be a war without cost, the White House withheld from public view the "imagery of return." From the beginning, journalists were banned from photographing the flag-draped coffins of dead soldiers arriving at Dover air base. Such censorship established parameters of coverage early on that successfully hid the war's human costs over time, and even when images of returning bodies were later made available over the Internet they rarely became the subject of national news. By the spring of 2008, just after the fifth anniversary of the invasion of Iraq, when the U.S. military death toll reached 4000, only two newspapers reported the figures on their front pages. Yet U.S. military personnel have been far more visible in death than the people of Iraq. Enemy soldiers have been shown killed and captured at times, but the tens of thousands of civilian dead remain outside the boundaries of U.S. media coverage.[8] In the fall of 2007, reasonable estimates using standard sampling and cluster analysis set the number of Iraqis killed by violence during the five years of occupation at over 1 million.[9] Yet a poll conducted in 2007 for the AP revealed that Americans believe on average that fewer than 10,000 Iraqis have died.[10] In the twenty-first century, the notable absence of public knowledge and acknowledgment of the death and destruction of modern warfare is a phenomenon deeply interconnected to media representations, and that lack of knowledge confers great power to those who wage war.

There are notable exceptions in which powerful visuals slip into the public conscience. An image that conveys the horror of the war's underreported slaughter was published in the *New York Times* in June 2008, as an illustration for a review of the book *Final Salute* by investigative reporter Jim Sheeler of the *Rocky Mountain News*. The book bears witness to the many ways in which U.S. casualties are hidden from the public: "Dead soldiers' coffins have been hidden in cardboard boxes (ostensibly to protect the coffins), toted by forklifts and stowed in the cargo holds of passenger planes."[11] In the photograph that accompanied the review, airline passengers struggle to see out their windows as a flag-draped coffin is offloaded from the belly of the aircraft. Each face peering out is tightly framed by the plane's small windows. They form a collective metaphor for the confining spaces of a world atomized and reduced by the loss of public knowledge.

TRANSFORMING THE IMAGERY OF WAR

Something must replace the empty spaces once occupied by the photojournalism of war's human costs. When no images of flag-draped coffins returning home are shown to the sound of taps playing, and when no soldiers in formal dress are seen carrying the remains of their brothers and sisters across the tarmac, the public is invited not to notice that the American president was not there to greet them and acknowledge their sacrifice. Other images that tell a different story about war must be designed and made available to a press willing to disseminate a more favorable view of conflict. Take, for example, the Thanksgiving Day celebrations in 2003, and the photographic session with the president – only one of the many choreographed occasions that resulted in a barrage of widely distributed images. Early that Thanksgiving morning, Air Force One left Washington, DC, on a secret trip that would land a small group of aides and journalists with the president at the Baghdad airport for a two-and-a-half-hour visit with 600 U.S. troops. Pictures show a beaming president wearing an Army flight jacket, cradling a bountiful golden-brown turkey generously garnished with grapes and all the trimmings. He appears to be serving dinner to the grateful soldiers that surround him. A moment of high patriotism, the pictures were ubiquitous in the days that followed and the president's poll numbers shot up five points as criticism for his seeming indifference to the suffering of American troops was quieted for a time.

It would take a week for the *Washington Post* to report that the president was not actually serving the soldiers who were eating presliced turkey from canteen-style hot plates. But little was made of this fact in the press, or other details that revealed the nature of the staged event. It was six o'clock in the morning and the turkey Bush held was inedible. White House spokespersons rebuked those who called the turkey fake, insisting it was not a presidential prop, but a standard decoration supplied by contractors for the chow hall. In a burst of spontaneous enthusiasm the president had raised the platter and the shutter clicked. If we suspend disbelief for the claims that the moment was not entirely choreographed beforehand (as was claimed) we must then assume that the president is a master at visual self-coding. His ability to stand in at Norman-Rockwell moments comes naturally, just as he can mimic the scripts of so many Westerns where the man in the badge says, "Wanted Dead or Alive." To the company that produced a limited-edition turkey-dinner-action figure for $34.95, however, there was nothing about the staging of the event that diminished its power. It had become "a piece of our nations history." Such is the nature of visual power, even as so much of photographic legitimacy is based on the assertion of the camera's ability to convey truth in a more accurate mode then text.

THE NEW CHOREOGRAPHY OF WAR IMAGES

By the twenty-first century, professional image choreographers defined the public gaze for a president in ways that had not been achieved before. But the power of some of these visions changed as they reverberated through new interpretive landscapes and were recontextualized over time.

To announce the formation of the new office of Homeland Security in 2002, White House public relations professionals merged George W. Bush with historically revered past leaders. To do so they employed a visual gimmick, creating a setting and camera perspective that placed him among the enduring stone portraits of Mount Rushmore.

The creation of such an image invites historical comparisons, even as it turns history into a frozen moment of visual staging. The image endures, though the power of the association shifts. It carries a new meaning by the end of a decade, as the 43rd president has become the least revered leader in modern history.[12] The legacy of such a once-so-powerful image resides now, mainly in the negative registers.

Such is the power of the image that in constructing a variety of "photographic moments" during the invasion and occupation of Iraq, military planners and the president allowed their passions for the image to shape their actions. They created victories for the camera, such as the president's "Mission Accomplished" landing of the fighter jet onto the aircraft carrier, the *USS Abraham Lincoln*, off the coast of San Diego. Alternative media commentators noticed at the time that the assembled images bore a striking resemblance to the visual choreography of the film *Top Gun*.

Yet a plethora of TV anchors and mainstream commentators lauded the president's forceful demeanor, confident gait, and manly stature that day in 2003.

With the "rescue" of Private Jessica Lynch, filmed and edited by "Combat Camera" – the military's own media producers – the Pentagon conducted military actions during the invasion of Iraq for the sole purpose of providing triumphal pictures to the press. The invasion was stalled by desert windstorms and heavy Iraqi resistance, and the war's narrative needed a thrilling plot sequence to propel the themes of power and heroism. At the press conference featuring green-lit night video to illustrate the daring rescue, Army spokesmen spoke of "no soldier left behind," and Hollywood director Jerry Bruckheimer was referenced, especially in the British press, as the mentor for the new hybrid of storytelling and graphic styles that merged entertainment fictions with actual military procedures in what is now called militainment.

The Bush administration has left a visual legacy of war like no other. The *New York Times* published a series of some of the most horrific photographs of war. Down the page, column right, the disquieting images register each war, their cumulative signature an indelible mark on the human psyche. At the bottom, from the war in Iraq, stands George W. Bush cradling the huge turkey, in a symbolic gesture that hides the visual register of the death and horror of Iraq, of all the civilians, the fighters on all sides.

These images have not faired well under the cold stare of history. The legacy of chaos and destruction of the now unpopular war (with no end in sight) that the visuals promoted reveals the falsity of their claims to be real and has robbed them of their power to signify in controlled ways. The general cultural attitude, reinforced weeknights on late night "comedy news," now accepts that the victory was faked and the courage and compassion that the president displayed were just pretend. Mission Accomplished is an on-going, ubiquitous joke, and cartoon characters now have their pictures taken against the backdrop of Mount Rushmore.

ANOTHER KIND OF PHOTOGRAPH

No historical assessment of contemporary war imagery is meaningful without seeking to come to terms with the images taken at Abu Ghraib. Here the more simple, straightforward dichotomies between accidental and staged, war and myth, and between reality and interpretation become more complicated. Photographs from Abu Ghraib were not accidental in the conventional terms of war photojournalism. They were not the chance, battlefield witness of the actualities of conflict documented by independent observers. They were taken not on a battlefield, but within the confining walls of a military prison, and they were taken by soldiers themselves of events and actions that implicated their photographers in crimes against humanity. Though shot by soldiers, they will forever damage the image of the military, yet, as we will see, the images also failed to challenge hierarchical military structures and neocolonial military power. Equally important in understanding the ultimate nature of their power, and its limits, is the conflicting ways in which these visions can be interpreted. In addition, essential historical frames of interpretation have been neglected in the on-going battle over the politics of war.

THE IMAGES FROM ABU GHRAIB

In November of 2003 what was actually happening in Iraq could not have been further from the American mythic icon of a Thanksgiving turkey, especially for those locked naked and hooded in places across Iraq and the world where American military and civilian contract personnel abused and tortured prisoners under directives issued from the highest levels of the U.S. government.[13]

When digital photographs taken at Abu Ghraib prison outside Baghdad were aired by CBS on April 28, 2004, the images reverberated through the press, were widely reprinted, and were uniformly described as shocking. The photos of nude Iraqi prisoners – some in piles, some hooded, one on a leash, one dead – showed Americans smugly posing in positions of domination. One image shows a black-cloaked and hooded figure standing on what looks like a box, his arms held out from his sides at an unnatural angle, wires trailing from his hands. The posed figure is alone, attached to the instruments of torture in a bare chamber, the gray walls riddled with ugly stains. Though the pictures were released in the spring of 2004, the abuse had taken place late in 2003, and the Red Cross had been documenting the mistreatment of prisoners well before the story broke.

The figure who has become known across the globe as "The Hooded Man" will forever hold a prominent position in the global catalogue of human misery as visual rendering of evil itself, not as an abstract construct, but as the brutality humans inflict upon one another. The power of the images was undeniable, and torture perpetrated by Americans shattered – at least for a moment – the simple choreography of the measures justifying the Iraq war. They confronted the rhetorical basis for the war on terror, defined as a way to "rid the world of evil."

As more pictures from the prison emerged, they began to be interpreted and understood through the codes of the Vietnam War, a framing perspective that had been resisted by news commentators up to that point in the war. On the front page of *USA Today* (May 10, 2004), a naked Iraqi prisoner, backed up against cell bars, holds his hands behind his head, the fear etched plainly in his face. The photograph is part of a sequence that shows the man surrounded by uniformed

Americans and being set upon by dogs. Placed to the left of the page in *USA Today* is a photograph of a North Vietnamese soldier being summarily executed on the streets of Saigon during the Tet Offensive in 1968. The pictures of Abu Ghraib had become the twenty-first-century equivalent of the Vietnam War.

It should come as no surprise that attempts were made by the military to censor the pictures from Abu Ghraib prison. General Richard Myers of the Joint Chiefs of Staff reportedly called Dan Rather to urge CBS not to air the photographs, and though the *60 Minutes II* segment was delayed for two weeks, the network refused to comply, and as feared by the military, the brutality evident in the pictures registered a highly negative response. A *Washington Post*/ABC poll found that by 69 to 28 percent, the American public felt that such abuse by American military personnel was unacceptable.[14] The legitimacy of the war in Iraq had already been called into question by the failure to find and display the weapons of mass destruction that justified the war. In their absence, the Bush White House had argued that Iraqis would be better off on the road to democracy. The victims of Abu Ghraib presented a visual challenge to that assertion. On May 6, speaking from the Rose Garden in an attempt to deflect global criticism, President George W. Bush assured King Abdullah of Jordan that "wrong-doers will be brought to justice" and that "the actions of those folks in Iraq do not represent the values of the United States of America."

The power of the images of torture taken at Abu Ghraib prison is undeniable, but the interpretive field they occupy continues to expand, as their accepted historical significance is still evolving. What truth do they tell about the torture that took place within those walls? What is the nature of their power? What role have they played in ending the brutality that they documented? In a recent documentary titled *Standard Operating Procedure*, filmmaker Errol Morris revisits the imagery of Abu Ghraib to question the meaning of the photographs and the culpability of the perpetrators that they depict. Ultimately, he questions the fundamental power of the pictures to convey knowledge about what went on at Abu Ghraib. Most important, Morris opens a national dialogue on torture and justice. How do the images interconnect with Bush's assertion of May 2003, that the wrongdoers would be brought to justice, and what do they say about American values?

THE SMILING PICTURE

Morris is especially concerned with one image that he selects for particular focus. It is a picture of Specialist Sabrina Harman, one of the eight soldiers who were prosecuted for the abuses at Abu Ghraib.[15] The photograph is horrific because of Harman's facial expression and the thumbs-up sign she is gesturing over the mangled dead body of a man identified as Manadel al-Jamadi. Harmon is leaning down over the corpse. For stability, her left hand is touching the black plastic spread under the body, in an awkward pose that frames her face directly above the corpse in close proximity to the dead man's open mouth. Morris spends considerable time both in the documentary and in subsequent writing on this one photograph, examining the image for meaning as he comes to terms with what he finds most distressing about the shot – Sabrina Harman's broad, beaming, white-tooth-gleaming smile.

Morris consults the expertise of psychologist Paul Ekman, a renowned specialist on facial expression and the author of *Emotions Revealed: Unmasking the Face*, and *Telling Lies*. After analyzing a CD of over 20 pictures of Harman in Iraq, including Photograph No. 2728, the smile picture, Ekman tells Morris that Harman "is showing a social smile or a smile for the camera. The signs of an actual enjoyment smile are just not there."[16] Morris fills significant amounts of column inches in an article that includes illustrations of facial expressions and musculature, explaining the science behind the analysis of the smile. His argument concludes that the photo captures nothing more than a posed, socially false "say cheese" expression.

Though the smile is not genuine, it evokes in the viewer an almost irresistible urge to smile back at the photograph. The revulsion at wanting to do so quickly follows, and the viewer's horror intensifies. The experience communicates a sense of becoming complicit with the smile and the celebratory attitude toward a death. In the moment of viewing, the photograph acts like a mirror reflecting an image to Americans of an identity they are determined to deny.

The human being who was once Manadel al-Jamadi exists in the picture only as a corpse. Human empathy with such an objectified sight is difficult to achieve. A viewer cannot easily connect with a corpse.[17] It evokes only a feeling of pity or terror at such a death, and possibly a demand for justice. We know nothing about who the living person was – he is a stranger. We connect with the living, and Sabrina Harman is very much alive, yet smiling over a dead man. These emotions, combined with the conflicted feeling brought about by the smile, create a toxic emotional mix. For Americans, another impulse to identify with Harman is the familiar uniform she wears – Army fatigues. The viewer quickly recoils, discomforted by the complicity with the images. In doing so, anger sets in. The result is indignation and the denial of any connection to such a scene. The viewer protests that he or she is not involved in any way, could never condone such a thing, had nothing to do with it. Sabrina becomes the depraved bad apple, an aberration, not like us. She could not possibly represent American values, a visual affirmation of Bush's proclamation. The dynamics of the picture demand her prosecution.

The picture shocks with a jumble of complicated emotions, but one thing it cannot do is narrate any details about what actually happened. From this terrible sight, we know nothing about the victim, either the details of his journey to Abu Ghraib or the way he was killed. And we certainly do not know, and now never will, whether he was guilty of the crimes he was suspected of committing. The picture is powerless to convey the information needed to find justice.

MANADEL AL-JAMADI

Early in the morning on November 4, 2003, al-Jamadi was apprehended by Navy Seals as a suspect in a bombing that took place outside the office of the International Committee of the Red Cross on October 27. Two Iraqi employees had been killed, and al-Jamadi was suspected of supplying the explosives. He was first taken to Camp Pozzi, an interrogation unit operated by the Seals and also used by the CIA. He was then moved to Abu Ghraib to a holding cell on Tier 4B, where he was also interrogated. Some time later he was taken to the shower room on Tier 1B, adjacent to the now infamous "hard site," Tier 1A, where most of the pictures of prisoner abuse were taken. There he was interrogated by CIA operative, Mark Swanner. Jane Mayer, writing for the *New Yorker*, reports that there was another person in the shower room, a private contractor working as a translator referred to in court documents as "Clint C." One hour after being taken into the shower room, al-Jamadi was dead.

Morris describes in detail the furious chain of events that occurred when it was discovered a prisoner had died in custody, even though he was a "ghost," an anonymous detainee not officially recorded or given an ID number. In an interview with Morris, Hydrue Joyner, a noncommissioned officer in charge on the day shift, describes the scene at the prison as a version of the movie *Weekend at Bernie's*, "where two sad-sack employees pretend that their murdered boss is still alive so that they can avoid being implicated in his death." When al-Jamadi was finally listed in the prison log book (since he was a ghost detainee), "he was simply identified as 'Bernie'. A good joke."[18]

THE PICTURES NOT SEEN

The "smiling picture" was one of the most sensational of the Abu Ghraib images and was widely disseminated in the press. Of course, there were many other pictures in the catalogue of horrors from Abu Ghraib that, to this day, have been withheld from the public. In court, military prosecutors selected the smiling picture to use as evidence of Harman's extreme depravity. But there are an additional 15 or so relatively unknown pictures of the body of al-Jamadi taken by Sabrina Harman with her commanding officer, Sergeant Ivan (Freddi) Frederick. Later that night, about an hour and 40 minutes after Corporal Chuck Graner took her picture smiling over the corpse, she went back into the shower room with Freddi and took more pictures. According to Morris, these photographs "provide unmistakable evidence of the gruesome treatment al-Jamadi received: broken teeth, a mangled lip, contusions, bruises, the cartilage of his nose crushed, a gash under his right eye."[19] This very different set of photographs constitutes a visual record motivated by the desire to document the evidence of al-Jamadi's death. Harman wanted to keep her superiors from achieving what she was beginning to understand was a cover-up. Quoting from her letter at the time to her female partner, who she refers to as her "wife" and from her answers to his own questions, Morris makes the case that Harman was actually documenting the murder that the officers in charge were attempting to deny. As Harman explained,

> His knees were bruised; his thighs were bruised [around] his genitals. He had restraint marks on his wrists. What else? You had to look close. They did a really good job cleaning him up. I mean, he had ice all over his body, so unless you removed things, you couldn't really see the actual physical damage that they had done.
>
> You don't think your commander [Brinson] is going to lie to you about something, first of all. And then you realize wait, maybe he did lie because there's no way somebody would die of a heart attack and have all these injuries. It just didn't add up.[20]

Ironically, for taking this later set of pictures, Harman was charged with tampering with government evidence. Indeed, the military was not pleased with any of the pictures of al-Jamadi because without them the world would not have known about the death of this one Arab suspect who was killed in custody.

Morris' arguments are coherent, and his investigation into events is thorough and convincing. Harman clearly had no part in the chain of brutal events that led to al-Jamadi's death. Morris concludes that the picture has been misinterpreted, that viewers have been shocked by the photo into believing that Harman was happy about the death, even responsible for the murder of al-Jamadi, when in fact she was not. In the end, he concludes, the image helped the government block the prosecution of those who actually perpetrated the torture, the superiors at the prison in numerous branches of the Armed Forces and intelligence agencies, including private contractors. Mayer's investigations demonstrate that those who perpetrated torture continue to do so, the Bush White House and its close advisors, and Vice President Dick Cheney and his council, David Addington. Yet torture remains illegal. The limits of the visuals of Abu Ghraib were their failure to disclose pathways to end the practice of torture, in spite of the visceral reactions they evoked initially.

Morris' inquiry is unflinching, sophisticated, and nuanced, and a much-needed examination that expands our knowledge of what happened at Abu Ghraib. Yet his discussion is as disturbing as it is incomplete. We are left with unanswered questions about the connection between human rights and public compassion and the mystery of why Sabrina Harman smiled over the corpse of Manadel al-Jamadi.

Harman herself has tried to give answers, but her words seem inadequate to the task.

> Like when you get into a photo, you want to smile. It's just, I guess, something I did.... I mean, even when I look at [the photographs], I go, "Oh Jesus, that does look pretty bad." [But] if a soldier sees somebody dead, normally they'll take photos of it. I don't know why, maybe it's a curiosity thing."[21]

Ultimately, Errol Morris has no answers that could explain why any of the pictures were taken at Abu Ghraib, though he openly wonders at times: "There will always be questions about why any of these photographs were taken. Were they simply yet one more way to humiliate and dehumanize the prisoners? Were they soldiers' trophies from the war in Iraq? An attempt to collect evidence against the military?"[22] There is no doubt that some of the pictures were taken to further humiliate the victims, as reported in the *Washington Post*. Indeed, Morris shows that some were also taken as evidence. But Morris has touched on another explanation – the photograph as trophy picture – but he drops the point as quickly as he raises it.

THE SMILE OF EMPIRE

Yes, it is a trophy picture. The smile picture and many of the others, of soldiers posed against the backdrop of piles of humiliated bodies, are best understood as symbolic texts, as part of a visual convention with a long history that reveals a set of power relations in which a dominant force demonstrates its control over the wild and unruly bodies of the vanquished. True to American media culture, Morris' lengthy analysis remains at the level of the psychosocial, never recognizing that the visual is only the latest iteration of the tradition of using the photograph to claim the rights of imperial power and domination. To fully understand the meaning of the Harman photograph the layers of interpretation must include the historical, global plane. A fine book by Pauline Wakeham probes the traditions of the trophy picture. Though speaking of the sight of animals on display, in *Taxidermic Signs* she points out that such images confirm the reverence for conquest and domination.[23] Such visual reflections of power relations move across texts from the colonialization of human cultures to the displays of the heads, skins, and furs of wildlife. The same position of dominion accounts for the pose and attitude expressed in the Harman picture. Apparently not cognizant of the long convention she followed, of the explorer towering over "the natives," the conqueror over the vanquished, or the hunter claiming the body of the dead prey, the soldier over the enemy, Harman smiles over the corpse.

Trophy pictures are unacceptable and powerless in civilian discourse because they have been so widely understood and critiqued in the postcolonial world. Take, for example, an education film titled *The Eyes of Empire*, which argues that photography of the nineteenth century was a "tool of imperial science and exploration."[24] Featuring museum collections of photographs from Oxford and Cambridge, the images of native peoples are shown to be humiliating documents that tamed wild and naked bodies and classified "savage" creatures as oddities of the natural world. Large Europeans tower over their less-than-human discoveries.

Yet within the military, the trophy picture is not unique. Take, for example, an image in the film *Winter Soldier*, shot in Detroit between January 31 and February 2, 1971, during a gathering of over 200 Vietnam veterans who came together to tell their own stories of infamy. The conference and the film made from it (never shown on American television) were attempts to expose the truth and stop the war that the veterans now considered brutal and immoral. One sequence shows a still photograph bearing an uncanny resemblance to Photograph No. 2728, the smile picture from Abu Ghraib. A young American GI stands grinning over dead bodies of Vietcong at an interrogation site. In the film, the words he speaks over the image warn: "Don't ever let your government do this to you." This statement is an acknowledgment of another cost of war, the brutality that soldiers find themselves capable of after the conditioning of military training and the conditions of trauma perpetrated by war. The winter soldiers of Vietnam recognized the influence of forces larger them themselves on their conduct in acts of war. Soldiers in Iraq, like Vietnam, and in any war, are trained to become desensitized to killing. Iraq vets at *Winter Soldiers II* explained some of cognitive techniques used to habituate recruits to the process of killing.[25] Peter Sullivan explained that throughout his training he and comrades frequently chanted such things as "left, right, left, right, left, right kill!!! Left, right, left, right, yes we will!!" The extreme conditioning and acceptance was best illustrated by the repeated call and response, "What's the heel of the boot for? Crushing baby skulls!"[26] Only after he left the military did he fully appreciate the psychological conditioning he underwent to accept killing, and the imperative, "kill or be killed." Sergeant Ben Flanders, who ran hundreds of military convoys in Iraq, described to journalist Chris Hedges his loss of empathy. "I felt like there was this enormous reduction in my compassion for people."[27] Under such conditions, a dead body does not provoke compassion. A picture over a dead body is only the visual expression of far more horrific conditions of death and killing that surrounds soldiers. It is a powerful affirmation of the training, purpose, and realities of war – to kill those identified as an "enemy."

But Sabrina Harman was beginning to question her surroundings, her mission, and her purpose, and the brutal aspects of standard operating procedures carried out by the U.S. military in Iraq. Harman admits in a letter to her partner written only a few days after the murder, that she doesn't feel good about anything she is experiencing in the military; she explains

> if I want to keep taking pictures of those events – I even have short films – I have to fake a smile every time. I hope I don't get in trouble for something I haven't done. I hate this. I hate being away from home and I hate half the people I'm surrounded by. They're idiots. I can't be here. I don't want to be a part of the Army, because it makes me one of them. I don't like it here. I don't like what we do.

Morris is certainly correct when he concludes from this letter that "In a sense, Harman was deliberately falsifying the evidence of her own photographs to seem more at home than she was." Indeed, sharing the visual convention of the military trophy picture was no doubt a very effective way to convince her fellows and superiors that she was one of them. She went along with the visual displays of demonstrating the military's power over the enemy.

Though Harman seeks to document the wrongdoings of senior officers, she admits her lack of compassion for the person that was once al-Jamadi. "I guess we weren't really thinking, 'Hey, this guy has family,' or anything like that, or 'Hey, this guy was just murdered.' It was just, 'Hey, it's a dead guy, it'd be cool to get a photo next to a dead person."[28] And that is what some civilian viewers may find most disturbing about the picture. Even if the smile is fake, her pose is still a triumphal claim over a dead man, something unacceptable in civilian life but very much part of military culture.

Ultimately, coming to terms with the pictures from Abu Ghraib cannot be done without an assessment and critique of this inhuman culture of the military. Though Morris exposes the malfeasance of the hierarchy of the Armed Forces, he fails to address the loss of human compassion of the victors at the heart of the Abu Ghraib controversy. His investigation revolves around the smile, the sequence of events, the culpability, and the cover-up. Though he describes what was done to al-Jamadi, he never invites the reader or viewer to empathize with him as a person or a victim.

THE DEADLY INFLUENCES OF MILITARISM

Some of the details of al-Jamadi's ordeal are included in Morris' writings. Specialist Jason Kenner, who escorted al-Jamadi to the shower room 1B, says, "I could see the prisoner in the corner of the cell in a seated position like a scared child with the translator and interrogator leaning over him yelling at him." Morris comments, "Kenner's statement...comes alive at several moments. One of them sticks with me: 'I could see the prisoner in the corner of the cell...like a scared child.'" He offers no explanation as to why that part of Kenner's testimony "sticks" with him. He then jumps back to a summary of portions of his chronology of that night.

Manadel al-Jamadi had been put in what Secretary of State Donald Rumsfeld called a stress position. In the shower room he was positioned in what is called a Palestinian hanging – a "a low-budget crucifixion without the nails. His arms were handcuffed behind him and then the handcuffs were suspended from a window frame. (As a prisoner becomes weaker and weaker, greater and greater pressure is put on the arms, potentially pulling them out of the sockets.)"[29] At about 7 a.m., after about an hour in the shower room, three MPs (military police) on the tier were called in to help Swanner; al-Jamadi was "sagging," and Swanner wanted him tied up higher. Morris writes, "Al-Jamadi was unresponsive. The hood was removed. Almost immediately, blood started streaming from his nose. He was dead."[30] These horrific details are left without comment, interwoven in a story line as the backdrop to an investigation that primarily concerns the defense of Sabrina Harman.

Viewing death and torture demand that we do something to stop it. If we are not invited to care, the viewer becomes detached, a voyeur. If left as an abstraction, as only a piece of lifeless evidence, the picture of a corpse fails to realize its most important power, to evoke the power of empathy and to make viewers aware of the terrible human costs of war. Thus, through seeing these disgusting pictures and reading about them, Americans are not invited to adopt the position or perspective of the person being tortured, to pause and consider what it might be like to die with your chest caving in on your lungs with a hood holding in the blood coming out of your ears, nose, and mouth. Without empathy for the human, the public call to stop such inhumanity cannot be fully realized.

CONCLUSION

We occupy a visual landscape that at once overwhelms us with the weight of its vivid content while at the same time is barren and strangely denuded. A tiny fraction of a highly circumscribed view of the surface of the real is all we see, all the time, over and over. The vast majority of life, events, conditions, and the people who experience them around the globe, are outside our field of vision. If information is power, we are surely disempowered, and if knowledge and "truth" are freedom, we are close to being enslaved. This unity of generosity and lack characterize every aspect of images of war and conflict. Without more thorough public information, our humanity as global citizen will always be lacking.

The images of empire and the "trophy picture," once the domain of acceptable representations, are now rejected as too obvious and blatant. Other visual means to express and promote the relations of global power became necessary with the advent of twenty-first century.

As American foreign policy became more "preemptive," employing military aggression instead of other means to insure U.S. national interests, the justification for the invasion of Iraq leaned on rhetorical and visual strategies that avoided and denied an imperial discourse. Enlightenment values (always part of colonial language) were emphasized as the need to bring democracy to Iraq. Fears of weapons of mass destruction were also powerful persuasions. Equally important, if not more so, were the entertainments developed by public relations professionals of pictures and narratives that reveled in themes of victory, heroism, and the exciting weaponry controlled by the commander-in-chief clad in military uniform.

After five years of war, commentators and opinion elites now often admit that the war in Iraq was a war fought for oil reserves in the gulf.[31] The staged and choreographed visions of mythic war, like the photographs of empire once so powerful, have lost their flavor, yet remain as a reminder of war's folly. History will continue to judge the images and interpretations of Abu Ghraib, and they will remain part of the visual record. They will fully realize their visual power when viewers are asked to care about the victims, and not the victors.

NOTES

1. Quoted by Peter Jennings on *ABC Nightly News*, March 11, 2003.
2. Harold Evans (1980). *Eyewitness: 25 Years through World Press Photos*. New York: William Morrow. pp. 24–30.
3. "New Torture Photo Release Delayed by Obama," *The Huffington Post,* May 14, 2009. http://www.huffingtonpost.com/2009/04/24/obama-to-release-new-tort_n_191015.html
4. See The Freedom Forum, "Front Lines and Deadlines: Perspectives on War Reporting," *Media Studies Journal*. Vol. 15, No. 1 (Summer 2001).
5. See Robin Andersen (2006). *A Century of Media, A Century of War*. New York: Peter Lang. Chapter 4.
6. Phillip Knightley (2003). *The Eye of War: Words and Photographs from the Front Line.* Washington, DC: Smithsonian Books. p. 193.

7. In March of 2007, the Tillman case underwent public scrutiny when Henry Waxman, the chair of the House Government Oversight Committee, held hearings titled "Misleading Information on the Battlefield." The hearings featured testimony from Jessica Lynch and the family of Patrick Tillman. See http://www.prwatch.org/node/6005
8. See Michael Massing (2004). "Iraq, the Press, and the Election." *Tomdispatch.com*, November 24. See http://www.alternet.org/story/20569/
9. Peter Beaumont and Joanna Walters (2007). "Greenspan Admits Iraq Was about Oil, as Deaths Put at 1.2m," *The Observer*, September 16. See http://www.guardian.co.uk/world/2007/sep/16/iraq.iraqtimeline
10. Associated Press (2007). "Americans Unaware of Iraqi Death Toll: Poll Shows Knowledge of U.S. dead, but Huge Underestimation of Iraqis," February 24. See http://www.msnbc.msn.com/id/17310383/
11. Janet Maslin (2008). "Bearing Witness to the Fallen and the Grieving," June 5. See http://www.nytimes.com/2008/06/05/books/05maslin.html
12. Paul Steinhauser (2008). "Poll: More Disapprove of Bush than Any Other President," *CNNPolitics.com*, May 1. See http://www.cnn.com/2008/POLITICS/05/01/bush.poll/
13. See Jane Mayer (2008). *The Dark Side: The Inside Story of How the War on Terror Turned into a War on American Ideals.* New York: Doubleday, and Philippe Sands (2008). *Torture Team: Rumsfeld's Memo and the Betrayal of American.* New York: Palgrave Macmillan.
14. David Morris and Gary Langer (2004). "Terror Suspect Treatment: Most Americans Oppose Torture Techniques." See http://abcnews.go.com/sections/us/polls/torture_poll_040527.html
15. See Errol Morris (2008). "The Most Curious Thing," *The New York Times,* May 19. See http://morris.blogs.nytimes.com/2008/05/19/the-most-curious-thing/
16. Ibid.
17. This point has long been made by critics; see Susan Sontage (1977). *On Photography.* New York: Farrar, Straus & Giroux; Susan Sontage (2003). *Regarding the Pain of Others.* New York: Farrar, Straus & Giroux; and John Berger (1980). *About Looking.* New York: Pantheon Books.
18. Morris, "The Most Curious Thing."
19. Ibid.
20. Ibid.
21. Ibid.
22. Ibid.
23. Pauline Wakeham (2008). *Taxidermic Signs: Reconstructing Aboriginality.* Minneapolis: University of Minnesota Press
24. *The Eyes of Empire*, (1991). Films for the Humanities and Sciences. Princeton, NJ.
25. Veterans of the Iraq and Afghanistan conflicts, similar to what Vietnam veterans had done almost 40 years before, conducted a second Winter Soldiers hearing in the spring of 2007 and dozens gave harrowing testimony about conduct, procedures, and atrocities they had witnessed or participated in directly. Though offering eyewitness accounts of conditions too dangerous for most journalists to document, the mainstream press, including the *New York Times*, declined to cover the hearings. Covering the war in Iraq is difficult for journalists, therefore, it would seem logical that they would be interested in eye-witness accounts, and therefore should have covered the Iraq Winter Soldier hearings. And yes, the Iraq winter

soldier hearings were very open to the press - with lots of outreach in hopes that the media would cover them. See Fair (2008) "Why Are Winter Soldiers Not News?" March 19,

26. Peter Sullivan (2008). "Hindsight of a Trained Killer," April 18. See http://ivaw.org/membersspeak/hindsight-trained-killer
27. Chris Hedges (2008). "War and Occupation, American Style," *Tomgram*, June 3. http://www.tomdispatch.com/post/174939/chris_hedges_war_and_occupation_american_style
28. Morris, "The Most Curious Thing."
29. Ibid.
30. Ibid.
31. For example, in his 2007 book, *The Age of Turbulence: Adventures in a New World* (New York: Penguin Press) Retired Chairman of the Federal Reserve, Alan Greenspan, wrote: "I am saddened that it is politically inconvenient to acknowledge what everyone knows: the Iraq war is largely about oil."

CHAPTER SEVEN

Public Pedagogy, Cultural Politics, and the Biopolitics of Militarization

HENRY A. GIROUX

> We educate people toward the possibility of something better... [W]e must educate people toward the idea that they are more than what simply exists. Otherwise education is altogether complete nonsense.
>
> THEODORE W. ADORNO[1]

Cultural studies has long focused on the intersections of culture, media power, and power, on the one hand, and pedagogy and the politics of everyday life on the other. In its early history, particularly in its Birmingham tradition, cultural studies embraced its responsibility to address the most pressing social issues undermining a substantive democracy, and this sense of social responsibility was complemented by the belief that pedagogy is central to any viable notion of a transformative and collective politics. While current cultural studies theorists have made an enormous analytic investment in critically addressing the interface of race, class, gender, and identity politics, largely through various symbolic and material circuits of power, they have had little to say about Raymond Williams' earlier concept of "permanent education," the broader notion of pedagogy as central to the educational force of culture in the latter half of the twentieth century.[2] In fact, current criticism largely ignores the importance of public pedagogy to a politically efficacious model of cultural studies.[3] In what follows, I reassert the centrality of cultural politics and public pedagogy to the actual practise of cultural studies, particularly its intersection among media, the politics of representation, and power relations. In doing so, I analyze the developing biopolitics of militarization in the wider culture, the various ways in which it legitimizes the emerging national security state, and how it might be contested through a materially and symbolically informed cultural politics. In the current historical moment, militarization has become bipolitical in that it now saturates every aspect of daily life, blurring the traditional distinctions between the economic and cultural, on the one hand, and the private and the public on the other.

Under the Bush administration, American power *was restructured* domestically around a growing culture of fear and a rapidly increasing militarization of public space and popular culture. Military presence and economic militarization abroad coupled with the rhetoric of an elaborate civilizing mission that combined the hard reality of military violence with the soft rhetoric of democratization.[4] Even with the election of Barack Obama, little has been done to curb the spread of US military action abroad under the guise of an unlimited war against terrorism, as popular spheres on the domestic front are increasingly being organized around values supporting a highly militarized, patriarchal, and jingoistic culture that is undermining "centuries of democratic gains."[5] Americans are not merely obsessed with military power; rather, according to Andrew J. Bacevich, "it has become central to our national identity."[6] Bacevich develops this position by arguing that Americans have "fallen prey" to a dangerous form of militarism

> manifesting itself in a romanticized view of soldiers, a tendency to see military power as the truest measure of national greatness, and outsized expectations regarding the efficacy of force. To a degree without precedent in U.S. history, Americans have come to define the nation's strength and well-being in terms of military preparedness, military action, and the fostering of (or nostalgia for) military ideals.[7]

Even the media have become militarized, adopting the rhetoric of war to shape their news reporting, largely dealing with military violence as an aesthetic, and constantly drawing its news stories from the battlefronts of Iraq and Afghanistan. If "Shock and Awe" represented the most blatant example of elevating a war, in this case the invasion of Iraq, to the level of spectacle, the culture of force, violence, and war has now become an integral part of most television and radio networks. Stripped of any critical analysis, the dominant media trade in euphemism as part of the production of violence. Invasions are called regime change, civilian war casualties are demoted to collateral damage, and journalists who get their cues from the Pentagon are now labelled as embedded, and so it goes. Chalmers Johnson argues that America's history of "standing armies, almost continuous wars, an ever growing economic dependence on the military-industrial complex and the making of weaponry, and ruinous military expenses as well as a vast, bloated defense budget...might in the end, produce a military dictatorship or – far more likely – its civilian equivalent,"[8] a position that is never addressed in the dominant media. American militarism is evident not only in the 969 military bases on American soil and in the fact that the United States spends more on "defence" than all the rest of the world put together, but also

> in the network of 823 American military bases we maintain around the world (according to the Pentagon's own 2008 official inventory). Not including the Iraq and Afghanistan conflicts, we now station over half a million U.S. troops, spies, contractors, dependents, and others on military bases located in more than 130 countries, many of them presided over by dictatorial regimes that have given their citizens no say in the decision to let us in.[9]

The notable historian, Tony Judt, is right in insisting that the United States is

> obsessed with war: rumors of war, images of war, "preemptive" war, "preventive" war, "surgical" war, "prophylactic" war, "permanent" war. [And] as President Bush explained at a news conference on April 13, 2004, "This country must go on the offense and stay on the offense."[10]

The growing influence of military presence and ideology in American society is made visible, in part, by the fact that the United States now has more police, prisons, spies, weapons, and soldiers than at any other time in its history. This radical shift in the size, scope, and influence of the military is apparent in the redistribution of domestic resources and government funding away from social programs into military-oriented security measures at home and war abroad. As Richard Falk has pointed out, "The US Government is devoting huge resources to the monopolistic militarization of space, the development of more usable nuclear weapons, and the strengthening of its world-girdling ring of military bases and its global navy, as the most tangible way to discourage any strategic challenges to its preeminence."[11] According to journalist George Monbiot, the federal government "is now spending as much on war as it is on education, public health, housing, employment, pensions, food aid and welfare put together."[12] Moreover, the state itself is being radically transformed into a national security state, increasingly put under the sway of the military–corporate–industrial–educational complex.[13]

The process of militarization – the increasing centrality of the military in shaping American culture, society, and foreign policy – has a long history in the United States and takes on different forms under different historical conditions.[14] Furthermore, it involves a radical and socially pernicious reallocation of resources, the reduction of human beings to narrow and hierarchically organized identity positions, and the development of a discourse that glorifies militarism at all costs. Catherine Lutz elaborates on the ways in which militarization is

> an intensification of the labor and resources allocated to military purposes, including the shaping of other institutions in synchrony with military goals. Militarization is simultaneously a discursive process, involving a shift in general societal beliefs and values in ways necessary to legitimate the use of force, the organization of large standing armies and their leaders, and the higher taxes or tribute used to pay for them. Militarization is intimately connected not only to the obvious increase in the size of armies and resurgence of militant nationalisms and militant fundamentalisms but also to the less visible deformation of human potentials into the hierarchies of race, class, gender, and sexuality, and to the shaping of national histories in ways that glorify and legitimate military action.[15]

Unlike the old style of militarization in which all forms of civil authority are subordinate to military authority, the new biopolitics of militarization is organized to engulf the entire social order, legitimating its values as central rather than peripheral to American public life. Moreover, the values of militarism are no longer limited to a particular group or sphere of society. On the contrary, Jorge Mariscal points out:

> In liberal democracies, in particular, the values of militarism do not reside in a single group but are diffused across a wide variety of cultural locations. In twenty-first century America, no one is exempt from militaristic values because the processes of militarization allow those values to permeate the fabric of everyday life.[16]

Following the events of 9/11 and the wars in Afghanistan and Iraq, the military has assumed an even more privileged place in American society. Bush endlessly played on his image as the most powerful living symbol of America's might. Bush lived up to billing; he did his best to embody military strength by endlessly giving public talks before military audiences, staging military-designed spectacles, such as the Shock and Awe campaign, and doing all he could to use his administration's resources to celebrate and cultivate the military presence in American culture. He often wears a military uniform when speaking to "captive audiences at military bases, defence plants, and on aircraft carriers," and he goes out of his way to give speeches at military facilities, talk to military personnel, and address veterans' groups.[17] In order to attract media attention, Bush also took advantage of the campaign value of military culture by using military symbolism as a political prop. One glaring example took place on May 1, 2003, when Bush landed in full aviator flight uniform on the *USS Abraham Lincoln* in the Pacific Ocean and officially proclaimed the end of the Iraq war. There was also the secret trip to Baghdad in 2003 to spend Thanksgiving Day with the troops, an event that attracted world-wide coverage in all the media. Since his re-election in 2004, Bush has showcased defence experts, such as Dick Cheney, Donald Rumsfeld (until he was replaced in 2006), and Condoleezza Rice as the most visible and key representatives of a government whose power reflects what President Eisenhower had long ago labelled the "military–industrial complex" and identified as a dire threat to American democracy.[18] But Bush has done more than take advantage of the military as a campaign prop to sell his domestic and foreign policies. His administration, along with the Republican Party, has developed a new, dangerous, "and unprecedented confluence of our democratic institutions and the military."[19]

Writing in *Harper's Magazine*, Kevin Baker insists that the military "has become the most revered institution in the country."[20] Soon after the war in Iraq, a Gallup Poll reported that over 76 percent of Americans "expressed 'a great deal' or 'quite a lot' of confidence in their nation's military." A poll of 1200 students conducted by Harvard University revealed that 75 percent believed that the military would "do the right thing" most of the time. In addition, the students "characterized themselves as hawks over doves by a ratio of two to one."[21] The mainstream has played an important and crucial role in promoting a culture of fear, one that mobilized moral panics about domestic safety and internal threats, accentuated by endless terror alerts, creating, in part, a society that increasingly accepted the notion of a "war without limits" as a normal state of affairs (while increasingly being opposed to the Iraq war). But fear and insecurity do more than produce collective anxiety among Americans, who are exploited largely to get them to believe that they should vote Republican because it is the only political party that can protect them. In addition to producing manufactured political loyalty, such fears can also be manipulated into a kind of "war fever" that normalizes war and idealizes its institutions. In such cases, as Robert Lifton points out, "War then becomes heroic, even mythic, a task that must be carried out for the defense of one's nation, to sustain its special historical destiny and immortality of its people."[22] The mobilization of war fever carries with it a kind of paranoid edge, endlessly stoked by government alerts and repressive laws, and it has been used "to create the most extensive national security apparatus in our nation's history."[23] Military support is also reproduced in the Foxified media that, in addition to constantly marketing the flag and implying that critics of American foreign policy are traitors, offer up seemingly endless images of brave troops on the front line, heroic stories of released American prisoners, and utterly privatized commentaries on those wounded or killed in battle.[24] *Time Magazine* embodied this representational indulgence in military culture by naming "The American Soldier" as the 2003 "Person of the Year."[25] Such ongoing and largely uncritical depictions of war inject a constant military presence in American life and simultaneously help to create a civil society that has become aggressive in its warlike enthusiasms.

But more is at work here than the media's exploitation of troops for higher ratings or the attempts by right-wing political strategists to keep the American public in a state of permanent fear so as to remove pressing domestic issues from public debate. We also witnessed an attempt by the Bush administration to convince as many Americans as possible that, under the current "state of emergency," the use of the military in domestic affairs is perfectly acceptable. This new domestic focus is evident in the increasing propensity to use the military establishment "to incarcerate and interrogate suspected terrorists and 'enemy combatants' [a term the Obama administration no longer uses] and keep them beyond the reach of the civilian judicial system, even if they are American citizens."[26] It is also apparent in the attempts by the federal government to try suspected terrorists in military courts and to detain prisoners "outside the provisions of the Geneva Convention as prisoners of war…at the US Marine Corps base at Guantanamo, Cuba because that facility is outside of the reach of the American courts."[27] This state of emergency with its onslaught of legal illegalities was not only legitimated in the dominant media but was used by the media to mobilize public opinion and sanction a growing authoritarian state. In this sense, the media functioned as a form of right-wing public pedagogy providing the ideas, values, and framing mechanisms to win over the consent of many Americans to the "dark side" of many of the policies pushed by the Bush administration.

The flipside of the shift towards viewing civilians as objects of military surveillance is that civilians were also being recruited as foot soldiers in the war on terrorism, urged to spy on their neighbours' behaviour, watch for suspicious-looking people, and supply data to government sources in the Bush administration's war on terrorism. Even now as the American public grows suspicious of the war in Iraq, patriotism renders inseparable the call for supporting the troops from the madness of empire building. Similarly, for all of the dissent about the war, the media are dominated by images of flags on storefront windows, lapels, cars, houses, and SUVs in a show of support for the increasing militarization of the culture and social order at home. The mainstream media also detract any criticism of militarization in American society by endlessly reducing the imperatives of citizens to the narrow demands of consumption. Critical thought and civic courage are now replaced by the urge to shop, consume, and add to the garbage pile of waste.

Just as individuals fall prey to the current high-pitched appeals to hyperpatriotism, so do institutions, whether willingly or not, and educational institutions are particularly vulnerable. Major universities now compete for defence contracts and rush to build courses and programs that cater to the interests of the Department of Homeland Security. Obama's Secretary of Defence, Robert Gates, heralds academia as part of an intensive campaign to offer grants to academics in order to enlist them in the officially sanctioned production of violence. In its eagerness to assist in the militarization of higher education, Congress passed a legislation that would "stiffen penalties for colleges that bar military recruiters from their campuses."[28] JROTC programs are fast becoming a regular part of the school activities. As a result of former president Bush's No Child Left Behind Act, "schools risk losing all federal aid if they fail to provide military recruiters full access to their students; the aid is contingent on complying with federal law."[29] Unfortunately, President Obama is simply recycling NCLB rather than dismantling it. What both Bush and Obama miss is that schools should be democratic public spheres that teach students how to resist the militarization of democratic life, understand how media power has become central to political life, learn what it means for young people to have stake in the resources of their country, address the importance of economic justice and cultural rights, and understand what it would mean to engage the complexities of power on both the domestic and international fronts. Instead, they serve as recruiting stations for students to fight as part of an occupying force in a war that is largely condemned by the rest of the world and that frequently sends young Americans back home either in body bags or with serious bodily and psychological injuries.

Worse still, schools represent a nexus of this bizarre coupling of trends: the criminalization of civilians and the pervasive militarization of civilians and civil institutions. Not only are penal policies changing as youth are tried as adults but schools are also increasingly modelled after prisons. Schools represent one of the most essential public spheres to come under the influence of military culture and values. Tough love translates into zero tolerance policies, which transform public schools into disciplinary institutions that deliberately fail to recognize students' rights. Additionally, as educators turn over their responsibility for school safety to the police, the new security culture in public schools has turned them into "learning prisons," "reformed" through the addition of armed guards, barbwired security fences, and lockdown drills.[30] Not too long ago in Goose Creek, South Carolina, police conducted an early morning drug sweep at Stratford High School. When the police arrived, they drew guns on students, handcuffed them, and made them kneel facing the wall. No drugs were found in the raid.[31] Though this incident was aired on the national news, there were barely any protests from the public.

Unfortunately, during the last 30 years, the Republican Party, which has been the governing party in the United States, has done everything it can to allocate funds for "educational reforms" that undermine democracy. These reforms often strip young people of the capacity to think critically by teaching them that learning is largely about test taking and by preparing them for a culture in which punishment is the central principle of reform. Bush could not even fully fund his own educational reform act, but in his 2005 State of the Union Address he pledged an additional $23 million to promote drug testing of students in public schools. Once again, fear, punishment, and containment overrode the need to provide healthcare for 9.3 million uninsured children; increase the ranks of new teachers by at least 100,000 (as then-president Bill Clinton suggested in 2000)[32]; fully support Head Start programs; repair deteriorating schools; and improve those youth services that could break for many poor students the direct pipeline from school to the local police station, the courts, or prison. The Obama administration is reversing some of these policies, but Arne Duncan, the new Secretary of Education, has a long record as the head of the Chicago Public System of also relying on fear, surveillance, and punishment as central to defining educational reform.[33]

The rampant combination of fear and insecurity that is so much a part of a permanent war culture in the United States seems to bear down particularly hard on children. In many poor school districts, specialists are being laid off and crucial mental health services are being cut back. As Sara Rimer pointed out in the *New York Times*, much-needed student-based services and traditional, if not compassionate, ways of dealing with student problems are being replaced by the juvenile justice system, which functions "as a dumping ground for poor minority kids with mental health and special-education problems.... The juvenile detention center has become an extension of the principal's office."[34] In some cities, for example, ordinances have been passed that "allow for the filing of misdemeanor charges against students for anything from disrupting a class to assaulting a teacher."[35] Children are no longer given a second chance for minor behaviour infractions, nor are they simply sent to the guidance counsellor, principal, or to detention. Instead of being viewed as young people with future potential, who, therefore, deserve and require nurturing and support, children are largely portrayed in the media as yet another source of anxiety, best dealt with by the courts and juvenile justice system. Media discourses increasingly cast children as either commodities or as dangerous.[36]

Yet no matter how closely schools come to resemble prisons, they continue to teach, not only through the approved curriculum but also through the culture they create; increasingly, this is a militarized culture. For example, in the summer of 2006, the city of Baltimore "spent over $1.1 million to install about 575 cameras in 11... schools, averaging 52 cameras per school."[37] School administrators often justify such actions as part of the need for school safety and "school reform," but rarely do they ask what kids who are put under constant surveillance learn from the experience. Students are not only subjected to diverse forms of control and surveillance, but they are also taught to believe that these basic intrusions on their freedom and privacy are matters of routine and commonsense. This is hardly a lesson in critical citizenship. While children encounter a profound distrust on the part of adult society, they are also being educated to accept passively the military-sanctioned practises that maintain control, surveillance, and unquestioned authority, all conditions central to a police state and to protofascism. Some schools actually use sting operations in which undercover agents pretend to be students in order to catch young people suspected of selling drugs or committing any one of a number of school infractions. The consequences of such actions are far-reaching. As Randall Beger points out,

> Opponents of school-based sting operations say they not only create a climate of mistrust between students and police, but they also put innocent students at risk of wrongful arrest due to faulty tips and overzealous police work. When asked about his role in a recent undercover probe at a high school near Atlanta, a young-looking police officer who attended classes and went to parties with students replied: "I knew I had to fit in, make kids trust me and then turn around and take them to jail."[38]

Clearly, the militarization of America's home front does more than undermining the fair use of social and material resources; the very social relations that bind us are at risk. Children are taught not to trust that adults will keep them safe by nurturing them, but that adults will keep themselves safe by monitoring youth and violating their rights. Further, we teach youth that the violation of rights is morally acceptable and even essential to the maintenance of a civil society.

This climate, with its assumption that rights are entirely alienable, restricts the ability of young people to think critically and to learn how to question authority. Under the auspices of the national security state and the militarization of domestic life, containment policies are the principal means to discipline working-class youth. Marginalized students learn quickly that they are among America's surplus populations and that the journey from home to school no longer means they will next move into a job; on the contrary, school is now a training ground for their "graduation" into containment centres such as prisons and jails that keep them out of sight, patrolled, and monitored so as to prevent them from becoming a social canker or political liability to those white and middle-class populations concerned with their own safety. Schools increasingly function as zoning mechanisms to separate students marginalized by class and colour and, as such, have become prison-like in their role as social institutions. This supports the argument of David Garland, who points out that "Large-scale incarceration functions as a mode of economic and social placement, a zoning mechanism that segregates those populations rejected by the depleted institutions of family, work, and welfare and places them behind the scenes of social life."[39]

The recreation of schools in the image of prisons and the rise of the prison–industrial–educational complex reflect the militarization of the criminal justice system. The traditional "distinctions between military, police, and criminal justice are blurring."[40] The police now work in close collaboration with the military, receiving surplus weapons and technology/information transfers, introducing SWAT teams modelled after the Navy Seals, and relying more and more on military models of crime control.[41] This growth of the military model in American life has played a crucial role in the paramilitarizing of the culture, which provides both media-produced narrative and legitimation "for recent trends in corrections, including the normalization of special response teams, the increasingly popular Supermax prisons, and drug war boot camps."[42] In the para-militaristic perspective, crime is not a social problem; it is instead constructed as both an individual pathology and a matter of punishing rather than rehabilitating the "enemy." Unsurprisingly, paramilitary culture typically embodies a racist and class-specific discourse, and it "reflects the discrediting of the social and its related narratives."[43] This is particularly evident as America's inner cities are being singled out as dangerous enclaves of crime and violence. The consequences for those communities have been catastrophic, as can be seen in the cataclysmic rise of the prison–industrial complex. As Sanho Tree writes,

> With more than 2 million people behind bars (there are only 8 million prisoners in the entire world), the United States – with one-twenty-second of the world's population – has one-quarter of the planet's prisoners. We operate the largest penal system in the world, and approximately one quarter of all our prisoners (nearly half a million people) are there for nonviolent drug offenses.[44]

With 2.2 million people behind bars, nearly 70 percent of the inmates are people of colour: 50 percent are African American and 17 percent are Latino. Between June 2004 and June 2005, prisons and jails were adding more than 1000 inmates each week. The Bush administration had estimated that by the fall of 2007 "about 27,500 immigrants will be in detention each night."[45] Justified by America's para-militarization, jails are increasingly used to render disposable people of colour who are either poor or marked as the "illegal" *other*. As the social state collapses, the punishing state criminalizes a range of social problems; instead of addressing what it might mean to enable and co-operate with citizens, especially those of marginalized race and class, to create a state that places power in the hands of all of its members, it confronts social suffering with punitive measures, suggesting that certain populations are by default worthy of nothing but contempt. Angela Davis is right in claiming that such policies represent the logic of what she calls the imprisonment binge. She writes:

> Instead of building housing, throw the homeless in prison. Instead of developing the educational system, throw the illiterate in prison. Throw people in prison who lose jobs as the result of de-industrialization, globalization of capital, and the dismantling of the welfare state. Get rid of all of them. Remove these dispensable populations from society. According to this logic the prison becomes a way of disappearing people in the false hope of disappearing the underlying social problems they represent.[46]

When poor youth of colour are not being warehoused in dilapidated schools or prisons, they are being aggressively recruited by the Army to fight the war in Iraq. For example, Carl Chery recently reported that

> With help from *The Source* magazine, the U.S. military is targeting hip-hop fans with custom made Hummers, throwback jerseys and trucker hats. The yellow Hummer, spray-painted with two black men in military uniform, is the vehicle of choice for the U.S. Army's "Take It to the Streets campaign" – a sponsored mission aimed at recruiting young African Americans into the military ranks.[47]

It seems that the Army has discovered hip-hop and urban culture and, rather than listening to the searing indictment of poverty, joblessness, and despair that is one of their central messages, the Army recruiters appeal to their most commodified elements by letting the "potential recruits hang out in the Hummer, where they can pep the sound system or watch recruitment videos."[48] Of course, they won't see any videos of Hummers being blown up in the war-torn streets of Baghdad.

What they will see each day in multiple modes of screen culture, however, is the widespread imagery of militarization that pervades popular culture and functions as a mode of public pedagogy. From video games to Hollywood films to children's toys, popular culture is increasingly bombarded with militarized values, symbols, and images that aim to instil the values and the aesthetic of militarization through a wide variety of pedagogical sites and cultural venues. For instance, Humvee ads offer up the fantasy of military glamour and machismo, marketed to suggest that ownership of these military-designed vehicles, first used in Desert Storm, guarantees virility for its owners and promotes a mixture of fear and admiration from everyone else. One of the fastest growing sports for middle-class suburban youth is the game of paintball, "in which teenagers stalk and shoot each other on 'battlefields' (In San Diego, paintball participants pay an additional $50 to hone their skills at the Camp Pendleton Marine Base)."[49] Military recruitment ads flood all modes of entertainment, offering messages that resonate powerfully with young people. Typically, these marketing tools depict particular forms of masculinity that are inseparable from violence in order to entice new recruits. For example, the website for the US Marines, www.marines.com, contains various images of marines in battle, sounds of gunfire, and an array of messages such as "Everyone gets knocked down but the tough get up." An earlier ad campaign contained the following message:

> We are the warriors, one and all. Born to defend, built to conquer. The steel we wear is the steel within ourselves, forged by the hot fires of discipline and training. We are fierce in a way no other can be. We are the marines.[50]

As alluring as this hypermasculinity is to young people, it also reveals the assumptions on which it is based, that young people are surplus – *born* to defend – and that our responsibility to young people is merely to prepare and educate them for life and death as soldiers – these young people are *built* to conquer. There is no room in this model of subjectivity for critical thought or practise, and there is no purpose for this militaristic subject position outside of the interrelated registers of war and violence.

As luck would have it, the infiltration of military culture into popular culture creates the impression of constant war. This is evident in the numerous ways the military has found to take advantage of the intersection between popular culture and the new electronic technologies. Even as such technologies are being used to recruit and train military personnel, they are also tapping into the realm of popular culture with its celebration of video games, computer technology, the Internet, and other elements of visual culture used by teenagers.[51] Video games such as *Doom* have a long history of using violent graphics and shooting techniques that appeal to the most excessive modes of masculinity. The Marine Corps was so taken in the mid-1990s with *Doom* that they produced their own version of the game, *Marine Doom*, and made it available to download free of cost. One of the game's developers, Lieutenant Scott Barnett, claimed at the time that it was a useful game to keep marines entertained. The interface of military and popular culture has not only been valuable in providing video game technology for diverse military uses but has also resulted in the armed forces developing partnerships "with the video game industry to train and recruit soldiers."[52] The military uses the games to train recruits, and the game makers offer products that have the imprimatur of a first-class fighting machine.[53] Moreover, the popularity of militarized war games is on the rise. Nick Turse argues that the line between entertainment and war is disappearing:

> [A] "military-entertainment complex" [has] sprung up to feed both the military's desire to bring out ever-more-realistic computer and video combat games. Through video games, the military and its partners in academia and the entertainment industry are creating an arm of media culture geared toward preparing young Americans for armed conflict.[54]

Combat teaching games offer a perfect fit between the Pentagon, with its accelerating military budget, and the entertainment industry, with annual revenues of $479 billion, which include $40 billion from the video game industry. As the production of violence morphs into a media combat game, the militarization becomes ludic, enticing in a hypermasculine mode that provides both a legitimation for violence and a media-centred cultural sphere where young people can narrate their desires, hopes, and wishes. This collaboration brings in human and financial resources for both parties and creates a legitimizing cycle: the entertainment industry offers a stamp of approval for the Pentagon's war games, and the Defence Department provides an aura of authenticity for corporate America's war-based products. While collaboration between the Defence Department and the entertainment industry has been going on since 1997, the permanent war culture that now grips the United States has given this partnership a new life and has greatly expanded its presence in popular culture.[55]

The US Army purchased and now maintains its own video game production studio, developing online software that appeals to computer-literate recruits. Capitalizing on its link with industry, the Army is working to produce a host of new war games. Among these is a shooting game "that actually simulates battle and strategic-warfare situations."[56] When asked about the violence such games portray, Brian Ball, the lead developer of the game, was crystal clear about its purpose: "We don't downplay the fact that the Army manages violence. We hope that this will help people understand the role of the military in American life."[57] One of the most popular and successful recruiting video games, *America's Army*, teaches young people how "to kill enemy soldiers while wearing your pajamas [and also provides] plenty of suggestions about visiting your local recruiter and joining the real US Army."[58] Clive Thompson notes that "more than 10 million people have downloaded...*America's Army* [which] the Army gives away as a recruiting tool."[59] The game, free to use on many gaming websites and also distributed as a free CD-ROM, has become so popular that the Army staged a tournament in New York City and had recruiters waiting at the door.[60] In fact, *America's Army* is one of the most popular video games of all time.[61]

Using the latest versions of satellite technology, military–industry collaboration has also produced *Kuma War*. This game, released in 2004, was developed by the Department of Defence and Kuma Reality Games. It is a subscription-based product that "prepares gamers for actual missions based on real-world conflicts" and is updated weekly.[62] The game allows players to recreate actual news stories such as the raid American forces conducted in Mosul, Iraq, in which Saddam Hussein's sons Uday and Qusay were killed. Gamers can take advantage of "true to life satellite imagery and authentic military intelligence, to jump from the headlines right into the frontlines of international conflict."[63] As of March 2009, more and more technically sophisticated war video games become available to young people through a variety of media. Of course, the realities of carrying 80-pound knapsacks in 120-degree heat; the panic-inducing anxiety and fear of real people shooting real bullets or planting real bombs to kill or maim you and your fellow soldiers; and being away from family for months, if not years, are not among those experiences reproduced for instruction or entertainment. This cleansed fantasy of military life means that young people no longer learn military values in training camp or in military-oriented schools. Instead, these values are now disseminated through the pedagogical force of popular culture itself, which has become a major tool used by the armed forces to educate young people about the ideology and social relations that inform military life – minus a few of the unpleasantries. The collaboration between the military and entertainment industry offers up a form of public pedagogy that "may help to produce great battlefield decision makers, but... strike[s] from debate the most crucial decisions young people can make in regard to the morality of a war – choosing whether or not to fight and for what cause."[64] What is disturbing about the military–entertainment complex is that it has been enormously successful in promoting video games as a central type of media that are increasingly important as a central force in creating a web of power that encompasses a wide range of sites, and powerful economic agents.

In light of the militaristic transformation of the country, attitudes toward war play have changed dramatically and can be observed in the major increase in the sales, marketing, and consumption of military toys, games, videos, and clothing. Corporations recognize that there are big profits to be made at a time when military symbolism gets a boost from the war in Iraq and from the upsurge in patriotic jingoism, and this has not changed with the election of Obama to the American presidency. The popularity of militarized culture is apparent not only in the sales of video combat games but also in the sales of children's toys. Major retailers and chain stores across the country are selling out of war-related toys. KB Toys retail stores in San Antonio, Texas, sold out in a single day an entire shipment of fatigue-clad plush hamsters that dance to military music, and store managers were instructed "to feature military toys in the front of their stores."[65] Moreover, sales of action figures have soared. Hasbro reported that, "between 2001 and 2002, sales of G.I. Joe increased by 46 percent, and when toy retailer Small Blue Planet launched a series of figures called 'Special Forces: Showdown With Iraq,' two of the four models sold out immediately."[66] KB Toys took advantage of the infatuation with action toys related to the war in Iraq by marketing a doll that is a pint-sized model of George W. Bush dressed in the US pilot regalia he wore when he landed on the *USS Abraham Lincoln*. Japanese electronic giant Sony attempted to cash in on the war in Iraq by patenting the phrase "Shock and Awe" for use with video and computer games. The phrase, referring to the massive air bombardment planned for Baghdad in the initial stages of the war, was coined by Pentagon strategists as part of a scare tactic to be used against Iraq. Additionally, the *New York Times* reported that after 9/11, "nearly two-dozen applications were filed for the phrase, 'Let's Roll.'"[67] The term was made famous by one of the passengers on the ill-fated hijacked plane that crashed in a field in Pennsylvania. Respect for people killed in violent attacks is no deterrent to the commodification of war or to the spread of its paraphernalia and catch phrases through the diverse circuits of mass and popular culture. Of course, the media have always aligned itself with corporations that provide toys, videos, films, and other elements of screen culture as a way to deploy corporate and military power.

Even in the world of fashion, the ever-spreading chic of militarization and patriotism is making its mark as part of a broader media–military complex. Army–Navy stores are doing a brisk business selling American flags, gas masks, aviator sunglasses, night-vision goggles, and other military equipment, as well as clothing with the camouflage look.[68] Even chic designers are getting into the act. For instance, a few years ago at a fashion show in Milan, Italy, many designers were "drawn to G.I. uniforms [and were] fascinated by the construction of military uniforms." One designer "had beefy models in commando gear scramble over tabletops and explode balloons."[69] Fashion critic Vince Carducci claims that "Military fashion was being conscripted into the mainstream at what seemed to be unprecedented levels [and] sales of camouflage and fatigue apparel are brisk."[70] Military fashion apparently is not simply for adults and young people. Coolbaby Clothing sells camouflage gear for toddlers and babies, offering everything from baby combat pants and camouflage diaper shirts to diaper bags and crib sets. Clearly, in a culture in which military symbols dominate, it is cool to dress babies like soldiers.[71]

The pervasiveness of the militarization of American culture reveals the extent to which our democratic values have been eroded: the glorification of military values is quickly approaching the level of fascist idealization. Fascism in both its old and new forms views life as a form of permanent warfare and, in doing so, subordinates society to the military, rather than viewing the military as subordinate to the needs of a democratic social order. Militarism in this scenario diminishes both the legitimate reasons for a military presence in society and the necessary struggle for the promise of democracy itself. As Umberto Eco points out, under the rubric of its aggressive militarism, protofascist ideology argues that "there is no struggle for life but, rather, life is lived for struggle."[72] The ideology of militarization is central to understanding protofascism since it appeals to a form of irrationality that is at odds with any viable notion of democracy. For instance, militarization uses fear to drive human behaviour, and the values it promotes are mainly distrust, patriarchy, and intolerance. Within this ideology, masculinity is associated with violence, and action is often substituted for the democratic processes of deliberation and debate. Militarization as an ideology is about the rule of force and the expansion of repressive state power. In fact, democracy appears as an excess in this logic and is often condemned as being a weak system of government. Echoes of this anti-democratic sentiment can be found in the passing of the Patriot Act in 2001, with its outrageous violation of civil liberties, and in the Military Commission Act of 2006, which

> authorizes the president to seize American citizens as enemy combatants, even if they have never left the United States. And once thrown into military prison, they cannot expect a trial by their peers or any protections of the Bill of Rights.[73]

The fanaticism that cultivates authoritarian tendencies can also be seen in the rancorous patriotism that equates dissent with treason, and in the discourse of public commentators who, in the fervour of a militarized culture, fan the flames of hatred and intolerance. One example that has become all too typical emerged after the 9/11 attacks. Columnist Ann Coulter, in calling for a holy war on Muslims, wrote, "We should invade their countries, kill their leaders and convert them to Christianity. We weren't punctilious about locating and punishing only Hitler and his top officers. We carpet-bombed German cities; we killed civilians. That's war. And this is war."[74] A similar rhetoric of hate and divisiveness can be found in Dinesh D'Souza's politically fatuous but inflammatory book, *The Enemy at Home*, which argues that the alleged "cultural left" (which includes everyone from Hilary Clinton to Noam Chomsky) is responsible for causing the horrible events of 9/11.[75] More recently with the election of Barack Obama, the right-wing media, typified by Glenn Beck, a rising star on Fox news, have become almost hysterical in promoting a discourse of hate, suggesting, for instance, that Obama's administration will be building concentration camps for conservatives. While such statements do not reflect the mainstream of American opinion, the uncritical and chauvinistic patriotism and intolerance that inform them have become standard fare among many conservative radio hosts in the United States and are increasingly produced and legitimated in a wide number of cultural venues. As militarization spreads through the media culture, it produces policies that rely more on force than on dialogue and compassion; it offers up modes of identification that undermine democratic values and tarnish civil liberties; and it makes the production of both symbolic and material violence a central feature of everyday life. As Kevin Baker points out, we are quickly becoming a nation that "substitute[s] military solutions for almost everything, including international alliances, diplomacy, effective intelligence agencies, democratic institutions – even national security."[76] By blurring the lines between military and civilian functions, militarization deforms our language, debases democratic values, celebrates fascist modes of control, defines citizens as soldiers, appropriates popular culture as a form of symbolic violence, and diminishes our ability as a nation to uphold international law and support a democratic global public sphere. Unless militarization is systematically exposed and resisted at every place where it appears in the culture, it will undermine the meaning of critical citizenship and do great harm to those institutions that are central to a democratic society. At stake here is the recognition that the biopolitics of militarization has become a form of public pedagogy asserting its values and assumptions through a wide range of media, popular, and cultural sites.

As the forces of militarization are ratcheted up within multiple spaces in the body politic, they increasingly begin to produce the political currency of fascism in the United States, and it is these fascist discourses that discourage and disable acts of resistance. As the mainstream media spread the influence of militarization both at home and abroad, a culture of fear is mobilized in order to put into place a massive police state intent on controlling and manipulating public speech, while making each individual a terrorist suspect subject to surveillance, finger printing, and other forms of "electronic tattooing." But the increasing danger of militarization is also evident in the attempt by the corporate–military–media complex to create those ideological and pedagogical conditions in which people become convinced either that the power of the commanding institutions of the state should no longer be held accountable or that citizens are powerless to challenge the new reign of state terrorism. And as militarization spreads its values and power throughout American society and the globe through a range of media extending from television broadcasts and news papers to the Internet, it works to eliminate those public spaces necessary for imagining an inclusive democratic global society. Militarization and the culture of fear that legitimates it have redefined the very nature of the politics and, in doing so, have devalued speech and agency as central categories of democratic public life.

Both exposing and resisting such anti-democratic and authoritarian tendencies should be among the primary responsibilities of intellectuals, activists, parents, youth, community members, and others concerned about the fate of democracy on a global scale. Working both within and without traditional public spheres, such as the media, churches, schools, and universities, individuals and groups can expose the ideology of militarization in all its diversity and the ways in which it threatens to turn the United States into a military state while it simultaneously undermines crucial social programs, constitutional liberties, and valuable public spaces. Such intellectual work should take place across nation-states and among researchers, academics, intellectuals, and others who produce ideas in the service of social justice, and this work should promote indignation and collective resistance. This is the pedagogical task that must confront the politics and ideology of militarization. The spreading militarization at home and abroad demands a new politics of resistance that expands the relationship between politics and everyday life. According to Arundhati Roy, this new politics of resistance requires

> fighting to win back the minds and hearts of people.... It means keeping an eagle eye on public institutions and demanding accountability. It means putting your ear to the ground and listening to the whispering of the truly powerless. It means giving a forum to the myriad voices from the hundreds of resistance movements across the

> country which are speaking about *real* things – about bonded labor, marital rape, sexual preferences, women's wages, uranium dumping, unsustainable mining, weavers' woes, farmers' suicides. It means fighting displacement and dispossession and the relentless, everyday violence of abject poverty. Fighting it also means not allowing your newspaper columns and prime-time TV spots to be hijacked by their spurious passions and their staged theatrics, which are designed to divert attention from everything else.[77]

Thus, in addition to making clear the threat that the biopolitics of militarization poses for democracy, especially that highlighted by the political role played by different media, cultural studies theorists and progressives everywhere are faced with the challenge of constructing a broad social movement capable of developing real strategies of resistance at both the local and glogal levels to the forces of militarization. This suggests that there is more to it than simply working through traditional spheres of political contestation, such as elections or union struggles or various means of education. Collective struggle must also combine the tasks of a radical public pedagogy and cultural politics with massive acts of non-violent collective disobedience. Such acts can serve to educate, to mobilize, and to remind people of the power of alliances, demonstrations, long-term commitments, and of the importance of struggles that change both ideas and relations of power.

In order to be efficacious, however, acts of resistance must have a clear focal point. Militarism, which so greatly undermines democratic spaces, practises, and principles, is one such focal point that requires urgent attention. By making militarization visible through the force of images, words, and peaceful resistance, politics can become both meaningful and possible as a contested site through which people can challenge, locally and within international alliances, the obscene accumulation of power symptomatic of the increasing militarization of public space as well as the fascism that is spreading throughout the United States and across the globe. Arundhati Roy is right in her incessant and courageous call to globalize dissent, but if dissent is to work, it must have a focus that cuts across empires, nation-states, and local space, a focus that cuts to the heart of a clear and present danger to democracy and social justice. Challenging militarization in all of its expressions is a direct strike at the heart of a policy that has exceeded its usefulness for democracy and has now formed a dreadful pact with authoritarianism. Cultural studies theorists can take on the responsibility of making dominant power visible, unpacking its authoritarian values in media discourses and representations, and revealing the violence and social suffering it promotes all over the world. The examination of militarization at the level of everyday life makes visible how personal problems can be translated into public issues. For instance, such analyses can be useful in revealing how militarization recreates public schools as boot camps; undercuts basic civil rights; provides the foundation for a military dictatorship; diverts resources from important social projects; promotes the global movement of arms; and creates a vast machinery of war built on greed, profits, and the accumulation of capital, all the time exhibiting an egregious indifference to human suffering and democratic public life.

Cultural studies theorists must be part of the challenge to the politics of militarization, the emerging national security state, and the power the two have to reproduce and legitimate themselves. Zygmunt Bauman insightfully suggests that part of such a challenge points to the necessity for what he calls an "ethic of distant consequences," one that addresses "the globalization of responsibility."[78] This "taking responsibility for our responsibility" suggests that responsibility is the first act of any involvement in public life, one that ties us both to the integrity and dignity of the other and to the meaning and possibility of a global democracy.[79] Such responsibility should not only be the basis for individual and collective resistance to the biopolitics of militarization but should also provide the normative framework for the greater role intellectuals might play in opposing large media corporations; creating a new politics of daily life; and fostering social relations that refuse to reproduce the existing social order of violence, impoverishment, and social suffering. Cultural studies theorists can rethink and help to revitalize a cultural politics that links political economy and the economy of representations, desires, and bodies to scholarly work, public conversations, the educational force of the larger culture, and everyday life. Moreover, such work engages in the attempt to reclaim the culture of politics, to reconceptualize and expand the possibilities for social agency, to reverse the evisceration of public goods, and to prevent the increasing commodification and privatization of public spaces. Similarly, cultural studies can take on the task of imagining how to build global political alliances and social movements. In order to forge these productive alliances, intellectuals need to develop the theoretical tools, political strategies, and pedagogical practises necessary to wage multiple struggles in a variety of sites against those institutions and cultural formations that provide social guarantees only to the privileged, and offer suffering, uncertainty, and insecurity to everybody else.

Clearly, then, there is great potential in cultural studies to challenge and rethink not only diverse articulations of culture, media, and power but also how such relations both close down and open up democratic relations, spaces, and transformations, and what the latter mean theoretically, pedagogically, and strategically for how we envision the meaning and purpose of politics under a revitalized military–industrial–academic complex. Equally important is the challenge of recognizing that any viable political struggle must nurture, in pedagogical and political terms, the act of translation and the ability of individuals to connect their personal lives to broader public issues and to take seriously that if politics is in part defined through acts of deliberation, translation, and struggle, there is a desperate need to create the public spheres that make such pedagogical tasks possible. As admittedly difficult as these challenges might appear, they offer the opportunity for cultural studies advocates to rethink their role as oppositional public intellectuals within a global context, and they provide incentives for mastering new technologies of communication, exchange, and distribution as part of an act of collective global resistance.

In opposition to the alleged guardians of "authentic" radicalism who believe that cultural politics undermines "real" struggles, cultural studies theorists must demonstrate that cultural questions are central to understanding struggles over resources and power as well as organizing a politics that enables people to have a voice and an investment in shaping and transforming the conditions through which they live their everyday lives.[80] Such a collective movement requires that people experience themselves as critical social agents along multiple axes of identification, investment, and struggle. Only then can we provide the basis for opening up the space of resistance by making power visible as it is manifest in different media and diverse public and private spheres. Democracy does not come cheap and one step in creating the conditions for young people and adults to imagine different and more democratic futures lies in trying to understand how power and politics come together in diverse media while simultaneously developing a language of critique and possibility that makes visible the urgency of politics and the promise of a vibrant and radical democracy.

NOTES

1. Theodor W. Adorno, *Critical Models: Interviews and Catchwords*, trans. Henry W. Pickford (New York: Columbia University Press, 1998), 303.
2. Raymond Williams, *Communications* (New York: Barnes and Noble, 1967), 15.
3. There are some exceptions to be found in the work of Doug Kellner, Roger Simon, Henry Giroux, Susan Searls Giroux, Stanley Aronowitz, Richard Johnson, Nick Couldry, and a few others, though this work is marginal to the diverse field of cultural studies.
4. Christopher Newfield, "The Culture of Force," *The South Atlantic Quarterly* 105, no. 1 (Winter 2006): 241–63. The literature on militarization is immense. An exceptional bibliography can be found in Molly Wallace, "Preliminary Bibliography of Recent Research on Militarization and Demilitarization," Center for the *Watson Institute for International Studies*, Brown University, December 3, 2006, www.watsoninstitute.org/pub/Militarization_Demilitarization_Bibliography.pdf (accessed January 10, 2008).
5. Susan Buck-Morss, *Thinking Past Terror: Islamism and Critical Theory on the Left* (New York/London: Verso, 2003), 33.
6. Andrew J. Bacevich, *The New American Militarism* (New York: Oxford University Press, 2005), 1.
7. Ibid., 2.

8. Chalmers Johnson, "Empire v. Democracy: Why Nemesis Is at Our Door," *TomDispatch.com*, January 31, 2007, www.commondreams.org/views07/0131–27.htm (accessed February 17, 2006).
9. Chalmers Johnson, "Chalmers Johnson on the Cost of Empire," TruthDig, May 15, 2009, www.truthdig.com/arts_culture/item/20090514_chalmers_johnson_on_the_cost_of_empire (access May 15, 2009).
10. Tony Judt, "The New World Order," *The New York Review of Books* 52, no. 14 (July 14, 2005): 14–18.
11. Richard Falk, "Will the Empire Be Fascist?" *Transnational Foundation for Peace and Future Research*, March 24, 2003, www.transnational.org/forum/meet/2003/Falk_FascistEmpire.html (accessed July 26, 2006).
12. George Monbiot, "States of War," *The Guardian/UK*, October 14, 2003, www.commondreams.org/views03/1014–09.htm (accessed August 3, 2006).
13. Henry A. Giroux, *The University in Chains: Confronting the Military-Industrial-Academic Complex* (Boulder: Paradigm, 2007).
14. John R. Gillis, ed., *The Militarization of the Western World* (New Brunswick: Rutgers University Press, 1989). On the militarization of urban space, see Mike Davis, *City of Quartz* (New York: Vintage, 1992) and Kenneth Saltman and David Gabbard, eds., *Education as Enforcement: The Militarization and Corporatization of Schools* (New York: Routledge, 2003). Some of the more recent work on militarism in American life can be found in Noam Chomsky's *Towards a New Cold War* (New York: New Press, 2003), *Rogue States* (Boston: South End Press, 2000), *Hegemony or Survival* (New York: Metropolitan Books, 2003), and *Failed States: The Abuse of Power and the Assault on Democracy* (New York: Metropolitan Books, 2006); also Howard Zinn's *On War* (New York: Seven Stories Press, 1997) and *Terrorism and War* (New York: Seven Stories Press, 2002); Gore Vidal's *Imperial America: Reflections on the United States of Amnesia* (New York: Nation Books, 2004) and *Perpetual War for Perpetual Peace* (New York: Nation Books, 2002). Other important works include Chalmers Johnson, *The Sorrows of Empire: Militarism, Secrecy, and the End of the Republic* (New York: Metropolitan Books, 2004); Andrew J. Bacevich, *The New American Militarism*; and Carl Boggs, *Imperial Delusions: American Militarism and Endless War* (Denver: Paradigm Publishers, 2005); and Chalmers Johnson, *Nemesis: The Last Days of the American Republic* (New York: Metropolitan Books, 2006).
15. Catherine Lutz, "Making War at Home in the United States: Militarization and the Current Crisis," *American Anthropologist* 104, no. 3 (September 2003): 723–35.
16. Jorge Mariscal, "'Lethal and Compassionate': The Militarization of US Culture," *Counter Punch*, May 5, 2003, www.counterpunch.org/mariscal05052003.html (accessed January 26, 2006).
17. Ibid.
18. David Harvey, *The New Imperialism* (New York: Oxford University Press, 2005), 192.
19. Kevin Baker, "We're in the Army Now: The G.O.P.'s Plan to Militarize Our Culture," *Harper's Magazine*, October 2003, 38.
20. Ibid., 37.
21. Ibid.
22. Ruth Rosen, "Politics of Fear," *San Francisco Chronicle*, December 30, 2003, www.commondreams.org/views02/1230–02.htm (accessed February 7, 2006).

23. Ibid.
24. Fox News's and MSNBC's Iraq war coverage was named by *Time Magazine*, no less, in its "The Year in Culture" section as "the worst display of patriotism" for 2003. See *Time Magazine*, January 5, 2004, 151..
25. Nancy Gibbs, "TIME Person of the Year, 2003: The American Soldier," *Time Magazine*, December 21, 2003, www.time.com/time/personoftheyear/2003/story.html (accessed March 2, 2006).
26. Richard H. Kohn, "Using the Military at Home: Yesterday, Today, and Tomorrow," *Chicago Journal of International Law* 94, no. 1 (Spring 2003): 165–92.
27. Ibid.
28. Kelly Field, "Colleges Risk Losing More Funds for Banning Military Recruiters," *Chronicle of Higher Education, Daily News Online*, October 22, 2004, http://search.epnet.com (accessed October 23, 2006). See also the print article, Kelly Field, "Colleges Risk Losing More Funds for Banning Military Recruiters," *Chronicle of Higher Education*, sec. A, October 22, 2004.
29. David Goodman, "Covertly Recruiting Kids," *Baltimore Sun*, September 29, 2003, www.commondreams.org/views03/1001–11.htm (accessed February 23, 2006).
30. Gail R. Chaddock, "Safe Schools at a Price," *Christian Science Monitor*, August 25, 1999, p. 15.
31. Tamar Lewin, "Raid at High School Leads to Racial Divide, Not Drugs," *New York Times*, sec. A, December 9, 2003.
32. Nancy Johnson and Charles Rangel, "CEC Public Policy Update 3/23," *ConnSense Bulletin*, March 23, 2000, www.connsensebulletin.com/cec5.html (accessed December 26, 2006).
33. take up this issue in Henry A. Giroux and Ken Saltman, "Obama's Betrayal of Public Education," December 17, 2008, www.truthout.org/121708R (accessed December 12, 2009).
34. Sandra Rimer, "Unruly Students Facing Arrest, Not Detention," *New York Times*, sec. 1, January 1, 2004.
35. Ibid.
36. I take this issue up in great detail in Henry A. Giroux, *Youth in a Suspect Society: Democracy or Disposability*? (New York: Palgrave Macmillan, 2009).
37. Sara Neufeld, "10 More City Schools to Get Surveillance," *Baltimore Sun*, October 20, 2006, www.populistamerica.com/10_more_city_schools_to_get_surveillance (accessed December 28, 2006).
38. Randall Beger, "Expansion of Police Power in the Public Schools and the Vanishing Rights of Students," *Social Justice* 29, no. 1 & 2 (2002): 119–129.
39. David Garland cited in Melange, "Men and Jewelry; Prison as Exile: Unifying Laughter and Darkness," *Chronicle of Higher Education*, sec. B, July 6, 2001.
40. Peter B. Kraska, "The Military-Criminal Justice Blur: An Introduction," in *Militarizing the American Criminal Justice System*, ed. Peter B. Kraska (Boston: Northeastern University Press, 2001), 3.
41. See Christian Parenti, *Lockdown America: Police and Prisons in the Age of Crisis* (London: Verso Press, 1999).
42. Kraska, "Military-Criminal Justice Blur," 10.

43. Jonathan Simon, "Sacrificing Private Ryan: The Military Model and the New Penology," in *Militarizing the American Criminal Justice System*, 113.
44. Sanho Tree, "The War at Home," *Sojourner's Magazine*, May/June 2003, 5.
45. See Elizabeth White, "1 in 136 U.S. Residents Behind Bars," *Associated Press*, May 22, 2006, www.commondreams.org/headlines06/0522–03.htm (accessed January 1, 2007); Meredith Kolodner, "Private Prisons Expect a Boom: Immigration Enforcement to Benefit Detention Companies," *The New York Times*, July 19, 2006, http://select.nytimes.com/search/restricted/article?res=F60B13F83D5B0C7A8DDDAE0894DE404482 (accessed February 10, 2007).
46. Angela Y. Davis, *Abolition Democracy: Beyond Empire, Prisons, and Torture* (New York: Seven Stories Press, 2005), 40–41.
47. Carl Chery, "U.S. Army Targets Back Hip-Hop Fans," *The Wire/Daily Hip-Hop News*, October 21, 2003, www.sohh.com/article_print.php?content_ID=5162 (accessed January 27, 2006).
48. Ibid.
49. Mariscal, "'Lethal and Compassionate.'"
50. See the US Marine's official website, www.marines.com/page/usmc.jsp?flashRedirect=true (accessed December 20, 2006).
51. For a list of such "toys," see Nicholas Turse, "Have Yourself a Pentagon Xmas," *The Nation*, January 5, 2004, 8. For a more extensive list, see www.tomdispatch.com (accessed June 7, 2007).
52. Matt Slagle, "Military Recruits Video-Game Makers," *Chicago Tribune*, October 8, 2003, p. 4.
53. Anthony Breznican, "Army Recruiting Through Video Games, " *The Washington Post*, sec. A, May 23, 2002; Joan Ryan, "Army's War Game Recruits Kids," *San Francisco Chronicle*, sec. B, September 24, 2004; Sheldon Rampton, "War Is Fun as Hell," *AlterNet*, August 2, 2005, www.alternet.org/story/23840 (accessed January 4, 2006).
54. Nick Turse, "The Pentagon Invades Your XBox," *Dissident Voice*, December 15, 2003, www.dissidentvoice.org/Articles9/Turse_Pentagon-Video-Games.htm (accessed November 3, 2006).
55. In the late 1990s, the military reached out to game designers to help them develop new video technologies and war games. See Clive Thompson, "The Making of an XBox Warrior," *New York Times Magazine*, August 22, 2004, 33–37.
56. R. Lee Sullivan, "Firefight on Floppy Disk," *Forbes Magazine*, May 20, 1996, 39–40.
57. Gloria Goodale, "Video Game Offers Young Recruits a Peek at Military Life," *Christian Science Monitor*, May 31, 2003, p. 16.
58. Wayne Woolley, "From 'An Army of One' to Army of Fun: Online Video Game Helps Build Ranks," *Times-Picayune*, September 7, 2003, p. 26.
59. Thompson, "The Making of an XBox Warrior," 35.
60. Ibid., 34–37.
61. Ibid., 35.
62. This description comes from *Gaming News*, October 10, 2003, www.gamerstemple.com/news/1003/100331.asp (accessed March 19, 2006).
63. Ibid.
64. Turse, "Pentagon Invades."

65. Maureen Tkacik, "Military Toys Spark Conflict on Home Front," *Wall Street Journal*, sec. B, March 31, 2003.
66. Amy C. Sims, "Just Child's Play," *Fox News Channel*, August 21, 2003, www.wmsa.net/news./Fox News/fn-030822_childs_play.htm (accessed October 18, 2006).
67. Sabra Chartrand, "Patents," *New York Times*, sec. C, April 21, 2003.
68. Mike Conklin, "Selling War at Retail," *Chicago Tribune*, p. 1, May 1, 2003.
69. Both quotes are from Cathy Horyn, "Macho America Storms Europe's Runways," *New York Times*, sec. A, July 3, 2003.
70. Vince Carducci, "America: Dressed to Kill," *PopMatters*, May 10, 2004 www.popmatters.com/features/040510-dressed.shtml (accessed April 1, 2006).
71. See CoolBaby Clothing at www.coolbabyclothing.com/longoveralldlh.html (accessed February 17, 2007).
72. Umberto Eco, "Eternal Fascism: Fourteen Ways of Looking at a Blackshirt," *Utne Reader*, November/December 1995, 13.
73. Bruce Ackerman cited in Heather Wokusch, "Now That You Could Be Labeled an Enemy Combatant…" *Common Dreams News Center*, October 4, 2006, www.commondreams.org/views06/1004–35.htm (accessed October 5, 2006).
74. This quotation by Coulter has been cited extensively. See *Coulter Watch* at www.coulter-watch.com/files/BW_2–003-bin_Coulter.pdf (access January 10, 2008).
75. Dinesh D'Souza, *The Enemy at Home* (New York: Doubleday, 2007).
76. Baker, "We're in the Army Now," 38.
77. Arundhati Roy, *War Talk* (Cambridge, MA: South End, 2003), 37–38.
78. Zygmunt Bauman and Keith Tester, *Conversations with Zygmunt Bauman* (London: Polity, 2001), 145.
79. Ibid.
80. See, for instance, the recent hoopla over the utterly reductionistic and economistic book by Walter Benn Michaels, *The Trouble with Diversity* (New York: Metropolitan Books, 2006), as covered in Jennifer Howard, "Ideology Instead of Identity – and a Lot More Extremism," *The Chronicle of Higher Education*, September 22, 2006, http://chronicle.com/weekly/v53/i05/05a01401.htm (accessed February 1, 2007) and in David Moberg, "Is Diversity Enough?," *In These Times*, October 9, 2006, www.inthsetimes.com/site/main/article/2848 (accessed February 1, 2007).

PART IV: MEDIA AND ACADEMIA

CHAPTER EIGHT

Bringing Power Back In: The Herman–Chomsky Propaganda Model, 1988–2008

ANDREW MULLEN

Money and power are able to filter out the news fit to print....[1]

INTRODUCTION

October 2008 marked the 20th anniversary of the publication of *Manufacturing Consent: The Political Economy of the Mass Media* by Edward Herman and Noam Chomsky.[2] This chapter demonstrates that the Propaganda Model (PM) developed by Herman and Chomsky has been systematically marginalized within the field of media and communication studies. It also argues that, despite such neglect, there is a pressing need to bring power back into the study of the media and their role in capitalist, liberal-democratic societies. The chapter is divided into six sections. The first section highlights the contrast between the liberal-pluralist perspective and the Marxist-radical critique of how political and media systems operate in capitalist, liberal-democratic societies. The second section provides an overview of the PM, more specifically its three hypotheses, its five operative principles and the evidence put forward in support of the model. The third section assesses how the PM has been received within the field of media and communication studies since 1988. The fourth section presents empirical evidence which suggests that the PM is applicable in countries other than the United States. More specifically, it compares British press coverage of European integration in the 1970s and the 2000s and finds that the PM possesses the capacity to (a) account for the different editorial positions adopted in these two periods and (b) explain the changes in press coverage over time. The fifth section suggests a number of reasons to explain why the PM has been generally ignored, while the sixth section investigates whether recent economic, political and technological transformations have bolstered or undermined the explanatory power of the PM. The chapter concludes that a political economy approach, with its sophisticated analysis of power, is essential to any attempt to understand and explain media behaviour in the 21st century, and it recommends that the PM should be central to any such an endeavor.

UNDERSTANDING AND EXPLAINING POLITICS AND THE MEDIA: THE LIBERAL-PLURALIST VERSUS MARXIST-RADICAL DEBATE

An informed electorate, with access to accurate and unbiased information and news, is widely accepted as an essential precondition for the effective functioning of a democratic society. The liberal-pluralist perspective on how the political system works in such a society holds that there is a healthy "marketplace of ideas".[3] In other words, there are different opinions, policy proposals, worldviews and so on which the general public can choose from. Moreover, the most popular of these will be reflected in the laws and policies adopted by the political system. The liberal-pluralist view of how the media system operates is based upon the notion that it constitutes the "fourth estate".[4] Put simply, it is claimed that the media serve as a guardian of the public interest and a watchdog on the exercise of power; the media thereby contribute to the system of checks and balances that comprise the modern democratic system. Importantly, Herman and Chomsky observed that the "leaders of the media claim that their news choices rest on unbiased professional and objective criteria, and they have support for this contention in the intellectual community,"[5] thus ensuring that the liberal-pluralist standpoint is the dominant, mainstream one.

Going beyond the classical and modern elitism theories put forward by Gaetano Mosca, Vilfredo Pareto, James Burnham, Robert Michels, C. Wright Mills and Joseph Schumpeter,[6] the Marxist-radical critique of the political system purports that it reflects the class-based nature of society and that the laws and policies that are enacted are those which serve to bring about and to maintain ruling-class domination and exploitation.[7] The Marxist-radical account of the media system posits that

> the media are...part of an ideological arena in which various class views are fought out, although within the context of the dominance of certain classes; ultimate control is increasingly concentrated in monopoly capital; media professionals, while enjoying

> the illusion of autonomy, are socialized into and internalize the norms of the dominant culture; the media, taken as a whole, relate interpretive frameworks consonant with the interests of the dominant classes, and media audiences, while sometimes negotiating and contesting these frameworks, lack ready access to alternative meaning systems that would enable them to reject the definitions offered by the media in favour of consistently oppositional definitions.[8]

Working within the Marxist-radical tradition, and in a direct challenge to the liberal-pluralist approach, Herman and Chomsky warned that if "the powerful are able to fix the premises of discourse, to decide what the general populace is allowed to see, hear and think about, and to "manage" public opinion by regular propaganda campaigns, the standard view of how the system works is at serious odds with reality."[9] Herman and Chomsky, in advancing and empirically testing a number of hypotheses concerning media performance, attempted to answer this fundamental question.

THE PROPAGANDA MODEL

The PM developed by Herman and Chomsky proposed three hypotheses and was based upon five operative principles.

Hypothesis 1 – elite consensus and media compliance. The first hypothesis put forward by Herman and Chomsky was that where there was consensus among the corporate and political elite on a particular issue, the media tended to reflect this in their coverage of that issue, to the exclusion of rival viewpoints. The elite, Herman and Chomsky stated, was composed of "the government, the leaders of the corporate community, the top media owners and executives and the assorted individuals and groups who are assigned or allowed to take constructive initiatives".[10] Herman asserted that "where the elite are really concerned and unified, and/or where ordinary citizens are not aware of their own stake in an issue or are immobilised by effective propaganda, the media will serve elite interests uncompromisingly."[11] A similar thesis was advanced by Thomas Ferguson, who found that where the major investors in political parties agree on an issue, the parties will not compete on that issue, no matter how strongly the public might want an alternative.[12]

Conversely, Herman and Chomsky conceded that the propaganda system did not work as efficiently where there was dissensus: "the mass media are not a solid monolith on all issues. Where the powerful are in disagreement, there will be a certain diversity of tactical judgements on how to attain generally shared aims, reflected in media debate."[13] Herman acknowledged that "there are often differences within the elite which open up space for some debate and even occasional (but very rare) attacks on the intent, as well as the tactical means of achieving elite ends."[14] In this situation, "news media coverage might have the ability to *influence* executive policy processes" rather than just reflect elite interests.[15] Indeed, the political contest model put forward by Gadi Wolfsfeld and the policy–media interaction model formulated by Piers Robinson both suggest that the media can sometimes play an active role in elite policy formation.[16] Critically, however, the media do not stray from the bounds of "thinkable thought": Herman and Chomsky reasoned that "views that challenge fundamental premises or suggest that the observed modes of exercise of state power are based on systemic factors will be excluded from the mass media even when elite controversy over tactics rages fiercely."[17] The existence of elite consensus or dissensus is a matter of empirical investigation; Herman and Chomsky offered no ready-made rules on this matter.

Hypothesis 2 – the five filters. The second hypothesis put forward by Herman and Chomsky was that in liberal-democratic regimes such as the United States, where the mass media worked under corporate rather than state control, media coverage was shaped by what was, in effect, a "guided market system" underpinned by five filters – the operative principles of the PM. Herman and Chomsky agreed that the use of propaganda was an integral and long-standing mechanism of population control employed by economic and political elites in capitalist, liberal-democratic regimes. In totalitarian societies, the state controlled the general public's access to information and this was generally understood to constitute a propaganda system; in capitalist, liberal-democratic societies, by contrast, the notion that there was an open "marketplace of ideas" created the misleading impression that the general public was free from manipulation. In reality, however, the corporate sector and their political allies have long conspired to ensure that some ideas are elevated and others are excluded from the "marketplace".[18]

In terms of the operative principles of the PM, the five filters, Herman and Chomsky suggested that

> Money and power are able to filter out the news fit to print, marginalise dissent and allow the government and dominant private interests to get their message across to the public. The essential ingredients of our propaganda model, or set of news "filters", fall under the following headings: (1) the size, concentrated ownership, owner wealth and profit orientation of the dominant mass-media firms; (2) advertising as the primary income source of the mass media; (3) the reliance of the media on information provided by governments, business and "experts" funded and approved by these primary sources and agents of power; (4) "flak" as a means of disciplining the media; and (5) "anti-communism" as a national religion and control mechanism. These elements

> interact with and reinforce one another. The raw material of news must pass through successive filters, leaving only the cleansed residue fit to print. They fix the premise of discourse and interpretation, and the definitions of what is newsworthy in the first place.[19]

The methodological approach underpinning the PM and the wider work of Herman and Chomsky, both individually and together, rested upon three principles. The first principle was the use of empirical data rather than polemic or theoretical treatise. Alison Edgley, the author of *The Social and Political Thought of Noam Chomsky*, noted that

> In [their] analysis of the media, [Herman and] Chomsky can be seen employing a rigorous empirical method. [They] look at the data available on a particular issue and contrast it with that used and highlighted by the media. ... [They] can be found measuring column inches and looking at where in a report an issue gets raised. Very often, [they] argue, all the data on an issue are actually used by the media, but what is significant is the amount of attention given to some issues over others.... [It] is the observed disparity which is important and indicative, rather than accuracy of some data over other data.[20]

The second principle was the use of official sources rather than "left-wing" and marginalized ones. Edgley recorded that

> Chomsky's work...sets out to demonstrate the disparity between [the elite's] purported morality and the outcome of [their] policies. The disparity between the two, Chomsky suggests, is often suggestive not of their purported morality but rather indicates an alternative morality *rational* to an elitist view of human nature. [In terms of sources] official data is the elite's own record of their action. In other words their own interpretation of [policy] outcome can be found to contradict their own political rhetoric. In this sense official data becomes the most "objective" source.[21] (emphasis in original)

The third principle was the use of paired examples to highlight the process of dichotomization within newspaper coverage. The comparison of cases in this way enabled the contradictions and double standards, and the explicit or implicit distinction between "worthy" and "unworthy" victims, to be exposed. To give just one example, why were the concurrent cases of state terror unleashed by the Pol Pot regime in Cambodia and the military dictatorship in Indonesia in the 1970s treated so differently in terms of US newspaper coverage? The answer, Herman and Chomsky suggested, was the serviceability of such reporting to elite interests. In short, the crimes of enemy states, such as Cambodia, were newsworthy, while comparable actions committed by allies and client states, such as Indonesia, were not; as Herman and Chomsky explained, "a propaganda system will consistently portray people abused in enemy states as *worthy* victims, whereas those treated with equal or greater severity by its own government or clients will be *unworthy*" (emphasis in original).[22]

The data presented by Herman and Chomsky in support of the PM consisted of a series of case studies based upon content analysis of newspaper coverage. These included studies of the coverage of the murdered Polish priest, Jerzy Popieluszko, and other religious victims in Latin America; elections in El Salvador, Guatemala and Nicaragua; the "KGB-Bulgarian plot" to kill the Pope; and the wars in Cambodia, Laos and Vietnam. The 2002 edition of *Manufacturing Consent*[23] expanded the studies to include mainstream media usage of the term "genocide" to describe events in East Timor, Iraq, Kosovo and Turkey, and the coverage of elections in Cambodia, Kenya, Mexico, Russia, Turkey, Uruguay and Yugoslavia. Herman and Chomsky also claimed that, in addition to foreign policy matters, the PM could be applied to domestic issues such as the North American Free Trade Agreement, anti-globalization protests, the long-standing elite assault on the labour movement and the chemical industry and its regulation. Herman and Chomsky concluded that the PM "fits well the media's treatment of this range of issues'[24] and pointed out that, despite its general neglect, the PM remains one of the most tested models in the social sciences. Indeed, as Chomsky observed

> we've studied a great number of cases, from every methodological point of view that we've been able to think of – and they all support the "Propaganda Model". And by now there are thousands of pages of similar material confirming the thesis in books and articles by other people too – in fact, I would hazard a guess that the "Propaganda Model" is one of the best-confirmed theses in the social sciences. There has been no serious counter-discussion of it at all, actually, that I'm aware of.[25]

Hypothesis 3 – marginalization. The third hypothesis put forward by Herman and Chomsky related to the way in which the PM would be received:

> [The] "Propaganda Model" makes predictions at various levels. There are first-order predictions about how the media function. The model also makes second-order predictions about how media performance will be discussed and evaluated. And it makes third-order predictions about the reactions to studies of media performance. The general prediction, at each level, is that what enters the mainstream will support the needs of established power.[26]

Chomsky declared that, as discussed above, "the first-order predictions of the model are systematically confirmed."[27] The second-order prediction, which is concerned with the marginalization of the PM, is dealt with in the next section.

THE RECEPTION OF THE PROPAGANDA MODEL

Since its publication in 1988, the PM has received very little attention within the field of media and communication studies, the wider social sciences or society more generally, as Herman and Chomsky predicted. Those who did engage with the PM were overwhelmingly negative, again as predicted. Such criticisms, emanating from a variety of sources on the left and right of the political spectrum, included the notion that the PM presented a conspiratorial view of the media[28]; that it overstated the power of the propaganda system and downplayed popular opposition to elite preferences[29]; that it was deterministic, functionalist and simplistic[30]; that it neglected of impact of journalistic professionalism[31]; that it was overly ambitious, projecting a "total and finalising view'[32] and that, in the post-Cold War period, "as traditional ideological divisions have broken down to be replaced with new alignments, the propaganda model has looked increasingly creaky."[33] Furthermore, John Corner questioned whether the PM supported or opposed liberal principles; whether those involved in the propaganda system were conscious of its operation and effects and whether, by deploying notions such as "brainwashing under freedom" and "thought control', the PM was indeed concerned with media effects rather than just media behaviour and performance.[34]

Since its publication, several scholars have presented evidence in support of the central hypotheses of the PM.[35] As predicted, however, this work received very little attention. Furthermore, although they did not utilize the PM, a number of other scholars in Britain and in the United States concurred that the mass media tended to manufacture consent for elite preferences, both in terms of domestic and foreign policy.[36] While the PM has been applied within the Canadian and US contexts, and while David Edwards and David Cromwell, plus David Miller, have alluded to its explanatory potential in terms of the British media,[37] there has been no attempt to systematically test the PM within the British context. Indeed, one critic questioned whether it "could be applied in countries with very different media systems and political structures".[38] Nevertheless, studies by Alex Doherty and Andrew Mullen presented evidence which suggested that it may indeed be applicable in Britain (the latter is set out in the next section).[39]

APPLYING THE PROPAGANDA MODEL IN BRITAIN

British media coverage of European integration is a relatively neglected subject within European studies/political science. Nevertheless, several studies have been conducted. Uwe Kitzinger focused upon the editorial stance of the main newspapers during the negotiations preceding Britain's accession in 1973.[40] David Butler and Kitzinger, Philip Goodhart, Anthony King and Mark Hollingsworth analyzed the national press coverage during the 1975 Referendum.[41] George Wilkes and Dominic Wring identified three distinct phases in reporting during the post-World War II and post-Cold War periods: a pro-European consensus from 1948 until 1975, near-unanimous enthusiasm from 1975 until the early 1990s and a growing Euroscepticism in sections of the media thereafter.[42] David Morgan conducted a survey of leading journalists to ascertain their views on access, constraints, sources and the European Union (EU) "news story" itself.[43] Roy Greenslade traced the emergence of the pro-EU consensus in the early 1960s and described its effects during the 1975 Referendum.[44] Julie Firmstone evaluated the editorials of six national newspapers following the introduction of the euro in January 2002, concluding that "the lack of consensus evident within the political system on the euro may well serve to intensify the influence and role of the press in the debate,"[45] while Paul Statham conducted a cross-national study of press coverage of European integration between 2001 and 2004, finding that "with the exception of *The Sun* in Britain, there is little evidence for the press as a source of Euroscepticism, and covering Europe is really 'business as usual'."[46] The existing literature, however, is limited in two senses. First, it tended towards description rather than analysis, specifically neglecting the question of why newspapers adopted particular positions on the EU. Second, with the exception of Wilkes and Wring, it focused upon particular time periods and failed to attend to, or account for, changes in national press coverage over time. This section, utilizing the PM, attempts to transcend these limitations.

CASE STUDY 1

The National Press in the 1970s

The editorial line on accession pursued by the main national newspapers between May 1971, when the French veto on Britain's application was lifted, and January 1973, when Britain officially joined the EU, is shown in Table 1.

With the exception of the *Daily Express* (owned by Beaverbrook Newspapers[47] with a readership of 3.4 million) and the *Morning Star* (linked to the Communist Party of Great Britain, with a readership of 70,000), the rest of the national newspapers, with a readership of 10.8 million, supported Britain's accession to the EU in the early 1970s.

Colin Seymour-Ure studied the national press coverage of European integration during the 1975 Referendum using a content-analysis approach.

Table 1: National Newspapers' Editorial Position on Joining the EU (between May 1971 and January 1973; Circulation Figures in June 1971 Are in Parentheses)

Newspaper	For accession	Against accession
Daily Express (3,436,000)		X
Daily Mail (2,007,000)	X	
Daily Mirror (4,380,000)	X	
Daily Telegraph (1,455,000)	X	
Financial Times (168,000)	X	
The Guardian (328,000)	X	
Morning Star (70,000)		X
The Sun (2,083,000)	X	
The Times (341,000)	X	

This survey, which is summarized in Table 2, details how much support the (pro-EU) Yes campaign and (anti-EU) No campaign received between 9 May and 5 June (Referendum day).

Consolidating these figures illustrates

> the grossly unequal treatment of the two sides [the No and Yes campaigns] as far as sympathetic column inches were concerned. Omitting the extreme case of the *Morning Star* the mean balance was 54 per cent pro-EU and 21 per cent anti-EU (with the rest neutral content).[49]

Furthermore, with the exception of the *Morning Star*, the rest of the national newspapers, with a readership of 14.2 million, campaigned for a Yes vote.

The Economic and Political Elite in the 1970s

The position on European integration adopted by the key institutions that constitute the economic and political elite is shown in Tables 3 and 4.

Table 2: National Newspapers' Referendum Coverage (between May and June 1975)

Newspaper (circulation figures, in May 1975, in parentheses)	Pro-EU column inches (% in parentheses)	Anti-EU	Neutral	Total*
Daily Mirror (4,001,000)	2,436 (69)	538 (15)	561 (16)	3,535 (100)
The Sun (3,419,000)	1,408 (55)	529 (20)	646 (25)	2,583 (100)
Daily Express (2,819,000)	1,722 (48)	665 (19)	1,185 (33)	3,572 (100)
Daily Mail (1,742,000)	1,672 (61)	476 (17)	605 (22)	2,753 (100)
Daily Telegraph (1,333,000)	2,492 (55)	884 (19)	1,163 (26)	4,539 (100)
The Guardian (338,000)	3,420 (46)	2,112 (29)	1,868 (25)	7,400 (100)
The Times (320,000)	2,652 (42)	1,607 (25)	2,086 (33)	6,345 (100)
Financial Times (182,000)	3,563 (55)	1,405 (21)	1,567 (24)	6,535 (100)
Morning Star *(not available)*	102 (2)	3,077 (95)	59 (2)	3,238 (100)

Source: Butler and Kitzinger.[48]
*includes adverts, articles, cartoons and photographs.

The elite united around a pro-EU consensus in the 1970s. It was motivated by a number of economic and political factors, as revealed in the declassified and official records: (a) the belief that entry would deliver a bigger home market for British companies; (b) the anticipation that Britain's economy would become more efficient as a result of greater competition from continental European rivals; (c) the expectation that Britain would benefit from an increase in the rate of economic growth and, therefore, a higher standard of living; (d) the hope that entry would provide a new power system upon which Britain could preserve its "great power" status and its world influence; (e) the wish to maintain the "special relationship" with the United States, which favoured British entry and (f) the determination to derail any attempt to construct a European bloc that was independent of the United States.[50] Accordingly, the Conservative and Labour governments, the Conservative and Liberal parties, a minority within the Labour Party, most of the Civil Service and much of the corporate sector backed Britain's accession in 1973 and recommended a vote in favour of continued membership in the 1975 Referendum. Furthermore, the elite deployed its substantial power resources to achieve such objectives.

Table 3: Position of Key Institutions on Accession, between 1971 and 1973

For accession
• Conservative Government • Conservative Party – the 1971 Conference voted by 2,471 to 324 in favour of entry, while • the 1972 Conference called for the EU to be shaped in Britain's "national interest' • Liberal Party • Civil Service – with the exception of the Ministry of Agriculture and the Treasury • Corporate sector – the Confederation of British Industry (CBI) published two reports in 1970 recommending entry, the CBI Small Firms Council voted in favour of entry, while CBI Regional Councils reported that small, medium and large companies across Britain backed entry
Against accession
• Labour Party • Ministry of Agriculture • Treasury • Trades Union Congress (TUC) and the wider trade union movement – with the exception of the municipal workers' trade union • British Left

Table 4: Position of Key Institutions on Continued Membership in the 1975 Referendum

Campaigned for a Yes vote (continued membership of EU)
• Labour Government • Conservative Party • Liberal Party • Civil Service • Corporate sector – a CBI survey of 419 chief executives of major companies (April 1975) found that 415 supported continued membership of the EU
Campaigned for a No vote (withdrawal from EU)
• Labour Party • TUC and the wider trade union movement – with the exception of the municipal workers' trade union • British Left

CASE STUDY 2

The National Press in the 2000s

The editorial line on the euro pursued by the main national newspapers between January 2002 (when the euro was launched as an actual currency) and June 2003 (when the Treasury published its assessment of the five economic tests) is shown in Table 5.

The main national newspapers were divided over whether Britain should adopt the euro. Five national newspapers, with a readership of 4 million, supported euro entry, while five newspapers, with a readership of 7.5 million, opposed it.

The editorial line on the European Constitution pursued by the main national newspapers between December 2001 (when the Convention on the Future of Europe was established) and May/June 2005 (when the Netherlands

Table 5: Number of Editorials on the Euro (between January 2002 and June 2003; Circulation Figures, in July 2002, Are in Parentheses)

Type of newspaper	Pro-euro		Anti-euro	
Tabloid	*Daily Express* (936,091)	30	*Daily Mail* (2,350, 689)	27
	Daily Mirror (2,092,034)	32	*The Sun* (3,609,269)	30
Broadsheet	*Financial Times* (432,883)	12	*Daily Telegraph* (946,926)	28
	The Guardian (375,432)	8	*The Times* (632,638)	18
	The Independent (191,875)	34	—	—
Left-wing	—	—	*Morning Star*	—

Table 6: Number of Editorials on the European Constitution (between December 2001 and June 2005; Circulation Figures, in September 2004, Are in Parentheses)

Type of newspaper	Pro-European constitution		Anti-European constitution	
Tabloid	*Daily Express* (893,614)	35	*Daily Mail* (2,346,229)	45
	Daily Mirror (1,793,718)	28	*The Sun* (3,336,322)	31
Broadsheet	*Financial Times* (406,530)	36	*Daily Telegraph* (866,041)	51
	The Guardian (350,409)	27	*The Times* (620,870)	50
	The Independent (228,174)	36	—	—
Left-wing	—	—	*Morning Star*	—

and France rejected the European Constitution in their referendums) is shown in Table 6.
The main national newspapers were divided over whether Britain should ratify the European Constitution. Five national newspapers, with a readership of 3.7 million, supported the European Constitution, while five national newspapers, with a readership of 7.2 million, opposed it.

The Economic and Political Elite in the 2000s

The position on the euro and the European Constitution adopted by the key institutions that constitute the economic and political elite is shown in Table 7.

The elite was divided on the question of further European integration in the early 2000s. However, it was primarily concerned with tactics and timing rather than fundamentally challenging the issue of continued membership of the EU. Instead, the elite disagreed about whether and when to support euro entry and the ratification of the European Constitution. Some fractions of the elite supported the euro and the European Constitution on the basis that, economically, the EU constituted an important market and, politically, Britain needed to fully engage with the European integration process so as to shape its nature and trajectory. Other fractions, however, were opposed to the construction of a social Europe, manifest in the Social Chapter, European Commission directives, the Charter of Fundamental Rights and so on, and, therefore, were opposed to any attempt to impose such a model on Britain. In short, the corporate sector feared the development of a social democratic or socialist EU. The opinion polls conducted within the corporate sector illustrate that there were significant divisions within and between the financial and manufacturing sectors of the economy, and within and between small, medium and large companies, over these matters.

The debate within the corporate sector is mirrored in the debate among the political elite. The New Labour government and the then-prime minister, Tony Blair, supported the principle of a European single currency and favoured early euro entry, while the then-chancellor of the exchequer, Gordon Brown, was more cautious. Likewise, Blair supported the European Constitution, while Brown was more equivocal. The Liberal Democrats, the nationalist parties, the Foreign Office, the engineers' trade union, the municipal workers" trade union and the TUC supported the Blair line, preferring early euro entry and the ratification of the European Constitution, while the Labour Party, the Treasury, the TGWU and Unison backed the Brown position. Meanwhile, the Conservative Party, as the official opposition, was hostile towards the euro and the European Constitution. Indeed, in March 2000 an anti-EU faction of the Conservative Party persuaded a

Table 7: Position of key institutions on the euro and the European Constitution (between 2001 and 2005)

For the euro and the European constitution

- New Labour Government
- Labour Party
- Liberal Democrats
- Plaid Cymru
- Scottish National Party
- Civil Service – with the exception of the Treasury
- The TUC and sections of the wider trade union movement, particularly the engineers' trade union and municipal workers" trade union – a MORI poll of trade unionists (September 1999) found that 38 per cent supported euro entry. An ICM poll of trade unionists (August 2002) found that 32 per cent supported euro entry
- Parts of the corporate sector:
  - (a) A MORI survey of FTSE 500 companies (September 1998) found that 77 per cent supported continued membership of the EU and 48 per cent favoured euro entry
  - (b) An HSBC survey of small companies (1999) found that 23 per cent supported euro entry
  - (c) A MORI survey for the Engineering Employers Federation (March 2001) found that 74 per cent supported euro entry
  - (d) An ICM survey (September 2002) found that 31 per cent of companies supported euro entry
  - (e) An HSBC survey of small companies (2002) found that 61 per cent supported euro entry
  - (f) An Institute of Directors survey of 1,000 members (February 2005) found that 29 per cent backed the European Constitution
  - (g) A MORI survey for the British Chambers of Commerce (January 2003) found that 35 per cent supported euro entry
  - (h) A MORI survey of finance directors (April 2005) found that 32 per cent favoured the European Constitution
  - (i) A Clifford Chance survey (April 2005) found that 62 per cent of companies of all sizes believed that the EU Single Market was good for business
  - (j) A YouGov survey of 50 FTSE 100 and FTSE 250 chief executives (March 2006) found that 68 per cent believed that the Single Market was good for business, 70 per cent supported EU enlargement and 78 per cent favoured continued membership of the EU
  - (k) An ICM survey for Open Europe of 1,000 chief executives (September 2006) found that 43 per cent believed that the benefits of the Single Market outweighed the costs of extra EU regulation, while 36 per cent felt that the EU was a success and that Britain should join the euro and cede more power to the EU

(*continued*)

Table 7: (*continued*)

Against the euro and the European constitution
• Conservative Party – a survey of party members, announced at the 1998 Conference, found that 85 per cent opposed euro entry for the duration of the 1997–2001 parliament and the subsequent parliament • Treasury – its assessment of the five economic tests ruled out euro entry • Transport and General Workers' Union (TGWU) and Unison (the public sector trade union) – a MORI survey of trade unionists (September 1999) found that 55 per cent opposed euro entry. An ICM survey of trade unionists (August 2002) found that 49 per cent opposed euro entry • British Left • Parts of the corporate sector: (a) A MORI survey of FTSE 500 companies (September 1998) found that 16 per cent supported withdrawal from the EU and 28 per cent opposed euro entry (b) A MORI survey for the Engineering Employers Federation (March 2001) found that 22 per cent opposed euro entry (c) An ICM survey (September 2002) found that 66 per cent of companies opposed euro entry (d) A MORI survey for the British Chamber of Commerce (January 2003) found that 13 per cent opposed euro entry (e) An Institute of Directors survey of 1,000 members (February 2005) found that 49 per cent opposed the European Constitution (f) A MORI survey of finance directors (April 2005) found that 68 per cent opposed the European Constitution (g) A Clifford Chance survey (April 2005) found that 27 per cent of companies of all sizes did not believe that the Single Market was good for business (h) A YouGov survey of 50 FTSE 100 and FTSE 250 chief executives (March 2006) found that 12 per cent did not believe the Single Market was good for business, 8 per cent opposed EU enlargement and 18 per cent opposed continued membership of the EU (i) An ICM survey for Open Europe of 1,000 chief executives (September 2006) found that 54 per cent believed that the costs of extra EU regulation outweighed the benefits of the Single Market, while 52 per cent felt that the EU was failing and that Britain should not adopt the euro and should repatriate power from the EU

US Senate committee to investigate the possibility of Britain leaving the EU and joining the North American Free Trade Agreement. However, the committee report, published in August, opposed such a move on the basis that withdrawal from the EU would cause considerable damage to the British economy.

Applying the Propaganda Model

Applying the operative principles of the PM to the case studies helps to explain the difference in national press coverage in the 1970s compared to the 2000s.

Ownership. Media ownership in Britain, like the United States, has long been highly concentrated, as shown in Table 8.

In the early post-war period, "a substantial section of the press remained subject to the personal control of aggressively interventionist proprietors." For these businessmen "ownership of newspapers" became one strategy by which they "sought to influence the environment in which they operated".[51] Following the decimation of the centre-left press in the 1960s and 1970s as a result of market forces, more specifically the lack of advertising revenue, these corporations progressively increased their share of the market such that by 1988, three corporations controlled "57 per cent of the *total* daily and Sunday circulation, and "three out of the four *national* newspapers sold in Britain".[52] Furthermore, these corporations, often linked through cross-ownership, diversified their holdings to become multinational conglomerates which were thoroughly integrated into the "core sectors of financial and industrial capital". Indeed, "British newspapers and other media interests were, in many cases, merely the northern outposts of global media empires."[53] The national press, whether in 1970s or the 2000s, was not an independent "fourth estate"; rather it was an integral part of the corporate sector. Consequently, it is reasonable to expect that the "guided market system" identified in the PM is applicable within the British context. Furthermore, given the corporate nature of the British media, it is logical to assume that any consensus or dissensus among the elite on European integration will be reflected in the national press coverage of that issue, as was indeed the case.

Table 8: Ownership of the Main National Newspapers in Britain

Newspaper	Owner in 1970s	Owner in 2000s
Daily Express	Beaverbrook Newspapers	Northern and Shell
Daily Mail	Associated Newspapers	Daily Mail and General Trust
Daily Mirror	Reed International	Trinity Mirror
Daily Telegraph	Viscount Camrose	Sir David and Sir Frederick Barclay
Financial Times	Pearson	Pearson
The Guardian	Scott Trust	Scott Trust
The Independent	—	Independent News and Media
The Sun	News International	News International
The Times	Times Newspapers	News International

Advertising. The abolition of newsprint rationing in 1956 "had the effect of restoring the national press's heavy dependence on advertising. It also resulted in a net redistribution of advertising away from the reformist press to its Conservative opponents."[54] Furthermore, commercial pressures precipitated the general de-politicization of the national press. One of the fears on the part of the corporate sector in the 1970s was that a failure to join the EU and, once Britain was a, a vote to withdraw, would bolster anti-EU forces on the left and risk a resurgence of economic nationalism. Indeed, contingency planning by the Foreign Office in the event of a No vote in the 1975 Referendum included the possible reintroduction of some form of rationing to cope with the expected economic crisis.[55] Such a situation would have detracted from the "buying mood" sought by advertisers and the corporate sector more generally.[56] In the 2000s, however, there was no such threat from the left. Consequently, even if referendums on the euro and European Constitution had been staged, and the British people had voted against, the cases of the referendums in Denmark (2000), Sweden (2003), France (2005) and the Netherlands (2005) suggest that advertisers and the corporate sector would have continued to thrive in the outer lane of a "two-speed" EU. In short, the economic and political environment and the interests of the corporate sector were very different in the 2000s compared to the 1970s.

Sourcing. Herman and Chomsky argued that "the mass media are drawn into a symbiotic relationship with powerful sources of information by economic necessity and reciprocity of interest."[57] Private corporations, the state and other bureaucracies "turn out a large volume of material that meets the demands of news organizations for reliable, scheduled flows". Furthermore, these sources are viewed as credible and are treated as "'objective' dispensers of the news".[58] The main sources of information in Britain include the government (e.g. the Central Office of Information), political parties (e.g. the New Labour "spin machine"), corporate organizations (e.g. the CBI) and international organizations (e.g. the European Commission Information Service). The pro-EU consensus among the elite in the 1970s resulted in most of the main sources issuing material that was positive about European integration. This was reinforced by Britain's second concerted pro-EU propaganda campaign in 1971, which was allegedly part-funded by the US Central Intelligence Agency.[59] Ernest Wistrich, then director, reported that the European Movement alone spent over £1 million on this campaign, while Douglas Evans noted that anti-EU forces spent only £50,000.[60] In short, the attempt by anti-EU forces to influence the "great debate" on accession was swamped by the pro-EU campaign. The imbalance was even more pronounced as a result of Britain's third concerted pro-EU propaganda campaign during the 1975 Referendum. The No and Yes campaigns both enjoyed access to government grants of £125,000. However, the Yes campaign managed to raise an additional £1.8 million from the corporate sector and other sources, while the No campaign merely secured an extra £8,610.[61] Once again, anti-EU forces were overwhelmed. The elite dissensus in the 2000s, by contrast, resulted in some of the main sources issuing material that was sceptical of further European integration. Likewise, the use of propaganda was more evenly balanced. Material was disseminated by the New Labour government that Britain was positive about euro entry and the European Constitution. However, Eurosceptic forces had increased their financial resources and organizational capacity, manifest in the formation of Business for Sterling, New Europe and Open Europe. These forces, which were sceptical of, if not hostile towards, the euro and the European Constitution, were successful in influencing the national press agenda.

Flak. Herman and Chomsky explained that "'flak' refers to negative responses to a media statement or programme" which "may be organized centrally or locally, or it may consist of the entirely independent actions of individuals". They further argued that the "ability to produce flak, and especially flak that is costly and threatening, is related to power."[62] Pro-EU forces dominated the production of flak in the 1970s. During the 1975 Referendum, for example, the anti-EU Secretary of State for Industry, Tony Benn, warned that "we have probably lost half a million jobs as a result of our trade deficit" with the EU. The fear that the No campaign would exploit the public's concern about unemployment prompted a series of attacks on Benn from his pro-EU Cabinet colleagues and from the national press. The *Daily Mirror*, for example, talked of "Lies, More Lies and Those Damned Statistics", dubbing Benn the "Minister of Fear".[63] In the 2000s, pro-EU forces continued to deploy flak in an attempt to shape the national press agenda. The European Commission, for example, issued a pamphlet in 2000 attacking what it saw as the unfair reporting of the EU.[64] However, given their greater resources and power, anti-EU forces also began to deploy flak. In 2000, the Global Britain think tank commissioned Minotaur Media Tracking (2000, 2001) to investigate the allegation that the coverage provided by the British Broadcasting Corporation (BBC) was biased in favour of the EU.[65] This prompted the BBC Board of Governors to commission its own report[66] and to issue a public statement defending BBC impartiality on the issue.[67]

Anti-communism. The Western ideology of anti-communism "helps mobilize the populace against an enemy, and because the concept is fuzzy it can be used against anybody advocating policies that threaten property interests or support accommodation with Communist states and radicalism".[68] Hollingsworth and James Curran and Jean Seaton documented the long history of national press campaigns against the Labour Party and the wider left in Britain in the name of "anti-communism". During the 1975 Referendum, pro-EU forces attempted to associate the No campaign, and Benn in particular, with the spectre of "communism". One of the civil servants active during the 1975 Referendum later complained that

> Most of my colleagues thought that [anti-EU Cabinet Minister] Peter Shore was a "fellow traveller" and Tony Benn was regarded as a Communist. In the whole of Whitehall, at the middle level, there was fear all over the place and the "antis" were being labelled as Communists and "fellow travellers".[69]

Meanwhile, Benn was portrayed by many national newspapers as a "dangerous radical". The *Sunday Express*, for example, claimed he aspired to become the "Commissar of an Iron Curtain Britain" (1 June 1975). Such reporting led Hollingsworth to argue that the personalization of the referendum "was so intense that a Yes or No vote really meant whether you were "for" or "against" Tony Benn as an individual politician."[70] By the 2000s, however, the ideology of "anti-communism" was redundant. Herman suggested that in the post-Cold War period the ideology had been replaced by the ideological "belief in the market",[71] while Chomsky argued that the new fifth filter was fear: "because if people are frightened, they will accept authority."[72] There is evidence that both anti- and pro-EU forces deployed fear in the 2000s. The former claimed that pro-Europeans were "regulators" intent on imposing a social Europe and destroying British jobs in the process, while the latter claimed that Eurosceptics were "extremists" whose explicit or implicit support for withdrawal threatened trading relations and the millions of jobs that depended upon continued membership of the EU.

In terms of explaining editorial positions, the PM predicted that the elite consensus of the 1970s would be reflected in the national press coverage, as indeed was the case; nearly all the main national newspapers adopted a pro-EU position during this period. Likewise, the PM predicted that the elite dissensus of the 2000s would be reflected in the national press coverage, which was also true; newspapers were evenly divided on the euro and the European Constitution. In terms of explaining the difference in coverage between the two periods, transformations in the operation of the five filters further demonstrated the utility of the PM. Although Britain's media system and political structure are different to that in the United States, the corporate nature of the British media in the 1970s, and its thorough integration into the capitalist global economy by the 2000s, renders it ripe for analysis using the PM. The interests of advertisers and the corporate sector in the 1970s, namely, the desire for the economic and political stability provided by the EU, had altered significantly by the 2000s, when further European integration carried considerable risks for business. In the 1970s, the pro-EU elite dominated the sourcing of information, the use propaganda, the deployment of flak and the manipulation of fear. By the 2000s, however, Eurosceptic sections of the elite were also engaging in such activities. In short, the modification of the five filters precipitated a dramatic shift in national press coverage of European integration over time.

EXPLAINING THE MARGINALIZATION OF THE PROPAGANDA MODEL

The criticisms of the PM set out above, which were rebutted by Herman and Jeffery Klaehn,[73] were little more than obfuscation, for none of these critics, some of whom used to work within the political economy tradition, had actually addressed or engaged with the operative principles of the PM, its predictions or the vast amount of empirical, supportive data presented by Herman and Chomsky. Why was this? First, scholars neglected the PM, and the work of Herman and Chomsky more generally, because they were seen as "outsiders" to the discipline; consequently they were not considered to be "legitimate" analysts within the field of media and communication studies. Second, Chomsky in particular had been regularly smeared by his opponents as an apologist for totalitarian regimes and a "self-hating Jew". Consequently many scholars avoided such a seemingly "controversial" figure. Third, following the "cultural turn" in media and communication studies in the 1980s and 1990s, with its focus on culture, discourse and identity, there had been move away from empirical and political economy-based studies of the media, of which the PM was exemplary. Fourth, the PM challenged the mainstream consensus. That the PM should be ignored by liberals and those on the centre-left should come as no surprise; after all, the PM, or more specifically, its predictions and the wealth of empirical evidence that support these, effectively demolished their worldview of how media and political systems operated. What was more surprising was how many academics on the left, who claimed to be empirical social scientists, had also neglected the PM and its radical implications for the operation of the mass media in contemporary capitalist societies.

The practical implications of such marginalization were lamentable. Media and communication students were often not exposed to the PM, as it rarely featured in mainstream textbooks and seldom appeared in the curricula of undergraduate and postgraduate courses. Likewise, media and communication scholars did not engage in debates about the PM in their journals or at their conferences. The result has been 20 years at the margins; a devastating indictment of the state of academia given that the PM was, as Chomsky argued, one of the most tested models in the social sciences.

THE CONTINUED RELEVANCE OF THE PROPAGANDA MODEL

In the updated 2002 edition of *Manufacturing Consent*, Herman and Chomsky attended to some of the economic, political and technological transformations that had occurred since the book's original publication in 1988. In terms of economic factors, they highlighted

> the media's gradual centralization and concentration, the growth of media conglomerates that control many different kinds of media... and the spread of the media across borders in a globalization process. [They] also noted the gradual displacement of family control by professional managers serving a wider array of owners and more closely subject to market discipline.[74]

The end result was that "two dozen firms control nearly the entirety of media experienced by most US citizens."[75] Herman and Chomsky also argued that, as a consequence of the neoliberal globalization process, media corporations have actively encouraged governments in the West, together with the International Monetary Fund and the World Bank, to open up media markets across the globe, thus further entrenching their dominance. They pointed to the increased commercialization of the global media and its promotion of consumerism.[76] They described the deleterious impact of increased competition, deregulation and privatization on the non-commercial media and public service broadcasting, arguing that those which remained were increasingly forced to emulate commercial systems.

In terms of political factors, Herman and Chomsky conceded that the end of the Cold War effectively undermined the anti-communist ideology that so figured in their earlier writings. Nevertheless,

> this is easily offset by the greater ideological force of the belief in the "miracle of the market".... The triumph of capitalism and the increasing power of those with an interest in privatization and market rule have strengthened the grip of market ideology, at least among the elite, so that regardless of evidence, markets are assumed to be benevolent and even democratic... and non-market mechanisms are suspect.... Journalism has internalized this ideology. Adding it to the residual power of anti-communism in a world in which the global power of market institutions makes non-market options seem utopian gives us an ideological package of immense strength.[77]

To this package could be added the ideological power of the "war on terror" and the "us and them" dichotomy, promoted by many academics, journalists and politicians across the political spectrum, which have helped to galvanize public support for elite interests since the end of the Cold War.

In terms of technological factors, Herman and Chomsky reflected upon the argument that "the Internet and the new communications technologies are breaking the corporate stranglehold on journalism and opening an unprecedented era of interactive democratic media."[78] While acknowledging that the new media had increased the efficiency and scope of individual and group networking, resulting in some important victories for protest movements, they determined that such a claim was not justified as

> [The Internet] has limitations as a critical tool. For one thing, those whose information needs are most acute are not well served by the Internet – many lack access, its databases are not designed to meet their needs, and the use of databases (and effective use of the Internet in general) presupposes knowledge and organization. [Furthermore] the privatization of the Internet's hardware, the rapid commercialization and concentration of Internet portals and servers and their integration into non-Internet conglomerates – the AOL–Time Warner merger was a giant step in that direction – and the private and concentrated control of the new broadband technology, together threaten to limit any future prospects of the Internet as a democratic media vehicle.[79]

These developments were compounded by the "rapid penetration of the Internet by the leading newspapers and media conglomerates, all fearful of being outflanked by small pioneer users of the new technology, and willing (and able) to accept losses for years while testing out these new waters".[80] In short, the traditional media, dominated by corporations, are colonizing the new media.

The end result, Herman and Chomsky reasoned, was that the five filters, and thus the explanatory power of the PM, had been strengthened, rather than diminished, by such developments. Ownership, the first filter, had become more concentrated than it was in 1988. Advertising, the second filter, had become more important as the global media became increasingly commercialized, seeking out new ways to sell products by expanding into the new media. Sourcing, the third filter, continued to be dominated by corporate and government bodies – witness, for example, the emergence of "embedded journalists" during recent wars,[81] the covert media operations before and during the 2003 Iraq war,[82] the "full spectrum dominance" objective of the strategic communication documents issued by the US government and so on.[83] Flak, the fourth filter, remained an effective weapon in the hands of elites, while anti-communism, the fifth filter, had been superseded by the ideology of "the market". In short, "the changes in politics and communication over the past dozen years have tended on balance to enhance the applicability of the "Propaganda Model"."[84]

To focus upon one of the filters, sourcing, Herman and Chomsky stated that "studies of news sources reveal that a significant proportion of news originates in public relations releases. There are, by one count, 20,000 more public relations agents working to doctor the news today than there are journalists writing it."[85] Further evidence to support this view was advanced by Nick Davies in his book, *Flat Earth News*.[86] Davies described how he commissioned research which surveyed more than 2,000 British news stories from the four quality dailies (*Times*, *Telegraph*, *Guardian*, *Independent*) and the *Daily Mail*. The researchers found that only 12 per cent of the stories were wholly composed of material researched by reporters; 80 per cent of the stories were wholly, mainly or partially constructed from second-hand material provided by news agencies and by the public relations industry. They also found that facts had been thoroughly checked in only 12 per cent of the stories. Davies commented:

> The implication of those two findings is truly alarming. Where once journalists were active gatherers of news, now they have generally become mere passive processors of unchecked, second-hand material, much of it contrived by PR to serve some political or commercial interest. Not journalists, but churnalists. An industry whose primary task is to filter out falsehood has become so vulnerable to manipulation that it is now involved in the mass production of falsehood, distortion and propaganda.[87]

CONCLUSION

Despite its systematic marginalization within the field of media and communication studies over the last 20 years, the PM has stood the test of time. While intellectual fashions and media theories have come and gone, the three hypotheses advanced by Herman and Chomsky, which have been repeatedly confirmed by a wealth of overwhelmingly supportive empirical evidence, have been shown to be robust and enduring. Indeed, recent economic, political and technological transformations, more specifically globalization, the ideological hegemony of "the market", and the corporate colonization of the new media have strengthened the explanatory power of the PM. In undertaking this work, Herman and Chomsky have helped to answer the fundamental question alluded to earlier. Quite simply, the liberal-pluralist view of how the media system operates is fanciful, while the Marxist-radical critique is more in accord with reality. Herman and Chomsky also demonstrated the importance and continued relevance of the political economy approach to media analysis. Power is central to this type of conceptual framework and is critically important when trying to understand and explain how media systems operate. Power is reflected in, and exercised through, media ownership, advertising, sourcing, flak and ideology – the key factors within the PM. Furthermore, as suggested by several studies, including the data presented earlier on the transformation over time of British press coverage of European integration, the PM is not only appropriate in the US context but it is also applicable in media systems in other capitalist, liberal-democratic countries. Indeed, the globalizing nature of the media suggests that the PM may have a much wider, perhaps near-universal, application. Such a bold claim, however logical, could only be substantiated by a concerted and transnational research effort. What is clear, though, is that Herman and Chomsky have substantially advanced our knowledge of the media over the last 20 years. Furthermore, any attempt to understand and explain the media in the 21st century should acknowledge and build upon the PM.

NOTES

1. E. Herman and N. Chomsky, *Manufacturing Consent: The Political Economy of the Mass Media*, New York: Pantheon, 1988, p. xi.
2. Published by Pantheon (New York).
3. B. Ginsberg, *The Captive Public: How Mass Opinion Promotes State Power*, New York: Basic Books, 1986, p. 86.
4. The first estate under the French *Ancien Régime*, before the 1789 revolution, was the church; the second estate was the nobility; the third estate was the commoners and the fourth estate was the press.
5. Herman and Chomsky, *Manufacturing Consent*, p. xi.
6. G. Mosca, *The Ruling Class*, translated and edited by A. Livingstone, New York: McGraw-Hill, 1939; V. Pareto, *The Mind and Society*, translated by A. Livingstone and A. Bongiaro, New York: Harcourt-Brace, 1935; J. Burnham, *The Managerial Revolution*, New York: Day, 1941; R. Michels, *Political Parties*, Glencoe, IL: Free Press, 1949; C. Wright Mills, *The Power Elite*, New York: Oxford University Press, 1956; J. Schumpeter, *Capitalism, Socialism and Democracy*, London: Allen and Unwin, 1976.
7. It is important to note, however, that the Marxist-radical tradition is not a monolithic bloc; there are important disagreements and debates between classical and modern Marxists, and between anarchists and Marxists, on the primacy of the economy, ideology, the role of the state and many other questions.
8. M. Gurevitch, T. Bennett, J. Curran and J. Woollacott (Eds.), *Culture, Society and the Media*, London: Methuen, 1982, p. 2.
9. Herman and Chomsky, *Manufacturing Consent*, p. xi.
10. Ibid., p. xii.
11. E. Herman, "The Propaganda Model Revisited", *Monthly Review*, Vol. 48, July–August 1996.
12. T. Ferguson, *Golden Rule*, Chicago: University of Chicago Press, 1995.
13. Herman and Chomsky, *Manufacturing Consent*, p. xii.
14. Herman, "The Propaganda Model Revisited".
15. P. Robinson, "Theorizing the Influence of Media on World Politics: Models of Media Influence on Foreign Policy", *European Journal of Communication*, Vol. 16, No. 4, p. 527, 2001.

16. G. Wolfsfeld, *The Media and Political Conflict*, Cambridge: Cambridge University Press, 1997; Robinson, "Theorizing the Influence of Media".
17. Herman and Chomsky, *Manufacturing Consent*, p. xii.
18. See, for example, E. Fones-Wolf, *Selling Free Enterprise: The Business Assault on Labor and Liberalism, 1945–60*, Chicago: University of Illinois Press, 1994; M. Hughes, *Spies at Work*, Bradford, UK: 1 in 12 Publications, 1994; A. Carey, *Taking the Risk Out of Democracy: Propaganda in the US and Australia*, Sydney: University of New South Wales Press, 1995; S. Ewen, *PR! A Social History of Spin*, New York: Basic Books, 1996; S. Beder, *Suiting Themselves: How Corporations Drive the Global Agenda*, London: Earthscan, 2006; S. Beder, *Free Market Missionaries: The Corporate Manipulation of Community Values*, London: Earthscan, 2006; W. Dinan and D. Miller, *Thinker, Faker, Spinner, Spy: Corporate PR and the Assault on Democracy*, London: Pluto, 2007; D. Miller and W. Dinan, *A Century of Spin: How Public Relations Became the Cutting Edge of Corporate Power*, London: Pluto, 2008.
19. Herman and Chomsky, *Manufacturing Consent*, p. 2.
20. A. Edgley, *The Social and Political Thought of Noam Chomsky*, London: Routledge, 2000, p. 29.
21. Ibid., pp. 27, 28, 29.
22. Herman and Chomsky, *Manufacturing Consent*, p. 37.
23. Published by Pantheon (New York).
24. Herman and Chomsky, *Manufacturing Consent*, p. xlii.
25. P. Mitchell and J. Schoeffel (Eds.), *Understanding Power: The Indispensable Chomsky*, New York: New Press, 2002, p. 18.
26. N. Chomsky, *Necessary Illusions: Thought Control in Democratic Societies*, London: Pluto, 1989, p. 153.
27. Ibid., p. 154.
28. N. Lemann, "Book Reviews", *The New Republic*, 9 January 1989.
29. W. LaFeber, "Whose news?" *New York Times*, 6 November 1988.
30. P. Schlesinger, "From Production to Propaganda", *Media, Culture and Society*, Vol. 11, pp. 283–306, 1989; P. Golding and G. Murdock, "Culture, Communications and Political Economy" in J. Curran and M. Gurevitch (Eds.), *Mass Media and Society*, London: Edward Arnold, 1991; J. Eldridge (Ed.), *Getting the Message*, New York: Routledge, 1993.
31. D. Hallin, *We Keep America on Top of the World*, New York: Routledge, 1994; C. Sparks, "Extending and Refining the Propaganda Model", *Westminster Papers in Communication and Culture*, Vol. 4, No. 2, pp. 68–84, 2007.
32. J. Corner, "Debate: The Model in Question – A Response to Klaehn on Herman and Chomsky", *European Journal of Communication*, Vol. 18, No. 3, p. 369, 2003.
33. B. McNair, *News and Journalism in the UK*, Fourth Edition, London: Routledge, 2003.
34. Corner, "Debate: The Model in Question".
35. E. Herman, *The Real Terror Network: Terrorism in Fact and Propaganda*, Boston: South End Press, 1982; M. Parenti, *Inventing Reality: The Politics of the Mass Media*, New York: St Martins, 1986; E. Herman and G. O'Sullivan, *The "Terrorism" Industry: The Experts and Institutions That Shape Our View of Terror*, New York: Pantheon Books, 1989; J. Aronson, *The Press and the Cold War*, Revised Edition, New York: Monthly Review Press, 1990; M. Lee and N. Solomon, *Unreliable Sources: A Guide to Detecting Bias in News Media*, New York: Lyle Stuart, 1990; E. Herman, *Beyond Hypocrisy: Decoding the News in an Age of Propaganda*,

Boston: South End Press, 1992; J. Winter, *Common Cents: Media Portrayal of the Gulf War and Other Events*, Montreal: Black Rose Books, 1992; G. Gunn, *A Critical View of Western Journalism and Scholarship on East Timor*, Sydney: Journal of Contemporary Asian Studies, 1994; J. McMurtry, *Unequal Freedoms: The Global Market as an Ethical System*, Toronto: Garamond Press, 1998; J. Winter, *Democracy's Oxygen: How the Corporations Control the News*, Second Edition, Montreal: Black Rose Books, 1998; P. Hammond and E. Herman (Eds.), *Degraded Capability: The Media and the Kosovo Crisis*, London: Pluto Press, 2000; E. Herman and N. Chomsky, *Manufacturing Consent: The Political Economy of the Mass Media*, Updated Edition, New York: Pantheon Books, 2002; J. Winter, *MediaThink*, Montreal: Black Rose Books, 2002; R. Babe, "Newspaper Discourses on Environment" in J. Klaehn (Ed.), *Filtering the News: Essays on Herman and Chomsky's Propaganda Model*, London: Black Rose Books, 2005; J. Klaehn, "Corporate Hegemony: A Critical Assessment of *The Globe* and *Mail's* News Coverage of Near-Genocide in Occupied East Timor, 1975–1991" in J. Klaehn (Ed.), *Filtering the News: Essays on Herman and Chomsky's Propaganda Model*, London: Black Rose Books, 2005; J. Winter and J. Klaehn, "The Propaganda Model under Protest" in J. Klaehn (Ed.), *Filtering the News: Essays on Herman and Chomsky's Propaganda Model*, London: Black Rose Books, 2005.

36. R. Miliband, *The State in Capitalist Society*, London: Weidenfeld and Nicholson, 1969; W. Domhoff, *The Powers That Be: Processes of Ruling Class Domination in America*, New York: Vintage Books, 1979; L. Curtis, *Ireland: The Propaganda War*, London: Pluto, 1984; Glasgow University Media Group, *War and Peace News*, Milton Keynes, UK: Open University Press, 1985; D. Hallin, *The Uncensored War*, Berkeley: University of California Press, 1986; M. Hollingsworth, *The Press and Political Dissent: A Question of Censorship*, London: Pluto, 1986; L. Bennett, "Towards a Theory of Press–State Relations in the United States", *Journal of Communication*, Vol. 40, No. 2, pp. 103–125, 1990; R. Entman, "Framing US Coverage of International News: Contrasts in Narratives of the KAL and Iran Air Incidents", *Journal of Communication*, Vol. 41, No. 4, pp. 6–27, 1991; G. Philo and G. McLaughlin, *The British Media and the Gulf War*, Glasgow, UK: Glasgow University Media Group, 1993; S. Carruthers, *Winning Hearts and Minds: British Governments, the Media and Colonial Counter-Insurgency, 1944–1960*, London: Leicester University Press, 1995; J. Zaller and D. Chui, "Government's Little Helper: US Press Coverage of Foreign Policy Crises, 1945–1991", *Political Communication*, Vol. 13, pp. 385–405, 1996; P. Lashmar and J. Oliver, *Britain's Secret Propaganda War, 1948–1977*, Gloucestershire, UK: Sutton Publishing, 1998; J. Mermin, *Debating War and Peace*, Princeton, NJ: Princeton University Press, 1999; R. Greenslade, *Press Gang: How Newspapers Make Profits from Propaganda*, London: Pan Books, 2003; P. Knightley, *The First Casualty: The War Correspondent as Hero, Propagandist and Myth-Maker from the Crimea to Iraq*, Third Edition, London: André Deutsch, 2003; D. Miller (Ed.), *Tell Me Lies: Propaganda and Media Distortion in the Attack on Iraq*, London: Pluto, 2004.
37. D. Edwards and D. Cromwell, *Guardians of Power: The Myth of the Liberal Media*, London: Pluto, 2006; D. Miller in J. Klaehn (Ed.), *Bound by Power: Intended Consequences*. London: Black Rose Books, 2006.
38. Corner, "Debate: The Model in Question", p. 367.
39. A. Doherty, "The BBC and the Propaganda Model" *Z Magazine*, 7 February 2005.
40. U. Kitzinger, *Diplomacy and Persuasion: How Britain Joined the Common Market*, London: Thames and Hudson, 1973.

41. D. Butler and U. Kitzinger, *The 1975 Referendum*, Basingstoke, UK: Macmillan, 1976; P. Goodhart, *Full-Hearted Consent: The Story of the Referendum Campaign – and the Campaign for a Referendum*, London: Davis-Poynter, 1976; A. King, *Britain Says Yes: The 1975 Referendum on the Common Market*, Washington, DC: American Enterprise Institute, 1977; Hollingsworth, *The Press and Political Dissent.*
42. G. Wilkes and D. Wring, "The British Press and European Integration: 1948 to 1996" in D. Baker and D. Seawright (Eds.), *Britain for and against Europe: British Politics and the Question of European Integration*, Oxford: Clarendon Press, 1998.
43. D. Morgan, "British Media and European Union News: The Brussels News Beat and its Problems", *European Journal of Communication*, Vol. 10, No. 3, pp. 321–343, 1995.
44. R. Greenslade, *Press Gang.*
45. J. Firmstone, "Britain in the Euro? British Newspaper Editorial Coverage of the Introduction of the Euro', *European Political Communication Working Paper 5/2003*, p. 10. Available at http://ics.leeds.ac.uk/eurpolcom/discussion_papers.cfm (accessed 1 March 2007).
46. P. Statham, "Political Journalism and Europeanization: Pressing Europe?" *European Political Communication Working Paper 13/2006*, p. 1. Available at http://ics.leeds.ac.uk/eurpolcom/discussion_papers.cfm (accessed 1 March 2007).
47. Beaverbrook Newspapers was owned by Lord Beaverbrook, a long-standing supporter of the British Empire, and then the Commonwealth, and an opponent of Britain's engagement with Europe.
48. Butler and Kitzinger, *The 1975 Referendum*, pp. 226–227.
49. Ibid. p. 224.
50. See A. Mullen, *The British Left's "Great Debate" on Europe*, London: Continuum, 2007.
51. J. Curran and J. Seaton, *Power without Responsibility: The Press and Broadcasting in Britain*, Fourth Edition, London: Routledge, 1991, pp. 85, 101.
52. Ibid. p. 91.
53. Ibid. pp. 93–94.
54. Ibid. p. 106.
55. Mullen, *The British Left's "Great Debate".*
56. Herman and Chomsky, *Manufacturing Consent*, p. 17.
57. Ibid. p.18.
58. Ibid. p.19.
59. A. Mullen, *Anti- and Pro-European Propaganda in Britain*, London: Continuum, forthcoming.
60. D. Evans, *While Britain Slept: The Selling of the Common Market*, London: Victor Gollancz, 1975; E. Wistrich, "Lessons of the 1975 Referendum" in R. Beetham (Ed.), *The Euro Debate: Persuading the People*, London: Federal Trust, 2001.
61. Butler and Kitzinger, *The 1975 Referendum.*
62. Herman and Chomsky, *Manufacturing Consent*, p.26.
63. Hollingsworth, *The Press and Political Dissent.*
64. European Commission, *A Glossary of Eurosceptic Beliefs: An Exposé of Misunderstanding*, London: European Commission Representation in the UK, 2000.
65. Minotaur Media Tracking, *The BBC and Europe*, London: Global Britain, 2000; Minotaur Media Tracking, *BBC "Europe and Us" Week*, London: Global Britain, 2001.
66. MORI, The EU: Perceptions of the BBC's Reporting, London: MORI, 2004.

67. British Broadcasting Corporation, *BBC News Coverage of the European Union: Statement by the Board of Governors*, London: BBC, 2005.
68. Herman and Chomsky, *Manufacturing Consent*, p. 29.
69. R. Broad and T. Geiger, "The 1975 Referendum on Europe: A Witness Seminar," *Contemporary Record*, Vol. 10, No. 3, p. 103, 1996.
70. Hollingsworth, *The Press and Political Dissent*, p. 48.
71. E. Herman, "The Propaganda Model: A Retrospective", *Journalism Studies*, Vol. 1, No. 1, p. 109, 2000.
72. Chomsky in P. Mitchell and J. Schoeffel, *Understanding Power*, chapter 1 footnotes. Available at: www.understandingpower.com (accessed 1 March 2007).
73. Herman, "The Propaganda Model Revisited"; "The Propaganda Model: A Retrospective"; J. Klaehn, "A Critical Review and Assessment of Herman and Chomsky's "Propaganda Model", *European Journal of Communication*, Vol. 17, No. 2, pp. 147–182, 2002; J. Klaehn, "Debate: Model Construction and Various Other Epistemological Concerns – A Reply to John Corner's Commentary on the Propaganda Model", *European Journal of Communication*, Vol. 18, No. 3, pp. 377–383, 2003; J. Klaehn, *Filtering the News*.
74. Herman and Chomsky, *Manufacturing Consent* (Updated Edition), p. xiii.
75. Ibid.
76. This would include the "dumbing down" by the media, with its increasing obsession with celebrities, fashion, gossip and so on – in short "infotainment".
77. Herman and Chomsky, *Manufacturing Consent* (Updated Edition), pp. xvii–xviii.
78. Ibid. p. xv.
79. Ibid. p. xvi.
80. Ibid.
81. See Miller, *Tell Me Lies*.
82. See D. Barstow, "Message Machine: Behind TV Analysts, Pentagon's Hidden Hand", *New York Times*, 20 April 2008.
83. See US Department of Defence, *Joint Vision 2020*, Washington, DC: Department of Defence, 2000; Department of Defence, *Report of the Defense Science Board Task Force on Strategic Communication*, Washington, DC: Department of Defence, 2004; Department of Defence, *Quadrennial Defense Review*, Washington, DC: Department of Defence.
84. Herman and Chomsky, *Manufacturing Consent* (Updated Edition), p. xvii.
85. Ibid.
86. Published by Chatto and Windus (London), 2008.
87. N. Davies, "Our Media Have Become Mass Producers of Distortion," *The Guardian*, 4 February 2008.

CHAPTER NINE

The Faculty Filter: Why the Propaganda Model is Marginalized in U.S. Journalism Schools

ROBERT JENSEN

Looking back, 1988 was a fairly important time in my life. That was the year I left my career as a reporter and editor in the corporate commercial newspaper industry and began my Ph.D. studies, focusing on media ethics and law. Since high school I had loved the craft of journalism–the process of searching through records and interviewing people about their lives, trying to understand a complex world, and then translating that understanding in an elegantly concise form using plain language for ordinary people. More than 30 years after publishing my first news story, I still love the craft of journalism, evidenced by the haste with which I abandoned the conventional scholarly world after receiving tenure to return to researching and writing for popular audiences.

But in the last few years of my career in mainstream journalism, a vague dissatisfaction grew evermore troubling, as I couldn't ignore the gap between the ideals that brought me into journalism (telling the truth, helping right wrongs, standing up for the underdog, etc.) and the reality of what much of my daily work seemed to be (filling the space between the ads in a fashion that seemed to have more to do with efficiency than ideals). That dissatisfaction led me back to graduate school, in the hopes that the intellectual and political engagement I had hoped to find in journalism would be more common in the academy.

Fortuitous for me, 1988 was also the year that *Manufacturing Consent*[1] was published. As I read, I felt as if Herman and Chomsky had published the book just for me, to help me understand how a craft that I truly loved could leave me so dissatisfied. When I studied the book in conjunction with other analyses of journalistic practices by sociologists,[2] I came to understand my previous vocation in a new way; I felt liberated by this knowledge, eager to incorporate it into my teaching. I understood my job as a journalism professor to be teaching students—most of who came into the endeavor with the same ideals I had—the basics of the craft, along with a deeper understanding of the industry than I had when I had begun my reporting career. The goal of that kind of honest assessment of the constraints of the industry was not to undermine students' idealism but to help them cope with the real-world conditions they would face in newsrooms. Because most of the other Ph.D. students I knew had spent some time in the news industry and seemed to have experienced similar frustrations as working journalists, I expected that the propaganda model would become part of the standard curriculum in journalism education. Well, it turns out that was a bit naive.

To be honest, it wasn't just naive—it was just plain stupid. I hadn't read *Manufacturing Consent* closely enough.[3] Even if I couldn't figure this out on my own, I should have noted this passage from Chomsky's 1989 book, *Necessary Illusions*:

> However well-confirmed the model may be, then, it is inadmissible, and, the model predicts, should remain outside the debate over the media.... Note that the model has a rather disconcerting feature. Plainly, it is either valid or invalid. If invalid, it may be dismissed; if valid, it *will* be dismissed.[4]

First, is the model valid? I conclude that it is, though like any model it does not (and could not, as Herman and Chomsky acknowledge) account for every decision made by every journalist in every news media outlet in the United States. Like any model in the humanities and social sciences, it tries to understand—and allows us to predict—patterns of behavior. Many have critiqued the model, which is appropriate for any serious intellectual venture.[5] Unfortunately, most of the critiques have contributed little to our understanding.[6]

As I made my way through graduate school and then landed a teaching job, my uneasiness with journalism was to be matched by my uneasiness with journalism education, which is hardly surprising. Journalism schools are trade schools, closely connected to the industry, in several obvious ways.

First, most of the personnel who staff a journalism faculty come from the industry, sometimes cycled through a graduate program and sometimes not. Many journalism schools, especially at larger universities such as the University of Texas at Austin, strive to shore up their status in the academy by employing faculty members who conduct scholarly research, along with the faculty directly from the industry who teach many of the bread-and-butter skills courses. But even most of the research faculty members have roots in the industry. More on the role of faculty later.

Second, the majority of graduates of a journalism school will go to work in corporate commercial news media outlets, and the connections that faculty members maintain with managers, editors, and reporters are important to help secure those positions for graduates. The curricular decisions of faculty members and administrators clearly reflect the role of journalism schools in this system—providing a steady supply of trained journalists willing to work within the existing industry.

Third, the media corporations and their related foundations supply some funding for research and scholarships. Every journalism school administrator knows that such relationships are crucial to a "successful" program, especially as public universities become increasingly more dependent on such external funding.

In short, whatever the high-minded rhetoric of mission statements, the actual role of journalism schools in this system is to subsidize some of the basic training costs of the industry, while at the same time indoctrinating students into the journalism-as-the-bulwark-of-freedom ideology that makes it more palatable for many students to accept low-wage entry-level jobs. Although there are occasional tensions between faculty members and industry managers, both the journalism schools and the corporate media are reasonably comfortable with this arrangement, which gives the schools a mission and a reason for existing and contributes to the industry's ability to generate considerable profits.[7]

With this context, we can return to a question that echoes Chomsky's comment: Do faculty members in journalism schools routinely ignore the propaganda model and its implications for journalism education because the model is invalid or because it's too valid? A couple of stories might help us make a determination.

Anecdote #1: I am waiting for a meeting to start with two faculty colleagues from the College of Communication at the University of Texas. One of the participants is late, and I strike up a conversation with another colleague, someone with centrist politics who is a critic of the worst excesses of the mass media but generally supportive of the industry. The subject of the propaganda model comes up, and I mention that I find it a compelling analysis. "Well," my colleague says, "there are some real problems with that model." I ask him what those problems are. He says, "That would be a great discussion to have sometime." Well, what about now? I suggest. We have time to kill waiting for this meeting to start, so why don't you give me some idea of your criticisms? "That would be a great discussion to have sometime," he repeats, indicating he has no intention of starting that discussion, then or ever. I shrug and let it pass.

Anecdote #2: I am having coffee at a scholarly conference with a professor who studies news media and teaches in the communications department of an elite university. This colleague has left/liberal politics and is critical not just of the excesses of the industry but also of some basic journalistic practices. We are talking about the state of journalism, and I mention that I include the propaganda model in my teaching. He scoffs, suggesting the model is inadequate to understand the complexity of journalism and the politics of the industry. I am somewhat surprised by this and ask him to elaborate. "Ever since the Romano article,[8] one can't take that model seriously," he explains. I counter that I had read Romano's critique and had found it, to be polite, less than persuasive. What was so compelling about it for you? I asked. "The Romano article destroys the propaganda model," he repeats. I press for more, and he sidesteps again. I shrug and let it pass.

These two exchanges help explain why journalism education is unlikely to take the propaganda model seriously. I am not arguing, nor would Herman and Chomsky, that the model must be accepted uncritically by everyone. Instead, I am claiming that the model, at minimum, is a plausible framework for analysis that would be part of the discussion in an intellectually healthy institution. That is unlikely in journalism schools in the United States, where there tend to be two basic kinds of faculty members, what we might call the professionals and the professors:

The professionals. Those whose main identification is with practicing journalists, who typically see the world in the same way as those in the industry. For these people, who tend to be centrist in political orientation, there's no reason to even consider these questions. They see the question like most journalists: The right and the left both critique journalism, therefore journalism is doing its job. They typically lack the intellectual tools to step outside the journalism profession and evaluate it, not because they aren't smart enough but because such folks tend to be trained not to think systematically and to distrust any critical political analysis that falls outside the conventional wisdom of the dominant culture. Many have never read critical works such as *Manufacturing Consent;* if they have, they typically feel no reason to respond in a serious manner.

The professors. Those whose main identification is with other academics, who are willing to critique some of the assumptions of the industry. For these people, who tend to be centrist or liberal, some constraints on journalists in a corporate commercial media system can be acknowledged. They typically lack the moral capacity to step outside the privileges that come with their university positions and are generally unwilling to risk a direct confrontation with the industry over such basic issues. They almost always have some exposure to the propaganda model, and they often do their best to denigrate it in order to assert their position as the "serious" critics, the kind who should be included in serious debates.

Just as the propaganda model does not posit that all journalistic accounts that conflict with elite opinion will be eliminated from mainstream news media, neither would we expect that all professors who teach the model in journalism schools will be eliminated. Again, attempts to understand human societies lead to an understanding of patterns, not a declaration of absolutes. As a result, in my 15 years of full-time teaching, I have been able to teach the model in my classes without interference. But it's also true that in a department with 20 to 25 full-time faculty members, there have been at any given time in my career no more than two or three others who would include this work in a syllabus. In many departments, there are no faculty members to address these questions.

But we should be teaching the propaganda model, for a number of reasons. Primary, of course, is that after nearly two decades it remains the most compelling account of why mainstream news ends up looking as it does, as a reflection of the point of view of the centers of power. The model is consistent with the best of other scholarship that I teach and, in my case, consistent with my past experience as a news worker in the industry and my ongoing interaction with journalists as a political activist outside the academy. There also are other good reasons to teach the Herman and Chomsky model, for the ways it can be used to make larger points about the nature of research and analysis.

First, the propaganda model offers an opportunity to teach about the nature of theory. When it comes to engaging theory in the classroom, students are often either (a) intimidated by theory, having been conditioned to believe it is something complex and beyond their reach; (b) bored by theory, having been exposed to countless dreary lectures that put forward various irrelevant or impenetrable theories; or (c) both. In teaching the propaganda model, the first thing I emphasize is that Herman and Chomsky call it a model, not a theory. There is very little, if anything, in the humanities and social sciences that rises to the level of real theory, in scientific terms. Human beings and their social institutions are far too complex for there to be theories that have the kind of predictive capacity that is demanded of theory in the physical sciences. In the humanities and social sciences, the best we can hope for is models that help us understand complex systems, models which can be judged as better or worse at giving us a rough guide as to how the world has worked and can be expected to work in the future. All our actions in this world are, of course, based on some kind of model, implicit or stated; the propaganda model gives us an example of an attempt to work out such an understanding in a systematic and principled way.

Second, Herman and Chomsky's work also highlights the difference between models that look primarily at systems and structures of power, and those that focus on individual behavior within the institutions created by power. This doesn't suggest we should be looking for a magic-bullet answer to the longstanding structure/agency debate; instead, we can make it clear that individuals have various levels of agency depending on the nature of the structure. In assessing news media, the propaganda model trains our attention on the structures so that we can make sense of what actual level of agency individuals routinely exercise within this particular system. Both the conventional industry defense (journalists make professional decisions, insulated for the most part from internal corporate or external political influence) and the standard right-wing critique (news media reflect a bias in favor of the left or liberal political ideas that working journalists are said to hold) must ignore structure to be even marginally intelligible. These models obsess about the individual attributes of working journalists—either their professionalism (in the case of the industry defense), or their alleged left/liberal attitudes (in the case of the right-wing critique)—to make a case. Teaching the propaganda model can help students clarify the levels at which analysis can go forward.

The use of the propaganda model to teach about theory/models and structure/agency is increasingly important in a culture in which people are routinely trained never to think about these matters. It's not that people are stupid; this is a sophisticated society in which many people develop considerable skills in a variety of intellectual arenas. The question is: What kinds of thinking, applied to what subjects, are encouraged. It is a society in which, for example, a brilliant computer scientist may well be unable to apply that rigorous thinking to questions of politics and power. We live in a world in which business people who have developed considerable analytical skills in their work can't transfer that ability to understanding the social world. We should always be teaching in a way that combats that problem. In other words, we should not be talking about critical thinking in the abstract, but applying it in the real world in a way that focuses on how power operates at the ground level.

For the past few years, I have been using the propaganda model this way in a large introductory lecture course called "Critical Issues in Journalism." In addition to covering the industry's understanding of its own practices, which is the bulk of most introductory courses, I have students read Herman's summary of the model[9] and sections of Brent Baker's book on liberal bias in the media.[10] I lecture about the very different approaches each takes, and then I assign students to review the material from two media watchdog groups that mirror these different perspectives, Fairness and Accuracy in Reporting (FAIR) and the Media Research Center (MRC). Students are asked to describe the basic approach each takes, and then compare and contrast the groups' analysis of a specific media issue.

Many of the students come into this class having absorbed and accepted either the industry's middle-of-the-road defense or the right-wing claim that the news media are dangerously liberal. So, rather than simply dismissing those positions as being without merit in intellectual terms (which is, I believe, an honest assessment of both those views), I seek to give students the tools to make their own assessment. The risk in this approach is that it implicitly suggests there is some equivalence in the competing models, that by adopting this "teach the controversy" approach I am putting them on equal footing, rather like biology professors would if they taught creationism and "intelligent design" alongside evolutionary theory in an introductory biology class.

This is a problem, but if I were to dismiss the industry and right-wing critiques in a lecture, my fear is that—no matter how thorough the assessment of the strengths and weaknesses of each—some students would conclude that I'm just another liberal professor trying to force my political views on them. Because the issue has been politicized so effectively in the public arena, it can be difficult for many students to see that there is an intellectual question—with political implications, of course—that can be addressed through research and careful analysis.

Such are the struggles to teach honestly in a culture in which the major ideological institutions, especially the mass media and educational institutions, are encouraged to move in directions that are more acceptable to those who wield power. For daring to teach this, and other material that critiques that power, I have been charged—mostly by conservative campus groups[11] or right-wing groups outside the university that specialize in attacks on left/progressive intellectuals[12]—with inappropriately politicizing the classroom. While this kind of "flak" intimidates some, we should see these critiques as an opportunity to talk in public about the responsibilities of professors to engage with students about the realities of the systems and structures of power.[13] Such attacks are a reminder that while teaching should be more than the assertion of one's politics, every professor's teaching is based on some political judgments.[14] If one stays safely within the conventional wisdom, those political judgments will remain invisible, precisely because they don't conflict with the powerful. Coming to judgments critical of concentrated power likely will lead to critique. We should encourage such critique—of all teaching—and vigorously defend the intellectual grounds for our judgments.[15]

When teaching the propaganda model, the ground on which we stand is firm.

NOTES

1. Edward S. Herman and Noam Chomsky, *Manufacturing Consent: The Political Economy of the Mass Media* (New York: Pantheon, 1988).
2. Gaye Tuchman, *Making News: A Study in the Construction of Reality* (New York: Free Press, 1978); Herbert Gans, *Deciding What's News* (New York: Pantheon, 1979); Mark Fishman, *Manufacturing the News* (Austin: University of Texas Press, 1980).
3. I later learned that a media scholar had addressed this. See Elli Lester, "Manufactured Silence and the Politics of Media Research: A Consideration of the 'Propaganda Model,'" *Journal of Communication Inquiry*, 16:1 (Winter 1992): 45–55.

4. Noam Chomsky, *Necessary Illusions* (Boston: South End Press, 1989), p. 11.
5. For a review, see Edward S. Herman, *The Myth of the Liberal Media* (New York: Peter Lang, 1999), pp. 259–271.
6. For an example, see Kurt Lang and Gladys Engel Lang, "Noam Chomsky and the Manufacture of Consent for American Foreign Policy," *Political Communication*, 21 (2004): 93–101. That issue of the journal includes Herman and Chomsky's reply (pp. 103–107) and the Langs' response (pp. 109–111).
7. In my view, there's nothing wrong with including some professional training in a university-level education, but it should be training with a critical edge rather than instruction that merely uncritically imposes the industry standards on students. There's also nothing wrong with teaching the best ideals of journalism with passion, but not in a context that encourages students to ignore their economic self-interest.
8. Carlin Romano, "Slouching toward Pressology," *Tikkun*, 4:3 (1989): 41–44, 120–123.
9. Herman, *The Myth of the Liberal Media*, pp. 23–29.
10. Brent H. Baker, *How to Identify, Expose, and Correct Liberal Media Bias* (Alexandria, VA: Media Research Center, 1994).
11. The Young Conservatives of Texas 2004 "Watch List" identified "professors who push an ideological viewpoint on their students through oftentimes subtle but sometimes abrasive methods of indoctrination." http://studentorgs.utexas.edu/yct/events/watchlist/.
12. David Horowitz, *The Professors: The 101 Most Dangerous Academics in America* (Washington, DC: Regnery Publishing, 2006), pp. 238–340.
13. For examples of my approach, see "They'll 'watch' but won't hear of prof's politics," *Houston Chronicle*, November 5, 2003, p. A-35, http://www.commondreams.org/scriptfiles/views03/1105–01.htm; "'Dangerous' academics: Right-wing distortions about leftist professors," *Alternet*, February 9, 2006, http://www.alternet.org/rights/31986/; "Florida's fear of history: New law undermines critical thinking," Common Dreams, July 17, 2006, http://www.commondreams.org/views06/0717–22.htm.
14. Robert Jensen, "The Myth of the Neutral Professional," in Jeffery Klaehn, ed., *Bound by Power: Intended Consequences* (Montreal: Black Rose Books, 2006), pp. 64–71.
15. Robert Jensen, 'Academic Freedom on the Rock,' in Malini Johar Schueller and Ashley Dawson, eds., *Dangerous Professors: Academic Freedom and the National Security Campus* (Ann Arbor: University of Michigan Press, 2009), pp. 291–306.

CHAPTER TEN

Reporting on the Pharmaceutical Industry: Profit before People

JAMES WINTER

As I write this we are one week into the so-called swine flu "pandemic" in April 2009. If there's any pandemic about, it's one of fear and greed. News media have filled their pages and newscasts with reports of deaths in Mexico, Texas and (God forbid) even Canada, where one toddler was reported dead on the East coast. Politicians debated a national vaccination program, while shares skyrocketed in firms making germ-killing medical masks. Canwest News helped out by prominently featuring a photo of a man wearing a medical mask while waiting at Vancouver Airport for his cousin's return from a vacation in Mexico.[1] The Toronto Stock Exchange was reportedly "pulled down" by "swine-flu fears." Airlines and tour operators suspended trips to Mexico. Airports increased screenings as the virus reportedly infected "13 Canadians in four different provinces."[2]

Blatant fear-mongering by the media manufactured hysteria and then pointed to the solution: "Until a vaccine is ready, the primary line of defence will be the government's national stockpile of antiviral drugs... Tamiflu and Relenza... [which] some experts believe can prevent infection and slow the spread of a pandemic," reported Andrew Mayeda of Canwest News Service.[3]

In 2005, Tamiflu was administered to Japanese children in response to an outbreak of the bird flu. At the time, James Ridgeway wrote in the *Village Voice* that "... last week Japanese newspapers told how children who were administered Tamiflu went mad and tried to kill themselves by jumping out of windows. In a cautionary statement the FDA noted 12 deaths among children, and said there are reports of psychiatric disturbances, including hallucinations, along with heart and lung disorders."[4]

For the corporate media, history seldom repeats itself as previous events have long since disappeared down the memory hole, no longer constituting "news." Thus, few recalled what happened in 1976 when there was a previous outbreak of swine flu at the Fort Dix military base in New Jersey. U.S. President Gerald Ford ordered a national vaccination campaign, at a cost of about $125 million (U.S.). Canada followed suit with free vaccinations, although no cases were reported north of the border. The inoculations were halted in the U.S. after 40 million out of 220 million people were vaccinated. In the end, only one person died of the swine flu, but 500 people contracted Guillain-Barré, a rare paralyzing nerve disease believed to be a side-effect of the vaccine, and more than 30 people died.[5]

In the context of the swine flu hysteria of spring 2009, we need to inquire, not only about public safety, but also about who will get rich from the manufactured crisis. For example, in 2005 former U.S. Secretary of Defense Donald Rumsfeld, himself former CEO of drug company Searle, owned stock in the one company that owns Tamiflu patents—to the tune of at least $18 million.[6] So, when media corporations use their power over public opinion to create hysteria, governments then use the hysteria to justify purchasing vaccines which sometimes harm and even kill the public. At the same time, people in government/business such as Rumsfeld and others realize huge profits at the public expense, in a blatant example of greed and abuse of power.

HERBOLOGY

Herbal cures have been around on the North American continent for thousands of years. When the Iroquois living around the St. Lawrence River discovered Jacques Cartier and his men on their shores, in around 1534, the Europeans were deathly ill with scurvy. European civilization was so backward at the time that they believed scurvy was caused by the "bad air" encountered on voyages. One of their cures for this and any other ailment was bleeding. The medical doctors just cut people open until enough bad blood flowed out. It either killed you or it cured you. Fortunately for old Jacques and the remainder of his men, the Iroquoian people knew that if you drank a tea made with white pine bark, it would cure your scurvy. This is because white pine bark is rich in vitamin C.

While herbal remedies such as white pine bark, garlic, and so forth will cure ailments, ranging from scurvy to the common cold or the swine flu (garlic has both antiviral and antibiotic properties), drug manufacturers and governments ignore this and continue to seek chemical "cures" and vaccinations. Anyone can grow garlic in their backyard, or pick it up for pennies in the supermarket. So, it can't be patented. Herbal pill manufacturers can make a good profit, but there's no captive and exclusive market, no MDs prescribing it, no drug plans to pay for it, and no billions of dollars in profits.[7]

BIG PHARMA

Big Pharma makes huge profits, using patents, captive and sometimes exclusive markets, MDs, and drug plans. The pharmaceutical industry is a dirty business. They falsify research, risk people's health and lives, use celebrities to push drugs, use medical doctors to push drugs, manufacture nonexistent diseases they can then "cure," and try to enlist lifelong patients. Big Pharma revised the cholesterol level guidelines so they could create a "high cholesterol epidemic," and profit from statin drugs which have serious side effects. But it doesn't stop there. They "educate" medical students and doctors, provide freebie incentives or bribes such as free vacations to those who prescribe their drugs; they control the release of research results with big bucks and tight contracts. Then, they try to ruin the careers and reputations of MDs and other whistleblowers who defend public safety.

That still isn't the end of the corruption. Big Pharma "ghostwrites" articles for well-known medical researchers, who put their names on the articles—sometimes without ever seeing the data—in return for payoffs. Of course, these ostensibly "objective, scientific" articles are published in academic medical journals, and serve to play up the benefits of company drugs and downplay their problems.

Any student who has ever been warned about avoiding plagiarism should take note: these professors are plagiarizing, using other people's work as their own, and making a bundle in the process. We'll look at some concrete case studies of these unethical, immoral, and sometimes illegal actions in this chapter.

As a result of drug company efforts, we have become pill-popping nations. Americans alone consume about 40% of all the drugs prescribed annually, throughout the world. In Canada in 2005, pharmacists filled an average of 14 prescriptions for each and every Canadian, and five times as many—74 prescriptions—for Canadians who were 80 years and older. A study published in 2008 in the *Canadian Medical Association Journal* revealed that adverse drug reactions accounted for 12% of all emergency room visits. It's now at the point where we are getting pharmaceutical drugs through our drinking water, because there are so many of them out there. In Germany, where prescription levels are much lower than North America, researchers have found from 30–60 drugs in a typical drinking water sample.

THE PFIZER EXAMPLE

Let's begin with the example of Pfizer Inc. In January 2007, Pfizer announced it was slashing 10,000 jobs to save annual costs of $2 billion, "amid fierce competition from generic drugs."[8] Pfizer blamed generic drugs, as its U.S. sales of Lipitor, one of the statin drugs for treating high cholesterol, slipped 6% to U.S. $1.9 billion , according to an article in *The Toronto Star*. Globally, Pfizer sells about $12 billion worth of Lipitor annually. The company's after-tax profit in 2006 was U.S. $7.9 billion.

In 2007, American drug companies had a median profit margin of 15.8% , compared with an average of 6.3% for the most profitable *Fortune 500* industries.[9] For most of the 1990s and the early part of this decade, the pharmaceutical industry was the most profitable business sector in the U.S. According to the nonprofit watchdog group *Public Citizen*, the combined profits of the top ten pharmaceutical companies in the *Fortune 500* exceeded the combined profits of the other 490 companies.[10]

When Pfizer blamed generics, the popular media merely echoed the company's claim, but that's not the real story.

SPIN DOCTORING

In common parlance, "spin doctoring" refers to the way politicians spin their own account of events, using public relations. But there is another type of spin doctoring going on.

Pfizer is the largest drug manufacturer in the world, with U.S. $50 billion in annual sales, and familiar names such as Lipitor, Viagra, and antidepressant Zoloft (which admittedly did lose its patent protection in 2006). Every weekday, about 38,000 Pfizer sales reps whistle their way to work around the globe. The sales reps cost Pfizer U.S. $170,000 per year, including their company car, personal computers, and benefits. Pfizer can afford it. In 2004, the company generated $45 billion in gross profits, or $1.2 million per sales rep.[11] With their briefcases full of free drug samples and lavish expense accounts for wining and dining their prey, the sales reps head into hospitals, clinics, pharmacies, and medical doctors' offices. In some cases they buy lists of MDs' prescribed drugs from pharmacies, so they know whom to target. One 2001 report in the *Journal of the American Medical Association* indicated that drug companies such as Pfizer spend as much as U.S. $13,000 annually on every MD targeted.[12] The goal is to get Pfizer drugs prescribed by the MDs. And it works.[13]

Phyllis Adams, a former drug rep in Canada, was told by a doctor that he would not prescribe her product unless her company made him a consultant. For another doctor, she arranged a $35,000 "unrestricted educational grant" for him to use for a swimming pool in his back yard.[14] Another U.S. example involves a drug rep paying $50,000 for a consulting accountant to turn around a failing medical clinic with about 50 MDs who didn't know how to run a business. He turned the practice into a smoothly running financial machine, all the while promoting the drug rep's company, and its prescriptions and profits soared. Why? The MDs were grateful for the economic bonanza.

Drug giant GlaxoSmithKline has been accused of using exotic holidays, stereos, World Cup soccer tickets, and cash to bribe thousands of Italian and German doctors into prescribing its products. In the U.S., AstraZeneca paid a $355 million court settlement for a kickback scheme in 2003, where doctors billed insurance providers for drugs they received free from the company. TAP Pharmaceutical Products pulled the same stunt and settled for $875 million in 2001.[15]

Some MDs avoid reps like the plague. But, it must be difficult. They are young, good-looking, and frequently women. They have large expense accounts. As one American MD writes, it's "virtually impossible to demonize them."[16] MDs who accept gifts deny that it influences the prescriptions they write, but the evidence shows otherwise: gifts turn into scripts. As one former rep noted, "If you could get ten minutes with a doctor, your market share would go through the roof." These bribes are changing MDs' prescribing habits. For example, a review paper by Ashley Wazana—then a resident at Montreal's McGill University—found that doctors who attended pharma-sponsored CME received free drug samples, or accepted pharma funds for travel expenses, were more likely to prescribe the sponsor's drug. The Canadian company Biovail paid American MDs $1,000 for signing up 11 patients each, in 2003.[17] This is another form of spin doctoring. Indeed, the *Journal of the American Medical Association* admitted in their February 2, 2002, issue that 87% of their medical experts formulating the practice guidelines with which doctors must comply are tied financially to the pharmaceutical companies.[18]

A MARKETING BLITZ

In addition, of course, for Pfizer and other pharma companies, there are the other elements of a vast marketing blitz: such as more than $3 billion in annual advertising, placing Pfizer, for example, fourth among all American companies in 2003, behind only *General Motors, Proctor & Gamble*, and *Time Warner*. And it doesn't matter that these are prescription drugs being advertised. The commercials coax us to "ask your doctor" if this pill is for you. Consequently, MDs are bombarded by patients as well as drug reps. Apparently, it works. As a recent *Health Canada/*

British Medical Journal study reported, "physicians often prescribe drugs requested by patients, even when the doctors aren't convinced the advertised medication is better than older, often cheaper pills."[19] By one estimate, Americans consume 40% of all the drugs prescribed around the world every year. In 2004, Americans averaged 12 prescriptions each. Developing countries bear a disproportionate part of the world's disease burden. But with 80% of the world's population they account for only 10% of global drug sales. The drug bill for the whole continent of Africa is just 1% of the world total.[20]

Advertising expands the market, promoting diseases to fit drugs. Thus, "millions of normal people come to believe that they have dubious or exaggerated ailments such as 'generalized anxiety disorder,' 'erectile dysfunction,' 'premenstrual dysphoric disorder,' and GERD (gastroesophageal reflux disease)."[21]

As American MD and bioethics professor Carl Elliott points out, Americans have become reliant on pill popping. Baseball players in the U.S. take drugs to improve their performance; college students take Ritalin to improve their academic performance; musicians take beta blockers to improve their onstage performance; middle-aged men take Viagra to improve their sexual performance; shy people take Paxil to improve their social performance.[22]

This incredible drug use impacts on all of us as it shows up in our drinking water. Drugs given to people and animals have been showing up in water samples: surface water, groundwater, and tap drinking water, dating back to the early 1990s. Researchers have found antibiotics, hormones, strong pain killers, tranquilizers, and chemotherapy chemicals given to cancer patients, for example. German scientists report that between 30 and 60 drugs can be measured in a typical water sample.[23]

As for Big Pharma's much-vaunted research and development, far more money is spent on marketing than on research. According to Dr. Marcia Angell, a Harvard professor of medicine and former editor of the prestigious *New England Journal of Medicine,* from 1998 through 2003, 487 drugs were approved by the U.S. Food and Drug Administration (FDA). Of those, 379 (78%) were classified by the agency as "appear[ing] to have therapeutic qualities similar to those of one or more already marketed drugs," and 333 (68%) weren't even new compounds (what the FDA calls "new molecular entities"), but instead were formulations or combinations of old ones. Only 67 (14% of the 487) were actually new compounds considered likely to be improvements over older drugs.[24] Fourteen percent!

Most marketing is aimed at persuading doctors and patients to choose one of these "me-too" drugs over another, without any scientific basis. So most free samples are recently patented me-too drugs. Says Dr. Marcia Angell, "AstraZeneca was reported to have spent a half-billion dollars in a year to switch Prilosec users to Nexium." That may explain why we were suddenly bombarded with ads for "the purple pill." There's another danger with new drugs, in that they are tested on relatively few people; so less frequent side effects aren't detected. If you test a drug on 5,000 people, and one death occurs as a result, that's not significant and will be ignored. But if 5 million people subsequently go on that drug, this translates into 1,000 people who will die from it.

The next blockbuster drug in the Pfizer lineup was called by the chemical name of *Torcetrapib*. In clinical trials, it was found to raise HDL or "good cholesterol" levels. Pfizer was three years into 100 clinical trials involving 15,000 patients on three continents. The company reportedly invested between $1 billion and $2.1 billion on the drug, with hopes of a very high payoff. "If it works, it will be the biggest blockbuster ever," CEO Hank McKinnell Jr. told the business press in 2005.[25]

Suddenly, the wheel fell off. In early December 2006, the company learned from independent monitors that the drug was increasing people's risk of dying by an alarming 161%. It was also causing other problems, related to heart failure, etc, for people who had not died in the trials. In all, 82 people died taking the drug in the trials, versus 51 who were not taking it. These were very scary numbers, and Pfizer pulled the plug on the drug tests. The discontinuation of Torcetrapib was the second major failure in Pfizer's development program in less than a week. Earlier, Pfizer said it would no longer collaborate with Akzo Nobel, a European company, on asenapine, a drug for schizophrenia.[26]

Although to the media—and even in my wording above—this incident was seen as a "failure," in reality it is a success story, as the problems with the drug were divulged before the testing was completed, and before the drug was sold to the public. We're not always so lucky. For example, *Vioxx*. By the time it was withdrawn in September 2004, Merck & Co. Inc.'s painkiller Vioxx had been taken by an estimated 80 million people, and its sales reached U.S. $2.5 billion in 2003.

According to a report in the *New Scientist*, Cox-2 inhibitors such as Vioxx were licensed for the treatment of chronic inflammation as a safer alternative to traditional anti-inflammatory drugs such as ibuprofen, for people at high risk for specific side effects. Ibuprofen can cause gastrointestinal bleeding and stomach ulcers in some people, such as those over 65 years of age. In September 2004, Merck's Vioxx was voluntarily withdrawn amid revelations that its long-term use might double the risk of heart attack and stroke among users.

Soon after, in December 2004, it emerged that another Cox-2 inhibitor—Pfizer's *Celebrex*—might triple the risk of heart attacks and stroke, although other studies found no additional risk and the drug was not withdrawn. And a previous study suggested that Vioxx increased the risk of coronary heart disease compared with a traditional NSAID called naproxen, which may have actually protected the heart.[27] A study published in 2005 suggested that huge numbers of people may have been put at risk by taking Cox-2 inhibitors. *The Lancet* suggested Vioxx could have caused between 88,000 and 140,000 extra cases of serious coronary heart disease in the U.S., because it was not withdrawn sooner.[28]

As was eventually reported even in the popular press, "When a study found that patients on Vioxx were three times more likely to have heart attacks than patients on Naproxen, Merck-funded scientists decided it was because naproxen prevented heart attacks. It wasn't until four years later that Merck pulled Vioxx off the market because of concerns it increased the risk of heart attacks."[29]

Researchers at the British medical journal, *The Lancet,* looked at the studies conducted between 1999 and 2004, concluding,

> If Merck's statement in their recent press release that "given the availability of alternative therapies, and the questions raised by the data, we concluded that a voluntary withdrawal is the responsible course to take," was appropriate in September, 2004, then the same statement could and should have been made several years earlier, when the data summarised here first became available. Instead, Merck continued to market the safety of [Vioxx].[30]

Vioxx and Merck are not alone. As one pharmaceutical watchdog summed things up, in 2004, one of Wyeth's weight-loss drugs harmed so many people that the manufacturer "put aside more than $16 billion to compensate victims."[31]

In 1975, Canadians spent an average of $46.50 on drugs. By 1985, this had risen to $4 billion, averaging about $150 each. By 2005, drug spending was forecast to be up by more than 600% , to over $24 billion. Per capita, we're now spending almost $800, instead of $46.50. Prescription drugs account for $20 billion, or 83%.[32] This latter amount was more than we paid for all of the physicians' services in the country, combined, annually. The *Canadian Medical Association Journal* reports that the annual increase in prescription drug spending alone—now $1.5 billion—could pay for 3,500 more MDs, annually.[33]

CHAMPIONING CHOLESTEROL

For the last couple of years, my own wonderful medical doctor has been urging me to go on a statin drug, for reducing cholesterol. I've resisted, because I'm a firm believer that exercise and weight loss will accomplish the same thing—once I get around to it. I'm particularly wary of statins, however, since reading a *Toronto Star* Series, which I'll come to shortly. Not everyone feels the same way that I do, however. More than 23.6 million prescriptions for cholesterol reducers were dispensed from Canadian retail drug stores for the 12-month period ending September 30, 2006, according to the drug-tracking firm IMS Health. In Canada alone, statins are a $2-billion market. There were more than 12.3 million prescriptions over the same period for Pfizer's Lipitor, the No. 1-selling drug in the country. It can be sold in subtle ways, for example by former Maple Leaf hockey coach Pat Quinn, praising his cholesterol medication at a media brunch.[34]

Quinn is part of a select group of celebrity drug pushers, including actors Olympia Dukakis and *West Wing*'s Rob Lowe, pop singer Carnie Wilson, and U.S. presidential candidate Bob Dole, who promoted Viagra for Pfizer. Wyeth hired supermodel Lauren Hutton to hawk hormone replacement therapy for menopause. Gymnast Bart Connor, Olympic figure skater Dorothy Hamill, who promoted Merck's Vioxx, jockey Julie Krone, former NFL coach Bill Parcells, San Francisco 49er legend Joe Montana, actors Rita Moreno, Bob Uecker, and Debbie Reynolds—all are celebrity pill pushers. Joan Lunden promoted Claritin. Kathleen Turner apparently suffers from rheumatoid arthritis, and has appeared on *Good Morning America* to quietly plug Wyeth's Enbrel, a drug for arthritis sufferers.

Wayne Gretsky touted Tylenol arthritis formula, even though he didn't have osteoarthritis, but this was openly paid advertising. This was part of a long tradition of celebrity endorsements: the star's connection to the company was obvious; the pitch was straightforward promotion. It was like Ricardo Montalban pushing coffee, or Mean Joe Green touting Coke. But with drugs there were controversies, and the pitches weren't as effective as they could be, so the drug companies went underground. They gave us celebrity-driven public awareness campaigns which completely obscured the financial relationship between the star and the drug company, allowing both parties to avoid any talk of side effects or potential problems with the drug. With all hints of drugs and money hidden, celebrities were again willing to sign up, taking fees as high as $1 million to do a series of television and newspaper interviews in which they speak about a particular illness and urge sufferers to seek treatment. Sometimes the celebrities don't mention their sponsor or its product by name, instead urging people to see their doctors about the latest treatments, or, in the case of Kathleen Turner, suggest that viewers or readers visit a specific web site that offers information about a condition.[35] When *Frasier* star Kelsey Grammer and his wife were promoting irritable bowel syndrome on top-rated TV shows, viewers thought the pair was speaking on behalf of an independent foundation. In fact their fee came from GSK, which was at that time preparing the market for alosetron (Lotronex), a controversial new drug that carried modest benefits and "severe side effects, including possible death."[36]

These awareness campaigns also happen to be a way for the drug companies to avoid the remaining U.S. FDA regulations on TV advertising of prescription drugs. In a straightforward television commercial for a drug, viewers must be told about the drug's major side effects or be directed to another source—a web site, or 800 number, for example—where they can get more information. Awareness campaigns are exempt from these restrictions because the FDA doesn't consider them to be advertisements.[37]

What Pat Quinn didn't mention—likely didn't know—was that statins can cause muscle damage or myopathy, which can lead to muscle pain and weakness, and can be a sign of a rare, potentially fatal muscle-wasting disease called rhabdomyolysis. In its worst form, patients can die due to muscle breakdown leading to kidney damage. As well, doctors are seeing more cases of statin-induced peripheral neuropathy, where the long nerves in the body die off, causing numbness and pain in the feet. A number of studies and case histories have reported memory loss due to statins, with recovery after the drug use was halted. In August 2001, Bayer's *Baycol* was pulled from the market because of dozens of cases worldwide involving rhabdomyolysis, the muscle-wasting disease. As of October 2004, *Health Canada* reports for statins on the market showed that there were 62 reports of rhabdomyolysis in patients taking Lipitor, 18 for Zocor, 12 for Merck's Mevacor, five for Pravachol, made by Bristol-Myers Squibb, and 11 for AstraZeneca's Crestor.[38]

TAKE A NAP INSTEAD

What one has to weigh against these risks is the benefit of using a cholesterol drug. One 2004 study indicated, for example, that a 42-year-old man with high cholesterol who took statins for ten years would reduce his risk of a heart attack or stroke by only 2% .[39] Let's compare this to what you can do naturally, by exercising, eating a low-cholesterol diet, or even snoozing. Yes, I said snoozing. *The Toronto Star* reported in February 2007 that in a longitudinal study of over 23,000 Greeks, those who napped three times a week for a half hour, had a 37% lower risk of dying from heart attacks or other heart problems compared to those who didn't nap.[40]

Researchers now have found that patients who don't have evidence of occlusive vascular disease, which leads to clogged arteries, should not be taking the drugs. Yet, only one quarter of statin users fall into this category. Statins have also been found to be ineffective on women.[41]

So part of the problem is that statins are prescribed so broadly, where they may not be appropriate, or as a—perhaps costly—preventative measure. The cure could be worse than the disease, as they say. But why all the sudden concern about high cholesterol? Was it junk food bingeing, a lack of exercise? What created the problems which resulted in skyrocketing high cholesterol levels and soaring prescription drugs? Was it really well-intentioned physicians recognizing an international epidemic and trying to make people healthy again? Or was it something else?

REVISING CHOLESTEROL GUIDELINES

Even some physicians may not be aware that the definition of just what constitutes "high cholesterol" is regularly revised. As with other conditions, the definition can be broadened in ways that describe more and more healthy people as "at risk," and hence requiring prescriptions. A minor scandal erupted in the U.S. in 2003, when it was learned that eight of the nine experts who wrote the 2003 cholesterol guidelines also served as paid speakers, consultants, or researchers for the world's major drug companies. Some of the members had multiple ties to companies and one "expert" had taken money from ten of them.[42] In 2005, the *Canadian Medical Association Journal* reported that the "new Canadian guidelines have so changed the threshold for 'high' cholesterol that an additional 500,000 Canadians should be getting statin medication," at a cost of another $250 million.[43] This may or may not be good for us, but it's undoubtedly good for the drug companies.

Dr. Jacques Genest, a cardiologist at the Royal Victoria Hospital at Montreal's McGill University, acknowledged in an interview that he and the other doctors involved in revising the Canadian guidelines for prescribing statins have all worked as consultants for at least some of the six pharmaceutical giants that make statins. Genest himself has worked for four of them, including Pfizer.[44]

As the Big Pharma companies do studies to demonstrate the value of their drugs, miraculously, these cut-off points for high cholesterol have gradually lowered. "Once it was reserved for blood cholesterol levels over 280mm per deciliter," says Dr. Marcia Angell. "Then it fell to 240. Now most doctors try to knock it down to below 100."[45]

These seemingly distant events are ultimately played out in my own doctor's office. Recently a colleague and friend whose brother is a Seattle MD was, like my doctor, telling me about a cholesterol epidemic. "You should get on a statin," he advised.

Of course, the problem is not restricted to just cholesterol levels or statin drugs. "Abnormal" levels of blood pressure, obesity, and bone density have all changed over the years to expand the markets for disease. High blood pressure (hypertension) was once defined as blood pressure above 140/90. An expert panel then introduced something called prehypertension in 2003, which embraces readings between (120/80 and 140/90). "Overnight, people with blood pressure in this range found they had a medical condition," says Dr. Angell.[46] Bipolar disorder, irritable bowel syndrome, male and female sexual dysfunction, and attention deficit hyperactivity disorder (ADHD) which has become pandemic are all part of what has been called "disease mongering" on the part of Big Pharma and the medical establishment. So-called disease awareness campaigns are underwritten by pharmaceuticals. Of course, there will be some individuals who suffer severe forms of these problems, who will benefit from treatments and from the publicity given to the disorders. But there is a difference between legitimate public education about an under-diagnosed disease and turning us all into patients, with crude attempts to build markets for potentially dangerous drugs.[47]

The Eli Lilly-sponsored promotion of premenstrual dysphoric disorder to help sell a rebranded version of fluoxetine (rebranded from Prozac to Sarafem) is a case in point, according to some medical doctors. "Considered by some as a serious psychiatric illness, premenstrual dysphoric disorder is regarded by others as a condition which does not exist."[48]

UNTIL DEATH DO US PART

In his analysis of the selling of "bipolar disorder," Dr. David Healy notes that the whole concept of "mood stabilizer" drugs was invented around 1995, and by 2001, around a 100 scientific articles a year featured this term.[49] Although the academic psychiatric community hasn't come to a consensus about what the term means, many physicians are convinced that bipolar disorders must be detected and treated with these mood stabilizers. Bipolar disorders entered the literature in 1980, and involved acute cases of manic depression involving hospitalization. Since 1995, the definition has been expanded to include other disorders, and estimates for their prevalence have risen from 0.1% of the population to 5% or more. While treatment of the acute manic states of bipolar disorders has been effected using antipsychotic drugs, no drugs have been successfully scientifically tested for the prevention of the broadened definition of "bipolar disorder." Despite this, a whole new industry has cropped up. Dr. David Healy writes that "With the possible exception of lithium for bipolar I disorder, there are no randomized controlled trials to show that patients with bipolar disorders in general who receive psychotropic drugs are better in the long term than those who receive no medicine."[50]

Healy notes that any slight evidence of benefits for these drugs must be weighed against a consistent body of evidence that regular treatments with antipsychotic drugs in the long run may increase *mortality*, through suicide and for other reasons.

In 2002, the *British Medical Journal* reported the text of a secret, internal memo obtained through a whistleblower at GlaxoSmithKline (GSK). GSK was working on a three-year program (2000–2003) to "create a new perception of irritable bowel syndrome as a concrete disease [which] must be established in the minds of doctors as a significant and discrete disease. Patients also need to be convinced that [it] is a...medical disorder." Commented University of British Columbia medical researcher, Barbara Mintzes: "Not content with providing a pill for every ill, the drug companies now push an ill for every pill."[51]

DISEASE MONGERING

In her book, *Disease-Mongers: How Doctors, Drug Companies and Insurers Are Making You Feel Sick*, Lynn Payer describes it as "trying to convince essentially well people that they are sick, or slightly sick people that they are very ill." She Lists the ten major disease-mongering tactics. These include identifying an "abnormality," imputing suffering to people, identifying a (large) population of potential sufferers, defining new diseases, spin doctoring, framing the issues, selective use of statistics, using the wrong end point, promoting technology as risk-free magic, and calling a common ambiguous symptom a disease.[52]

One example of disease mongering is the Hormone Replacement Therapy (HRT) scandal. Professor of medicine at Harvard University, Dr. JoAnn Manson, recently cited the 20 million women on HRT in the U.S. alone. She blamed the rise of HRT on patients and doctors both swallowing the industry propaganda which began in 1966 with Dr. Robert Wilson's book *Feminine Forever*. Financed in its entirety by the pharmaceutical company Wyeth-Ayerst, the manufacturers of Premarin, this book promised: "Breasts and genital organs will not shrivel. Such women [on HRT] will be much more pleasant to live with and will not become dull and unattractive." Dr. Manson added that rather than conducting proper trials, "it was just assumed that there would be an overall favorable benefit-to-risk ratio."[53]

A study of 16,608 postmenopausal women in a U.S. nationwide study reported in the July 2002 issue of *The Journal of the American Medical Association* (*JAMA*) that women taking the dual-hormone therapy for five years had 26% more cases of breast cancer than women receiving a placebo. Moreover, compared with the placebo, the hormones doubled the incidence of blood clots, hiked stroke incidence by 41% , and upped the occurrence of heart disease by 29%.[54]

The Journal of the American Medical Association announced recently that estrogen/progesterone-combined synthetic HRT doesn't protect you from anything much and increases your risk of getting breast cancer by 60–80%. In some circumstances, it also seems to trigger ovarian cancer. The study known as the Women's Health Initiative was halted as the evidence became undeniable.[55]

By 2003, with millions of women on HRT, the mainstream began to report problems. One *Canadian Press* story reported that HRT was previously "believed to protect women against heart disease, colon cancer, age-related mental decline and osteoporosis," however, based on recent research, the story said "women were actually at greater risk of having a heart attack, stroke or life-threatening blood clot." While reporting this—even belatedly—is a good thing, such articles continued to present mixed reports, which would be confusing for the public. For example, this article went on to quote Dr. Robert Reid, a medical professor at Queen's University who said, "Hormone replacement therapy is still, by far, the best treatment for symptomatic women with hot flashes and...night sweats."[56] Well, which would you rather have, hot flashes or a heart attack or stroke, or cancer?

Another example of disease mongering is male and female "sexual dysfunction." Leonore Tiefer has reviewed this history, concluding that "...the pharmaceutical industry has taken an aggressive interest in sex, using public relations, direct-to-consumer advertising, promotion of off-label prescribing, and other tactics to create a sense of widespread sexual inadequacy and interest in drug treatments."[57] Tiefer writes that in the 1980s and 1990s, urologists created organizations, journals, and "sexual health clinics" focusing on men's erection problems. The creation of "erectile dysfunction" as a serious, prevalent, and treatable medical disorder was firmly in place by the time Viagra was launched in 1998 with an unprecedented global public relations campaign, as Joel Lexchin has described. Lexchin wrote, "Pfizer's well-financed campaign was aimed at raising awareness of the problem of ED, while at the same time narrowing the treatment possibilities to just a single option: medication."[58] Though journalists began calling for a "female Viagra" only days after the U.S. Food and Drug Administration (FDA) approved Viagra in March 1998 (examples of journalists' calling for a "pink Viagra" are collected on http://www.fsd-alert.org/press.html), it was "far from clear what medical condition Viagra was supposed to treat in women."[59]

In the early years, key players in the medicalization of women's sexual problems were a small group of urologists who, capitalizing on their relationships with industry, recruited many sex researchers and therapists. Irwin Goldstein of Boston University, an active erectile dysfunction researcher, opened the first Women's Sexual Health clinic in 1998. Goldstein convened the first conference on female sexual function in October 1999 in Boston. Goldstein is the editor of a journal which was launched in 2004—*The Journal of Sexual Medicine* (http://jsm.issir.org)—which has already published an industry-supported supplement on FSD.[60]

Pfizer was the main promoter of FSD from 1997 to 2004, when its attempts to have Viagra approved to treat "female sexual arousal disorder" ended because of consistently poor clinical trial results. In a public statement, Pfizer said that that several large-scale, placebo-controlled studies including about 3,000 women with female sexual arousal disorder, showed inconclusive results.[61]

DRUG COMPANIES EDUCATE MEDICAL STUDENTS, FACULTY

One of the ways disease mongering is advanced is through medical education. Although most of us tend to think of the academic community as being largely independent of outside business, this independence is under attack. Cutbacks to government spending on education mean educators and administrators increasingly look to corporations to replace lost funding. But such funding doesn't come without a price.

The medical profession has largely abandoned its responsibility to educate medical students and doctors in the use of prescription drugs. Instead, it's the drug companies themselves that support continuing medical education, medical conferences, professional association meetings, and even university classroom education. The billions of dollars to do this with come out of Big Pharma's marketing budgets.[62] In an *Atlantic Monthly* article titled "The Drug Pushers," American academic Dr. Carl Elliott described how medical students of another professor who were given a "pharm lecture" with PowerPoint slides courtesy of *Cialis*, sarcastically commented that they should have gotten "a free lunch" with the lecture.[63]

According to two medical educators, psychiatry residents may be particularly susceptible to the influences of pharmaceutical marketing practices, because, "the residents have assumed the dual roles of learners and practicing physicians." Consequently, "their prescribing preferences have yet to be established and their fund of knowledge, though developing, is limited."[64]

As one commentator has pointed out,[65] it's perfectly reasonable to require teaching faculty to disclose a conflict of interest to students and residents. Meaningful disclosure would include research grants and honoraria received from industry, and any other significant relationship between the faculty member and the pharmaceutical company, including stock ownership and work as a company speaker, adviser, or consultant. Any other legal or business relationship between the company and the faculty member which might exert influence over the faculty member's teaching activities should be disclosed, as well as the specific relevancy of the conflict to the subject matter.

But simply disclosing conflicts of interest doesn't resolve them. Key opinion leaders list relationships with Big Pharma when presenting at medical conferences and publishing in peer-reviewed journals. But the process of disclosing conflicts reveals nothing about how they're actually managed, which is a crucial point. When a person has disclosed a relationship, or ended it, any associated conflict of interest may be resolved, but it's naive to believe that clinician–researchers will permanently sever ties to industry, and even if they do, prior interactions with industry may still influence future behavior.[66]

What's necessary is that the medical community, including its educators, replace its apparent lackadaisical acceptance of Big Pharma's PR with—at a minimum—healthy skepticism, and even outright rejection. But given the money involved, this won't happen anytime soon.

As bad as this situation is in the developed west, it's worse for the underfunded nations of the south. According to Dr. Dennis Ross-Degnan, a Harvard professor who studies pharmaceutical policy, "The only people providing meaningful education for doctors in developing countries are the drug companies. The problem is it is biased education."[67]

WHISTLEBLOWERS

As I have detailed elsewhere citing the cases of Nancy Olivieri and David Healy,[68] not only has academia been corrupted by Big Pharma, but so too have supposedly independent government agencies which review, test, and approve drugs in the public interest: such as Health Canada. In July 2004, three Health Canada scientists, Drs. Shiv Chopra, Margaret Haydon, and Gerard Lambert, were fired for insubordination on the same day. The researchers were fired a few months after federal legislation to protect whistleblowers died on the order paper with the previous, 2003, federal election.

The scientists, from the government office that tests new drugs used on animals raised for food, said publicly they were being pressured to approve drugs despite human safety concerns. In the late 1990s, they publicly opposed bovine growth hormone, a Monsanto product that enhances milk production in cows.

GETTING THE LAWS THEY NEED

The big drug companies don't just work around and against the laws: they *actually make them*. Billions of dollars in profits means they can afford to hire political lobbyists, who in turn pressure legislators to pass favorable laws. In 2003, the big drug companies employed an army of 675 lobbyists in Washington D.C., more than one for every member of Congress. Coincidentally, in that year the U.S. Congress passed a law which explicitly prohibits Medicare from using its purchasing power to bargain for low prices or discounts, which is done by every other large insurer, including the U.S. Department of Defense.

In 1992 the U.S. Congress passed the Prescription Drug User Fee Act, which allows drug companies to pay a variety of fees to the FDA, to speed up drug approval. This makes the drug industry a major funding resource of the agency which was set up to regulate it. In 1997, the FDA dropped most restrictions on direct-to-consumer advertising of prescription drugs.[69] All these laws help the drug companies.

In June 2006, the FDA approved a Merck vaccine named *Gardasil* for treatment of two kinds of human papilloma virus, or HPV, that cause 70% of cervical cancer cases. Some 11,000 women a year in the U.S. are diagnosed with cervical cancer; nearly 4,000 die. Merck wanted to make sure Gardasil would be as widely used as possible. Even before the FDA approved Gardasil, Merck was lobbying with state governments to make the vaccine mandatory for school girls. At the same time, it was making donations to state legislators. For example, California assemblyman Ed Hernandez introduced a bill mandating the vaccine in California. He also received a $5,000 campaign donation from Merck.[70]

GHOSTWRITING OR FALSIFYING MEDICAL RESEARCH

> "No man but a blockhead ever wrote, except for money."
>
> —SAMUEL JOHNSON, 1709–1784

In a recent article in the *Bioethics Forum*, Dr. Kate Jirik asked, "What kind of fraud could possibly involve academic researchers and universities?"[71] The answer, as I noted above, is that Big Pharma "ghostwrites" articles for well-known medical researchers, who put their names on the articles—sometimes without ever seeing the data—in return for payoffs. Ghostwritten articles are by someone working directly or indirectly for a pharmaceutical company. A second person, frequently a well-known academic researcher, is paid for letting his/her name appear as the author of the article. This conceals the article's origin, and of course is highly unethical. Dr. Jirik writes,

> According to recent studies in *JAMA* and the British Journal of Psychiatry, somewhere between 11% and 50% of articles on pharmaceuticals that appear in the major medical journals are thought to be ghostwritten.[72]

The people selling their names are some of the best and brightest because "the pharmaceutical companies want the support of key opinion leaders." Unfortunately, the articles are anything but impartial analyses. According to a study in *JAMA,* "the industry sponsored articles report more favorably on a drug than those done by independent researchers by an 8:1 margin." And yet, the ghostwritten articles appear in more prestigious journals and are more often cited by other researchers.[73]

Dr. Adriane Fugh-Berman was approached in the summer of 2004 by a medical education company, to write a review article on *Warfarin*, a blood-thinner (and rodent poison!).[74] The article's sponsor was a pharmaceutical company which manufactured neither herbal products nor *Warfarin*. On August 24, 2004, she was sent a draft article with a title, her name and institution, and suggestions for potential journals. The medical education company asked for a one-week turnaround. The ghostwritten article didn't name any pharmaceuticals manufactured by the drug company sponsoring the article: it just described numerous problems with *Warfarin*. Coincidentally, the pharmaceutical company had developed a competitor to *Warfarin*. Dr. Fugh-Berman refused to sign off as author of the paper. Just by chance, a few months later she was asked to peer-review the ghost-written article when it was submitted to the *Journal of General Internal Medicine* by a different researcher.[75]

Recently it's been revealed that numerous "scientific" studies have actually been ghostwritten by specialized PR firms representing the drug industry, minimizing harmful effects of drugs such as *Zoloft*.[76] In "Ghostly Data," a commentary on a web site, Dr. David Healy lists a number of concrete instances, where it can be certain that some ghostwriting happened.[77] In one of these, Healy was approached by the pharmaceutical company Pierre Fabre, which provided a ghostwritten Healy article called "Bridging the Gap." Healy writes, "This was subsequently published with the apparent author as Siegfried Kasper."

In 2005, an anonymous MD noted that "Several years ago, editors at the New England Journal of Medicine lamented that they were almost unable to find an expert academic psychiatrist without industry links who could review a clinical trial involving anti-depressants."[78] In June that year, the editor of the *Cleveland Clinical Journal of Medicine* decided to stop publishing articles from private (non-academic) researchers. The editor wrote, "We and others have noted an increase in submissions produced by medical education companies at the behest of pharmaceutical companies, with an academician's name appended as author."

Obviously, if you have megabucks at your disposal the way Big Pharma does, then you can mount pretty serious public relations campaigns. When problems arise with their drugs or allegations surface, whether from a David Healy, Nancy Olivieri, or Betty Dong, Big Pharma trots out the heavy duty PR artillery. Aside from the usual smear campaign such as that which was unleashed on Dr. Jeffrey Wigand by Big Tobacco, there are a number of methods employed.[79] A special issue of *The New Internationalist* reviewed these, among other related matters.[80] The fight back strategies are as follows: Denial, shutdown, extrication, purging, and compensation. In some respects, this differs little from the crisis management strategies long propagated by the public relations industry, in crises ranging from the Union Carbide gas leak in Bhopal, India, to the Dalkon Shield UID, Dow Corning's leaky silicone breast implants, the cyanide-laced Extra Strength Tylenol incident, the selling of the Gulf War, or the Exxon Valdez oil spill, to name a few.[81] Another aspect of this is the way pharmaceutical companies can muddy the waters of just about any debate, by using their own high-priced academic talent. Virtually any research may be criticized for shortcomings in one fashion or another. This would probably fall under the first stage of reactions: Denial.

THE ROLE OF THE MEDIA

Obviously, public relations and crisis management, as with sales generally, have a lot to do with the media. The news media are instrumental as a means of delivering audiences to advertisers, for example. They also cooperate in the marketing blitzes, and their uncritical—indeed promotional—coverage of new drugs is virtually another form of advertising. One extensive study of newspaper reporting, for example, found 68% of articles examined mentioned a drug's benefits but made no mention of possible harm or side effects. No articles failed to mention a drug's benefits. Overall, there were five times as many benefits as harm reported. Financial links to pharmaceutical companies were mentioned for only 3% of all nongovernment, nonindustry spokespeople.[82]

Since the drug industry is so predominant in the area of research, and because news media love to report on medical studies, their reporting can amount to a PR arm for the industry. And, because pharma spokespersons are influential MDs, professors, and opinion leaders, they warrant positive coverage by news media, by default.

Another way to examine news media coverage is to look at what they leave out. There have been a number of books written in recent years which are critical of Big Pharma: from Lynn Payer's *Disease-Mongers* in the early 1990s through to John Abramson's best-seller, *Overdosed America*, in 2005. I put six of these into a computer full-text data search of Canadian daily newspapers to see how many reviews and how much attention they warranted. They ranged from zero articles for *Disease-Mongers* to six for *Selling Sickness*. There was a total of 14 reviews for the six books, or an average of about two reviews per book. That's among 20 newspapers, stretching from Victoria's *Daily Colonist* to the St. John's *Evening Telegram* in Newfoundland. So, another way to look at it is that for each book, there was an average of one book review in every ten newspapers.[83] Here's how they fared:

- *Selling Sickness* (6)
- *The Truth About Drug Companies* (3)
- *Generation Rx* (2)
- *Prescription Games* (2).
- *Overdosed America* (1)
- *Disease-Mongers* (0)

So, criticism of Big Pharma doesn't exactly find a receptive audience in Canadian daily newspapers.

If the critical message is missing from the news, what about the drug companies' side of things? Drug companies also respond to the charges against them by hiring someone to write a column defending them: for example, Kevin Hassett of the corporate-sponsored American Enterprise Institute, who wrote an article for Bloomberg titled, "The Misguided Assault on the U.S. Drug Industry."[84]

The web site *mediadoctor.ca* indicates that the Canadian news media get a failing or barely passing grade for articles about new medical drugs and treatments, ranging from 22% to 53% . The worst offender in this bad lot was *The Times-Colonist* of Victoria (22%) and the *Montreal Gazette* (36%), the "best," with bare passing grades, were *The Globe and Mail* (53%) and *Ottawa Citizen* (52%). But overall, the differences are small and may well not be statistically or socially significant, as no statistical test was reported.[85]

If *The Globe and Mail* is indeed at the high end of the reporting, we're really in trouble. A *Globe* story reporting on academic research near Love Canal, New York, indicated that the researchers found "No link between cancer and Pesticide." *The Globe*'s editors liked the story so much that they ran a front page paragraph pointing to the story inside. Unfortunately, the *Globe and Mail* has gravely distorted the study's findings. An accurate headline would read, "Breast-feeding reduces risk of cancer from pesticides." Two very different conclusions. The researchers found that breast feeding flushed carcinogens such as DDT and PCBs from women's breasts. Unfortunately, the story was picked up and run in the same way by other newspapers as well.[86]

SELLING PRIVATE MEDICINE

The impact of selling Big Pharma and indiscriminate pill popping is horrid, as we have seen from the impact of these drugs on the lives and deaths of patients. When you multiply this problem by the number of drugs and the number of serious side effects and deaths, you have a healthcare crisis. But there is another way the news media are promoting problems, potentially on an even larger scale, and that is their consistent promotion of privatized healthcare.

As Linda McQuaig documented in *Shooting the Hippo*, in the early 1990s, manufactured hysteria in the press about government deficits and accumulated debt, credit ratings, and the "debt wall" paved the way for drastic cuts to social program spending in Canada. The neoliberals or "business liberals" of the Chretien Liberal government and finance minister Paul Martin cut health and education transfer payments to the provinces from $17.3 billion in 1995, to $12.9 billion in 1996, and then $10.3 billion in 1997—a 40% cut in two years. Murray Dobbin notes, "Mulroney had cut Ottawa's contribution to health, education and welfare programs from 20 percent to 15 percent of provincial spending in nine years; Martin would cut it to nine percent in four years."[87]

These deliberate and unnecessary actions manufactured a crisis in Canada's healthcare system, which was the best health system in the world. It's still a very good system, especially compared with its American counterpart, but problems related to MD shortages and long waits for surgery and emergency room treatment have been greatly exacerbated. And why not? The 1996 cuts alone meant that Quebec, for example, lost $1.1 billion, *equivalent to half of its payments for all MDs' services.*[88]

I have intentionally called this a manufactured crisis, for two reasons. First of all, the cuts were unnecessary, as McQuaig and a host of economists have pointed out. The ballooning debt was the result of interest payments related to *Bank of Canada*'s obsession with inflation, rather than social program spending. Second, the Chretien/Martin Liberal governments fatally undermined the "most important core principle of Canadian social democracy," the philosophy of universality, the principle that everyone, regardless of income would receive key public services, paid for through progressive taxation.[89] I'll return to this topic momentarily, but first, a comparative analysis.

The Canadian single-provider healthcare system is still demonstrably more cost efficient and effective than its American counterpart, as we will see. On a per-capita basis, the Canadian system costs 48% less, with 100% coverage. In the U.S., approximately 47 million people, perhaps one in six people, are without healthcare insurance, although they pay 91% more for their system. The U.S. system is based on the ability to pay, rather than need, and Canada's system compares quite favorably, according to Marcia Angell, a Harvard professor and the former editor of *The New England Journal of Medicine.*[90] All Canada's system requires is a cash infusion to return it to its former speedy efficiency, while the U.S. system must be totally revamped.

Let's explore the figures. In Canada, healthcare spending comprised 10.3% of Gross Domestic Product in 2006.[91] In the U.S., this was about 55% higher, at 16% of GDP. U.S. expenditures are higher, both per capita and as a percentage of GDP, than for any other major industrialized country. Despite this, 16% of Americans, or 47 million, lack healthcare coverage altogether.[92] This is more than the aggregate population of 24 states, plus Washington D.C. One out of three Americans below age 65—or 85 million people—lacked private or public health insurance for all or part of 2003–2004. Millions more are underinsured, lacking adequate coverage for medical expenses.[93] As of 2003, Canadian per capita spending on healthcare was $2,989 versus $5,711 for Americans, a difference of 91%.

The U.S. does not have guaranteed universal healthcare. Most Americans have health insurance which is paid for through their employment, or which they purchase directly from private insurers. There are some publicly funded healthcare programs for the elderly, disabled, and the poor, and U.S. federal law is supposed to guarantee public access to emergency services regardless of ability to pay. A number of free clinics also provide free or low-cost care for poor, uninsured patients, in non-emergency situations. However, according to Ron Pollack, founding executive director of *Families USA*, "In 42 states a childless adult can be literally penniless but not fit a 'deserving' category and therefore be ineligible for assistance."[94]

A *New York Times/CBS* poll in January 2006 found that 90% of respondents said the U.S. healthcare system needs fundamental changes or to be completely rebuilt (56% and 34%, respectively).[95] This finding has been fairly consistent over the past 15 years. However, the Employee Benefit Research Institute's annual Health Confidence Survey has found from 1998 to 2004 that the percentage of respondents rating the U.S. healthcare system as "poor" has doubled from 15% to 30% .[96]

In the words of Dr. Christopher Murray of the World Health Organization (WHO), "Basically, you die earlier and spend more time disabled if you're an American rather than a member of most other advanced countries."

Well, how well are we doing? According to the World Health Organization's 2006 comparison of health statistics for Canadians and Americans, although Canada had a smaller population and lower gross domestic product, per capita, it leads everywhere else. Life expectancy is three years longer, child mortality is 25% lower. Health expenditure per capita in Canada is only 52% of what it is in the U.S., and as a percentage of GDP it is only 65% of the U.S. proportion in Canada. In short, using these admittedly broad measures, Canada's universal healthcare system compares quite favorably, despite serious cutbacks in the last ten years or so. The report was published in 2006, but relies on data from 2002–2004.

In spite of this, powerful forces in Canada consistently have been pushing hard in the direction of a private healthcare system similar to that in the U.S. This is ironic given that opinion polls show Americans are in favor of a single-payer, "Canadian style" healthcare system. So, if the Canadian system is better, why is there this push for privatization? The answer is profits. Although the system of multiple private providers is less efficient and more costly, it is very profitable for the insurers and other corporations involved. Canadian insurance companies want some of these profits, and their chums in government who make the laws want their friends in business to profit greatly, even if it means adopting an inferior system.

In writing this, I don't have the "smoking gun," which might consist of an email from Paul Martin to his (and Chretien's, Bob Rae's, and Mulroney's) mentor at *Power Corporation*, Paul Desmarais Sr. But, as I pointed out in *Democracy's Oxygen*, the family ties are very close, and it doesn't take a huge stretch of the imagination to think of them sharing thoughts about policy initiatives over dinner. Chretien's daughter France is married to Paul Desmarais' son Andre; Paul Desmarais Sr.sold *Canada Steamship Lines* for $195 million to his then-employee Paul Martin, in 1981. Desmarais also hired Brian Mulroney as a lawyer to help settle a strike at his Montreal newspaper, *La Presse*, in 1972. Four years later, Desmarais was Mulroney's biggest backer in the latter's first bid for the leadership of the Progressive Conservative Party. It was Mulroney who started us down the path of the first Free Trade Agreement, and then Chretien with NAFTA, and in part these agreements have opened up Canada's public enterprise to privatization.[97]

As Peter C. Newman noted, "No businessman in Canadian history has ever had more intimate and more extended influence with Canadian prime ministers than Desmarais."[98]

Multibillionaire Desmarais' group of companies includes Great West Life Assurance Co., Canada Life Assurance Co., London Life Insurance Co., Great-West Lifeco Inc., Great-West Life & Annuity Assurance Co., London Reinsurance Group, and others, which stand to benefit enormously from privatization of medical care and medical insurance in Canada. Indeed, the Power Financial subsidiary Great-West Life & Annuity Assurance Co. is already a provider of self-funded employee health plans for businesses in the U.S., with 2 million health plan members and 2005 revenues of U.S. $3.3 billion.

Through Gesca Ltee. and Power Communications, Desmarais has also been a significant news media owner over the decades. In the 1990s, he partnered with Conrad Black in controlling the *Southam* newspaper chain, the largest in the country. Today, *Gesca* controls seven daily newspapers in Quebec and Ontario. This media ownership did not harm Desmarais or Black when it came to promoting their shared belief in private enterprise. And it may go some of the way toward explaining the news media's steady criticism of public healthcare, and advocacy of private healthcare.

A recent editorial in *The Montreal Gazette* was headed, "Two-tier medicine is here - live with it." Over at *The Globe and Mail*, columnist Jeffrey Simpson wrote, "Canadians are warming to private health-care delivery," while an editorial chastised the provincial government over "Ontario's dismissal of privately provided care." At *The National Post*, William Watson concluded, "Canadians ready to change medicare." On the west coast at the Vancouver *Province*, subscribers could read that, "Private care is a growing field: Public system is over-stressed."[99] The columnists and editorialists representing the news media and the Desmarais' of Corporate Canada are more than ready for privatization.

NOTES

1. See "Taking precautions," photo and cutline, page C1, *The Windsor Star*, April 29, 2009.
2. Meagan Fitzpatrick, "Canadian swine flu cases hit 13," *The Windsor Star*, April 29, 2009. Andrew Mayeda, "Vaccine debate heats up," *The Windsor Star*, April 29, 2009. Anonymous, "Medical-mask stock surges," *The Windsor Star*, April 29, 2009. Anonymous, "TSX

struggles with swine flu," *The Windsor Star*, April 29, 2009. Linda Nguyen and Becky Rynor, "Airlines, tour operators suspend trips to Mexico," *The Windsor Star*, April 29, 2009.

3. Mayeda, "Vaccine debate," *The Windsor Star*, April 29, 2009.
4. James Ridgeway, "Capitalizing on the flu," *The Village Voice*, November 15, 2005.
5. See anonymous, "The swine flu fiasco," *CBC News* Archives, February 21, 1983.http://archives.cbc.ca/health/disease/clips/12711/
6. James Ridgeway, "Swine flu: Bringing home the bacon," *Mother Jones*, April 27, 2009.
7. The best resource for environment and health news that I'm aware of is Rachel's *Environment and Health Weekly*, at www.rachel.org
8. Theresa Agovino, "Drug maker Pfizer to cut 10,000," *The Toronto Star*, January 23, 2007.
9. Cf. *Fortune* Magazine, The Fortune 500, Top Industries, Most Profitable, May 5, 2008. http://money.cnn.com/magazines/fortune/fortune500/2008/performers/industries/profits/; Also, Arnold S Relman, Marcia Angell, "A Prescription for controlling drug costs," *Newsweek*, December 6, 2004, p. 74.
10. Carl Elliott, "The drug pushers," *The Atlantic Monthly*, April, 2006.
11. Amy Barrett, "Pfizer's funk," *BusinessWeek* online, February 28, 2005.
12. Karen Van Kampen, "Triumph of the pill: A story of health, wealth and stealth," *The National Post Business* Magazine, September, 2002.
13. Van Kampen, "Triumph of the pill."
14. Elliott, "The drug pushers."
15. Tamar Wilner, "Freemarket freebies," *The New Internationalist*, #362, November, 2003.
16. Elliot, "The Drug Pushers."
17. Gregory Zuckerman, "Biovail's tactics on marketing heart medicine focus of probe," *The Wall Street Journal*, August 24, 2003.
18. Cited in, Helke Ferrie, "The HRT scandal," KOS Publishing, Toronto, undated, http://www.kospublishing.com/html/hrt.html;
19. Van Kampen, "Triumph of the Pill."
20. Martin Foreman, *Patents, pills and public health: Can TRIPS deliver?* (The Panos Institute 2002). Cited in Adriane Fugh-Berman, "The Corporate Coauthor," *Journal of General Internal Medicine*, 20(6), June, 2005, 546–548.
21. Marcia Angell, "Excess in the pharmaceutical industry," *The Canadian Medical Association Journal*, December 7, 2004.
22. Carl Elliott, "This is your country on drugs," *The New York Times*, December 14, 2004.
23. "Drugs in the water," *Rachel's Environment and Health Weekly*, #614, September 03, 1998.
24. Angell, "Excess in the pharmaceutical."
25. Barrett, "Pfizer's funk."
26. Alex Berenson, "End of drug trial is a big loss for Pfizer," *The New York Times*, December 4, 2006.
27. Shaoni Bhattacharya, "Up to 140,000 heart attacks linked to Vioxx," *New Scientist*, January 25, 2005, www.newscientist.com
28. Cited in Shaoni Bhattacharya, "Up to 140,000."
29. Kris Hundley, "Win-win partnership," *St. Petersburg Times*, February 2, 2007.
30. Peter Jüni, Linda Nartey, Stephan Reichenbach, Rebekka Sterchi, Paul A Dieppe, and Matthias Egger, "Risk of cardiovascular events and rofecoxib: Cumulative meta-analysis," *The Lancet*, 2004; 364, 2021–2029.

31. Elliott, "This is your country on drugs."
32. Canadian Institute for Health Information, statistical information, 2007. The statistical graphs contain actual figures up to and including 2003, with projections for 2004 and 2005, as of January 2007.
33. Judy Gerstel, "Pushing pills down our throats," *The Toronto Star*, September 2, 2005.
34. Rita Daly and Karen Palmer, "Side effects; Drugs called statins can lower cholesterol levels, a risk factor for heart disease. But they can also cause serious problems," *The Toronto Star*, December 4, 2004.
35. Cf. Lawrence Goodman, "Celebrity pill pushers," *Salon*, July 11, 2002. Lawrence Goodman, "Well, if Kathleen Turner says it works: Celebrities in the pay of the drug companies," *The Guardian*, July 23, 2002.
36. Ray Moynihan, "The intangible magic of celebrity marketing," *PLoS Med* 1(2): e42, doi:10.1371/journal.pmed.0010042, November 30, 2004.
37. Goodman, "Celebrity pill pushers."
38. Daly and Palmer, "Side effects."
39. Elaine Carey, "Cholesterol drug spending may soar; Guidelines say 27% more patients need statins. But few benefits for low-risk patients, study says," *The Toronto Star*, April 12, 2005.
40. Lindsey Tanner, "Midday snooze helps the heart: Study," *The Toronto Star*, February 12, 2007.
41. Sharon Kirkey, "Cholesterol drugs don't help 'bulk' of takers," *The National Post*, January 23, 2007.
42. Alan Cassels, "Selling sickness to the masses," *The Toronto Star*, September 21, 2005.
43. Ibid.
44. Carey, "Cholesterol drug spending."
45. Jacky Law, "It's a medical scandal. The pharmaceutical giants are making billions by persuading us we have illnesses that only their products can cure. This is the real Drug Abuse," *The Daily Mail*, April 13, 2006. http://campaignfortruth.com/Eclub/080506/CTM%20-%20drug%20abuse.htm
46. Law, "It's a medical scandal."
47. Ray Moynihan and David Henry, "The fight against disease mongering: Generating knowledge for action, *PLoS Med* 3(4): e191, April, 2006.
48. Moynihan and Henry, "The fight." See also Ray Moynihan and Allan Cassells, *Selling sickness: How the Worlds Biggest Pharmaceutical Companies Are Turning Us All Into Patients* (New York: Nation Books, 2005), 99–118.
49. David Healy, "The latest mania: selling Bipolar Disorder," *PLoS Med* 3(4): e185. doi:10.1371/journal.pmed.0030185, April 11, 2006.
50. Healy, "The latest mania."
51. Helke Ferrie, "The HRT Scandal," http://www.kospublishing.com/html/hrt.html
52. Lynn Payer, *Disease-mongers: How doctors, drug companies, and insurers are making you feel sick*, New York, Wiley & Sons, 1992.
53. See Ferrie, "The HRT scandal"; "Conference updates hormone replacement therapy," *Focus*, a Harvard Medical School Newsletter, November 8, 2002. http://focus.hms.harvard.edu/2002/Nov8_2002/womens_health.html
54. Nathan Seppa, "Hormone therapy falls out of favor," *Science News Online*, 162:4, www.sciencenews.org

55. Ferrie, "The HRT scandal."
56. Helen Branswell, "Study shows HRT of no use," *The Windsor Star*, March 18, 2003.
57. Leonore Tiefer, Female Sexual Dysfunction: A Case Study of Disease Mongering and Activist Resistance. *PLoS Med* 3(4): e178, doi:10.1371/journal.pmed.0030178, April 11, 2006.
58. Joel Lexchin, "Bigger and better: How Pfizer redefined erectile dysfunction," *PLoS Med*, 3(4): e132, doi:10.1371/journal, pmed.0030132, April, 2006. See http://medicine.plosjournals.org/perlserv/?request=get-document&doi=10.1371/journal.pmed.0030132. Lexchin writes, "Pfizer's well-financed campaign was aimed at raising awareness of the problem of ED, while at the same time narrowing the treatment possibilities to just a single option: medication."
59. Tiefer, "Female Sexual Dysfunction."
60. Ibid.
61. Ibid.
62. Arnold S. Relman, A. "Separating continuing medical education from pharmaceutical marketing," *Journal of the American Medical Association*,, 285: 2009–2012; 2001.. Cited in Angell, "Excess."
63. Elliott, "The drug pushers." Dr. Elliott is a professor in the Centre for Bioethics at the University of Minnesota.
64. Richard C. Christensen and Michael J. Tueth, "Commentary: pharmaceutical companies and academic departments of psychiatry: A call for ethics education," *Academic Psychiatry* 22:135–137, June 1998.
65. Arthur Lazarus, "Commentary: The role of the pharmaceutical industry in medical education in psychiatry," *Academic Psychiatry* 30: 40–44, February 2006.
66. Ibid.
67. Quoted in, Wilner, "Freemarket freebies."
68. See "Big Pharma," in James Winter, *Lies the Media Tell Us* (Montreal: Black Rose Books, 2007).
69. Elliott, "The drug pushers."
70. "On guard against big pharma's lobbying efforts," *Marketplace*, National Public Radio, Monday, March 19, 2007, http://marketplace.publicradio.org/shows/2007/03/19/PM200703195.html
71. Kate Jirik, "How great researchers get by-lines, get paid, and get medicine in trouble," *Bioethics Forum*, December 28, 2006.
72. Ibid.
73. Ibid.
74. Ibid. See also, Adriane Fugh-Berman, "The corporate coauthor," *Journal of General Internal Medicine*, 20(6): 546–548, June, 2005.
75. Jirik, "How great researchers"; Adriane Fugh-Berman, "The corporate coauthor."
76. Carl Elliott, "Not-so-public relations: How the drug industry is branding itself with bioethics," *Slate*, December 15, 2003. http://www.slate.com/id/2092442/
77. David Healy, "Ghostly data," in Let Them Eat Prozac (web site) http://www.healyprozac.com/GhostlyData/default.htm
78. Anonymous, "Industry involvement in preparation of articles," *The Cleveland Clinical Journal of Medicine*, 72:6, June, 2005. His/her reference is: Marcia Angell, "Is academic medicine for sale?" *The New England Journal of Medicine*, Vol. 342, No. 20, 342:1516–1518, 2000.

79. On Wigand, see Marie Brenner, "The man who knew too much," *Vanity Fair*, May 1996.
80. From, "Pressure points: How Big Pharma reacts when a drug scandal breaks," *The New Internationalist*, #362, November, 2003.
81. See John Staube and Sheldon Rampton, *Toxic sludge is good for you!* (Monroe, Maine, Common Courage Press, 1995). Also, The Center For Media and Democracy, www.prwatch.org
82. Alan Cassels, "Canada's newspapers get failing grade for coverage of new prescription drugs," editorial, *Canadian Centre for Policy Alternatives*, http://policyalternatives.ca/index.cfm?act=news&call=622&do=article&pA=BB736455; Alan Cassels, Merrilee Atina Hughes, Carol Cole, Barbara Mintzes, Joel Lexchin and James McCormack, "Drugs in the news: How well do Canadian newspapers report the good, the bad and the ugly of new prescription drugs?" *The Canadian Centre for Policy Alternatives*, April, 2003.
83. If the book was merely mentioned in a list, or in passing in an article, I didn't count this: I was looking for book reviews. Cf. Lynn Payer, *Disease-mongers*; Ray Moynihan and Alan Cassels, *Selling Sickness;* Marcia Angell, *The Truth About the Drug Companies: How They Deceive Us and What To Do About It* (New York: Random House, 2005; John Abramson, *Overdosed America: The Broken Promise of American Medicine* (New York: Harper Perennial, 2005); Greg Critser, *Generation Rx: How Prescription Drugs Are Altering American Lives, Minds and Bodies* (Boston: Houghton-Mifflin, 2005); Jeffrey Robinson, *Prescription Games* (New York: Simon & Schuster, 2001).
84. Kevin Hassett, "*The misguided assault on the U.S. drug industry*," Bloomberg Press, August 29, 2005.
85. *Mediadoctor.ca* is published by the Institute for Media, Policy and Civil Society, a group of academics and clinicians from the University of British Columbia, York University and the University of Victoria. The goal of Media Doctor Canada is to improve Canadian media coverage of new medical drugs and treatments.
86. Cf. "Study finds no link between cancer, pesticides," *The Kingston Whig–Standard*, August 21, 1997.
87. See Linda McQuaig, *Shooting The Hippo: Death by Deficit and Other Canadian Myths* (Toronto: Viking, 1996); Murray Dobbin, *Paul Martin: CEO For Canada?* (Toronto: James Lorimer & Company, 2003); Maude Barlow and Bruce Campbell, *Straight Through the Heart: How the Liberals Abandoned the Just Society and What Canadians Can Do About It* (Toronto: HarperCollins Canada, 1996).
88. Dobbin, *Paul Martin*, 77–78.
89. Ibid.
90. Quoted in, "Canadian health care system makes U.S. system look insane: editor," *Canadian Press NewsWire,* Toronto: July 4, 2000.
91. Canadian Institute for Health Information, 2007. Total expenditures in 2006 were $148 billion, or $4548 per capita. http://secure.cihi.ca/cihiweb/dispPage.jsp?cw_page=media_05dec2006_e#1.
92. Plunkett Research, Ltd. "Industry Statistics, Trends and In-depth Analysis of Top Companies. Health Care Trends. 1) Introduction to the Health Care Industry Health Expenditures and Services in the U.S.": http://www.plunkettresearch.com/HealthCare/HealthCareTrends/tabid/294/Default.aspx
93. Holly Sklar, "Time For Health Care For All On Medicare's 40th Anniversary," *ZNet* Daily Commentary, August 13, 2005, www.zmag.org

94. "Universal health care advocate speaks," The University of Pittsburgh, *University Times*, Vol. 39:5, October 26, 2006. Ron Pollack, founding executive director of Families USA. The October 19, 2006 lecture was part of the Rubash Distinguished Lecture Series, co-sponsored by the School of Law and School of Social Work.
95. *The New York Times/CBS News* Poll of 1,229 adults, conducted January 20–25, 2006.
96. Employee Benefit Research Institute and Mathew Greenwald & Associates, Inc. 1998–2004 Health Confidence Surveys. "Public Attitudes on the U.S. Health Care System: Findings from the Health Confidence Survey" EBRI Issue Brief No. 275. November 2004.
97. See Jim Grieshaber-Otto and Scott Sinclair, *Bad Medicine: Trade treaties, privatization and health care reform in Canada,* The Canadian Centre for Policy Alternatives, Ottawa, 2004.
98. Peter C. Newman, "Epitaph for the two-party state," *Maclean's*, November 1, 1993, p. 14.
99. See editorial, "Two-tier medicine is here - live with it," *The Gazette,* February 2, 2007; Jeffrey Simpson, "Canadians are warming to private health-care delivery," *The Globe and Mail*, February 21, 2007; William Watson, "Canadians ready to change medicare," *The National Post*, March 8, 2007; editorial, Ontario's dismissal of privately provided care, *The Globe and Mail,* Toronto, Ont.: Mar 19, 2007; "Private care is a growing field: Public system is over-stressed," *The Province,* January 14, 2007.

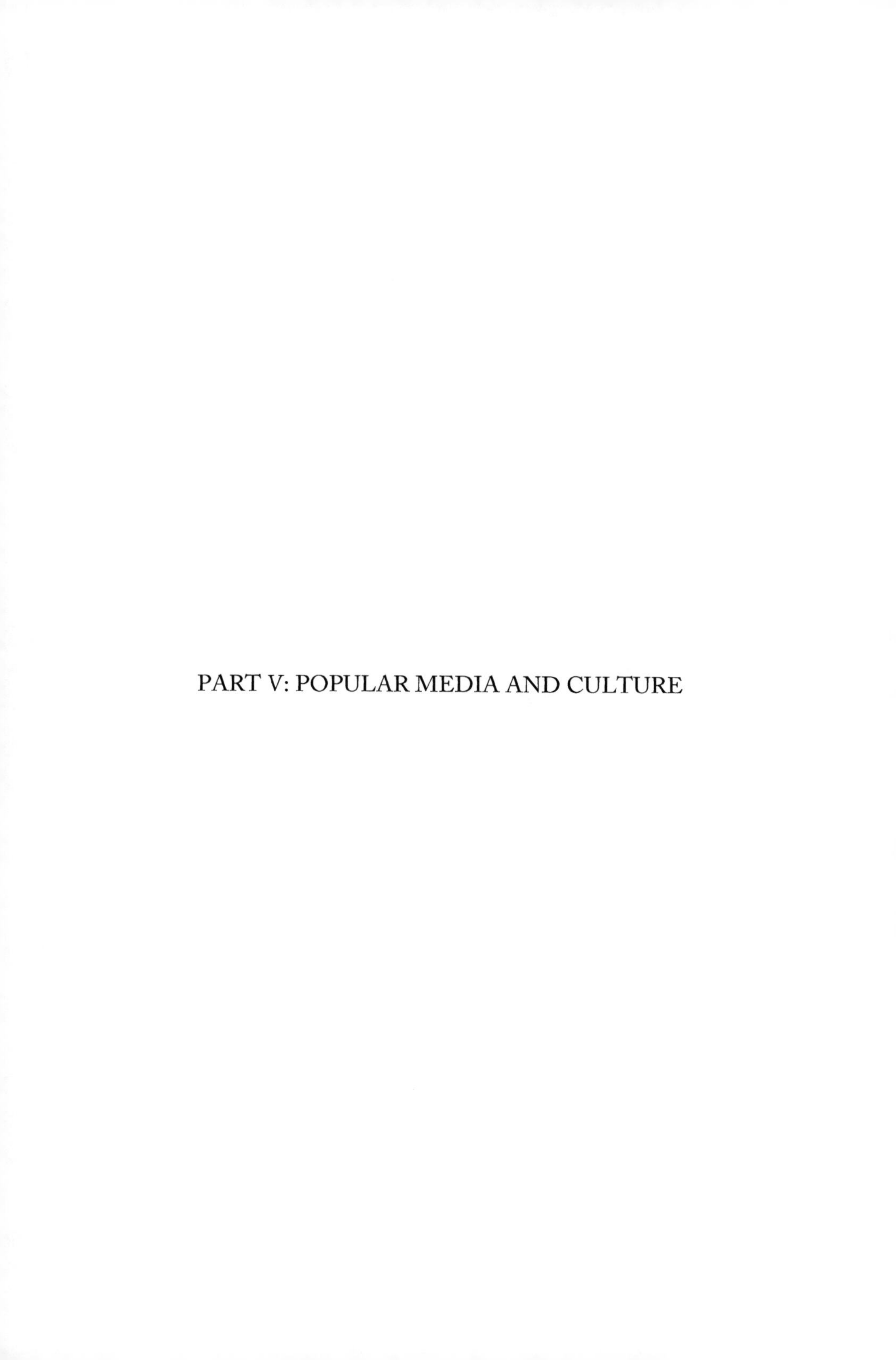

PART V: POPULAR MEDIA AND CULTURE

CHAPTER ELEVEN

Soft Power: Policing the Border through Canadian TV Crime Drama[1]

YASMIN JIWANI

> "Soft power" is the ability to achieve desired outcomes in international affairs through attraction rather than coercion. It works by convincing others to follow, or getting them to agree to, norms and institutions that produce the desired behavior. Soft power can rest on the appeal of one's ideas or the ability to set the agenda in ways that shape the preferences of others. If a state can make its power legitimate in the perception of others and establish international institutions that encourage them to channel or limit their activities, it may not need to expend as many of its costly traditional economic or military resources.[2]

In an article published in *Foreign Affairs*, Joseph Nye and Admiral William Owens[3] make an argument for the strategic use of information in winning the hearts and minds of people throughout the world. Though written for an audience specifically interested in foreign affairs and Americans working abroad, Nye and Owens's notion of soft power is not unfamiliar to those working on the margins, within the nonprofit activist circles or in academia. Soft power, as Nathan Gardels[4] observes, exemplifies the Gramscian concept of the hegemony of civil society in contrast to the hegemony of the state made explicit in its brute power to enforce. That hegemony, as Goldberg has argued in another context, is a veiling of violence where civility functions as "the iron hand in the velvet glove."[5] Thus, while the concept of soft power has most often been applied to, and anchored within, the domain of international relations and issues of cultural imperialism, it is apposite to domestic governance through the maintenance of a social order and the production of what Foucault[6] has described as "docile bodies."

In this chapter, I focus on the soft power of television crime dramas in constructing an imagined nation and, more particularly, on identifying the in- and out-groups within. While scholars have devoted some attention to the contemporary US crime drama genre, focusing on such programs as *Law and Order*, political dramas such as *West Wing*,[7] and talk shows (e.g., Oprah Winfrey), there have been few studies that have examined Canadian programming as popular cultural forms which reveal the complicated interstices of Canadian national identity vis-a-vis the U.S., and in relation to others within and outside the nation. *The Border*, a popular Canadian television crime show broadcasted on a weekly basis by the Canadian Broadcasting Corporation (CBC), offers an insightful avenue to examine issues of soft power. *The Border* debuted on January 7, 2008. Since then, the show has sparked considerable interest. It has been sold to the French market, and is now being showcased as a potential sale to the U.S. market.

SITUATING *THE BORDER*

Television crime drama has a particular structure of appeal. Closely resembling reality TV shows and borrowing from news and current affairs programming, crime dramas are particularly provocative in their identification of social problems, threats to safety, and offering resolutions to crises through the intervention of the state and its criminal justice system. The restoration of order and unraveling of mysteries are some of the compelling features that attract audiences. More importantly, "crime dramas are morality plays which feature struggles between good and evil, between heroes who stand for moral authority and villains who challenge that authority."[8] When such shows reference contemporary events, their realism is amplified thus blurring the lines between fiction and reality-based programming. It is this combination of melodrama and realism that makes the crime drama genre particularly effective as a vehicle of "soft power." Indeed, in the post-9/11 landscape of North American televisual culture, crises and threats have assumed an added potency, fueling crime dramas with scripts that reinvigorate embedded stereotypes of others[9] and that seek to appease public anxieties through a demonstration of effective technologies of surveillance and control.

PATROLLING *THE BORDER*

In some senses, *The Border* is a dilute, Canadian version of Fox's *24*—a program that has generated a wide and stable audience base.[10] However, unlike *24*, which pivots on a rogue/lone male hero working in a system but not yet quite a part of it, *The Border* tends to veer toward an institutionally structured team approach. What is quintessentially Canadian about *The Border* is its softer approach to issues of power and conflict that erupt in the various episodes. Lead actor, James McGowan described the show as "a clash between classic American and Canadian" approaches to security.[11] Tending more toward diplomacy, "smart action," and collaboration, *The Border*'s cast act as members of a specially mandated department of Immigration and Customs Security (ICS) that patrols the U.S.–Canada border, utilizing a "soft approach" tempered with what executive producer Peter Raymont describes as a "conscience."[12] At its debut, the show attracted 710,000 viewers[13] which is a sizeable number in the small Canadian market.

It is interesting to note that the show, in some implicit and explicit ways, attempts to defuse U.S. criticism of Canada's porous borders. The U.S. had charged that terrorists were slipping into the country through Canadian border posts in the immediate aftermath of 9/11. Since then, the Canadian state has sought to strengthen border control in various ways by arming border guards, increasing technologies of surveillance at airports, and engaging in information exchange with other state agencies.

Lindalee Tracey and her husband and partner Peter Raymont originally conceived *The Border* as a drama based on their previous work. They had originally produced an award-winning documentary *Invisible Nation* documenting the plight of illegal immigrants. Post 9/11, the team concentrated on issues of security and the threat of terrorism which culminated in their documentary television miniseries, the *Undefended Border*. The series focused on the different state agencies mandated to ensure national security, i.e., the Canadian Security and Intelligence Service (CSIS), the Royal Canadian Mounted Police, the War Crimes Unit, and the Immigration department.[14]

This focus on the Canadian state's security apparatus continues to be the focal point of *The Border*. The story's arc deals with the multiple agencies involved in securing the borders against terrorist and other threats. Within this context, *The Border*'s elite Immigration and Customs Security squad demonstrates its "good" and compassionate Canadian character in contrast to the brusque and ruthless character of America's Homeland Security, as well as the arrogance and deference (to the U.S.) of Canada's "spy" agency, CSIS. What comes through, in the final analysis, is that despite the "good" cop/ "bad" cop role played by each of these agencies, the security of the nation trumps all else.

DIFFERENT STROKES FOR DIFFERENT FOLKS—IMAGINING "THREATS" AND REPRESENTING DIVERSITY

The Border's 13 episodes that aired during its first season are instructive of the Canadian imaginary—how "we" like to think of ourselves. Each episode references contemporary political events thereby resonating with current concerns and invoking recall. This invocation is critical as it "fills in the gaps"—we, as the audience, input our remembrances of things past to make sense of the present situation. In this regard, the show performs its ideological labor by establishing materially grounded referents, and thus becomes "a vehicle for the communication of messages which embody, not our 'real social relationships, but rather cultural mythologies *about* these relationships."[15]

The very name of this team—Immigration and Customs Security— signifies what are perceived as being the central threats to the nation: immigrants, both legal and illegal, custom violations in the form of the trafficking of drugs, arms, and people, and, of course, threats to national security in the form of terrorism. Thus, throughout the series, the audience is treated to the team's capture of a Syrian terrorist; the smuggling of money and sale of Canadian arms; the arrest of Muslim detainees who have escaped from a crashed U.S. rendition flight; illegal strippers; stowaways; a human trafficking operation; criminal networks involving a child soldier from Darfur; a major terrorist attack in Toronto (again by Muslims); protecting a Cuban minister on Canadian soil; finding a pedophile and saving a child; and protecting Canadian immigrants and refugees from warlords and others who seek revenge. The list covers all manner of crime, and yet it is noteworthy that of the 13 episodes, five involve Muslim characters.

THE WEBSITE

The Border's website not only hosts all 13 episodes which are available for online viewing within Canada, but it also features a weekly poll, placed strategically after the description of each episode. The poll includes questions that emanate from and pertain to current political and social concerns. Hence, the first episode, titled "Pockets of Vulnerability" and featuring the arrest of a Syrian terrorist at the Toronto Pearson airport, asks viewers the following question: Do you feel security is too vigilant at Canada's international airport? Those viewing the episodes online can respond.

The website also features an interactive game titled "Interrogation." Here the viewer is presented with a typical case scenario: "You've just been pulled out of line at Customs as you land at Pearson Airport in Toronto. Try to keep your cool as you are being interviewed." The interview progresses with two members of the cast interrogating the player/viewer. On one side of the web page is a visual of a water cooler with the instructions, "press and hold, drink water to calm." Underneath is a digitized time clock, and on the left-hand side, immediately adjacent to the water cooler is a stress gauge. The sound accompanying the interrogation is of a rapid heartbeat. Viewers are invited to play the game at the end of which their potential is assessed insofar as their ability to qualify as an ICS field agent, or alternatively, to be condemned as a criminal. In the later part of this chapter, I address the technologies of surveillance that are incorporated in this website and that amplify fears of a constant and recurring threat, and legitimize insidious state mechanisms of control.

THE CAST

Filmed against Toronto's skyline, at the Toronto Port Authority's International Marine and Ferry Terminal (originally designed to be staffed by the Canadian Border Services Agency),[16] *The Border* establishes its Canadian identity. The cast itself is reflective of the multiracial composition of the city. At the lead is Major Mike Kessler, representing the "good" conscience-driven Canadian who attempts, against many odds, to maintain the semblance of Canada as a nation of fairness, tolerance, and compassion. Kessler's past experience as the leader of an elite counter-terrorism squad lends him the credibility to man this team. At the same time, his conscience, having witnessed the atrocities in Bosnia and realizing Canadian complicity in the genocide of a Muslim village, makes him cynical. Yet, he is the valiant hero that stands for good and attempts to rectify the moral corruption of Canadian politicians and their American counterparts. In this sense, he signifies a kind of hegemonic masculinity,[17] which is continually underscored by his sexual relationship with a human rights lawyer, his marital breakup with his wife, and his relationship with his rebellious daughter.

In contrast, Kessler's second in command, Superintendent Maggie Norton (played by Catherine Disher), represents the quintessential pleasant, nurturing figure. Smart and able to carry off various guises—as a border officer, passenger, grandmotherly figure—she embodies the traits commonly associated with "good women."[18] *The Border* website (www.theborder.ca) describes her as a mother who loves to bake, is a good shot, and can reduce "a vicious serial killer to a sobbing six-year-old, begging her forgiveness." Norton is counter-balanced by a traditional male archetypical Canadian figure—the burly, no-nonsense, overweight, and middle-aged police officer Detective Sergeant Al "Moose" Lepinsky (played by Mark Wilson). He is the traditional cop—loves doughnuts and has a stable family and a dog.

In contrast to Lepinsky, the cast also features the typical young, white Canadian male—Detective Sergeant Gray Jackson (played by Graham Abbey). He epitomizes the lone wolf—daring, charming, and a gambling addict.[19] Legendary for his survival skills and quick on his feet, he is a constant irritant to his partner, Sergeant Layla Hourani (played by Nazneen Contractor). A Muslim woman with a descent, background or origins and a previous RCMP officer, Hourani has issues with authority, especially with Kessler's. Fluent in seven languages, she represents the inside "informant" —teaching others about Muslims. Riddled with a conscience, she is shown as a somewhat weak character because of her emotional conflicts.

Aside from Hourani, the other person of color is Acting Inspector Darnell Williams (played by Jim Codrington). A Black man, he is described on the show's website as "tall, elegant, with a dry wit and a sexy smile" with an academic background in International Relations. He is noted as being "authentically" Canadian with "a family pedigree dating back to the Loyalists." Various episodes also allude to his previous positioning as "our man in Africa" (see Episode 9, "Restricted Access"). Other episodes have cast a shadow of doubt over his allegiance to ICS based on his role as ex-CSIS agent.

The other characters in the show include the typical "geek," Agent Hieroynmous Slade (played by Jonas Chernick), whose love interest in one episode is an Aboriginal woman from the Mohawk nation (Episode 12, "Grave Concern"). Slade is informal, socially inept, and constantly eating junk food. In contrast, Special Agent Bianca LaGarda (Sofia Milos) is formal, attractive, seemingly ruthless in the sense of adhering to a black and white view of reality, and hyper-patriotic. As a Canadian-based agent of Homeland Security, it is her responsibility to ensure that anything that bears on American interests is directly under her purview. Here, she is constantly in conflict with Kessler. However, what is most interesting about LaGarda is her Cuban background. As one of those who left Cuba as a child on a boat, and made it to Florida, she has an undying commitment to her adopted nation—the American people are her first and primary concern. She represents the immigrant who made it and whose loyalty cannot be questioned.

The final character in this team is the "evil" CSIS director, Agent Andrew Mannering (played by Nigel Bennett). Like LaGarda, he has a binary view of the world, and prefers to side with the U.S. Unlike Kessler, Mannering has no qualms about sending Canadians of Middle Eastern origins to Syria or elsewhere to satisfy U.S. desires (see Episode 1,"Pockets of Vulnerability"). He is portrayed as a lackey, serving powerful interests both in Ottawa and in Washington.

READING RACE AND GENDER

> Imaginative geography of the "our land/barbarian land" variety does not require that the barbarians acknowledge the distinction. It is enough for "us" to set up these boundaries in our own minds; "they" become "they" accordingly, and both their territory and their mentality are designated as different from "ours."[20]

The Border's cast orchestrates the kinds of meanings that are to be given to each element of the story. This is contingent on how each member acts, the sentiments and rationale they articulate to support their claims and ensuing actions. While the series, in totality, points to an overriding preoccupation and contestation with American power (which comes across as "hard" power), it is the underlying and more subordinate tropes through which this contestation is made possible that belie the ideological work involved in cementing a notion of *The Border*, as a "defended" in contrast to "undefended" boundary—separating "us" from "them." These subordinate tropes and stories cohere around the figure of the immigrant—whether an illegal, undocumented worker, a victim of human trafficking, a legitimate refugee, a newly arrived immigrant, or one with entrenched historical roots.

The immigrant/refugee in all of these various avatars remains the outsider of sorts, accepted gradually but only conditionally. Even the cast's three members who are racially marked as Black, South Asian, and Cuban reflect this conditional and tenuous acceptance, though they articulate a more "reasonable" and assimilated notion of the immigrant. Palumbo-Liu makes this same point in reference to Asian American bodies, remarking that "we have increased meditations on the workings of America upon the foreign body, which will wear away the marks of difference and mold Asia."[21] Similarly, in the Canadian context, the marking of the body through a wearing away of difference makes these bodies more acceptable, and they in turn buy into these "fictions of assimilation"[22] to gain a modicum of acceptance.

For example, in examining Darrell William's character as an assimilated Black man, it is significant to note how Blacks in general have been represented in the mass media. Deroche and Deroche examined Black portrayals in five police dramas in the 1985–1986 season. Though dated, their findings resonate with existing representations. They note, "black men are modeled for us as more bourgeois than their white counterparts, more self-directed and effectively well-managed, and more tasteful."[23] Deroche and Deroche argue that the currency of these representations rests on the need for "comforting images" that evacuate notions of structural racism and affirm the ethos of liberalism. As they put it, "The straight, upstanding image of the black man resonates well with white audiences that are tired of guilt and also with a black middle class constituency that is anxious to lay claim to a socio-economic rather than a racial master-status."[24] However, their findings contrast sharply with other literature focusing on race and crime in the news.[25]

Within television news, Black representations cohere around deviance and criminality.[26] Closer home in Canada, criminologist Scot Wortley[27] has demonstrated how crimes committed by Black people are given considerable media attention, while Black women as victims of crime are rarely accorded the same degree of publicity. These findings are corroborated by research in the U.S. In her review of the literature on race and crime, Mary Beth Oliver[28] observes that representations vary across the different genres and that within fictional entertainment, Blacks are less likely to be represented as perpetrators. However, for news and reality-based programming, an inverse relationship is apparent. Based on her findings and those cited above, I would argue that both these representations, i.e., of the Black male as criminal and as law enforcer, work in concert. In effect, they are part of the doubling discourse of race.

Hall[29] and Bhabha[30] argue that this tension and ambivalence between two diametrically opposite kinds of representations is inherent to all colonial stereotypes. For Bhabha, these polarities reflect the ambivalence between desire on the one hand, and disavowal on the other, or between the recognition of sameness and the demonizing of difference. Yet, in combination, they serve to suture an ideological framework that hinges on a "grammar of race,"[31] wherein power relations are kept unequal and intact, and difference is inferiorized and naturalized.

Hence, returning to *The Border*, Acting Inspector Darnell Williams's role can then be seen as "comforting" in the sense described above, and as a balancing trope to the continued stereotyping and marginalization of Black representations in Canadian news.[32] Or, as Sut Jhally and Justin Lewis[33] have argued in reference to the *Cosby Show*, Darnell Williams's representation could be an emblematic sign of "enlightened racism"—a racism which seeks to evacuate notions of racial inequality and emphasize upward mobility through progress while normalizing middle-class values and behaviors.

It is this notion of evacuating the history and continued presence of racial discrimination that I wish to pay particular attention to, with regard to both Acting Inspector Darnell Williams and Sergeant Layla Hourani's representations as detailed below.

THE VEILED AND UNVEILED MUSLIM WOMEN

As a Muslim woman of South Asian origins, Layla Hourani's character fits into the same prototype as that of Darnell Williams. Like him, she is educated, assimilated, and tolerably Muslim. She doesn't wear a veil, she can relate to others around her, and she speaks flawless English (Canadian style). However, unlike Williams, Hourani is more emotive and experiences considerable frustrations and crises of conscience while performing her duties. As mentioned before, she has repeated conflicts with her boss, Kessler.

In several episodes, Hourani attempts to dispel the stereotypes that others in her team have about Islam in particular, and Muslims, in general. Yet, her efforts to demonstrate that Islam is a religion of peace are continually frustrated by the show's repeated references to jihadists both in its story arc and in the footage that constitutes the content of the show. In this regard, her character demonstrates a certain nuanced quality in that she represents the dilemma of Muslims in the West that want to show that they are "good," "law-abiding" Canadians. Nevertheless, her roots, race, and religion situate her identity in a problematic manner. In one episode she attempts to enter a Wahhabi mosque (which embraces a fundamentalist interpretation of Islam). Though she covers her head, she is denied entry while her white male partner, Detective Sergeant Gray Jackson, is able to walk in. Hourani, in the meantime, is spat upon by other Muslim males outside the mosque. She is called a traitor and collaborator. She gets even when she pursues and catches a Muslim youth who has fled from the mosque upon seeing the white Sergeant Gray inside (Episode 1, "Pockets of Vulnerability"). This scene and others seal her representation as a subordinate in both worlds—Muslim and Canadian. In the Muslim context, it is the power of patriarchy and male supremacy that anchor her subordination. In the Canadian world of ICS, it is her difference that makes her subordinate.

The positioning of Hourani as an assimilated Other who survives on conditional acceptance, and who is denigrated by other Muslims, as well as by those in the team (except for Gray who tries to reach out to her), is problematized when contrasted with the role played by U.S. Homeland Security agent Bianca LaGarda. For LaGarda, the acceptance isn't conditional, it is not something that she thinks about, and it is not something that her own convictions or beliefs are in conflict with. In other words, though born a Cuban, LaGarda places her identity as an American first. Her commitment to the security and safety of the American people is her driving force. Yet, for all of her patriotic loyalty, LaGarda herself suffers from the quintessential stereotypical Latina flaw—her temper and inability to be diplomatic. In effect, this is what has consigned her to the outskirts of empire—Toronto, Canada! That her temper is a mark of her Latina identity is not as clearcut as it would seem here, because like other crime shows, within *The Border*, the political is transformed into the personal.[34] Thus, LaGarda's temperament is then ascribed to her personality rather than to a stereotypical national trait. Nonetheless, in contrast to other Americans, this temperamental slant combined with her accent and our knowledge of her background places her squarely in the realm of the "contained" and "domesticated" Other.[35]

Aside from LaGarda, Hourani's character as the conflict-ridden, conscience-driven, Westernized Muslim woman is also distinguished by contrast with other Muslim women characters in the show. In one episode which I detail below, she is confronted with unveiling a Muslim woman (who is wearing both the Hijab, the head scarf, and the Niqab, a face veil). In performing such an action, Hourani is well aware that she is working as an agent of the state and that she is violating her own ethics. In accomplishing these actions, she mimics colonial powers.

In mapping colonial fantasies, Meyda Yeğenoğlu argues that

> The veil attracts the eye, and forces one to think, to speculate about what is behind it. It is often represented as some kind of a mask, hiding the woman. With the help of this opaque veil, the Oriental woman is considered as not yielding herself to the Western gaze and therefore imagined as hiding something behind the veil. It is through the inscription of the veil as a mask that the Oriental woman is turned into an enigma. Such a discursive construction incites the presumption that the real nature of these women is concealed, their truth is disguised and they appear in a false deceptive manner. They are therefore other than what they appear to be.[36]

Interestingly, Hourani not only unveils and hence, unmasks the Muslim woman, but in so doing, reveals her for what she is—a terrorist rather than simply a woman and mother. However, this Muslim woman also turns out to be something other than the essentialized prototype of Muslim women, a point that I elaborate below.

ORIENTALIST ENCOUNTERS

> As two Canadian soldiers are held hostage by Afghani[37] militants, ICS and CSIS uncover plans for a deadly attack on Toronto. Kessler believes the key to preventing the attack may lie with an unlikely source – Sorraya, a burqa-clad wife and mother. Can ICS manipulate a mother's love to find out crucial information? And what collateral damage is Kessler willing to risk to prevent catastrophe?
>
> Weekly Poll: Do you feel collateral damage is ever justified in military action?
> Response: Yes 55% No: 45%
> (From *The Border* website: www.theborder.ca)

The above synopsis captures the gist of Episode 8. I focus on this episode because it represents, in a quintessential manner, the various orientalist discursive moves that were deployed by the characters in their encounters with a Muslim woman. It also highlights the support that this episode garnered with regard to naturalizing collateral damage.

The episode begins with a shot of the ICS crew tracking a car as it makes its way to the border patrol office. There, Superintendent Maggie Norton, dressed as a regular customs officer, asks to check the passport of the Arab and Muslim man driver. She also asks to look at his wife's face. The wife, Sorraya, is sitting in the back seat with a baby. The man, seemingly reluctant, agrees whereupon his wife reveals her face. The car drives away, and superimposed on the back seat window, on the body of the woman, is a reflection of the Canadian flag—sovereignty asserted.

The next sequence of events begins with opening shots of another scene with Kessler and CSIS agent Mannering in a car, watching a house in which the inhabitants of the car (mentioned above) and others are residing. Mannering asks Kessler to arrest the occupants, something that CSIS does not have the power to do. Kessler reluctantly obliges, given his suspicious and antagonistic relations with CSIS. Thereupon, the officers (all in plain clothes and located at different sites in close proximity to the house) are given the order and burst in to seize and arrest the occupants, all of whom are men. Inside the house, Kessler, while conversing with an officer, hears a baby crying, and upon opening the closet door, discovers Sorraya with her baby. While CSIS escorts the male prisoners out to interrogate them, ICS officers take Sorraya and her baby to their headquarters, where the baby is separated from his mother and Sorraya is interrogated. At the ICS headquarters, the multiple television screens portray a hostage situation in Afghanistan with two Canadian soldiers being held by an Afghan warlord.

Sorraya's interrogation begins with Maggie Norton who questions her about the baby's real identity (they have since discovered that the passports were forgeries). Using the motherly tack, Norton talks about how babies' cries are "calibrated" to drive mothers crazy and that Sorraya could lose her child if she didn't reveal all. This ploy does not work. Thereupon, our archetypal old-fashioned Canadian police officer, Detective Sergeant Al "Moose" Lepinsky, tries his tack. Sorraya begins to talk, but will not reveal anything. Lepinsky is followed by Darnell Williams, and subsequently, Layla Hourani. The interrogation resembles the game on the website, except that in this instance, it is not a game voluntarily engaged in by the viewer. Rather, the charge against Sorraya appears to be serious as she knows the plan that has been hatched to blow up a Toronto subway line. Her intransigence appears to be the motivating force for all the team members to try, in succession, to make her disclose her secret.

A transcript of this interrogation involving Lepinsky, Williams, and Hourani is detailed below. It is interesting to note how Sorraya responds and the kinds of counter-claims that she offers in response to her interrogators' questions.

Lepinsky: You're from Afghanistan, huh? The thing you're wearing on your head there; it's a burqa. Is that what it is called? That's Afghan, right? It gets hot as hell under there. No vitamin D. The whole country, all the women have their bones crumbling. You might wanna talk to the prison doctor. Do a bone scan. Maybe he'll get you some calcium supplements. Do you people like living in "A" hole? Is that it? Because you got Canadian kids coming over there helping you out and you send them home in boxes.

Sorraya: Help us?

Lepinsky: Yeah build roads. Set up clinics.

Sorraya:	They're soldiers. They're not aid workers.
Lepinsky:	They're nation-builders, lady.
Sorraya:	They are killers. You don't get it. Your soldiers are killing our people!
Lepinsky:	They're defending themselves. People are gun-crazy. They've got 10-year- olds running around with AK 47s. What's the matter with you people?
Sorraya:	26 years of uninterrupted war. My whole life.
Lepinsky:	The way I hear it you've been fighting since the beginning of time!
Sorraya:	Invaders have been attacking us since the beginning of time.
Lepinsky:	There were a few centuries there where you were fighting among yourselves.
Sorraya:	Did you wake up in a soft bed? You had a good breakfast? You drove yourself to work in a nice car. How could you understand? You've never been hungry. You've never felt your tongue swell and crack from thirst. You've never seen a child's leg blown off by an American cluster bomb.
Lepinsky:	Yeah an American bomb!
Sorraya:	Please. You fight alongside them. You hide behind their land mines. You send them your prisoners to be tortured.
Lepinsky:	You really do hate us, don't you? Fine. Climb up lady. But I know you've got something to say and you're gonna say it.

This dialogue, interrogation style, reflects how information from the news media seeps into and textures the crime drama. Lepinsky points out all of the pieces of information that we have heard about "our" troops in Afghanistan, about the aid workers who are there to help Afghan people and about the Vitamin D deficiencies that women in buraq are likely to suffer. Yet, Sorraya's rebuttal is powerful especially when she articulates how Lepinsky can never understand the situation of those in a warzone. Nonetheless, and in retaliation to her narrative of suffering, he invokes the "anger" card —with the statement "you really do hate us" implying that she is anti-American and against what the West stands for. This is reminiscent of Bush's speech delivered in the immediate aftermath of September 11. 'It effectively renders' a rational argument into an emotional expression of hate. Sorraya as a woman can be dismissed on the basis of emotionality, even though she has just articulated a sound argument.

Sorraya continues to bring up arguments and counter-claims as evident from her interrogation with Darnell Williams:

Williams:	I thought you might like this (he brings hot drink—maybe coffee). Go ahead; drink it. I hope you take sugar.
Sorraya:	You're being nice. Establishing a rapport.

Williams:	What is that accent? New England? Brenmar (?) maybe or Vass (?) or something like that?
Sorraya:	Don't you find it ironic that you, an African man, are interrogating me, a Muslim woman, while white men are watching us through a one-way mirror?
Williams:	Actually I am a Canadian man.
Sorraya:	Your ancestors were African.
Williams:	Everybody's ancestors were something.
Sorraya:	They were dragged here in chains.
Williams:	To America. They came to Canada to be free.
Sorraya:	They were treated like shit here!
Williams:	Everybody was treated like shit. Read your Canadian history. The Natives, the Chinese; hell even the Irish. That's what history is. People treating each other like shit.
Sorraya:	In Afghanistan the past is all we have. Even in the most primitive villages. We know our history. Thousand years back.
Williams:	Picking at it like a sore that never gets to heal. Who can live like that? Who can sustain being that pissed off every single day? Why are you so angry? What did we do to you?
Sorraya:	Your coffee sucks.

Again, one sees a discursive move here which denies history, levels all oppressions and concludes with Sorraya (and by proxy, all Afghans) as being driven by obsession, unwilling to let go of the past, and being overcome by an unresolved and unspent anger. The whole exchange affords one a tangible sense of the assimilation ethic—all of us were treated "like shit" so why complain. The equivalence between the Natives, Chinese, and Irish is revealing insofar as it levels differences between those who were directly colonized, and those who were used as agents of colonization. It also evacuates the history of Black settlement in Nova Scotia which, as Sorraya rightly notes, demonstrates how the Blacks were treated "like shit." Not all those who migrated to Canada were loyalists like Darnell Williams, nor do all Blacks in Canada identify as Canadian.

In a previous episode that was filmed in Mohawk territory, *The Border* inflects a similar message through its polling question online wherein it asks viewers: "Should Canadian border agencies control goods across First Nations land?"[38] While the poll results were not available, the particular episode makes it clear that First Nations communities do not have enough policing resources and while Kessler and his team are sensitive to boundary issues pertaining to land-claims, the necessity of catching criminals overrides all other considerations. The Natives then become like everyone else and the history of their colonization is erased.

GOOD MUSLIM/BAD MUSLIM

The final piece of the interrogation that I want to turn to involves an exchange between the "authentic" and "inauthentic" Muslim. This is when Hourani attempts to question Sorayya about the Anthrax found in the house:

Hourani:	Thousands of people will die.
Sorraya:	It is Allah's will.
Hourani:	No it's yours.
Sorraya:	Your mind is in turmoil, Sergeant.
Hourani:	My mind?
Sorraya:	Your life is a shadow.
Hourani:	What are you talking about?
Sorraya:	Western women. Obsessed with their looks.
Hourani:	At least I am free to choose the way I look.
Sorraya:	Choose what? $20 nail polish over the $10? The only freedom you have here is freedom to buy.
Hourani:	And what freedom do you have in Afghanistan?
Sorraya:	The only one we find here on earth. Surrender our will to Allah.
Hourani:	Allah doesn't wield murder of innocents.

Again, the counter-claims that Sorraya puts forward are illustrative of the main arguments that feminists have made in reference to the West's obsession with the veil.[39] The issue of consumption and its centrality in shaping the construction of gender is highlighted in her argument.[40] Yet, it is trivialized by reference to nail polish rather than say, body sculpting through cosmetic surgery. Sorraya's arguments are further deprived of any legitimacy once she reveals herself as a fundamentalist, bound to a literal and rigid understanding of Islam that is irrational. Islam literally means "surrender"—and the use of these terms within the dialogue suggests that the producers are well aware of the nuances and differences within Muslim sects and communities. It is this difference that marks Hourani and yet, that ultimately works against her—for she remains, after all, a Muslim. Against Sorraya's irrationality, Hourani's rationality is tentatively established through her reference to the murderous consequences of the crime, but it is unlike the rationality of the male interrogators that precede her. She responds more by questioning than by affirming or denying/defusing Sorraya's statements. She appears sympathetic to Sorraya.

Central in this exchange is the implicit and coded distinction between the "good" Muslim and the "bad" Muslim, a distinction that Mamdani makes in his book by the same name.[41] The good Muslim is the moderate Muslim, one who can be saved or one who is already on side, the bad Muslim is the angry, barbaric, resentful fundamentalist seeking to impose her/his views on the world. Sorraya represents the latter as evident in her last statement. Moreover, her wearing the Hijab and Niqab are also illustrative of her affiliation to a fundamentalist Islam—a "bad Islam." As a veiled woman, her representation signifies the oppression of women under Islam, a popular trope used by the news media and politicians to continually promote support for the intervention and war in Afghanistan.[42] The semiotic sign of an oppressed Muslim woman functions effectively because it stands in relation to her Western, liberated counterparts and, in relation to the Muslim man as irrational and ultra-patriarchal.

SORRAYA REVEALED

As the story progresses, we, as the audience, come to learn that Sorraya is in fact not the essentialized, born-as-Muslim woman that we had been led to believe, but rather a White woman (an American at that) who converted to Islam six years ago. Moreover, her parents were aid workers in Afghanistan. She, herself, was brought up and acquired her training as a biochemist in the U.S., and worked for the State department in that capacity. She had made the Anthrax that was to be used in metro Toronto's subway system. Thus, she was constructed as "one of us" who had gone native, and therein lay the problem. In other words, her ideals and values, fueled by her parents' beliefs and actions, had culminated in her affiliation to Islam and Afghanistan, an affiliation that might have, had ICS not intervened, resulted in a Canadian equivalent of tragic horrors of 9/11. In that regard, she is a traitor, but her one redeeming feature that recuperates her humanity (in contrast to that of her husband or the other Muslims that were arrested) lies in her maternal instinct. For it was only upon being shown film footage of her baby being carried in the same subway station where the Anthrax was to be released that impelled Sorraya to disclose the plot.

While Sorraya's husband and baby were returned to Afghanistan in exchange for the two Canadian soldiers being held hostage, she was escorted to prison. In her last exchange with Hourani, Hourani tells her that "she is alone." The White woman convert has been abandoned by Muslims, and other White Canadians, and Americans alike. Though American, Sorraya is not rescued by LaGarda—in fact, LaGarda is conspicuously absent in this episode.

If crime news depicts a morality tale, then *The Border* has certainly captured that element for, in presenting the Muslim convert in this fashion as the abject other, she becomes a living testament of what can go wrong should one sympathize too strongly with the "other" side. At the same time, as a woman, her fall is redeemed only by her maternal feelings toward her child and her irrationality—she is not quite in her senses, and hence cannot be held solely responsible in the same way as the men are. Nevertheless, despite articulating solid claims, Sorraya's legitimacy is denied and her positioning as a terrorist destroys any credibility that she might have had.

The analysis above demonstrates the interlocking nature of media representations. A representational economy prevails such that one sign/character depends on the other for meaning, but its signification also acquires meaning through the leakage of current political and social events via the news media. In this regard, *The Border* successfully sutures fictional and nonfictional programming. The news spills into its sets just as easily as do the various political machinations that underpin the Canadian political scene. The underpinning hierarchies of race and gender are thus kept intact.

CONCLUSION

While the preceding sections have focused on a raced and gendered reading of *The Border*, it should not be forgotten that these discourses are skillfully subsumed under the mantle of an overarching framing dealing with the rivalry, antagonism, and unequal power relation between Canada and the U.S. In this regard, *The Border* asserts and reasserts the Canadian national imaginary; that of a nation that is subordinate to yet more humane and compassionate than its powerful neighbor to the south. However, despite these differences, the core message underscores the necessity of uniting to confront a common enemy and enjoining the forces of law and order. Thus, soft and hard approaches to power are presented as equally necessary albeit not always tolerable. And in maintaining law and order, in patrolling the border, extreme vigilance is required. This is where surveillance technologies are vital and their use in this show, combined with human intelligence in the field, are rationalized and naturalized. *The Border* then performs a hegemonic function: it legitimizes the use of intrusive technologies of surveillance, of seizures and arrests, confinements and deportations.

Hegemony, as Hall has argued, is never stable, never completely achieved.[43] It is always in flux. The labor involved in obtaining consent is perpetual. To maintain this, *The Border* reflects a Canadian self-image that is tempered with compassion, with humanity—and this is why other episodes make a pointed attempt to "rescue" illegal immigrants and to provide shelter to those wrongfully accused or deported. But like the play between CSIS and ICS—the good cop and the bad cop— ultimately it is who the cops report to that seals their fate and that empowers them to do their work.

The work involved in seeking consent and in persuading the public of the necessity to engage in measures that violate fundamental freedoms and human rights is nowhere clearer than in the show's web description of the various episodes accompanied by polling questions. The public is invited to participate in this "game" of interrogation and approval, identifying what can and cannot be done in the name of national security. As active audience members, we too can be field agents for ICS and spy on our fellow human-beings. In the end, we are invited to become complicit in this game of power, maintaining hierarchies and race lines, dividing "us" from "them," and thereby defending the border.

NOTES

1. This research was supported by a grant from the Social Sciences and Humanities Research Council. I am especially indebted to Kenza Oumlil for her research assistance and critical feedback, as well as to Michele Aguayo for her assistance in editing and formatting this chapter. I would also like to acknowledge Sophia Poulin at Concordia library for her rigorous background searches on *The Border*.
2. Joseph Nye Jr. and William A. Owens, "America's Information Edge," *Foreign Affairs* 75, no. 2 (1996): 21.
3. Nye was at the time, a former Chair of the National Intelligence Council and Assistant Secretary of Defense for International Affairs in the Clinton administration, as well as Dean of the John F. Kennedy School of Government at Harvard University. Owens was former Vice Chair of the Joint Chiefs of Staff in the Clinton administration.
4. Nathan Gardels, "The Rise and Fall of America's Soft Power," *New Perspective Quarterly (NPQ)* 22, no. 1 (2005): 7–19.
5. David Theo Goldberg, "'Killing Me Softly': Civility/Race/Violence," *The Review of Education, Pedagogy and Cultural Studies* 27, no. 4 (2005): 354.
6. Michel Foucault, *Discipline & Punish, the Birth of the Prison* (New York: Vintage Books, 1978/1995).
7. Andrew Davison, "The 'Soft' Power of Hollywood Militainment: The Case of the *West Wing*'s Attack on Antalya, Turkey," *New Political Science* 28, no. 4 (2006): 467–87.
8. Gray Cavender and Sarah K. Deutsch, "*CSI* and Moral Authority: The Police and Science," *Crime Media Culture* 3, no. 1 (2007): 68.
9. Guy Dixon, "CBC's *The Border* Draws Good Numbers in Debut," *The Globe and Mail*, January 10, 2008, R3.
10. Interestingly, *The Border* debuted shortly after the film and television writers' strike in California. The show thus replaced *24* for the subsequent season.
11. Quoted in Robert Fulford, "Different Show, Same Message: 'The Border' Rereads the CBC's Favourite Theme," *National Post*, January 12, 2008, A18.
12. Leigh Stuart, "Raymont on 'The Border'," *Playback: Canada's Broadcast and Production Journal*, August 6, 2007, 20.
13. Dixon, "The Border' Draws Good Numbers in Debut."

14. Marc Glassman, "Hit Drama Was Tracey's Brainchild," *Playback: Canada's Broadcast and Production Journal*, April 28, 2008, 51.
15. John Fiske and John Hartley, *Reading Television* (London and New York: Routledge and Kegan Paul, 1978/1985), p. 170.
16. Bruce DeMara, "'A Production Designer's Dream': Customs Terminal Built for Rochester Ferry Ideally Suited for Role in CBC's 'The Border'," *Toronto Star*, December 18, 2007, L6.
17. See R. W. Connell and James W. Messederschmidt, "Hegemonic Masculinity, Rethinking the Concept," *Gender & Society* 19, no. 6 (2005): 829–59.
18. Yvonne Jewkes, *Media and Crime* (London, Thousand Oaks, CA, and New Delhi: Sage Publications, 2004/2005); Liesbet van Zoonen, *Feminist Media Studies* (Thousand Oaks, CA: Sage Publications, 1994).
19. See Ray Surette, *Media, Crime, and Criminal Justice*. 3rd edn. (Belmont, CA: Thomson Wadsworth, 2007).
20. Edward Said, *Orientalism* (New York: Random House, 1978), p. 54.
21. David Palumbo-Liu, *Asian/American Historical Crossings of a Racial Frontier* (Stanford: Stanford University Press, 1999), p. 85.
22. Melinda de Jesús, "Fictions of Assimilation: Nancy Drew, Cultural Imperialism, and the Filipina American Experience," In *Delinquents and Debutantes: Twentieth-Century American Girls' Cultures*, edited by Sherrie A. Inness, pp. 227–46. (New York and London: New York University Press, 1998).
23. Constance Deroche and John Deroche, "Black and White: Racial Construction in Television Police Dramas," *Canadian Ethnic Studies* 23, no. 3 (1991): 86.
24. Ibid, p. 87; see also Herman Gray, "Television and the New Black Man: Black Male Images in Prime-Time Situation Comedy," *Media, Culture & Society* 8 (1986): 223–42.
25. Lynn Chancer, "Playing Gender against Race through High-Profile Crime Cases," *Violence Against Women* 4, no. 1 (1998): 100–13.
26. Robert M. Entman, "Modern Racism and the Image of Blacks in Local Television News," *Critical Studies in Mass Communication* 7 (1990): 332–45; see also, Stuart Hall, Chas Critcher, Tony Jefferson, and Brian Roberts. *Policing the Crisis: Mugging, the State, Law and Order* (London: Macmillan Press, 1978).
27. Scot Wortley, "Misrepresentation or Reality?: The Depiction of Race and Crime in the Toronto Print Media," In *Marginality & Condemnation: An Introduction to Critical Criminology*, edited by Bernard Schissel and Carolyn Brooks, pp. 55–82 (Halifax: Fernwood Publishing, 2002).
28. Mary Beth Oliver, "Race and Crime in the Media: Research from a Media Effects Perspective," In *A Companion to Media Studied*, edited by Angharad N. Valdivia, pp. 421–35 (Maiden, MA: Blackwell, 2003).
29. Stuart Hall, "The Whites of Their Eyes, Racist Ideologies and the Media," In *The Media Reader*, edited by Manuel Alvarado and John O. Thompson, pp. 9–23 (London: British Film Institute, 1990a).
30. Homi Bhabha, "The Other Question—the Stereotype and Colonial Discourse," *Screen* 24, no. 6 (1983): 18–36.
31. Hall, "The Whites of Their Eyes, Racist Ideologies and the Media," p. 15.

32. Wortley, "Misrepresentation or Reality?" pp. 55–82.; Frances Henry and Carol Tator, *Discourses of Domination: Racial Bias in the Canadian English-Language Press* (Toronto, London, and Buffalo: University of Toronto Press, 2002).
33. Sut Jhally and Justin Lewis, *Enlightened Racism: The Cosby Show, Audiences, and the Myth of the American Dream* (San Francisco, CA: Westview Press, 1992).
34. Ina Rae Hark makes this argument in her reading of the crime drama *24*. She interprets the show as a continual replay of a sadomasochistic fantasy spurred on by the three male characters, their failed marriages, and their violent relationships with women. See Ina Rae Hark, "'Today Is the Longest Day of My Life': 24 as Mirror Narrative of 9/11." In *Film and Television after 9/11*, edited by Wheeler Winston Dixon, pp. 121–41. (Carbondale: Southern Illinois University Press, 2004).
35. Yasmin Jiwani, "The Eurasian Female Hero(Ine): Sydney Fox as the Relic Hunter," *Journal of Popular Film & Television* 32, no. 4 (2005): 182–91.
36. Meyda Yeğenoğlu, *Colonial Fantasies: Towards a Feminist Reading of Orientalism*. (Cambridge and Melbourne: Cambridge University Press, 1998), p. 44.
37. *The Border* uses the term "Afghani" which is a misnomer. Afghani is the name of the currency used in Afghanistan. The more accurate term is "Afghan." www.theborder.ca
39. Myra Macdonald, "Muslim Women and the Veil, Problems of Image and Voice in Media Representations," *Feminist Media Studies* 6, no. 1 (2006): 7–23.
40. See Stuart Ewen and Elizabeth Ewen, *Channels of Desire: Mass Images and the Shaping of American Consciousness* (New York: McGraw-Hill, 1982).
41. Mahmood Mamdani, *Good Muslim, Bad Muslim: America, the Cold War and the Roots of Terror* (New York: Pantheon, 2004).
42. Yasmin Jiwani, *Discourses of Denial: Mediations of Race, Gender and Violence* (Vancouver: University of British Columbia Press, 2006).
43. Stuart Hall, "The Work of Representations," In *Representation, Cultural Representation and Signifying Practices*, edited by Stuart Hall, pp. 15–74. (London: Sage in association with The Open University, 1997).

CHAPTER TWELVE

Appearance, Intimacy Exhibition, Hypersexualization and Pornography

RICHARD POULIN AND MÉLANIE CLAUDE

Seduce, it is to die as reality and to occur as lure.

—JEAN BAUDRILLARD[1]

Make your XXX film! Top ten erotic films guide. Pornographic films can feed your sexual life! Prepare popcorn and lubricant! Dance courses to boost the sexy seductress in us! Hurt me, honey! Hand-job festival!

These are not titles of pornographic DVD's or magazine articles for men. These titles are taken from the magazine *FA* (*Femmes d'aujourd'hui*—Women today—May 2008), published by TVA Publications, a company of the multinational Quebecor World, which also owns the most important private television in Quebec. *FA* solicits pornography by trying to convince women that it is glamorous, sexy and fulfilling. The magazine receives financial support from the Canadian government, through the Publications Assistance Program and the Canadian Fund for Magazines, for its postage and editorial costs. Quebecor World owns Videotron, a major cable and Internet connection company. The multinational also controls major commercial Internet portals in Quebec, including a search engine, dating agencies as well as networks of online communities. Hence, Quebecor is one of the main distributors of pornography on television and Internet. The group openly encourages pornographic diffusion in its many magazines and its free weekly newspapers.

Magazines like *FA* are the result of a trend at work since the 1990s. That's when pornography successfully emerged out of its ghetto, while imposing its standards on the society.

In this chapter, we investigate the links between the public sexualization and the hypersexualization—the excess of sexualization or its escalation—and the pornographization of the culture. Pornographization, which refers to the recycling of pornographic archetypes in the culture, is the novelty of the 1990s. This process is particularly evident in certain contemporary novels and biographies, in films, television programs, publicities, fashion, women and teenagers' magazines. More particularly, we examine the feminine press, notably the one that addresses teenagers, publicity, and fashion. We continue with the analysis of the public sexualization, which is influenced by the pornographic codes, what gives place to the implementation of a new tyrannical sexual order, particularly on younger people, as well as by the current tendencies to the public exhibition of the intimacy. Finally, we discuss the social influence of pornography in terms of social relationships of power.

MAGAZINES FOR WOMEN AND TEENAGERS

Women's magazines, which were traditionally sentimental, became "sexual." They clearly echo the pornographic imagery. The "if we became engaged" has evolved to "how to put a man in his bed" (*Isa*, March 2001). Like in pornography, the sexual act is separated from feelings: "Instantaneous sex, the guide of the fast and incognito love," titles *Vingt ans* (May 2000), a magazine read by teens and even preteen girls. In *Jeune et Jolie* (April 1999), the ideal lover "tears your low neckline, takes you on the chest of drawers, on the washing machine in drying position [...] a true wild boy." In April 2008, *Muteen*, a magazine "for girls in advance on their age" writes, "Sex, why men like X-rated films?" Answer: It's normal, men "have a spatial sexuality," nevertheless, be careful of addiction.

The goal is not only to "boost one's pleasure" (*Bien dans ma vie!* Summer 2005), and believe that everything that is pornographic is hot, it is most importantly about regulating feminine sexuality around the idea of sexual performance. Women and teenagers must absolutely live a full- bloom sexuality,[2], which requires at the same time a technical knowledge of the body, its conditioning (if it is not its transformation) and the adoption of pornographic practices: "Use sex toys!" (*Isa*, July 2003); "What if I did a striptease for him?" (*Bien dans ma vie*!, Summer 2005); "Sodomy 101: Pass by back door" — followed by practical advice: "First, open your mind. Secondly, open up your body" (*FA*, Summer 2005). "To give a great thrill to a gentleman ... nothing could be easier... Be somewhat trashy and terribly sexy" (*Adorable*, November 2005) — followed by a series of photos of a young "vamp" girl posing in ways that have nothing to envy to those found in pornography. "Please him every day,"commands a lingerie advertisement published by *Jeune et Jolie* (March 2007), which, in the same issue, raises the question "Do you have the body of his desires?"

Be audacious! Distinguish yourself! Do not hesitate to adopt body piercing, tattooing and even scarification (*Adorable*, November 2005). Since these practices are now "creating a sensation among women," you must be like others and be of your time, implies the magazine! It's like squaring the circle: One must successfully distance oneself from the others while being like everybody! Adopt other sexual positions, learn to like the sexual acts seen in pornography, have fun with sex toys, you will have a blooming sexuality and therefore self-fulfillment, prescribe magazines for girls. The use of prescription of standards to be followed clearly marks the current era. To feel good in her skin and in life, today's women and teens must adopt new sexual practices and consume the products of the sex industries. Women's magazines solicit for the sex shop, promote their gadgets. In November–December 2005edition, *Jalouse* offers its readers a vibrator. According to the director of the magazine, "to sell a vibrator with *Jalouse* corresponds perfectly to its avant-gardism."

In these magazines, feminine emancipation and empowerment are reduced to the accomplishment of high, individual sexual performance and the adoption of pornographic codes.

After reading these magazines, whether they are for teens or for women, we cannot be surprised by the growing number of women who consume pornography. That is what is new in comparison to what was practiced twenty years ago, when pornography consumption was mostly male.

THE "PORN CHIC" ADVERTISING

Luxury and sex mix together. Lesbianism, sadomasochism, collective rape (gangbang), fetishism, bestiality, etc., are subjects exploited in the commercial advertisements, which flirt with pornography or come very close to pornography. In advertising, "porn chic" is defined as an advertisement that draws its inspiration directly from pornography. The main purpose of this kind of publicity, besides the fact that it is intended to broaden the clientele, is to retain the public's attention and influence their opinion regarding the brand. Major luxury brands use this strategy to create a desire among consumers while making them remember the trademark. "By strongly implicating the consumer, the shockvertising guarantees the noticeability of the advertisement and significantly increase the chance that it will be memorized."[3] This type of communication strategy can be very effective. Researchers attest that "In an environment encumbered by advertising, shocking advertisement contents ensure that the message will be heard."[4]

Since 1993, advertisements have become more sexually explicit in both men's and women's magazines as well in those targeting a wider readership. At the end of the 1990s, this type of advertisement significantly increased.[5]

This trend—the "sex shop publicity"—was known to be the trademark of groups like Gaultier, Helmut Lang and Mugler.[6] In turn, luxury brands, such as Gucci, Versace, Dior and Vuitton, followed by the ready-to-wear brands like Eram and American Apparel, have adopted pornographic codes to advertise their products. It is fashionable to show a naked woman in a position submissive to a man (Weston) or licking a man in erection, full of dirty oil (Redwood jeans). Lesbians lick one another for an Ungaro handbag. A Tom Ford perfume bottle hides the genital area of a naked woman. Playboy.nl uses the same technique, but with a computer mouse. Alfa Romeo which conceals the genital area of a naked woman with its logo retakes this advertising trick. A man offers a Natan ring, the woman then opens her legs to show her sexual availability—the jewel is described as "the first remote control ever invented." "Concentrate on your goal," which is symbolized by the breasts of a woman. A woman dressed in Triumph underwear allows the airline company "low cost sky" to pride itself on being the "the first fashionable airline company." A naked woman in the snow biting on an apple symbolizes "the culture of pleasure" of Virgin.

The "pornographism" of the publicity does not use only female nudity nor does it exacerbate femininity; fundamentally, it gives full play to the submission of women and it contributes to their sexual subjection. The promoted product then becomes associated with the sexual access to women. This sexist objectification also eroticizes sexual aggression. In a Minute Maid advertisement, sailors engage in a gangbang, and so do men dressed in Dolce & Gabbana jeans. Models lying on the ground, partially stripped, soiled with dirty motor oil, promote a luxurious handbag for Dior, who reiterates: it shows a woman covered with sludge wearing, dirty and torn clothes, her face tumid and her eyes haggard. The ambiguity of the advertisement is its strength: a part of the public sees the representation of a rape, while another sees, in this extreme pleasure, a form of abandonment. An ad for Brother, a company that produces photocopying machines, asks in the view of a battered woman: "Sunstroke? Slap? Prudish?" The answer is however obvious. Publicity for the cream Babette reads, "I bind her, I whip her, and sometimes I pass her to the pan."

Sadomasochism (SM), fetishism and bondage are also in the spotlight. The sadomasochistic pornographic codes invaded publicity: leather, latex, spanking, flogging, bondage, handcuffs and metal chastity belts. Bestiality is commonplace.

The girl of Kookaï takes a doggie-style position in front of a sheep, because she "desires a pullover." Ungaro shows a woman in ecstasy while a dog is licking her. For Sisley, a woman, legs open, invites a bull to have sexual intercourse. Also for Sisley, a woman presses the udders of a cow spouting milk on her face, which mimics the facial ejaculation in pornographic movies. Sex tourism also finds its account. Around Christmas time, an ad for Thalys promotes a train trip to Amsterdam by showing a Santa Claus tourist in front of a window where a reindeer prostitute expects his visit.

Male pornographic fantasies are displayed without constraints. The "porn chic" advertising plays on all taboos, including that of pedophilia, although this is done with ambiguity. As models, kids are shown kneeling down, legs wide-open, and topless (Sisley), licking a lollipop (Lee), or holding a teddy bear ("Stop playing alone!" insists Goa).

Women's buttocks to promote a photocopier, breasts to sell perfume, legs for automobiles, stupid blondes for beer or other products... sexist advertisement has existed for a long time, but it has been tremendously growing since advertisers started using the pornographic codes.

HYPERSEXUALIZED FASHION

"How do we recognize a prostitute?" asks Florence Montreynaud.[7] To attract clients, prostitutes dress provocatively, expose themselves, make gestures and adopt "obscene" postures. They dress in a way that clearly shows their sexual availability. Florence Montreynaud stresses that nowadays these guides are scrambled. What was once thought of as raunchy is nowadays acceptable. The fashion industry caught up and even surpassed the "prostitute" style; it seems to have given itself the motto "to be more whore than the whores." The designers are "seriously competing with the outfits found in the sex-shops."[8]. Now, this fashion influences in an important way the tendencies of the ready-to-wear clothing: skirt, blouse, stiletto, waders, G-string, thong, etc. Today, prostitutes dress themselves like a number of teenagers or women and vice versa. Most of the prostitutes no longer use stereotyped clothing. Perhaps because these clothes have simply become the norm!

The conditioning of young girls to wear sexy clothing clearly illustrates the commercial nature of this pornographization. Towards the end of the 1990s, the string and the thong became the new must. Let us recall that the G-string draws its origin from the so-called exotic dancing. Primarily, it was used to cover "exotic" dancers' genitals, while allowing for a maximum exposure of the body. Fashion of the low-waisted pants became imperative. The thread of the G-string was to be shown. It is estimated that, in 2003, girls aged from 13 to 17 years would have spent nearly 152 million U.S. dollars for the purchase of G-strings.[9] Foam bras are now available to young girls who can feign to have breasts. La Senza Girls is capitalizing on this new market by offering 30-AA-cup stuffed bras. These types of fashion contribute to the early sexualization of girls by introducing them to the "charm, please and seduce" roles of Lolita and bimbos (hyperfeminine image). Also, these fashions inculcate in young girls the notion that their value is directly linked to their sex appeal.[10] The cult of the appearance objectifies girls by suggesting that they are objects of desire.[11]

Seven, nine or eleven-year-old girls are transformed into nymphets and mini-femmes fatales. Clothes of many brand names bring on this early sexualization. Now girls have their stores and specialty brands: Jennyfer, Tammy by Etam, NoBoys, Lulu Castagnette, Miss LM. Spaghetti straps, skin-tight T-shirts, G-strings and low-waist pants, more and more girls are being transformed into objects of desire even though they haven't had the chance to become subjects of desire. Girls learn to exist through the approving eyes of others, particularly men's. Adults who abhor pedophiles nevertheless show their children as sexual objects. Girls end up with an idea of sexuality and love that is centered on seduction and consumption.

The current social trends are worrisome. The early sexualization of girls is certainly not a new phenomenon.[12] However, its popularization and its universalization are recent. Early sexualization of girls is no longer a mere fact of the sex industry and of sexual aggression; it came out of its ghetto and has spread to a large number of young girls. Consequently, it is no longer a tangible sign of sexual aggression perpetrated by someone the victim most likely knew. Dr. Franciska Baltzer, a pediatrician and the director of the clinic for teenagers at the Children's Hospital of Montreal, reports, "In 1983, it was clear to us that the girls who wore sexy clothes at six years or seven years of age were victims of sexual abuse. Today, nothing is less certain given that these clothes are available in most stores."[13] In fact, wearing this type of clothing is now in fashion.

Traditionally, girls were sexualized through clothes like dresses, which required them to behave in an appropriate manner. Comparatively, the current sexualization is so radical that the concept "hypersexualization" was coined to reflect the deepening of the phenomenon. This term refers to excessive sexualization or its aggravation in society. It also refers to the concept of early sexualization, which is defined as girls who are "socially pushed to adopt attitudes and behavior of young sexy women."[14]

Today, children bathe in adult sexuality. At a very young age, they become acquainted with pornography— boys begin on average at the age of 12 and girls at the age of 13—[15] while teen magazines constantly write about sex and seduction, as if their universe was limited to these questions and to those relating to products they need to acquire to become sexy and, by that process, become so interesting that all will want to know them and become their friends. To have sex appeal, which is the main concern of these magazines, is now being imposed on a large number of girls. This imperative is also reinforced by music videos that they buy. To please has become a synonym of "to be sexy." To please, girls have to sexually objectify themselves and become just as feminine as women. Girls are now becoming sexually active at a younger age.[16]

This early sexualization is parallel while also being closely related with a more general phenomenon that is the emergence of a hypersexualized society inside which the female body is fragmented and objectified, and where the value of women is reduced to their physical attributes and their ability to please and seduce. This type of society overexposes an individual's intimacy in the public sphere; it is characterized by "extimacy."[17] It also focuses on sexual performance. Finally, this hypersexualized society praises juvenescence.[18] Everybody needs to feel, be and look young. Consequently, children behave as teenagers, teenagers as adults and many adults never emerge out of their adolescence crisis. There is not only a loss of generational references, but also a disturbance in social roles. The importance of juvenescence has been at work in the sex industries for a long time.

PUBLIC SEXUALIZATION AND PORNOGRAPHIZATION

The pornography industry is characterized mostly by the fact that it exploits girls. This exploitation is not only seen in pedophiliac pornography, which is criminal, but it can easily be found in mainstream pornography that is readily available and accessible. Pornography capitalizes on the Lolita fantasy. By typing "Lolita XXX" in a web search engine, 1,060,000 websites were offered to us. When we typed, "Lolita porn," we obtained 1,850,000 hits and for "Lolita sex," 2,510,000. For "teen XXX," 4,320,000 websites came up and for "teen porn," we found 12,700,000 websites. For "preteen XXX," i.e., young girls that are 13 years of age or less, we obtain 715,000 websites and for "preteen porn," 1,500,000. The number of hits is an indicator of the large amount of pornographic websites that use or abuse children or pseudo-children. On these websites, it is nearly impossible to tell the age of the girls being shown.

The phenomena of public sexualization, extimacy and hypersexualization are closely related to the pornographic invasion whose discourse and codes influence culture profoundly. Pornography is more than an industry; it is a culture in itself, while being a part of the popular culture.[19]

Pornography is only one aspect of a broader problem on which it acts, that of a society where sexualized representations of young people serve more and more to sell everything and anything, from perfumes to clothes. Furthermore, young ones are confronted with explicit sexual images in video games that they play, in magazines they read, or in films and television shows that they watch. From magazines to publicity, from television to the Internet, from films to pictures, the current society experiences a "boisterous sexual noise" that is characterized by an everyday acceptance of pornography[20] and sexual venality (merchandised sex)[21]. Sex is everywhere. It is bought, sold, rented, and it sells...

In the course of the past two decades, we have witnessed an explosion of the global sex industries, resulting in the pornographization of culture (imagination, attitude and behavior), the normalization of prostitution and consequently in an increased commodification of women and girls. Everyday we are bombarded with images of sexualized young women—when we watch television or surf the web, read through magazines or watch advertisements. Unfortunately, young women are being sexualized more and more at a younger age.

The concept of pornographization helps to highlight two elements that are intertwined: (1) the extent of the influence of pornography on the systems of representation and communication; (2) the standards adopted and promoted that arise from pornography and which contribute in forging gender roles that affect daily relations between men and women. Therefore, this concept refers to the fact that sexually explicit and sexist images are now widespread and that this process continues to grow and expand. Furthermore, it shows that the current period is not only one of suggestion, but also one of exhibition and prescriptive standards. To feel good, to live a fulfilling life and to be cool, it is necessary that women and young girls adopt new sexual practices and consume the sex industries' products. They must experience and learn to like sodomy, facial ejaculation, double penetration, group sex, etc. It is essential for them to dare everything!

To publish best sellers, writers tell their presumed or real sex life. Reality TV shows participants making love. Many women's magazines are promoting pornography as glamorous and inspiring. Talk shows expose the intimate life of ordinary citizens as well as famous people. "Sexy" clothes of prostitutes and porn stars inspire haute-couture and ready-to-wear fashion. Trademarks use in their advertisement sadomasochist, bestiality and gangbang codes. Popular brands of children's clothing sexualize their products. TV series focus on the life of swingers. Porn stars appear on television sets, produce shows for the mainstream media and pornographic reality TV shows. The World Wide Web is overrun with pornography. So-called documentaries on the busy and happy lives of porn stars and prostitutes abound. Mainstream television and pay-per-views offer an impressive lot of pornographic films. The praise of juvenescence and the stage setting of its sexualization also come into play.

This desire to be young in appearance is heightened by advertisement, pornography, magazines and fashion. Models for famous brands are mostly very young and often anorexic on a closer look. In 1970, the average weight of models was 11% less than the average weight of a woman. In 1987, this percentage had risen to 17%. Today, models weigh on average 23 % less than the average woman. This said, it should not be surprising that almost 90% of American women feel they are too fat and that 75% of women and girls follow or have followed a diet.[22]. According to Health Canada, eating disorders have become more prevalent and are affecting a significantly larger number of women than before. This problem especially concerns young women between 15 to 24 years, as well as girls who are less than 15 years. These age groups are more likely to be hospitalized because of an eating disorder. From 1987 until 2001, the number of girls who were hospitalized for eating disorders had increased by 34% for those under the age of 15 and by 29% among those aged 15 to 24 years.[23]

THE TYRANNY OF THE NEW SEXUAL ORDER

According to Jean-Claude Guillebaud, an "extraordinary sexual clamor colonizes all aspects of democratic modernity."[24] This clamor takes on a variety of forms, all of which take part in the pornographization of the culture.

The pornographic invasion has led to the establishment of a new sexual order. Women and teenagers' magazines multiply the occurrences of raunchy articles: "Posing naked, why not you?" "To be photographed for *Playboy*, yes it is possible" (*Le Mag des castings*, July–August 2005). "Fantasies, taboos, I dare it all" (*Bien dans ma vie!*, Summer 2005). "Darling! Let's make our own X-rated film!" (*OH!* Spring 2008). "I am addicted to cybersex. Is it good or not?" (*Jeune et Jolie*, September 2005). In many magazines, it is now common and recurrent to find information on the art of practicing sodomy, oral sex, etc…and to come across quizzes such as "What type of sex beast are you?" or " In bed, are you a genuine fire or a true ice cube?". The majority of these articles are followed by normative and prescriptive advice supposedly given by "experts."

The promotion of pornography is often accompanied by the normalization of prostitution. For example, in the July 2005 issue of the magazine *Adorable*, sex toys found in sex shops are praised, a glamorized history of pornography is proposed, advice on "quick sex" accompanied by "a range of sex toys" is given and the idea of "working" in prostitution and in the porn industry is valued. These magazines addressed to a feminine clientele, who often are teenagers, are not the only ones who promote "sex work." The magazine *Jobbom* "a leader in the on-line recruitment in Canada and a specialist of the labor market" which also offers "career advice and information on different fields of work," published in July 2007 a series of articles on the sex industries and "sex jobs."

When these phenomena are combined, recruitment for the sex industry becomes facile. The desire to enter the sex trade is one significant, but often overlooked, effect of the normalization of the global sex trades. For example, in the Eastern European countries, where prostitution, pornography and trafficking have known a significant increase in the 1990s, surveys revealed that, close to a sixth of Ukraine's girl students perceived prostitution in a positive way and believed that, in Western countries, prostitutes lived a luxurious and pleasant life. Also, a fourth of the girls who are in high school in Moscow, would consider becoming a prostitute.[25] When prostitution and pornography appear to be a profession like any other, they become a possibility for the future...for girls.

Since the past two decades, prostitution and pornography have become legitimate and normal. They were renamed "sex work," "sale of sexual services" and "recreational sex"; pimps are now "sex managers" or "erotic entrepreneurs"; stripping clubs or brothels are "entertainment places" and "erotic establishments." Strippers are called "exotic dancers" and they can obtain, from many governments, an "artist visa" to perform within a country. These visas are denounced by various international organizations, which consider them as a legal means to operate the trafficking in women and girls.

Women's magazines convey a message about sexuality that is far from subtle. In substance, it says: almost everyone has a fascinating and diverse sexual life...except you. Take on new sexual positions, learn to like the sexual acts seen in pornography, have fun with sex toys, as a result you will have an exciting sex life and, therefore, feel a personal blossoming!

These prescriptions, which benefit the sex industries, adopt other "transgression" and "liberation" forms that are quickly echoed by the media. For example, a "handjob competition" was organized by a sex shop in Montreal named *Venez tels quels*, the Quebecois subsidiary company of *Come as you are*, established in Toronto since 1988. Masturbators were not the only ones giving a hand; several artists accepted to give, free of charge, a benefit concert whose profits were given to Stella, an association in favor of the legalization of the prostitution. These two activities allowed Stella, who already receives important governmental subsidies, to receive 25,000 dollars. For Claire Thiboutot, the director at Stella, "it's very rare that people endorse our cause to the point of organizing from A to Z a fundraising campaign to help us. But, at the same time, it is normal. We share the same objective as *Venez tels quels*, which is demystifying sexuality.[26] Indeed, Stella is pursuing goals that correspond exactly with the interests of the sex industries, including the decriminalization of pimps. Therefore, it is not surprising that a sex shop, part of the sex industries, had an interest in financing such a group in order to strengthen its "fighting" capacities.

SEXUAL AND SEXIST SATURATION OF THE PUBLIC SPHERE

With neoliberal globalization, commercial sex in all its various forms is expanding its influence on social life, and as a result finding an unparalleled legitimacy. The public sphere accumulates commercial signs of sexuality; it is even saturated by them.

In a culture where there is a profusion of sexual imagery, naked or partially naked female bodies are exposed everywhere, they make the coverage of women's and men's magazines and they abundantly appear on billboards. "Erotic" and pornographic images are everywhere. Advertisers freely use this iconography to encourage people to buy their products. This rhetorical image aims to create an excitement, to identify a product with a persistent feeling. This technique is also known for its capacity to get that product into the consumer's head. The downfall of the saturation of sexual imagery is that it requires advertisers to do more, thus to develop advertisements that fit in the so-called porn chic and porn trash niche.

The focus of a great number of media is on "sexual entertainment." There are obviously men's magazines, whether they are pornographic or not, that abundantly exploit the female body. But there are also women's magazines, whose covers often resemble those of men's magazines—to the point that the distinction between them becomes blurred. In fact, a poster, that announced a seminar on pornography which took place in April 2008 at the University of Ottawa, was denied the right to be displayed in some buildings because the administration considered it to be pornographic. For the most part, it featured advertisements and covers taken from women's magazines.

Recently, the porn industry has decided to tackle a relatively untouched market: women. Women's magazines promote Web pornography as being "Your hottest new sex toy" (*Marie-Claire*, June 2007). Exhortations such as "expose yourself on Internet," "educate yourself by reading porn," "visit a sex shop," "adopt sex toys" are legion. New magazines, such as *OH!* "the smart and risqué magazine of today's women," are launched. Their purposes are obviously to promote sex and to praise the products of the porn industry. Some magazines suggest to their readers making their own pornographic films, taking as an example the success of such stars as Pamela Anderson and Paris Hilton. Others offer tips on how to reboot your libido or even offer free downloads for "erotic" MP3 "in which you are the heroine." Women are imperatively invited to spice up their sex life. Magazines dictate the "must in sexual gadgets." They explain to their readers what is in and what is out. In the spring 2008 edition of *OH!* Magazine, it was considered in to get tattooed, to wear lace, to visit sex shops and to drink cocktails, but it was considered unfashionable to wear clothes marked with logos and to buy low-end body care items. Other than being fascinated with products from the sex industries, these magazines also pretend to be at the forefront of the avant-garde tendencies, which allows them to dictate norms. The most important one is that the achievement of a fulfilling life necessitates sex and exhibition: women are given the order to do a striptease, to produce a porn video, to make their own XXX photo album...all this to attract and please men. When magazines write about male fantasies, the imprecation is for women to satisfy them.

Media encourage expanding consumption. This is particularly noticeable in women's magazines where at least half of the pages include advertisements while the rest discuss products from companies who bought advertising space. Magazines are intended "to inform" their readers. Properly speaking, these product placements cannot be considered publicity. Magazine editors are simply "informing" their readership of available products. This technique allows for greater revenues.

The main goal of mass media, which are themselves industries who must profit, is to sell a readership to advertisers. In 2004, the chairman of TF1, the main French television channel created a scandal by talking frankly about the roles of mass media: "Fundamentally, the job of TF1 is to help, for example, Coca-Cola to sell its product [...] For a paid advertisement to be received, television-viewer's brain must be available. Our shows have the role to make them available. What we sell to Coca-Cola, is available human brain time."[27] In order to sell "available brain time," one must not only "entertain" potential consumers, but also cultivate the desirability of consumable objects. Françoise Brune sees in this type of technique a serious implication: "There is desire only of object and thus [...] it is necessary to be objectified to be desired."[28] Thus, the production of the women-object by advertisement owes nothing to chance. Consumption and commodification of the woman's body go hand in hand.

Sexualized images of the female body abound in mass media. These women are young, thin and attractive. Their body is their asset. Above all, they are presented as sexually available and as seducers.

OVER-EXPOSED INTIMACY

Since the mid-1990s, our societies have been characterized by an overexposure of intimacy in the public sphere. This phenomenon results from a double process: the privatization of the public sphere and the "publicization" of the private sphere. We are in "the era of the *ordinary* individual, that is to say an era where everyone must reveal himself or herself in action in order to produce and show his own existence."[29] To be revealed as an individual, the *ordinary* citizen must find a way to be singled out in a society where mass consumption standardizes everything. To successfully acquire a unique identity, one is required to obtain social visibility. In turn, social visibility is the proof of one's success in the quest for identity. Nowadays, the social requirement is to behave as singular individuals. For Alain Ehrenberg, "the novelty is this impersonal process, this form of socialization that pushes everyone to be visible."[30] Everybody must make his/her life a success. Henceforth, one's happiness depends on personal visibility. In this respect, pop psychology injunctions are common and peremptory. People are burning with a desire to be on television shows in order "to grant a value to their life."[31] In such conditions, we can easily understand the success of reality TV. On these shows, people instantly become stars and are readily known and recognized. They can escape anonymity by integrating into the show business. But to do so, one must agree to expose himself/herself, give the public access to his/her intimacy (psychological and physical). Young contestants on *Big Brother* or *Loft Story* are willing to reveal their daily routines and their love-making scenes in front of cameras. The audience of these reality shows is predominantly young and composed of women.[32]

Nowadays, society commands people to expose their private life in great detail, including the most sordid ones, to make out of them consumable goods. This social trend resembles a lot the transformations seen in pornography. Pictures used in magazines like *Penthouse* reflect this progression towards the exhibition of intimacy. At the beginning of the 1970s, *Penthouse* started to reveal pubic hair and by gradually pushing the limits, they went on to expose a half-opened vulva. Lesbian and oral sex scenes evolved from simulating to displaying sexual contact. Penises were shown "in rest" and now they are in full erection. At the end of the 1990s, pornographic magazines presented, in delay plan, sexual penetration and now it appears in close-up. These magazines have pushed all limits; now, we can see dildos and urolagnia.[33]

In the past years, we have seen reality TV and talk show producers, who pretend they are showing the "true reality" of the participants or the stars. In parallel, we have witnessed an explosion of the production and the consumption of pornography. Producers want the consumers to believe they are looking at "true sex." The pornographic imagery, which was previously confined to private or hidden places, is now being displayed publicly and sometime even with arrogance.

The 1990s have made of the female body an object of transactions and commercial support. Women's liberation, a crucial conquest of the feminist movement, has been transformed by the neoliberal market into the submissiveness to male sexual pleasures. This time period corresponds, in Western countries (Germany, Netherlands, Greece, Switzerland, Australia, New Zealand, etc.), to the legalization of pimping and the prostitution of young women in brothels and in tolerance zones. It also coincides with the explosion of pornographic production and consumption. It reintroduced by the back door what had been driven out—the obligation for women to maintain a sexualized and feminine body. This imperative is very costly, both monetarily and physically: diets, cosmetics, surgery, clothing, fitness, etc. Every year since 1980, sales for lingerie have increased by 10%. The rise of the plastic surgery is phenomenal: "The number of interventions carried out globally has climbed vertiginously."[34] The obligation for women to look youthful is causing the female body to look childish: surgery to reduce the labia of the vagina, tightening of the vaginal walls, Brazilian waxing, etc.

New prescriptions are addressed to the female body. More than ever, the transformed and mutilated feminine body is marked by the dominant ideology (bourgeois and sexist). The body is now seen as an individual property for which each one is responsible. The increase in body transformation is paradigmatic of the new norms of feminine beauty and its "seduction power." The individual control over the body suggests one's control over one's life. The more a body is molded and exhibited, the more it is artificially constructed and stripped of its naturalness, the more *it exists*. Feminine beauty is now in the order of compulsion. To exist, a woman must reveal herself. This naked body is part of the daily representations found in a saturated public sphere. In the new version of capitalism, self-control is a prerequisite for selling oneself, which is a fundamental condition for social success. Véronique Guienne peremptorily affirms that in an era of neoliberalism, claiming "not to be a thing, an instrument, easy to handle and to commercialize, would be backward-looking and not a condition of dignity of the subject."[35] Appearances are crucial to emphasize one's value. The new spirit of capitalism pushes back the boundaries of what is marketable, which consequently increases the legitimacy of selling and renting bodies and sex, that is to say the commodification of women and children, primarily girls.

The regressions are both symbolic—the return of the objectified woman[36] —and tangible—an exploitation, without precedent, of the feminine bodies by the sex industries, setbacks on abortion rights, increase in poverty and inequality and so on.

New prescriptions are also sexual. They are inspired by pornography and its codes, which have became the new manual of the sexual liberation. In 1981, the G-spot, this supersensitive zone above the pubic bone, was "discovered." This erotic spot leads to an optimization of sexual performances and the obligation for women to have multiple orgasms. It has spawned the way to a new "regimented feminine sexuality." Most certainly, "sex doctors" will soon discover its anal equivalent...for women. The injunction to have an orgasm, which is considered to be a measure of sexual satisfaction, is now a condition for mental health stability. If the orgasmic Eldorado is now "within reach for all," the fact remains that young women consult mainly for their real or supposed "frigidity" and for pain during the sexual intercourse.[37]

This new bodily biopolitic[38] imposes on each one, particularly on women, to have a binding self-control. "Rather than a disappearance of the constraints, we are witnessing an internalization of controls and surveillances," explains Philippe Perrot, who continues: "By successive stages, accompanying the rise of individualism, the standards cease to be brutally imposed to be exerted insidiously and with flexibility, by the way of a blackmail disguised in solicitude and in an invitation to be fulfilled and to be well."[39] The internalization of social constraints is not only limited to issues relating to a plastic body and to clothing standards; it is increasingly linked to the pornographic codes. Pornographic derealization which exploits and focuses on younger-looking bodies with an exacerbated but always amazing libido influences attitudes and behaviors.

The invasion of sexual and pornographic representations leads to a new conformism. "The industrialization of the sexual image [...], from pornography to advertisement, renews the most reactionary gender norms (endocentrism and heterosexism) and the old control of the bodies, especially those of women," says François Cusset.[40] This representation of a hypersexualized woman, a great masturbator, whose lesbianism exists only for the pleasure of heterosexual men, this inveterate seductress who happens to be at the same time a bitch, a whore, a cum dumpster, holes to be filled with hands, feet and all kinds of objects, an insatiable and a masochist being, is proof that women live on sex and for sex.

To be beautiful, a woman must be young and remain so.[41] Since the 1980s, the youth are no longer associated with revolutionary ideas that disrupted archaic and stiff social frameworks. Youth's daringness limits itself to a normalizing, imperious, and commercial physical ideal. Teens' magazines repeat the imperative to "be daring." They are quick to complement this message with prescriptions such as "consume" this or that product, "be sexy" or "dare it all." For adult women, the "That's it, I'm taking care of me" (*Cosmopolitan*, September 2005) often means "have a face lift, botox injections, liposuction, adopt miraculous diets, especially before summer, put anti-wrinkle and anti-cellulite creams, do daily physical activities. Free yourself! Stay young, in your body and in your mind! Consume, consume, consume! Be of your time! Be inspired by sex shops and learn how to do a striptease in order to boost (the declining) desire of your man, for which you are responsible." In short, remain young, you will be attractive and, consequently, interesting...for others.

"Youthism is a major ideological movement of the 1980s."[42] It is implemented everywhere. Standards in pornography, publicity and fashion are largely "teencentrist." If youth, particularly young women and adolescent girls, are among the main targets of advertisers, they are also being transformed into consumable goods. Worldwide there is a rejuvenation of prostitutes[43] and an explosion of pseudo-child and child pornography. One certainly doesn't go without the other. There is also an early sexualization of girls impregnated by adult sexual references. Boys wear pimp style clothing and expect girls to act and physically look like the women they have seen in pornography. A pubis not depilated causes the rupture, testified young women.[44] The constraints have changed in nature. The new sexual morality, just as prescriptive as the old one, imposes a new tyrannical sexual order. It translates into high body standards and sexual relationships that focus on the male's pleasure. This new conformism is thundering but at the same time it makes women more docile. It is sexist, racist and pornographic. The permissive discourse, unprecedented in the Western societies' history,[45] is accompanied by an increase in violence. In contemporary pornography this violence is expressed, among other ways, by an accentuation of the humiliation and the degradation of women and by a tangible and normalized brutality.

THE PORNOGRAPHIC SOCIAL INFLUENCE

Pornography just as commercial literature is a place for the ideological crystallization of the expressed philosophy of an era.[46] In turn, pornographic representations affect the era by fortifying some of its traits. Pornography transforms the bodies of women into objects of fantasy. It feminizes children, by imposing on them the sexual maturity of adults, while it infantilizes the women. The pairing of the sensual young woman and the sexual nymphet is essential to pornography.

Officially, the sexual exploitation of children is condemned, although minors are shown as sexual objects and are stars of many pornographic productions. When applied, the repression of child pornography most likely affects the one who uses prepubescent children. In Quebec, police officers who track online child pornography worry only about the youngest victim, that is to say children below the age of puberty. Thus, the impunity of producers and consumers of child pornography (minor, but pubescent girls) is almost total. This absence of repression is an evidence of the growing social normalization of sexual exploitation of teens and also a contributing factor to its normalization. This staged sensuality of teens, who are temptresses, seducers and corrupters excite many men, who masturbate when looking at the images, either on their computer or television screens.

What we named "pedophilization[48]" takes into account three phenomena; (1) the juvenescence, an ideological movement that started in the 1980s; (2) the rejuvenation process in the recruitment for the sex industries; (3) and the "teencentrism" of representations. It also reflects the infantilization techniques used by the porn industry. However, the rejuvenation is not only seen in current methods of production, it also plays a role in consumption. Nowadays, people become aware of pornography at a younger age. The average age of the first consumption is 12 years for boys and 13 for girls. For a fair amount of youth, pornography has become their principal means of sexual "education" and a model for sexual intercourse. A recent study conducted among 213 university students found that the younger men and women consume pornography, the more likely it is that their sexuality and their relationship to their body will be influenced by these pornographic representations.. The younger they consume, the more their bodies are modified (tattoo, piercing, Brazilian wax). The younger they consume, the more they ask their partner to watch porn and reproduce sexual acts they have seen in pornography. The younger they consume, the more their actual consumption will be regular and frequent. The younger they consume, the more they are anxious about their bodies and their physical capabilities.[47] The survey also revealed that the consumption of pornography by young girls affects their self-esteem. This can be a critical fact, because previous studies showed that girls with low self-esteem engage early on in sexual activities. A survey done by Statistics Canada showed that among "girls whose self-image was low at the ages of twelve or thirteen were more likely than those who had a strong image to declare that from the age of fourteen or fifteen years they had already had sex intercourse."[48] While 10.9% of girls who had a good self-esteem reported having had sexual intercourses before the age of fifteen, the proportion almost doubles (19.4%) among those who have a poor self-esteem.[49] Unfortunately, those who engage in early sexual active are often seen or treated as sluts.

In short, the earlier consumption starts, the more tangible and durable its consequences.

It is important to highlight that youth aged 15 to 24 years are those who are most affected by sexually transmitted diseases (STDs). In Quebec, this age group represents 72% of female cases of Chlamydia and 49% of male cases. In regard to Gonococcus infection, the most recent data indicate that from 2004 to 2006, the number of reported cases has increased by 68%. This increase is 3.5 times higher among women than men. In fact, the number of reported cases for girls aged 15 to 19 years shows a drastic increase by 250%.[50]

The imperatives of beauty, which are universalized and weigh heavily on women and girls, require never-ending work. Women devote to these prescriptions a fair amount of time. Absolute thinness and flat stomachs—to keep one's shape at any price—is inducing anorexia bulimia in some teens. Breasts need to be firm and high and lips have to be luscious. Women's hair should be long, whereas all the body hair, including pubic hair, must completely disappear. Important markets are organized around feminine beauty. To stay competitive, "teenagers have to develop a 'worrisome listening' of their body."[51] Those who do not comply are out of fashion. "Save your body from disgrace, to shield it from the social penalization that it leads to, has become a new torment."[52]

Beauty can certainly open doors to women, but when they hit the "glass ceiling" these doors start to slowly close. Beauty is an indicator of a lack of intelligence. Therefore, beautiful women are often accused of obtaining their success thanks to their beauty, hence their difficulty to move beyond the "glass ceiling."[53]

Women, teenage girls and even young girls are now encouraged to expose themselves; their body is their most important asset that allows them a promising future. This imperative, which requires beauty and youthfulness, is disguised in the right to wellbeing. The body must be smooth, desirable and able to accomplish almost anything. Also, the body is fragmented in many parts that are alternately offered and available. This fragmentation is particularly obvious in publicity and even more so in pornography. Parts are preferred to the whole. The contemporary male eroticism is characterized by a "polymorphic fetishism": breasts, buttocks, feet. In addition, "the magnifying glass focused on all the details initially results in drawing aside the real bodies of the ideal body, the live bodies of the dreamed body."[54] A woman's "real" body despite all the efforts that they devote to it is bound to disappoint, particularly men who began to consume pornography at a very young age.

POWERS

Body representations, the values that they induce and the incessant work put into one's appearances in order to conform reproduce in their own way the powers within social structure. Fundamentally, social domination goes "through the control over the uses of the body and by the imposition of its standards."[55] The standards being imposed are historically correlated to the rise of the bourgeoisie and its subsequent victory.[56] The male domination requires not only a gender division of labor and an "essentialization" of sex roles—to men reason and the public sphere, to women reproduction, feelings, work on appearances and the private sphere—but also a control over the feminine body. This idea is interiorized by the dominated.[57] This idea is reflected in the clothes that historically women have worn. From the corset that highlighted femininity and stifled the body (which is fashion again) to the G-strings, the lingerie and the stiletto heels, women have been an "ostentatious showcase of the social success of their husbands."[58] If male domination dresses women from veil to the haute couture, it also strips them naked in publicity, pornography and elsewhere. It is men's regard that decides on the forms women's bodies will take.[59]

Advertising agencies, magazines and pornographers indefatigably claim to promote the "liberation" of women. Free women from what exactly? We do not know, but we do know that this so-called liberation implicates constant work on one's appearances and a perpetual self-surveillance. This in pornography reaches caricatural summits because femininity is paroxysmal. It also implies multiple body transformations, from tattoos, piercing, plastic surgery to repeated diets and the use of drugs (that above all diminishes appetite). To stay young is also an imperative of pornography, but the body undergoes constant stress and it ages very quickly (and undoubtedly very badly). This may explain the unusually high succession/rotation of porn actresses, who for the vast majority have a short life expectancy in the "business." Nevertheless, their performances will be long lasting, because once put on the Internet and duplicated on DVD, it is almost impossible to erase all footage. Consequently, some of them might feel the social stigma of their passage in pornography for a long time.

Bodies are issues of power while also being their symbolization. The current period inscribes systematically and massively the bodies of social disparities between genders and generations. Bodies are becoming an expression of the male and the capitalist social domination, which is heterosexist and, increasingly, "teencentric." In this context, the liberal sexual freedom "allows the strongest, the richest, and most cynical to guarantee their criminal desires to the detriment of the weakest or the poorest."[60] Money gives access to women and girls' bodies across the world, which contributes to the legitimacy their sexual exploitation.

This domination finds its ultimate expression in the pornographic productions that weigh considerably on the dominant representations that they "pedophilize." In her testimony, Raffaëla Anderson writes, "She finally finishes my make up. I am disappointed when I see the results. I look like a twelve-year-old kid."[61] The symbolic meaning is strong. To pretend that porn actresses look like a 12-year-old kid is one of the techniques used by pornographers to represent incest or sexual abuse of a minor and also "what is given to the consumer to think that the practices that are shown are not so *abnormal*, since they were able to produce, diffuse and sell these videos."[62] This child-pornographic imagery is combined with another normalized social trend: a growing number of men choose partners that are much younger than them or more fragile (by mail-order bride agency or not). Powerful men are often seen holding hands with younger women. This allows them to show their power and their aptitude to dominate.[63]

Sexual pleasure and power, sexual power and pleasure are combined: they excite and incite.[64] In pornography, power is expressed without restraint. When the archetype of the sexy and liberated girl is represented in a doggy style position, with her tongue out, wet lips, breasts that defy gravity, a body tattooed and pierced in erotic places, no pubic hair, and waiting for a manly male to come and fuck her, while he is insulting her, should we be surprised that young boys sexually take advantage of girls? That they leave a relationship if the girlfriend refuses sodomy or if she finds no pleasure in it? That they believe everything is due to them because women are at their sexual service?

Today's teenagers are bombarded by pornography. They are getting accustomed to a stereotypical and sexist vision of gender roles before they even reach sexual maturity. Products of the sex industry feed their sexual imagination. Feeling and tenderness are absent in pornography. Rather, pornographic material shows mechanical sex. Consequently, the objectification of women and girls is socially reinforced. Boys see girls of their age as potential sex objects. Psychotherapist James E. Wright observes that boys exhibit behaviors of great sexual control. These sexual attitudes and behaviors learnt at an early age, usually at the end of primary school, are closely related with their perception of masculinity.[65] Children are growing up in a social environment where pornographic codes influence culture. A survey of 3,000 Canadian high school students from Montreal, Kingston and Toronto found that three quarters of the students are sexually harassed by their peers.[66] Sexual harassment is an epidemic: in a sample of 315 students, it was found that 98.7% of women have been the target of sexual harassment before they were 18 years old.[67] In a society where sexuality especially that of young women is a consumer good used to sell products and to excite men, it is not surprising to find high rates of sexual harassment. Nor is it unexpected that most targets of sexual aggressions are teen girls.

In pornography, "women shout of joy and find pleasure in men's pleasures."[68] There is always a perfect equilibrium between men's desires and what women agree to offer as sexual services. "A woman has to learn to like her body, to be able to give pleasure."[69] Perhaps this is history's lesson: freedom is good, but only when it benefits men. Girls learn at a young age to exhibit their bodies to please. Today, young girls' bodies are shaped and forged according to dominant models, which are becoming increasingly pornographic.

NOTES

1 Baudrillard, Jean, *De la séduction* (Paris, Galilée, 1979), 98.

2 Moulin, Caroline, *Féminités adolescentes* (Rennes, Presses universitaires de Rennes, 2005), 44.

3 Lugrin, Gilles, *Âmes sensibles s'abstenir: entre surenchère homosexuelle et "glam trash," la polémique du porno chic*, ComAnalysis, no.25, September 2001, < http://www.comanalysis.ch/ComAnalysis/Publication25.htm > (retrieved August 3, 2002).

4. Dahl, Darren W., Kristina D. Frankenberger, and Rajesh V. Manchanda, "Does it pay to shock? Reactions to shocking and non-shocking and content among University students," *Journal of Advertising Research*, (vol. 43, no. 3, 2003), 268–280.
5. Reichert, Tom, and Courtney Carpenter, "An update on sex in magazine advertising: 1983 to 2003," *Journalism and Mass Communication Quarterly* (vol. 81, no. 4, 2004), 823–837.
6. Deleu, Xavier, *Le consensus pornographique* (Paris, Mango, 2002), 27.
7. Montreynaud, Florence, *Amours à vendre, les dessous de la prostitution* (Paris, Glenat, 1993), 44.
8. *Ibid.*, 48.
9. Paul, Pamela, *Pornified. How Pornography Is Transforming Our Lives, Our Relationships, and Our Families* (New York, Times Book, 2005), 184.
10. Bouchard, Natasha and Pierrette *La sexualisation précoce des filles peut accroître leur vulnérabilité*, Sisyphe, April 18, 2007, <http://sisyphe.org/imprimer/php3?id_article=917> (retrieved September 17, 2007).
11. Pommereau, Xavier, *Ado à fleur de peau* (Paris, Abin Michel, 2006), 56.
12. See Chapter II of Poulin, Richard, *Enfances dévastées. L'enfer de la prostitution* (Ottawa, L'Interligne, 2007), 50–79.
13. Baltzer, Franziska, *Sexualisation précoce des adolescentes et abus sexuels*, Sisyphe, April 13, 2007, < http://sisyphe.org/article.php3?id_article=2073 > (retrieved January 19, 2008).
14. Bouchard, Pierrette, *Consentantes? Hypersexualisation et violences sexuelles* (Rimouski, CALACS de Rimouski, 2007), 6.
15. See Poulin, Richard with the coll. of Mélanie Claude, *Enfances dévastées*, Tome II. *Pornographie et hypersexualisation* (Ottawa, L'Interligne, 2008). This book publishes the results of a survey on youth and the consumption of pornography.
16. According to the *Enquête sociale et de santé 1998* (Québec, Les Publications du Québec, 2000), 15% of the participants in a survey aged 15 to 29 years had their first sexual intercourse with penetration before the age of 15 years, whereas this proportion falls at 8% among the 30 to 39 years, to 4% at the 40 to 49 years and to 3% at the 50 to 59 years.
17. See Tisseron, Serge, *L'intimité surexposée* (Paris, Hachette Littératures, 2001).
18. Fourgnaud, Agathe, *La confusion des rôles. Les toujours-jeunes et les déjà-vieux* (Paris, Lattès, 1999).
19. Poulin, Richard, "Pornographie et sexualisation des enfants," *Actes de la Journée de réflexion sur la sexualisation précoce des filles* (Montréal, Y des femmes et Centre des femmes de l'UQÀM, 2005), 7.
20. Several authors tackled this question: Authier, Christian, *Le nouvel ordre sexuel* (Paris, Bartillat, 2002); Bouchard, *Consentantes ?*; Deleu, Xavier, *Le consensus pornographique*; Guyenot, Laurent, *Le livre noir de l'industrie rose* (Paris, Imago, 2000); Marzano, Michela, *La pornographie ou l'épuisement du désir* (Paris, Buchet-Chastel, 2003) and *Malaise dans la sexualité. Le piège de la pornographie* (Paris, JC Lattès, 2006); Paul, Pamela, *Pornified*; Robert, Jocelyne, *Le sexe en mal d'amour* (Montréal, Éditions de l'Homme, 2005).
21. Poulin, Richard, *La mondialisation des industries du sexe, Prostitution, pornographie, traite des femmes et des enfants* (Montréal, L'Interligne, 2004).
22. Garner-Moyer, Hélène, *Apparence physique et GRH: entre choix et discrimination*, Université Paris I < http://cergors.univ-paris1.fr/docsatelecharger/Garnermoyer.pdf > (retrieved May 25, 2008).

23 Santé Canada, *Rapport sur les maladies mentales au Canada*, Ottawa, Santé Canada, October 2002, < http://www.phac-aspc.gc.ca/publicat/miic-mmac/index_f.html > (retrieved October 15, 2005).
24 Guillebaud, Jean-Claude, *La tyrannie du plaisir* (Paris, Seuil, 1999), 16.
25 Aral, Sevgi O., Janet S. St Lawrence, Lilia Tikhonova, Emma Safarova, Kathleen A. Parker, Anna Shakarishvili, Caroline A. Ryan, "The social organization of commercial sex work in Moscow, Russia," *Sexually Transmitted Diseases* (vol. 30, no. 1, 2003), 39–46.
26 Dubreuil, Émilie, "Sexe Masturbation," *La Presse* (June 5, 2005).
27 In Bénilde, Marie, *On achève bien les cerveaux. La publicité et les médias* (Paris, Raisons d'agir, 2007), 19.
28 Brune, Françoise, *Le bonheur conforme* (Paris, Gallimard, 1985), 241.
29 Ehrenberg, Alain, *Le culte de la performance* (Paris, Hachette Littérature, 1991), 279.
30 Ibid., 280.
31 Verdu, Vicente, *Le style du monde. La vie dans le capitalisme de fiction* (Paris, Stock, 2005), 121–122.
32 Dupont, Luc, *Téléréalité: quand la téléréalité est un mensonge* (Montréal, Presses de l'Université de Montréal, 2007), 108.
33 Bertrand, Jean-Claude and Annie Baron-Carvais, *Introduction à la pornographie* (Paris, La Musardine, 2001), 13–14.
34 Taschen, Angelika (dir.), *La chirurgie esthétique* (Köln, Taschen, 2005), 10.
35 Guienne, Véronique, "Savoir, se vendre: qualité sociale et disqualification sociale," *Cahiers de recherche sociologique* (no. 43, January 2007), 13.
36 Détrez, Christine and Anne Simon, *À leur corps défendant. Les femmes à l'épreuve du nouvel ordre moral* (Paris, Seuil, 2006), 12.
37 See Poulin, *Pornographie et hypersexualisation*, 216.
38 Foucault, Michel, *Histoire de la sexualité tome 1. La volonté de savoir* (France, Éditions Gallimard, 1976).
39 Perrot, Philippe, *Le travail des apparences. Le corps féminin, XVIIIe-XIXe siècle* (Paris, Seuil, 1984), 206–207.
40 Cusset, François, *La décennie. Le grand cauchemar des années 1980* (Paris, La Découverte, 2008), 274.
41 Kaufmann, Jean-Claude, in *Corps de femmes, regards d'hommes. Sociologie des seins nus* (Paris, Nathan, 1998), has shown the strength of the ostracism faced by the elderly women in a place of apparent freedom and tolerance, the beach.
42 Cusset, *La décennie*,280.
43 Poulin, *Enfances dévastées. L'enfer de la prostitution.*
44 Poulin, *Pornographie et hypersexualisation*, 260.
45 Guillebaud, *La tyrannie du plaisir*, 36–37.
46 Concept of Antonio Gramsci, "Littérature populaire," in *Œuvres choisies* (Paris, Éditions Sociales, 1959).
47 These are results of a survey among 213 students conducted in the 2008 winter. Poulin, *Pornographie et hypersexualisation*, 205–234.
48 Statistique Canada, *Les relations sexuelles précoces*, May 3, 2005, < http://wwwstatcan.ca/Daily/Français/05053/q05053a.htm > (retrieved May 15, 2005).

49 Institut de la statistique du Québec, *Enquête sociale et de santé auprès des enfants et des adolescents québécois 1999* (Quebec, Les publications du Québec, 2002). The survey indicates that 61% of the 16-year-old girls who were seeing a boy in the year preceding the survey and who had low self-esteem have been abused. Among girls who claimed to have a high self-esteem, the rate dropped by half.

50 Bureau de surveillance et de vigie du ministère de la Santé et des Services sociaux, *Portrait des infections transmissibles sexuellement et par le sang (ITSS) au Québec année 2005 (et projections 2006)* (Québec, ministère de la Santé et des Services sociaux, 2006), 6.

51 Moulin, *Féminités adolescentes,* 78.

52 Perrot, *Le travail des apparences,* 205.

53 Amadieu, Jean-François, *Le poids des apparences. Beauté, amour et gloire* (Paris, Odile Jacob, 2005).

54 Perrot, *Le travail des apparencess,* 67.

55 Détrez, Christine, *La construction sociale du corps* (Paris, Seuil, 2002), 173.

56 See among others, Foucault, *Histoire de la sexualité tome 1*; Vigarello, Georges, *Le corps redressé* (Paris, Delarge, 2001); Corbin, Alain, *Le miasme et la jonquille* (Paris, Aubier, 1982).

57 Bourdieu, Pierre, *La domination masculine* (Paris, Seuil, 1998).

58 Détrez, *La construction sociale du corps,* 187.

59 Kaufmann, *Corps de femmes, regards d'hommes,* 181–189.

60 Folscheid, Dominique, *Sexe mécanique. La crise contemporaine de la sexualité* (Paris, La Table Ronde, 2002), 14.

61 Anderson, Raffaëla, *Hard* (Paris, Grasset, 2001), 17.

62 Le Rest, Pascal, *Des rives du sexe* (Paris, L'Harmattan, Paris, 2003), 56.

63 Mossuz-Lavau, Janine, *La vie sexuelle en France (*Paris, La Martinière, 2002), 49.

64 Foucault, *Histoire de la sexualité,* 66.

65 Wright, James E., *The Sexualization of America's Kids and How to Stop It (*New York, Lincoln, Shanghai, Writers Club Press, 2001).

66 In Bouchard, *Consentantes?,* 52.

67 Julia Whealin, "Women's report of unwanted sexual attention during chilhood," *Journal of Child Sexual Abuse* (vol. 11, no. 1, 2002), 75–94.

68 Dubost, Matthieu, *La tentation pornographique* (Ellipses, Paris, 2006), 66.

69 Détrez and Simon, *À leur corps défendant,* 245.

PART VI: THE POLITICAL ECONOMY OF MEDIA AND CULTURE

CHAPTER THIRTEEN

Radical Mass Media Criticism, History and Theory

DAVID BERRY

RADICAL MASS MEDIA CRITICISM: HISTORICAL BEGININGS: HISTORICAL BEGINNINGS

The debate over what exactly constitutes radical mass media criticism (RMMC) is largely based on two crucial and interlocking points. The first is the object of critique and the second is the intent attached to the critique. Radicals always seek outcomes, change and alteration as an objective of critique, which is far removed from *mere critique*. To assess this condition, this chapter is broadly split in two sections. The first section begins with an assessment of some of the key themes surrounding the beginnings and historical development of RMMC and evaluates the contribution of John Theobald in mapping out the framework of RMMC. The second section assesses the issue of press and media power by looking specifically at the work of a group of writers that Theobald believed to be either central to or at the margins of RMMC. The second section also assesses the work of the relatively unknown French sociologist and philosopher Jean Gabriel Tarde, the Danish philosopher Sören Kierkegaard and the German writers Max Horkeimer and Herbert Marcuse from the Frankfurt School in relation to Critical Theory. The choice of these particular writers is to highlight both the common ground of media criticism thus constituting a genealogy of thought, and also their distinctive differences in finding solutions to existing conditions of domination. This section also discusses the issue of resistance to press and media power, which is crucial to the debate mainly because there is an assumption that many writers in the field assume a prevailing dominant ideology too great to resist.

The mapping of radical mass media criticism normally begins with a number of writers such as Karl Kraus, Ferdinand Tönnies, Jean Gabriel Tarde and Sören Kierkegaard in the latter half of the nineteenth century. However, criticisms of news can be located as far back to the early period of sixteenth-century England with Royal condemnation of local news production as inherently heretical and pernicious to existing regimes of control. In this context the main reason for allowing the *Corantos*[1] to be imported from Holland was to satisfy the need for news from abroad whilst stifling home production. A little later the English dramatist Ben Jonson wrote a savage critical satire titled *The Staple of News* performed in 1625 claiming that "there cannot be any greater disease in nature" in Act III, Scene I under the title "To The Readers", which served as Jonson's warning to the public that news writing not only corrupted language, not unlike Kraus many years later, but equally of its power to influence the public thus distorting truth; once again not unlike Kraus who perceived a broken link between fact and the journalistic written word which for the latter as for the former had the propensity to distort truth thus creating a *false reality* through the power of the written word. As Bleyer notes in his impressive work *Main Currents in the History of American Journalism,* criticisms of "English newspapers in the seventeenth and eighteenth centuries"[2] were widely known as they were also in eighteenth-century North America. As Keeler et al. also noted during the mid-nineteenth century in the U.S. there was a "general debate" concerning the "ethical abuses"[3] in the press. Criticisms of the mass media (now including the press) emerged later with the introduction of mass communication systems, including television, radio, film and photography in the early part of the twentieth century onwards. Journalism, which as Conboy rightly reminds us, only entered the English vernacular as a term of reference to news writers in the earlier regions of the nineteenth century, and was becoming a central part of the liberal idea of the fourth estate. Thomas Carlyle in his work *The French Revolution* published in 1837 and later in his subsequent work *On Heroes, -Worship & the Heroic in History* published in 1841 laid out some of the rudimentary principles of journalism vis-a-vis the notion of the fourth estate, first discussed by Edmund Burke in the eighteenth century, as a necessary institution in the furtherance of democracy. But towards the end of the nineteenth century, the press were increasingly becoming the object of criticism not as the crusader of truth and democracy envisaged by Carlyle. One particular criticism was its apparent abuse of its seemingly privileged position as a fourth estate; hence the well-known phrase "Power Without Responsibility" the part cry of Stanley Baldwin in early-twentieth-century Britain; the liberal dream had turned decidedly sour.

In 2000, John Theobald produced "Radical Mass Media Criticism: Elements of a History from Kraus to Bourdieu"; this was the first attempt of its kind to begin to map out what John and myself would later refer to as a "cultural genealogy" or "tradition" of radical media critics throughout history to the present day. The chapter began thus:

> A full historical survey of radical mass media criticism has yet to be published. When it is, its early sections covering the late nineteenth and early twentieth centuries will surely be dominated by the seminal work of Karl Kraus. Despite being "shamelessly ignored" (Jameson 1990: 63), Kraus stands out as a major figure, many of whose ideas have been, often unknowingly, rediscovered by present-day writers on the media.[4]

Theobald made many astute observations and contributions towards RMMC, three of which are briefly detailed here. The first major contribution was to bring to the attention of the academic community the writings of the Austrian satirist Karl Kraus and his contribution to media criticism. This intervention by Theobald meant that we could now locate the beginnings of a radical tradition much earlier than the Frankfurt School, which for many writers mainly in cultural and media studies, were the founding figures and Theobald rightly reminded those who believed this latter point to be a truism that they had got it monumentally wrong: "Radical mass media criticism is habitually but inaccurately adjudged to have started with the Frankfurt School ..." but as early as the 1920s "Kraus had already produced over 500 numbers of his critical-satirical journal *Die Fackel (The Torch)*. . . ."[5]

The second major contribution came four years later in 2004 with the publication of *The Media and the Making of History* where Theobald was the first to present the "four generations" of radical media writers and perhaps more importantly how the writings of each overlapped and coalesced into a formal critique of mainstream media in liberal and neoliberal systems. It's important to note that many writers are missing from this account as noted by Theobald in the first line of the first quote above. Theobald also noted that "While other names can be put forward ..."[6] the writings of "the German Ferdinand Tönnies, the Frenchman Gabriel Tarde, and...the Austrian Karl Kraus standout as principal seminal thinkers in the lineage of radical mass media criticism".[7] This perspective applies to the other three generations of thinkers[8] which was updated to the "five periods" in his chapter titled "The Intellectual Tradition of Mass Media Criticism: A Framework", ranging from the "mid-nineteenth century to the present".[9]

Two years later in 2006 John and I published *Radical Mass Media Criticism: A Cultural Genealogy*, which led to his third contribution towards expanding the field of debate. During our work, John had an email exchange with Robert McChesney on the issue of addressing the history of radical mass media criticism, and at our book launch in 2006 it was noted that the result of that "conversation" was the production of *Our Unfree Press: 100 Years of Media Criticism* by McChesney and Scott which mapped out the North American tradition.

The key objective of our work was to begin to piece together hitherto seemingly disparate groups of writers who in many cases rarely referred to others in the "field" despite sharing substantial common ground. As Theobald claimed with reference to the first generation of critics, "There are considerable areas of overlap between the ideas of Tarde, Kraus and Ferdinand Tönnies ..."[10] which was to be extended throughout the entire intellectual system and this is what is meant with specific reference to both Nietzsche and later Foucault by "genealogy".[11] This identification of a tradition was not solely in relation to the critical approach towards a specific object of enquiry but moreover and perhaps more importantly to acknowledge an alternative view of history. Radical critics therefore produce what Scott Lash[12] referred to as a "different rationality" and in this context alone it is undeniably subversive in that it seeks to undermine and counteract official press/media accounts of events and history.

What is absolutely clear and undeniable amongst the three writers mentioned above is the nature of the critique, levelled in these cases at least towards the power and influence of the press to shape historical development; to leave its mark as an "official stamp" on what occurred. Kraus was certainly one of the first to challenge the press as an authority for making history but Kraus was equally concerned with what journalism was imposing on a cultural level; for Kraus the press were also responsible for corrupting language. As far as Tarde and Tönnies were concerned, public opinion was formed as a consequence of information distributed in society by the press thus becoming legitimate and dominant. Kraus also forcefully argued that the press were highly persuasive, distorted truth by using the cliché to subtly inculcate public opinion. Although there aren't specific and detailed references to ideology in the works on the press by the three, there is no doubt that their ability to recognise that the production of a rational press discourse was in fact transformed into an ideological structure in that what we come to know via the press is in fact manufactured.

One of the chief objectives of RMMC is to reveal the facade behind the liberal ideal of the fourth estate, as a supposedly independent critical body or a broadcast media system that contains similar ideals in terms of their approaches to the production of news and the idealised notion that deregulated media systems are pro-competitive, anti-monopolistic and inherently democratic in satisfying "consumer needs". The liberal rationale behind competitive commercial television that is broadly deregulated for instance is a business-oriented response to what is seen as the anti-competitive and pro-monopolistic public service broadcasting (PSB) systems. In Europe for instance the pro-liberal, anti-PSB perspective is written into the Treaty of Rome, 1957, and continues to govern media policy to this day within the European Union (EU). In essence, radical media critics have sought to reveal the contradictions and forms of political hypocrisy embedded in liberal philosophy that asserts freedom, individualism and attaining greater forms of knowledge, understanding and democracy through current media systems. This critique should now be extended to the EU's Media Literacy Programme, which in essence was developed in response to the increasing corporate character of media ownership. Importantly, it is also an admission of the inherent contradiction within liberal philosophy vis-a-vis individual rights of ownership that allows an individual to amass great swathes of power and control over media outlets. The Media Literacy Programme is therefore a measure to counter-balance the discrepancy between individual rights of ownership and the liberal notion of the public interest. The Media Literacy Programme therefore places great emphasis on the public having democratic rights of access to new technologies that allow the public to be able to access a broad range of news and informational outlets; to become less reliant on dominant mainstream media outlets and to be able to engage critically with content. The first problem to emphasise is that the EU have failed to confront corporate media ownership by explicitly accepting the central contradiction in liberal philosophy; the second is that there are no guarantees that individuals will multi-source away from dependency on mainstream media as *the* authoritative source of news, and third it does not consider poverty that disallow sections of society access to new technologies including the internet.

This modern day example is a good basis to lead into the following discussion concerning power and resistance, because, for all its flaws, the EU's Media Literacy Programme is in the final instance an attempt to enthuse the public to resist dominant mainstream media outlets. Whether it can be considered a *radical* response to become less dependent on mainstream media is perhaps a more difficult judgement to make because this would depend on the political position of each individual. As Anthony Giddens' book title *Beyond Left and Right* rightly suggests, the meaning of radical pierces right through various political positions and as we shall now see despite political and philosophical differences between the writings of Jean Gabriel Tarde, Sören Kierkegaard. Max Horkeimer and Herbert Marcuse they are all nevertheless considered to be radical vis-a-vis the object of enquiry at their related time of writing. Theobald rightly included them in his analysis of the five generations of thinkers. However, Tarde and Marcuse for instance wouldn't exactly be considered as compatible writers in terms of strategies to achieve political and economic objectives. I don't think it totally unreasonable to infer that Tarde for instance would have been sympathetic to the EU's response to corporate media power by allowing dispersed "publics" to emerge voluntarily. Marcuse, on the other hand, would have begged to differ and on that note we now proceed to review three positions of radical critics in relation to power and resistance.

POWER AND RESISTANCE

There is a perception that many writers of media criticism perceive the public mostly in passive terms, as uncritical consumers, unable or ill-equipped to cope with complex media messages or who simply accept discourse as truth. The view that people are ostensibly governed by a dominant ideology is certainly well documented and rehearsed as is the notion that the public is suffering from some fatal *false consciousness* unable to break free as ideology interpellates and conditions the essence of our very own subjective being. Even though the French philosopher Louis Althusser spent minimal time and effort in specifically analysing media, his Ideological State Apparatus contained the mass media as a key component for helping to reproduce existing relations of production inherent within the superstructure and the way reproduction proceeds is via ideology. In very broad terms this view embraces some of the core positions of what follows in this section of the chapter. Eagleton[13] noted that as opposed to dictatorship, ideology in liberal and/or neoliberal systems largely proceeds unnoticed and is subtly interwoven in social contexts; this was what Stuart Hall in many of his works called "taken-for-granted" contexts; largely accepted, and it is what Eagleton called "legitimate", "natural" and "rational" in that it forms our very boundaries of existence.

The three schools of thought discussed below by writers such as Jean Gabriel Tarde, the theologian–philosopher Sören Kierkegaard, Max Horkeimer and Herbert Marcuse from the Frankfurt School certainly regarded the press and broadcast media as an influential power over society. Tarde and Kierkegaard were more specifically interested in how public opinion was formed and informed by the press, whilst the Frankfurt writers broadened the debate out by assessing the media's impact on culture and in Marcuse's writings defining the necessary social components for liberation away from neoliberal systems. Whilst we can agree that all three positions advocated a dominating media power, they weren't, as is so often wrongly conveyed, entrenched fatalists, or, to use the over-popularised term, "pessimists"; there was always room for resistance and although there were political, philosophical and indeed psychological differences in their respective positions, they were without doubt *radical perspectives* vis-a-vis the object of critique. Whether one is satisfied with the proposed outcomes and objectives of sought-after strategies is a matter of both interpretation and subjective positioning.

JEAN GABRIEL TARDE

Taking these positions one by one, beginning with Tarde, we see on first viewing that his belief that public opinion was formed out of the power of the press to influence reads similar to the way in which Adorno for instance viewed the power of the culture industry to annihilate alternatives under capitalism. On closer scrutiny of Tarde's contribution to this debate, we find that although he levelled a critique against the power to influence, he wasn't pessimistic about the final outcome or consumption of how the various publics decoded the encoded message. This optimistic view of how communications operated and how consumption proceeds, in my mind, turns into a position not that dissimilar to some of the writings found in British Cultural Studies, although Tarde is rarely if ever mentioned in the studies from the 1980s and 1990s. Tarde[14] argued that publics were certainly produced in modern society but were able to interact collectively and/or individually, reproducing public discourse in conjunction with the press. I don't think it's unreasonable to suggest that Tarde was arguing that alternative realities could be achieved in this way, thus allowing greater subjective power vis-a-vis press power, thus the link to some of the writers in the British Cultural Studies field, although mysteriously, Tarde is as far as I'm aware not mentioned for providing the necessary information on what would later become "audience research".

Tarde's view of publics and public communication is also not that far removed from the philosophical writings of Richard Rorty on how truth is formed. In fact, Rorty's more detailed writings particularly on objectivity and truth can shed some fascinating insights into Tarde's earlier work, if only because Tarde didn't delve so deeply, but nevertheless, in essence, my intention is to connect his rationale and perhaps *ideals* to the work of Richard Rorty. To highlight this further in *Objectivity, Relativism and Truth* (1991) and later in *Truth and Progress* (1998), Rorty argued that truth is effectively created in relation to inter-subjective agreement between speakers who have entered into public discussion. Rorty, the pragmatist and post-modern thinker, claimed that truth is neither external and nor can it be imposed on rationally minded individuals. Grenz highlights this further in relation to postmodernism stating it

> ...affirms that whatever we accept as truth and even the way we envision truth are dependent on the community in which we participate...There is no absolute truth: rather truth is relative to the community in which we participate.[15]

Relativism over universalism and the negation of Platonic absolute knowledge with the replacement of the Platonic notion of "opinion" and the "inter-subjective agreement" in Rorty's work is equal to public opinion in Tarde and the ability for opinion to evolve unproblematically is what Rorty refers to as the "free discussion" of the members being able to take place in any given community, which is ultimately bound up with the liberal notion of free speech. Rorty maintained that the outcomes of any discussion are always uncertain, but it would be unwise to ignore the fact that some voices dominate proceedings or at least set the agenda for discussion. Here is what Rorty says:

> "Free discussion" here does not mean "free from ideology", but simply the sort which goes on when the press, the judiciary, the elections and the universities are free, social mobility is frequent and rapid, literacy is universal, higher education is common, and peace and wealth have made possible the leisure necessary to listen to lots of different people and think about what they say.[16]

Tarde[17] also acknowledged the power and position of the press and like Rorty there were safeguards and alternative regimes of power and information that somehow reduced its power to manipulate the minds of the public, plus the essential belief that human rationality was a product of the individual. To a certain degree, if this were true, then Tarde's, and certainly Rorty's views, can be seen as being essentially subversive if we hold to the view that the objective of media discourse is to persuade us of its validity and truthfulness. At worst, we can simply deride and denounce Tarde as an early liberal apologist. A more radical perspective, let's say Marxism for instance, would certainly argue that despite Tarde's interesting critique of the press, there is a failure to resolve power in society and that the multiple publics that Tarde argued existed in a liberal pluralistic society simply and only assured epistemological protection from the point of production.

There are problems with Tarde's and Rorty's *positive* evaluations of public opinion or inter-subjective agreement, particularly when we consider that some people rely heavily on limited sources of information on which to make informed judgements in the first instance, and such judgements not only help towards public opinion but they are also ultimately realised at the ballot box. "Free discussion" therefore can be highly infected with ideology that masks itself as truth, and gullibility is after all a human fact of life. Someone who is socially induced by obsessively watching Fox News believing it to be both authoritative and a trustworthy source of news will certainly have a skewed and hopelessly limited view of the world. Consider the following from World Public Opinion:

> A new study based on a series of seven US polls conducted from January through September of this year [2003] reveals that before and after the Iraq war, a majority of

Americans have had significant misperceptions and these are highly related to support for the war in Iraq.[18]

Whilst Rorty is from the school of pragmatism, can we also apply this label to Tarde? Certainly there are strong connections to John Dewey's philosophical works regarded as a form of pragmatism concerning the idea that publics *should* have as a central tenet a dynamic form in that they functionally interact with external institutions (media, political or otherwise) hitherto detached from the body politic.[19] Dewey argued that democratic participation by publics wasn't possible in present conditions at the time of writing and that radical transformations of social norms were required to ensure a closer dialectical unity between people and institutions that at the very least at all levels redress the imbalance of power. Technological communication, whether in the form of journalism or other related media, was pivotal to any transformation towards what Dewey called the "Great Community" through a kind of Kantian transcendentalism towards an enlightened condition.

We can see here also a connection to the work on culture by the German philosopher Georg Simmel who was concerned with the *crisis of culture* in relation to the separation between subjective and objective forms. Simmel claimed that institutions had created a "fateful autonomy" through the deliberate development of a detached "immanent developmental logic" based equally on separate "laws" and "rationale" distinct from cultural development in society or what Simmel preferred to call "subjective culture'. Simmel was concerned with the "improvement of the soul" primarily by intellectual engagement and profound understanding of our environs but this process or what Simmel called the "path of culture" was blocked by institutions who essentially were selfish and self-obsessed by creating an institutional "immanent logic which is by no means always appropriate to the process of individual development and self-realisation, which is the whole point of all the products of culture ...".[20] Dewey's concerns over the distribution of information and concomitant knowledge that may ensue is in an identical framework to the concerns of Simmel in that Dewey equally recognised the distant and oft impersonal position of production unrelated to the community. Whether we wish to directly discuss information and/or knowledge in relation to Dewey, the production of truth in the Rortian sense or Simmel's broader use of cultural production, we can nevertheless recognise the spirit of Tarde here in the manner in which publics function vis-a-vis the production of democracy and the constitution of community and its role in the production of meaning and accountability.

Finally, on closer reading of Tarde's work there are also strong connections with two of Latin America's most prominent writers in the field of mass communications, Jésus Martín Barbero and Nestor García Canclini who both in varying ways argue that "popular culture" is a site of alternative narratives and discourse that serve to resist dominant ideologies. When Tarde argued that multiple publics exist and that they interacted and coalesced outside the established regimes of power, this is what Martín Barbero called "mestizaje"[21] and Canclini called "hybrid culture"[22] – a fusion of cultural differences intermingling to form regimes of resistance that empowers publics, not subjugating them to a greater authority. Canclini's "Consumption is good for thinking" slogan highlights this process arguing that consumption is what Scott Lash,[23] basing his work on Immanuel Kant, called a different rationality not bound to dominant or dominating regimes of power.

SÖREN KIERKEGAARD

Similarly, Kierkegaard in his criticisms of the press argued that public opinion was ostensibly formed from the point of production, but differed significantly from the views held by Tarde. Rather than refer to "publics", Kierkegaard referred to the "crowd" and public opinion was in this view a product of crowd behaviour; in other words it not only negated truth but also negated *individuality*. Kierkegaard wrote scathing attacks against the press, so scathing were they that even Kraus, the arch critic, was duly impressed; the press "elevates the trivial into the important" states Theobald[24] with respect to the Dane.

Kierkegaard in my opinion occupies an interesting position within this present field of inquiry. On the one hand, reference to the crowd automatically assumes an elitist perspective with regards to what appears in this language as the hapless people. For instance, other writers who specifically used or referred loosely to the crowd included Gustave le Bon, Sigmund Freud, Wilhelm Reich, Ortega y Gasset and Oswald Spengler who all in one way or another took umbrage with the crowd as a product of "mass society". Gustave Le Bon took his lead from Tarde's notion of "group mind" although Tarde spoke in terms of publics rather than crowd. Wilfred Trotter eloquently summed up crowd behaviour with the word "herd"; where collective menial consciousness ruled over existential thought. The English phrenologist and artist William Powell Frith produced his celebrated work of art titled *The Derby Day* (1856–1858), which despite its name wasn't primarily about the famous horse race but rather was the first artistic representation of the crowd, mingling amongst the "cultured elite". A key part of phrenology was the belief that one could deduce character by the shape of a head and the essential features therein. One glance at Powell Frith's work reveals the unsettling and identical features of the crowd pitted against the individuality of the gentry. Ortega y Gasset referred to the crowd as "barbarians" and Wilhelm Reich in his complex work *The Mass Psychology of Fascism* asked how a foul dictatorship could manipulate the population.

Amongst the various views of crowd were various points of resolution. Powell Frith was perhaps at the most extreme perceiving the crowd mentally deranged and beyond the pale. Resolution could be sought by the "cultured" first by recognising the threat and then dealing with it by total detachment, both physical and mental. Ortega y Gasset believed in the ideal that only individuals would have to struggle for recognition and identity vis-a-vis the nation; this is not to be confused with *subjectivism* but rather was the *perspectivism* originally found in the works of Friedrich Nietzsche. Reich was more hopeful and compassionate arguing that mass psychology and manipulation could be overcome but not in the Marxist sense of a class-for-itself but rather by cultivating a democratic structure in which individual freedom would flourish against the ravages of the machine. Kierkegaard's view of the crowd contains the spirit of many of the writers above, some of which are detailed in *Upbuilding Discourses in Various Spirits*,[25] but as with Theodor Adorno, Kierkegaard also wrote with an ironic twist, which as we'll see shortly had a distinct social purpose.

Kierkegaard's polemics and satirical attacks against the press were partly linked to his views of the crowd as an antithetical force to the individual. Kierkegaard's views of the press and the formation of dire and conformist public opinion can be perceived as a closely interrelated relationship. He viewed the press as both representative of the public whilst simultaneously forming public opinion; in essence the press was intrinsic to crowd mentality creating and recreating in a never-ending vicious circle. Kierkegaard's journal entries titled "Our Journalistic Literature", "The Morning Observations in Kjøbenhavnposten No.43" and "On the Polemic of F'drelandet'[26] rank high as evidence of his dislike of the press. Interestingly, the American writer John C. Merrill has used Kierkegaard's writings on the crowd to inspire a journalistic resolution at the point of production rather than an individual/social resolution at the point of consumption:

> Kierkegaard argued that a person who forsakes personal freedom, follows the crowd, and does not choose his or her own identity as an individual cannot even be said to exist. I heartily concur in this sentiment and highly recommend it.[27]

For Merrill this position transfers into the notion of what he terms *existential journalism*. On the one hand, it concurs with Kierkegaard's view of the power and corruptive influence of the press/media, but on the other hand it differs by assuming a relatively passive audience, hence the desire to change at the production end to ensure truth which the audience can trust. Merrill's view appears to miss the point of Kierkegaard's savage wit, which admonished pretensions in society, of which the press were a part as they tried to impose external truth. It's also a negation of resistance because the purpose of Kierkegaard's writings was to force the reader to think and engage critically, or, to use a Cartesian term, to doubt. It's in this context that Kierkegaard certainly wasn't a hopeless pessimist but rather the eternal optimist, but what else could he have been when we consider his writings were inspired by his deep conviction in the belief of God. The issue of whether Kierkegaard's writings on the press can be viewed as radical meets with one resounding yes and one no on two points. The first, which Theobald first raised, is based on the savage critique in the first instance, but Theobald never expanded more than this. The second, discussed here and more decisive, is based on what proposals for alternative living were expressed by Kierkegaard (here readers may have mixed feelings) and his work *Either/Or* I believe holds the key to what decision can be made of his radicalism. In *Either/Or* (1992) the author proposed that we inhabit two "existence spheres"; the first is what Kierkegaard called "aesthetic" and the other was "ethical". For Kierkegaard both spheres were hardly satisfactory for perfect self-development because they entailed compromise with others but at the time of writing he was reasonably satisfied with the way in which Liberal-Bourgeois society was progressing, although that relatively conservative approach undoubtedly would have changed in a climate of media monopolisation where current capitalist economic conditions further crush the spirit of the individual.

THE FRANKFURT SCHOOL AND CRITICAL THEORY

The notion of Critical Theory espoused by thinkers from within the Frankfurt School (FS) is perhaps the epitome of early radical views concerning media in that the purpose of Critical Theory was to formulate understanding of social conditions with the objective of implementing alternatives to regimes of domination replaced with human emancipation. The tradition of RMMC continued through to the writings of many of the main thinkers within the FS, but unfortunately it has been tainted with a misunderstanding of the subtleties of the argument forwarded in certain academic quarters. Certainly the connection on one theoretical level between the FS writers with Kraus, Tarde, Tönnies and Kierkegaard is obvious in relation to their scathing attacks on the press/media and subsequent impact on society, although Theobald maintained that there was a subtle difference between a Krausian perspective and the Frankfurt school:

> We are not here, it should be added, dealing with an early advocate of the "hypodermic syringe" theory of media effects, wherein it is assumed that the media can inject a passive public mind with attitudes or ideas; rather, we are looking at a more stealthy

> process of gradual confusion and erosion of faculties by the press's substitution of the pure water of information with the seductive perfume of the cliché.[28]

The hypodermic syringe theory has probably been the most unhelpful concept in relation to the body of work produced by writers in the FS, and Theobald's reference assumed the common, and oft-mistaken view that passivity, conformity equalled absolute subjugation to authority. This view of the FS has also led, and once again wrongly, towards the criticism that FS writers were pathologically pessimistic in terms of the domination of capitalism in the absence of any notable resistance.

The hypodermic syringe theory is invoked in popular academic books on media consumption often without clear and concise analysis of the complexities of the arguments forwarded by the FS or fully explaining the origins of this term that has successfully entered the academic vernacular. The term in fact originates from Vance Packard's book *The Hidden Persuaders* (1957) that details the mastery of advertising techniques too powerful to resist. As Herbert Marcuse wrote in his introduction to *One-Dimensional Man,* Packard's book was just one of many "studies which are frequently frowned upon because of simplification, overstatement, or journalistic ease". Hypodermic syringe theory is not only endemic amongst the uninitiated in academia but also equally among hordes of students in the United Kingdom who enter university with this misplaced knowledge fed to them by school tutors based on the authority of the school textbook.

Despite the focus of the apparent pessimism, FS thinkers maintained that not all was lost and that Critical Theory itself was the means to re-exploring our relationship with dominant ideologies at the very least, and at the most was the conduit of social change. At one dialectical moment, Critical Theory serves as a form of enlightenment in a Kantian sense, to mature and to see and not be dependent on forces exogenous to oneself. At another dialectical moment, Critical Theory is akin and could be argued identical to Marx's notion of a class-for-itself whereupon the moment of epistemological realisation and the awakening to the real relations of production had arrived. In this sense FS writers were ultimately positive in their evaluation and outlook and not totally pessimistic, as most writers have argued. In fact, their pessimism served as a useful tool and justification for Critical Theory to help us escape the commercialised morass we find ourselves in. Perhaps the criticism of elitism is more apt, but even Gramsci wrote enthusiastically on the strategic position intellectuals occupy in society. Horkeimer argued that contradictory relationships between dominant ideas and values and the actual social conditions would impact upon social theory to critically engage this position and seek resolutions therein. If we take a leap into the now, we find in the works of Herman, Chomsky,

McChesney, Winter, Pilger, Media Lens, ZNet, Fifth Estate Online and many others too numerous to mention, a critical engagement, this time of the media, of which Horkeimer spoke.

Marcuse built on and broadened out the discussion concerning domination, Critical Theory, resistance and resolution. Marcuse noted systems were constructed of "administered individuals" who had derived self-gratification albeit from some form of misunderstanding or shall we say *false consciousness*? How could individuals under the sway of ideological regimes "liberate themselves from themselves as well as from their masters? How is it even thinkable that the vicious circle be broken?"[29] the author asked. The main aim for Marcuse was centralised control over the means of production to obtain "self-determination" and the production of the new "Subject" stating further:

> And yet, the facts are all there which validate the critical theory of this society and of its fatal development: the increasing irrationality of the whole; waste and restriction of productivity; the need for aggressive expansion; the constant threat of war; intensified exploitation; dehumanisation. And they all point to the historical alternative, the planned utilisation of resources for the satisfaction of vital needs with a minimum of toil, the transformation of leisure into free time, the pacification of the struggle for existence.[30]

Certainly, Horkeimer[31] spoke in terms of human enslavement, depicting a hopelessness of a given situation, which had led Martín-Barbero to denounce FS writers as elitist and for negating actual existing moments of liberation and cultural production by the people rather than passively accepting dominant forms. These are important criticisms, but sadly when focus remains fixed there we lose sight of the purpose of Critical Theory, despite its normative judgements on the restrictive character of capitalism. We can argue the toss as to what degree of domination and liberation exists within capitalist formations until the proverbial cows come home, but the means of transcending the restrictive practices remain important and if there's one criticism I would level at Martín-Barbero, it is that managing to survive is just that; Critical Theory seeks to go beyond the parameters of existence defined by what Grossberg called the "ruling bloc".[32] Horkeimer's insistence on explaining what is wrong in and with society automatically infers a normative imperative within the critique, and a normative resolution to attempt a successful rescue from it. Although Critical Theory in this sense may appear far removed from Tarde's, and therefore the pragmatists view on domination–emancipation, on closer scrutiny perhaps they are closer than one may think if all we are talking about is the transformation by radically reforming rather than overthrowing by violent means a capitalist society into a "true democracy". After all, an important part of Critical Theory is to highlight the main actors who can invoke change; for

Tarde, the key actors were members in publics; for Rorty, individuals within the community collectively produce truth statements based on contributions to social debate producing inter-subjective agreements. The transforming of capitalism into a real democracy was for Horkeimer an act of social consensus produced by a rational social system. Considering the emphasis on individuals as the source of meaning, it's not entirely unreasonable to witness the crossover between Critical Theory and the aforementioned thinkers who one would hardly claim as Left writers but would be more than content to place all under the heading of radical.

Whatever the substantive differences in outcomes, Critical Theory is therefore a form of resistance and is similar in basis to the way in which Kierkegaard wrote to stir the individual to read and engage critically in the first instance, but overall objectives differed significantly. Kierkegaard was no revolutionary but used irony as a form of subversive technical guide to criticism; Adorno, I would argue, used irony in a similar fashion despite the many protestations that the latter was some elitist thug.

CONCLUDING COMMENTS

What I have attempted to show in this chapter is the diverse range of radical media criticism that not only highlights common positions as a genealogical structure but equally the relative diversity of various positions. Tarde's relatively unknown contribution to the production of public opinion and the need for the creation of multiple publics to be able to competently respond to authoritative voices is not only reflected in the work of Rorty, Martín-Barbero and Canclini but equally in the works of Michel Foucault, who wrote on the disintegration of grand narratives in modern systems to be replaced by multiple, often, self-interested groups. Tarde's view in respect of the press is radical in the sense that he was able to identify it as an institution that attempted to impose a thought system onto society and despite its existence within a liberal democracy at the time of writing, it was essentially dictatorial in character. For Tarde solutions to such totalising could be found in the social, pluralistic and essentially democratic activity of groups that would effectively, and on their own fruition, produce alternative thought systems.

Kierkegaard was no revolutionary and relatively satisfied with the direction of liberalism whilst retaining sharp criticism of various institutional structures including the press. Kierkegaard differed from Horkeimer and Marcuse in that the latter two argued that the objective of Critical Theory amongst other concerns, was to identify the actors central to change and that a collective means of change took priority over the rights of individual sovereignty under liberal conditions. The objective was to transform a system that had successfully produced the illusion of individuality whilst in reality as Adorno had argued had merely standardised individuality as replicated multiple selves. Kierkegaard on the other hand had argued that *existentialism,* the opposite of what the FS writers were arguing for, was the true path to freedom, and in a sense education and understanding under the then political and economic climate were means to becoming aware of and enlightened to critical issues; in other words the ability to produce critical faculties was a means to achieving secular salvation, whilst for the FS writers true individual freedom could only be realised by radically transforming the landscape and whether this could be achieved by reform or revolutionary means is very much a key element of identifying factors within the method of Critical Theory. After all, the FS writers sought unity between philosophy and empirical research but maintained that normative philosophical judgements carry a greater weight in any end analysis. In other words social empirical research would always reveal the real relations of production but only normative judgements would help resolve ways forward to achieving resolution to the end of domination towards human emancipation. In fact the differences between FS writers and existentialism can be viewed in the works of Marcuse and Adorno, particularly the latter's *The Jargon of Authenticity*. Whether one is convinced by one argument or the other depends on various viewpoints of each reader, but perhaps the all-important point to bear in mind is the extent that the mainstream media today not confronts established power but rather what the British-based journalist John Pilger once said consorts and helps to maintain a legitimate control over society by current establishment forms. The realisation of this fact lay with the engager of the message!

NOTES

1. The early *Corantos* was a single-sided newssheet produced initially in Holland bringing news of Italy, Germany, Hungary and elsewhere in Europe to England.
2. Willard Grosvenor Bleyer, *Main Currents in the History of American Journalism* (Boston: Houghton Mifflin Company, 1927), 42.
3. John D. Keeler, William Brown and Douglas Tarpley, "Ethics" in William David Sloan and Lisa Mullikin Parcell (eds.) *American Journalism: History, Principles, Practices* (North Carolina: McFarland & Company, Inc., 2002), 49.
4. John Theobald "Radical Mass Media Criticism: Elements of a History from Kraus to Bourdieu" in David Berry (ed.) *Ethics and Media Culture: Practices and Representations* (Oxford: Focal Press, 2000), 11.
5. Ibid., 12.
6. John Theobald, *The Media and the Making of History* (Aldershot: Ashgate, 2004), 21.
7. Ibid.
8. Ibid. For the full list of writers in each generation see chapter titled "Radical Media Critics: The Four Generations",19–53.

9. John Theobald, "The Intellectual Tradition of Mass Media Criticism: A Framework" in David Berry and John Theobald (eds.) *Radical Mass Media Criticism: A Cultural Genealogy* (Montreal: Black Rose Books, 2006), 19.
10. Ibid, 26.
11. David Berry, "Radical Mass Media Criticism: An Introduction" in David Berry and John Theobald (eds.) *Radical Mass Media Criticism: A Cultural Genealogy* (Montreal: Black Rose Books, 2006).
12. Scott Lash, *Another Modernity a Different Rationality* (Oxford: Blackwell, 1999).
13. Terry Eagleton, *Ideology* (London: Verso, 1991).
14. Jean Gabriel Tarde, *L'Opinion et al foule* (Public Opinion and the Crowd) (Paris: P.U.F., 1989).
15. Stanley James Grenz, *A Primer on Postmodernism* (Grand Rapids: Cambridge University Press, 1995).
16. Richard Rorty, *Truth and Progress* (Cambridge: Cambridge University Press, 1998), 51.
17. Jean Gabriel Tarde, *On Communication and Social Influence*, trans. T. N. Clark (Chicago: University of Chicago Press, 1969).
18. Taken from "*Misperceptions, the Media and the Iraq War*" www.worldpublicopinion.org accessed February 2008.
19. See John Dewey, *The Public and Its Problems* (Athens: Swallow Press, 1991).
20. Georg Simmel, "The Crisis of Culture" in David Frisby and Mike Featherstone (eds.) *Simmel on Culture: Selected Writings* (London: Sage, 1998), 90–101.
21. See Jésus Martín-Barbero, *Communication, Culture and Hegemony: From Media to Mediations* (London: Sage, 1993).
22. Nestor García Canclini, *Hybrid Cultures: Strategies for Entering and Leaving Modernity*, trans. Christopher Chiappari and Silvia Lopez (Minneapolis: University of Minnesota Press, 1995).
23. Lash, *Another Modernity.*
24. Theobald, *The Media and the Making of History* , 22.
25. Sören Kierkegaard, *Upbuilding Discourses in Various Spirits*, trans. Howard Vincent Hong and Edna Hatlestad Hong (Princeton, NJ: Princeton University Press, 1993).
26. Howard Vincent Hong and Edna Hatlestad Hong (eds.) *Sören Kierkegaard s Journals and Papers*, assisted by Gregor Malantschuk (Bloomington: Indiana University Press, 1967–1978).
27. John Calhoun Merrill, "Communitarianism's Rhetorical War Against Enlightenment Liberalism" in Jay Black (ed.) *Mixed News: The Public/Civic Communitarian Debate* (Mahwah, NJ: Lawrence Erlbaum Associates, 1997), 64.
28. Theobald, "Radical Mass Media Criticism", 15.
29. Herbert Marcuse, *One-Dimensional Man* (Boston, MA: Beacon, 1991), 248.
30. Ibid., 249.
31. Max Horkeimer, *Critical Theory* (New York: Seabury Press, 1982).
32. Lawrence Grossberg, "History, Politics and Postmodernism: Stuart Hall and Cultural Studies" in David Morley and Kuan-Hsing Chen (eds.) *Stuart Hall: Critical Dialogues in Cultural Studies* (London: Routledge, 1992), 162.

CHAPTER FOURTEEN

The Myth of Commercialism: Why a Market Approach to Broadcasting Does Not Work

JUSTIN LEWIS

In recent decades we have seen a major shift in governmental approaches to television. The U.S. – where broadcasting has, since its infancy, been a creature of commercial imperatives – has succumbed almost entirely to the notion that what is good for the commercial broadcast industry is good for broadcasting. And despite the largely uninspiring consequences, governments around the world have been seduced and cajoled, from publicly funded, highly regulated broadcasting systems towards a more commercial, largely ad-based, multichannel ecology.[1] In the wake of a global drift towards pro-business neoliberalism, broadcasting policy has been increasingly subject to the terms of trade agreements that see broadcasting as a matter of commodity exchange rather than as part of the cultural quotidian.

This shift has come at a critical time, coinciding with a major expansion in the number of television channels people receive, with rapid increases in TV ownership in large and populous parts of the developing world (notably in Asia), and with the dismantling of many of the formerly restricted broadcasting environments in the old Soviet bloc and the Middle East. The multichannel systems that are now emerging worldwide are increasingly likely to be dominated by for-profit, transnational media conglomerates.[2]

The shift from public to private has generated its own momentum. As media corporations expand, so does their influence on public policy. This is partly because the control of information systems carries enormous political power. Attempts by government agencies to contain that power – or to regulate private broadcasters in the public interest – has become too risky for elected officials to contemplate.[3] But, it is also because they simply crowd both the lobby and the arena.

Let us be clear about what this means. While there are many debates about what a public service or democratic approach to broadcasting might look like, these debates are couched in terms of the quality and diversity of programmes and the ability of the system to meet the various needs and desires of audiences. The commercial sector, by contrast, begins with a very different motivation, famously expressed by former Disney CEO Michael Eisner thus: "We have no obligation to make history. We have no obligation to make art. We have no obligation to make a statement. To make money is our only obligation". Such eye-glinting avarice makes discussions about *any* form of programme-making operating outside the rules of commerce seem quaint and irrelevant. Non-commercial models are simply a restraint on profitability.

But Eisner's mantra – "speaking truth from power" – serves a more useful purpose. At a stroke it casts aside any notion that the best broadcasting system is one driven by business interests. Its table-thumping logic dismisses any conflation between what makes good commerce and what might inspire, engage or inform us as so much mealy-mouthed blather. And yet this conflation persists. Indeed, it now infests media policy documents with unashamed vigour, the knotweed that sucks the life out of a more diverse ecology.[4]

And yet even many advocates of public service broadcasting have failed to question the assumptions behind this shift. Indeed, many of the more high-minded attacks on commercialism begin with the assumption that commercial television is driven by popular taste – and *is* thereby inextricably linked to audience needs and desires. The problem, in this Reithian critique, is less with commercialism than with the vulgarity of the masses.[5]

The purpose of this chapter is to challenge this idea head on, and to debunk the idea that commercial broadcasting delivers audiences what they want. Even if we are driven by the notion of audience desire – notwithstanding the limits of its pragmatic and fickle philosophy – then commercial broadcasting is ill-quipped to provide it.

At the heart of this argument is a consideration of the central role of advertising in a commercial system. In debates about broadcasting policy, advertising is often regarded simply as a source of revenue, as if its voluminous presence in the schedule is entirely without consequence. If we regard advertising as a form of programming – as we should – then we must also consider its ideological consequences.

BROADCASTING POLICY AND PUBLIC OPINION

The for-profit broadcaster has been in the ascendancy since the 1980s. In the United States, the 1996 Telecommunications Act propelled commercial broadcasting further away from the idea of a public service model than at any time in US history.[6] Meanwhile, it is not just the old state broadcasters in former Soviet bloc countries that are being dismantled or swept aside: countries with more robust traditions of public service broadcasting – like Britain – have moved (albeit more slowly) in similar directions.

At the heart of this model is the classic neoliberal subject – the rational, independent citizen, who uses the market place to assert his/her wishes. And yet the citizen has been largely excluded from playing any real part in this policy shift. While this is in some ways ironic, it is in keeping with a top-down corporate model in which policy decisions are confined to the boardroom.

Unlike the era of consultation that surrounded changes in public service broadcasting systems before the 1980s (the debates around the creation of Channel 4 in Britain being a notable example[7]), more recent – and more profound – developments in broadcast media have taken place with very little reference to public discussion or opinion. So, for example, the siphoning away of major sporting events from widely available channels to more expensive and more exclusive satellite or digital services may have a certain kind of market logic, but it runs directly counter to popular desire. In this case, the "market" (insofar as such a metaphor is appropriate) produces an outcome that people would, if asked, almost certainly have voted against.

Although people undoubtedly care about what is (or is not) available to them on radio or television, broadcasting policy tends *not* to be regarded as an issue of major public debate. The US 1996 Telecommunication Act, for example, received almost no serious media attention (and when it did, more as a fait accompli than as a matter of debate).[8] While in the UK, an Ipsos-Mori survey in 2006 suggested that the majority of people had either never heard of or knew little about the main regulatory authorities for broadcasting or the press.[9] Thus, despite its significant presence in most people's lives, television *policy* is not generally seen as a sufficiently serious issue to make it onto the pollster's agenda. When opinion surveys on broadcasting issues *are* carried out, they tend to show strong support for certain principles of public service broadcasting,[10] and yet this kind of public opinion generally plays very little role in shaping policy. There are a number of reasons for this.

First, policy debates are often guided by an unthinking technological determinism. If technologies make it possible to have ten, twenty or a hundred TV channels, and the commercial sector see this as a profitable development, then the proliferation of commercial channels is seen as an inevitability – rather than as a possibility to be considered in the light of its effect on the system as a whole. In other words, we assume the technology – and the market – controls us rather than the other way around. Tied to this is an assumption that channel proliferation simply increases choice, without consideration of the finite resources available for broadcasting[11] (i.e. there may be more channels, but there isn't necessarily more money for programme-making).

Second, public debate is not encouraged because it is not in the interest of media companies who stand to benefit from regulatory changes. So, for example, research by Gilens and Hertzman found a direct relationship between newspaper ownership in the U.S. and coverage of the 1996 Telecommunication legislation, with those papers that stood to gain from the Act being most supportive.[12] Similarly, the Murdoch Press in the UK tends to adopt a critical stance towards the public service broadcasting in general and the BBC in particular, at least in part because Murdoch's ownership of the Sky and Fox TV networks makes this a matter of financial self-interest. This point was made particularly clear during the Hutton enquiry in 2003, when the media debated the BBC's coverage of the intelligence used to justify war with Iraq. As Jackie Ashley, writing in the *Guardian,* commented, "The Murdoch papers have acted as the most amazingly disciplined attack force...savaging the BBC in identical terms, from the *Sun,* to the *Times*, to *the News of the World*, using columnists, editorials and front-page splashes to pursue the cause".[13] In short, as commercial media grow more powerful, any public debate about broadcasting policy is constrained.

When "public opinion" is sought, it is generally within a narrow consumerist framework. As Caroline Pauwels has argued, the ideas of consumer sovereignty that inform such a framework are very limited, granting no space to forms of citizen subjectivity, action or desire that operates outside the market sphere.[14] There is, of course, a wealth of data measuring attitudes to television and radio, but most of it is in response to particular programmes or channels, rather than about the system as a whole.

People are rarely asked the big questions about broadcasting. What role should it play in society? What do we use it for, and how might it better serve our needs? Should there be commercials on children's TV? Are we better off spreading the money available for programme-making to a few well-funded channels or spreading it more thinly amongst a multitude? Even on the rare occasions when such questions *are* asked, little notice is taken of people's responses.

Indeed, policy makers not only disregard public opinion in its broader sense, they adopt a benevolent paternalism, not bothering to explain what lies in store secure in the knowledge that it will be good for us. In Britain, for example, the move towards the creation of a largely commercial multichannel digital system was made in a context in which most people are unaware of what such a move might mean. A Mori survey in the spring of 2001 found 75% people in the UK felt they knew little or nothing about digital TV – a fact that did nothing to modify the enthusiasm of the government's embrace of such a system.

The fact that governments *have* generally chosen to acquiesce to powerful private media interests comes either from belief in a neoliberal agenda (in which the motive of financial gain will always be preferred to notions of public service), or from the power of media corporations in the political process. But it does not come with any clear citizen mandate. On the contrary, it would be difficult to argue that most people, if asked, would want to give more power to private media corporations, that they want more advertising, wall-to-wall commercial programmes for children or significantly less access to major sporting events. And yet these are all outcomes of pandering to commerce.

Indeed, in the debate between public service and private models of television, *both* sides have tended to assume that audience desires rested on the side of commercial rather than public broadcasters. While commercial broadcasting *sometimes* has a better record of attracting big audiences (although there is nothing inevitable about this: BBC1 is the most popular channel in the UK, and the most popular British radio stations are all run by the BBC), there are many ways in which the move towards corporate, for-profit broadcasting is *opposed* to a broader notion of consumer sovereignty.

COMMERCIAL BROADCASTING VERSUS AUDIENCE DESIRE

The metaphor of the marketplace is far more limited than the advocates of neoliberalism generally acknowledge. The wistful image of a rational consumer moving from one stall to the next until they find the best product at the lowest price does not even describe what goes on in a supermarket, places designed to encourage "impulse" buying rather than to meet customer needs.[15] The main source of information about goods comes from an advertising industry that, as many advertising scholars point out, provides very little useful information about products that might allow consumers to make a rational choice.[16]

Applied to areas like health, transportation, the law or education, the benign simplicity of the "market stall" metaphor begins to look unrecognisable ('good health', for example, is hardly a matter of choosing from various options on display). The same is true of broadcasting, where the technicalities of allocating licences to broadcast are *necessarily* the product of regulatory structures – whether they are government bodies or cable operators – rather than consumer choice. Broadcasting is, in this sense at least, much like a railway system, where governments can both grant and police franchises held by private operators.

Broadcasting is complicated further by two other distinctive elements. First, it is an industry that is anti-competitive by design: it has an in-built ability to influence consumer preferences (and thereby to interfere with what might be seen by some as "natural" market mechanisms). Broadcasters therefore spend increasing amounts of time promoting their own programmes, messages designed to increase "brand loyalty" and to thereby *discourage* competition. Second, unlike most other forms of commodity production, it has traditionally been easier to distribute programmes or channels to everyone than to limit access to paying customers.

But this is only the beginning: once we begin to examine how basic economic principles apply (or do not apply) to broadcasting, the whole notion of "consumer sovereignty" as an abiding notion – even in narrow neoliberal terms - begins to look inappropriate.

Many of the critiques of lightly regulated commercial broadcasting[17] suggest that a commercial television system, left to its devices, serves commercial rather than public interests. The response from advocates of commercial broadcasting is to declare that commercial and public interests overlap. There is, of course, *some* truth in this, but commercial and public interests are also fraught with contradictions.

As I have suggested, the only form of "public interest" acknowledged by a commercial system is measured in the crude, monosyllabic language of ratings.[18] And yet even in these limited terms, audiences have very little sovereignty. When television is funded by advertising, as Dallas Smythe has pointed out, TV viewers are not the "market" but the commodity being exchanged.[19] The audience's value is determined largely by size and disposable income. The economic function of ad-based commercial television is to deliver the most valuable audiences at the highest price. If this seems quite a straightforward idea for economists to grasp, it is confusing for most people – including policy makers – who are used to understanding audiences (rather than advertisers) as the market, and who assume that the main commodities produced by commercial television are programmes rather than viewers.

This is hardly a trivial point, since the notion of consumer demand or sovereignty in such a system refers not to viewers but to advertisers. Of course, advertisers *tend* to prefer large audiences, and it is in this sense that the needs of advertisers and audiences may coincide. But policy makers overlook the many ways in which the needs and wishes of advertisers *conflict* with the needs and wishes of audiences. It is to these shortfalls in the commercial system that I now turn.

1. Advertising limits citizenship and political diversity

Advertisers have ideological – and practical – biases that have nothing to do viewer demand. This is, in part, because messages that contradict the pro-business, consumerist ideology – which most advertising either depends upon or promotes – are unlikely to please advertisers, *regardless* of the interests of viewers. But even if programmes do *not* extol the virtues of consumerism, the presence of commercials means that for every hour someone in the U.S. spends in front of the TV, they are watching at least 15 minutes of television devoted to celebrating the joys of consumption.

The critical literature on advertising is flattened beneath this onslaught: they are a few voices amidst a cacophony. And yet their insights, unlike those who celebrate advertising's semiotic superfluity in the name of freedom, are truly subversive. As Judith Williamson puts it in her well known analysis of ideology in advertising, "Advertisements are selling us something else besides consumer goods" ,[20] they sell us an image of ourselves *as* consumers.

Even Michael Schudson, regarded by critics like Stuart Ewen as an apologist for the industry, suggests that the industry "may shape our sense of values".[21] Television or radio programmes may vary, but there is a sense in which commercials themselves are, for all their symbolic excess, remorselessly repetitive. They tell us over and over and over again that health, happiness, freedom, beauty and human comfort "can be obtained only through commodities".[22] And with the spread of advertising like smog across the cultural firmament, "consumerism as an ethos and a practice is expanding in importance at a near exponential rate to incorporate everything from health and insurance to education and recreation".[23]

In the ad-world, the production and distribution of these commodities is a matter of no consequence. And, as Tim Edwards suggests, even "the analysis of consumption still tends to remain disassociated from the entire world of production on which it so fundamentally depends".[24] To this we might add the growing problems of post-consumption – the disposal of our increasingly toxic array of consumer goods. The problem here is not just that "consumer society remains socially divisive – inclusive and inviting to the affluent, mobile and able; exclusive of the poor, the isolated and the impaired',[25] but that in the ad world the inequities of global production and the environmental consequences of distribution and disposal remain resolutely hidden.

In an era when the foundations of a pro-corporate consumerist ideology are being increasingly challenged by advocates for the environment, social justice and wage labourers, the ideological consequences of these advertising messages cannot be underestimated. Even when regulators insist on it, there is no political balance here: as long as they refrain from explicit party advocacy, advertisers are immune from such strictures.

This point was graphically illustrated during the showing of a John Pilger documentary on ITV in Britain.[26] The documentary was intended as a critique of the way corporations treat workers in the global economic system, and yet every 15 minutes Pilger's argument was contradicted by advertisements, some of which, like a Peugeot ad featuring inspirational images of black women, were designed specifically to comfort consumer concerns about sweatshop production and corporate ethics. Whatever we think of it, Pilger's message was directly undercut by messages designed to soothe and divert. His freedom of speech was not so much silenced as smothered.

Advertising is, in this sense, not only a propaganda system for a whole way of life, but has something to say about two of the most vital issues facing citizens in the twenty-first century: climate change and the terms of trade in a globalised world. Campaigns against low wages in the third world or sweatshop labour are pitted against ad campaigns that provide soothing messages inspiring trust in brand names. Environmentalists concerned about global warming have to compete against a flood of commercial messages that urge us to consume without worrying about the consequences. Little wonder that climate change, for all its cataclysmic consequences for large sections of the planet's population, *still* struggles to become a serious electoral issue. Advertising is more than mere distraction, it is at the heart of how we have come to this point and why it is so difficult to come up with solutions.[27]

2. Advertising makes us unhappy

When Jerry Mander wrote that "the goal of all advertising is discontent'[28] he was, perhaps, indulging in a deliberate polemic against an industry predicated on the promise of happiness. Advertising, after all, is about happiness postponed, or what Wernick calls the "perpetual deferral of the promoted object".[29] Its relentless logic declares that satisfaction is always another product away. And yet, for advertising's main audience (those with disposable incomes), the evidence suggests that advertising *is* more a source of misery, insecurity and anxiety than it is of joy, pleasure and comfort.

This is not to belittle the genuine pleasures attached to particular moments of consumption. But the reams of data on happiness and quality of life suggest very little correlation between material possessions and personal satisfaction or fulfilment. As the economist Richard Layard points out,

> People in the West have got no happier in the last 50 years. They have become much richer, they work much less, they have longer holidays, they travel more, they live

longer, and they are healthier. But they are no happier. This shocking fact should be the starting point for much of our social science.[30]

The paradox, for some economists, is that *within* a society income *is* related to well-being.[31] But this is easily explained: briefly, in a society that links income with status, people like to feel they are doing well rather than doing badly.[32] In other words, those on higher incomes are happier than those on lower incomes because of the respect that accrues from their relative position, *not* because they have more stuff.

As Sut Jhally suggests, many advertisers are only too aware that fulfilment comes *not* from "the dead world of things" but from the social and physiological world, from good relationships, status, good health, relaxation and interaction.[33] TV advertising, in particular, rarely makes its pitch on the basis of the object being sold. The work of advertising is less to persuade than to juxtapose, so that we might associate images that connote popularity, attractiveness, family harmony, good health and so on with a product or a brand. A mobile phone is sold less on its functionality than its coolness. Research even suggests that democratic participation is linked to happiness,[34] a notion anticipated by the famously preposterous Pepsi commercials linking their cola with the collapse of the Berlin wall.

Advertising is, in this sense, deeply contradictory. Its purpose is to link fulfilment with consumption, and yet its strategy for doing so tacitly acknowledges the emptiness of the promise. But it is not just that, as Leiss, Kline and Jhally put it, "goods simply cannot deliver the promised happiness shown in advertisements"[35] the evidence suggests that the consumerism advertising promotes actually makes us unhappy. This is, Jhally argues, because it distracts us from the things that do bring satisfaction – we go shopping rather than taking a walk in the park, we engage with objects rather than with people.

This is more than plausible speculation. Tim Kasser's review of the literature on the psychology of materialism suggests that far from providing happiness or fulfilment, materialist values are associated with a *drop* in quality of life.[36] Similarly, Juliet Schor's study of children and consumerism suggests that "less involvement in consumer culture leads to healthier kids and more involvement leads kids' psychological well-being to deteriorate".[37] Her data analysis also suggests that this association is likely to be causal, with immersion in consumer culture being the key explanatory factor associated with various forms of unhappiness.

Reviewing similar data, Richard Layard argues that legislation banning advertising is a far more plausible policy for increasing quality of life than extending consumer choice.[38] In short, we'd all be better off with less advertising. The fact that policy makers have moved in the opposite direction is, quite literally, depressing.

3. An ad-based system favours some audiences over others

As political economists have long pointed out, advertisers discriminate in favour of certain groups – notably young people (who, to use the rather sinister parlance of the ad industry, are yet to be "branded"), and those with high levels of disposable income. Thus a programme that gets the largest share of the audience is not necessarily the most responsive to advertiser demand. An advertiser may well choose a smaller, wealthier, younger audience over a larger, poorer, older one: hence TV programmes have been cancelled even though they were often the most popular show in their time slot.[39] Popularity, in such a system, is trumped by youth and prosperity.

The irony of this is that many of the more rarefied critiques of commercial media tend to assume that the system panders not to the industry but to the vulgarity of popular taste. In fact, the role of advertising is to push broadcasters *up* market, where the best customers are. If commercial television fails to produce a diet of high quality, diverse, challenging or inspiring content, this cannot be blamed on the cultural limitations of a mass audience.

4. Advertising impoverishes the quality of programming

This brings me to my next point, which is more telling about the way that advertising degrades television content. Advertisers want to buy viewers who will be receptive to their commercial messages. Or as Edward Herman and Noam Chomsky put it, they want audiences to be in a "buying mood".[40] Such a system requires programmes that do not overshadow or detract from the commercials that punctuate them. Content that is too compelling, too profound or too serious to be easily interrupted is thereby producing a "bad" product (an audience irritated by the interruption).

Commercial television programmes – whether sport, drama, comedy, news or documentary – thus carry the significant aesthetic limitation of being suitable for commercial breaks. In well-developed commercial cultures like the U.S., programmes have been *written around* commercial messages ever since the early days of radio.[41] This is an obligation that makes the kind of sustained action, drama or mood we associate with quality television manifestly undesirable.

While Herman and Chomsky focus on the political consequence of this, the cultural consequences for broadcasting are legion. Advertisers *want* short attention spans, they *want* amusement rather than engagement, they *prefer* the trivial to the profound. If this suggests the kind of dystopian *Brave New World* of television that Neil Postman has railed against, we need to be clear about what drives it. The problem is not, as Postman has famously argued, with television per se.[42] While there is much to argue with in Postman's McLuhanesque critique, its most gaping hole is its lack of cultural specificity. His critique is not of television but of *American* television, which, in marked contrast to many European systems, has been built around the commercial message. It is not the medium "dumbing down" content, it is advertisers.

5. Advertising is impervious to qualitative measure of appreciation

It follows that while audiences will make qualitative judgements about the quality of television programmes, advertisers do not. The main "qualitative" criteria by which audiences are bought and sold are those that relate to buying habits and purchasing power. Although levels of audience appreciation are measured in some public service systems (like the BBC in Britain), most commercial systems pay little heed to such data. Thus a programme watched by ten million people who found it mildly entertaining is seen to be of greater value than a programme watched by nine million people, all of whom felt it was the best thing on television. Indeed, while advertisers may see an advantage in linking their product with a much-loved programme, they might also be put off by having to compete with it (the mildly entertained viewer, by contrast, is likely to be more receptive to a commercial interruption).

The most tangible motive for popular programme making – the use of ratings – only survives as the basic currency for establishing the value of an audience as a matter of convenience.[43] It is, after all, not the audience for *programmes* that interests advertisers, but the audience for the ads shown *during* the programme. This distinction may seem academic, but the technology exists for making judgements more finely attuned to the interest of advertisers, such that a popular show whose audience channel switches or leaves the room during the ad breaks can be deemed less valuable than a show whose audience does not.

For advertising to work in such a world requires higher levels of surveillance in data gathering and more manipulative techniques, all to discourage us from doing what we patently want to do, which is to avoid it.

6. Advertising dominates programming

The genre that dominates most multi-format commercial television networks is not drama, sport, film, comedy, quiz shows or soap opera, but advertising itself.

This point is, oddly enough, often overlooked. Indeed, the way we talk about television usually involves ignoring the commercials altogether – it is, after all, the programmes we tune in for.

This is certainly the case in terms of frequency of presence, as well as in total programming time. Advertisements now fill up over one quarter of the space on US networks – outperforming all other genres – and the permitted number of commercial breaks on British commercial television has crept up to four per hour (and more on cable, satellite and digital channels). A recent study suggested that British commercial news channels are showing 13 minutes of commercial per hour – in excess of the regulatory limits.[44]

While advertisements can be lavishly produced, witty or entertaining, the presence of advertisements on television has nothing to do with viewer demand. On the contrary, given a choice between equivalent programmes with and without advertising, most people are likely to opt for fewer commercial interruptions. A good test of this is in the UK, when the BBC and a commercial channel broadcast the same event simultaneously. Audience data show that the BBC will invariably get a *significantly* larger audience than its commercial rival – between three to five times the size[45] – simply because people would rather watch programmes without commercial interruptions.

In the U.S., the prospect of commercial free television is so enticing that audiences are willing to pay for it. The exclusivity of the "premium channel" is partly a matter of self-promotion,[46] but there is also a sense that when HBO promises a different kind of television – simply because it spares the viewer relentless commercial interruptions. This is not say that channels like HBO are commercial free – ads seep into programming in various ways, while it could be argued that with the proliferation of products and platforms, the programmes themselves have become ads for various spin-offs,[47] part of what Wernick refers to as the "promotional culture".[48]

Nonetheless, a pay-per-view or subscription system that *excludes* advertising is not as antagonistic to viewer demand in many of the ways that ad-based systems can be. It recognises the qualitative aspects of viewer demand (a highly motivated viewer can be charged more money); its focus on programme production is unhindered by the need to deliver audiences to advertisers at strategic moments; and while a commercial broadcasting company might be expected – as a private business – to have certain ideological preferences, it is not *obliged* to promote consumerism or to protect the specific interests of advertisers.

Because the market logic of an advertising-based system will be to maximise the volume of advertising, it is regulators – in the name of public interest – who will intervene to impose limits. In this instance it is the regulators rather than the advertisers who will have popular support (how many viewers or listeners express a desire for *more* advertising?). Consumer sovereignty, in this instance, works more through regulation than any market mechanism.

For these reasons commercial television funded by advertising is not a system designed, in the time-honoured mantra of free marketeers, to give people what they want. More to the point, the structure of the system means that we should not expect it to be. The various ways in which ad-based commercial broadcasting fails to respond to the interests of its viewers are not quirks in the system, they are the predictable outcome of a model in which viewers are treated as a commodity.

Advertising cheapens the medium, but it is not, as is often supposed, a cheap way to pay for broadcasting. It amounts, in effect, to a tax on advertised goods, and it requires us to support not only the production of programmes but the production of advertisements, which economists calculate costs us more than a publicly funded system.[49] The "invisible hand', in this instance, is picking our pockets. The fact that it is (for most people) invisible, however, means that it is cheap *politically*. Therein lies its success.

MORE IS LESS: THE LIMITS OF THE MULTICHANNEL ENVIRONMENT IN A COMMERCIAL SYSTEM

The move towards multichannel broadcasting has been made possible by cable, satellite and digital technologies, and such a move has generally been embraced in the name of technological progress and consumer choice. Thus a Mori poll for the British Department of Culture, Media and Sport in 2001 found the promises of increased choice and superior picture quality were the clearest selling points for multichannel digital television. The idea that more channels means more choices may seem self-evident, and yet the idea that you can create this by simply increasing the number of channels takes no accounts of the economics of broadcasting, since it assumes an increase in the supply of content without an increase in the demand.

Even in wealthy, developed countries where relatively large amounts of money are spent on broadcasting (and thus for providing a wide range of content across a range of channels), the prospects for significantly increasing the resources for programme-making are slim. Audiences have already reached saturation point – there is no untapped pool of non-viewers, and the available hours of leisure time for watching television are, if anything, decreasing in the face of competition from other entertainment technologies. Moreover, few would argue that we should spend *more* time watching television. For ad-based television channels, this means that there may be more spaces to sell to advertisers, - but there are no new audiences to sell. This has depressed the cost of advertising, decreasing a channel's revenue per viewing hour. In Britain, for example, the emergence of multichannel systems has already significantly dented the income of the main commercial channel, ITV – a trend that, if it continues, will make it increasingly difficult for ITV to invest in more expensive forms of programme-making.

In this context, there are only two ways to generate more revenue for programme production. The first is through increasing public investment, and the second is by persuading audiences to pay more money to watch television. On the first count, significant public investment in broadcasting is generally regarded as politically untenable. This is partly because of pressure from the private sector, but also because broadcasting is still viewed as something of a frippery – as a nonessential leisure activity with weak claims upon the public purse. Yet television's pivotal role as a source of information and culture in the developed world is indisputable. If we are prepared to spend huge amounts of money on public education, then why so little on something we watch for several hours a day from the cradle to the grave?

Indeed, given the centrality of television in most people's lives, the current levels of public investment in broadcasting is miniscule. In terms of its potential effect on most people's informational and cultural environment, investing in public service broadcasting would seem to be extraordinarily good value for money. The Blair government in Britain made some concession to this view by increasing the investment for the BBC's new digital services, although the multichannel system it has promoted is dominated by commercial channels in a way the terrestrial system was not.

Without such investment, it is left to the private sector to exploit the value we place on various forms of television. So, for example, the private sector has, in various countries, been allowed to remove various popular sporting events from terrestrial channels and to then significantly drive up the cost of watching those events on cable, satellite or digital channels. Their ability to do so is hardly in the viewer's interest, although it does demonstrate the extent to which, in purely market terms, television is worth more to most people than the amount they currently pay for it.

While there may be a demand for 24-hour news channels, music channels, movie channels or sports channels, it is not at all clear that the demand in most markets (with the possible exception of the U.S.) is sufficient to pay for innovative, diverse or high-quality programme provision on more than a few channels. Even in the U.S., the widespread shift to multichannel cable systems has produced a fairly meagre increase in new, innovative or quality programming. Most of the channels on U.S. cable survive on mainly cheap formats (like chat shows or music video), repeats of network shows, imports (such as British-made nature documentaries) or paid-for propaganda (mainly religious or party political). Those "premium" channels (like HBO) that do make a significant investment in programming are expensive, while the output is far less prolific than a well-funded public broadcaster like the BBC (so, for example, Miller and Kim have argued that much of HBO's sports coverage is cheap and banal).[50]

Perhaps the best way of thinking about this is to use the analogy of retail planning. Allowing the development of shopping complexes on the outskirts of towns and cities is often sold to people on the basis that it will increase their choice of places to shop. In practice, the new shops will inevitably affect the economic viability of the more established in-town stores. In short, in a commercial system we cannot simply "add on" a string of new channels to the broadcasting system without it having a deleterious impact on the existing channels.

This means, in practice, that without public investment we are faced with a long-term choice between having a few well-funded channels or lots of poorly funded channels. And yet in the current rhetorical climate, resistance to the move to a commercially funded multichannel environment is seen merely as old fashioned. We would do much better to investigate the cultural and economic consequences of technological change rather than rushing into an unthinking embrace.

Finally – and this is undoubtedly the most contentious point – many advocates for public service broadcasting argue that there is a cultural merit in creating non-market-based structures that *do* limit the choices available to people. So, for example, scheduling practices can be used in a limited-channel environment to encourage people to watch educational, challenging or innovative programmes. Who is making these choices and for what benefit is, of course, a crucial question, and it is easy to dismiss these arguments as straightforward cultural elitism (which they may well be).

But we also need to recognise the extent to which television and radio are now routine, well-ensconced parts of our cultural environment. To talk about individual responsibility ("you can always turn it off/over" etc.) in this context is unhelpful. Television and radio are the primary educational systems in our culture – certainly for adults as well as for many children. For good or ill, despite occasional flurries from other media (old and new), common knowledge in contemporary culture often depends upon a television presence. There is little point in arguing whether broadcasting *should* have an educational function, since it will do so regardless of intent. Few education systems are purely market driven (and few would argue that they should be), and it is not clear why broadcasting should be an exception.

ALTERNATIVES TO COMMERCIALISM: PUTTING THE POPULAR INTO PUBLIC SERVICE

In most industrialised countries – even in the United States, where the notion of public service broadcasting is distinctly under-developed – survey research suggests strong support for a range of public service broadcasting services and goals. Despite this, advocacy for public service broadcasting is often cast in broadly Reithian terms, in which a cultural elite defines what is of value and what is not.

There in no doubt that such paternalism underscores much of the thinking behind public broadcasting advocacy. All too often, the "problem" with commercial systems is deemed to be the quality of consumer taste, and it is this vulgarity which is seen as the instrument driving commercial broadcasting.[51] This creates a dichotomy in which the interests of a cultural elite are seen as antagonistic to the popular imagination, on whose behalf, it is supposed, commercial broadcasters toil.

It is argued, here, that the imperatives of commercial broadcasting systems are often *not* driven by consumer taste. On the contrary they systematically *fail* to reflect the interests and desires of both minorities *and* majorities. This is partly because the metaphor of the marketplace is simply too banal to reflect the political economy of broadcasting, and partly because, even if we accept the metaphor, the market and the audience for commercial ad-based channels are not the same thing. It is not only political folly to concede the notion of consumer sovereignty to the for-profit sector, it is sloppy thinking. If we cannot escape the mantra of consumer sovereignty, let us at least be clear about what it means and who can best provide for it.

Since public service broadcasting is free from the commercial interruptions and constraints imposed by advertisers, it is potentially better placed to avoid the many contradictions between the needs of advertisers and audience desire. And these are considerable freedoms: allowing broadcasters to take risks with innovative programming; schedule programmes to maximise choice in any given time slot (rather than compete for the same lucrative audiences), and generally appeal to both majorities and minorities without the need to deliver audiences receptive to commercial interruptions at regular intervals.

Unfortunately, advocates for public service broadcasting rarely speak the language of audience desire. On the contrary, the realm of the popular is often seen as something that is more suitably the property of commercial broadcasters. Indeed, much of the concern about the "dumbing down" of popular television assumes not only a contempt for popular taste, but that the popular is only imaginable within the confines of the audience-vending machinery of commercial television.

The British Government's response (as well as much of the broadsheet commentary) to proposals for new BBC digital channels in September 2001 was informed precisely by this notion. Those channels offering more traditional "public service" fare (such as children's programming, current affairs and the arts) were accepted, but the BBC's proposed channel for popular programming for young adults (BBC3) was seen as encroaching onto terrain more appropriately occupied by commercial broadcasters. And so it has, but under different conditions.

The idea that public service broadcasting is somehow in conflict with the popular is a mistake, both politically and philosophically. Faced with such high-minded paternalism, commercial broadcasters have been able to portray themselves as a more democratic alternative, in touch with popular taste and desire. This is most evident in the United States, where public television (PBS) has been allowed to develop (albeit on a shoestring) on the basis that it does *not* provide popular programming, since to do so would be regarded by the commercial networks as unfair competition, diminishing their ability to sell audiences.[52] Unlike the BBC, PBS has largely conceded the terrain of popular adult programming to the commercial networks.

Conversely, it could be argued that the regulated presence of commercial television and radio in Britain liberated the BBC from the stodgy, Reithian culture it inherited, forcing the Corporation to engage with the popular rather than try to mould it from above. By contrast, for PBS to cede the idea of popular television to the commercial networks has squeezed public service broadcasting in the United States into a cultural box, one marked "quality" and marketed only to the discerning few.[53] The BBC's popular appeal means that it provides a public service in a way that PBS cannot.

My argument is that it is both premature and politically ill-advised to *concede* the notion of audience desire to the advocates for commercial, for-profit broadcasting. I would argue, instead, that we should *extend* the notion so that it refers to citizens rather than consumers. This means moving away from the philosophy of market research towards a more open spirit of public consultation. We might then go beyond the narrow terms of consumerist measurement – in which people merely choose from a pre-packaged series of options – to think about more democratic forms of citizen involvement in broadcasting. Instead of asking people what they watch, we might begin by asking what the broadcasting system *as a whole* should provide.

Public broadcasting, in other words, should invoke the public from the bottom up rather than the top down. Most people rely upon television for much of their cultural, entertainment and informational needs; the least we can do is take the radical step of asking people what form it should take.

NOTES

1. See, for example, Tracey, M., *The Decline and Fall of Public Service Broadcasting*, London: Oxford University Press, 1998; Rowland, W. D. and Tracey, M. "Worldwide Challenges to Public Service Broadcasting', *Journal of Communication*, 40 (2), 1990, 8–27.
2. Herman, E. and McChesney, R., *The Global Media: The New Missionaries of Corporate Capitalism*, London: Cassell, 1997; also see Klaehn, J. (ed.), *Filtering the News: Essays on Herman and Chomsky's Propaganda Model*, Montreal: Black Rose, 2005; Klaehn, J. (ed.), *Bound by Power: Intended Consequences*, Montreal: Black Rose, 2006.

3. Tony Blair's visit to Rupert Murdoch before his election in 1997 was to strike a coy, very British version of the Faustian bargain.
4. In the UK, widely regarded as the home of public service broadcasting, media policy – such as the 2003 Communications Act – is now underwritten with the assumptions that inextricably tie the health of the commercial sector to the health of broadcasting.
5. See Ouellette, L. and Lewis, J., "Moving Beyond the Vast Wasteland: Cultural Policy and Television in the United States", *Television and New Media*, 1(1), 2000, 95–115.
6. See Aufderheide, P., *Communications Policy and the Public Interest: The Telecommunications Act of 1996*, New York: Guilford, 1998.
7. See Blanchard, S. and Morley, D., *What's This Channel Four.* London: Comedia, 1982
8. See McChesney, R., *Rich Media, Poor Democracy,* Chicago: University of Chicago Press, 2000.
9. A survey for the Press Complaints Commission found that 54% knew little about or had never heard of the PCC, and 58% knew little about or had never heard of Ofcom. Less than one in five knew more than "just a little" about either (www.pcc.org.uk/news, May, 2007).
10. So, for example, a survey by the Work Foundation for the UK Government found that people valued the BBC and were prepared to pay more for it and to see its services expanded www.theworkfoundation.com/Assets/PDFs/DCMS.pdf (Mat, 2007)
11. The UK government's championing of the move to digital television is invariably couched in terms of increased choice and interactivity.
12. Gilens, M. and Hertzman, C., "Corporate Ownership and News Bias: Newspaper Coverage of the 1996 Telecommunications Bill", *Journal of Politics* 62(2), 2000, 369–386.
13. Ashley, J. "This BBC row is not about sources – it is about power" *The Guardian 24* July 2003 (politics.guardian.co.uk/kelly/comment/0,,1004727,00.html).
14. Pauwels, C. "From Citizenship to Consumer Sovereignty: The Paradigm Shift in European Audiovisual Policy". Andrew Calabrese and Jean-Claude Burgelman (eds.), *Communication, Citizenship, and Social Policy: Rethinking the Limits of the Welfare State.* Lanham: Rowman & Littlefield, 1999.
15. The layout of most supermarkets are designed to make shopping, from the customer's point of view, inefficient and time-consuming, in order to encourage customers to walk down as many aisles as possible, thereby maximising opportunities for impulse buying.
16. See Jhally, S. *The Codes of Advertising,* New York: Routledge, 1990; and Williamson, J. *Decoding Advertisements: Ideology and Meaning in Advertising* (4th Impression), London: Marion Boyars, 1995. Jhally argues that advertising has little to say about the concrete meaning of commodities, and constructs meanings that speak to our identities rather than to the nature of the product. In his words, "their use-value is subsumed by exchange-value" (p. 173).
17. For example, Kellner, D., *Television and the Crisis of Democracy.* Boulder: Westview, 1990. Garnham, N., "Citizens, consumers, and public culture." *Media Cultures: Reappraising Transnational Media.* (eds.) Schroder, K.C., & Skovand, M. (pp. 17–41). London: Routledge, 1992; Gerbner, G., Mowlana, H. and Schiller, H., *Invisible Crisis: What Conglomerate Control of Media Means for America and the World.* Boulder, CO: Westview Press, 1996; Schiller, H., *Information Inequality: The Deepening Social Crisis in America.* New York: Routledge, 1996; McChesney, R., *Rich Media, Poor Democracy,* Chicago: University of Chicago Press, 2000.

18. See Ang, I., *Desperately Seeking the Audience*, London: Routledge, 1991, for an extended critique of the limits of ratings.
19. Smythe, D., *Dependency Road*, Norwood, NJ: Ablex, 1980. This idea has been developed by Leiss, W., Kilne, S. and Jhally, S., *Social Communication in Advertising*, New York: Methuen, 1986; and Jhally, S., *The Codes of Advertising*, New York: Routledge, 1990.
20. Williamson, *Decoding Advertisements*, p.13.
21. Schudson, M., *Advertising: The Uneasy Persuasion. Its Dubious Impact on American Society*. New York: Basic Books, 1986, p. 210, critiqued in Ewen, S., *Captains of Consciousness*, preface to 25th anniversary edition, 2001.
22. Mander, J., *Four Arguments for the Elimination of Television*, New York: William Murrow, 1977, pp. 126–127.
23. Edwards, T., *Contradictions of Consumption*, Buckingham: Open University Press, 2000, p.188.
24. Ibid., p.189.
25. Ibid., p.191.
26. *The New Rulers of the World* (ITV, 18 July 2001).
27. This argument is made in compelling and apocalyptic terms in Sut Jhally's video, *Advertising and the End of the World*, Media Education Foundation, 1998.
28. Mander, *Four Arguments*, p.128.
29. Wernick, A., *Promotional Culture: Advertising, Ideology and Symbolic Expression*, London: Sage, 1991, p.192.
30. Richard Layard, *Lionel Robbins Memorial Lectures* 2002/3, delivered on 3, 4, 5 March 2003 at the London School of Economics.
31. Oswald, A. "How Much do External Factors Affect Wellbeing? A Way to Use "Happiness Economics" to Decide', *The Psychologist*, 16, 2003, 140–141.
32. Layard, *Lionel Robbins Memorial Lectures*.
33. Jhally, S. "Advertising at the Edge of the Apocalypse" in S. Jhally, *The Spectacle of Accumulation*, 2006, New York: Peter Lang, pp 99–112.
34. Frey, B and Stutzer, A., *Happiness and Economics: How the Economy and Institutions Affect Human Well-Being*, New Jersey: Princeton University Press, 2001.
35. Leiss, Kline and Jhally, *Social Communication*, p.16.
36. Kasser, T., *The High Price of Materialism*, Cambridge MA: MIT Press, 2002.
37. Schor,J., *Born to Buy*, New York: Scribner, 2004, p.167.
38. Layard, *Lionel Robbins Memorial Lectures*.
39. Example in the U.S. include the *Beverley Hillbillies* and *Dr. Quinn, Medicine Woman*.
40. Herman, E., and Chomsky, N., The *Manufacture of Consent*, New York: Pantheon, 1988.
41. See Douglas, S., *Inventing American Broadcasting, 1899–1922*, Baltimore MD: John Hopkins University Press, 1987; Schiller, H., "Media, Technology, and the Market: The Interacting Dynamic', in Bender, G. and Druckrey, T.(eds.), Culture on the Brink: Ideologies of Technology, Seattle, WA: Bay Press, 1994.
42. Postman, N., *Amusing Ourselves to Death: Public Discourse in the Age of Show Business*, New York: Penguin Books, 1985.
43. Ang, I., *Desperately Seeking the Audience*, London: Routledge, 1991.
44. Lewis, J., Cushion, S. and Thomas, J., "Immediacy, Convenience or Engagement? An Analysis of 24-hour News Channels in the UK", *Journalism Studies*, 6 (4), 2005, 461–477.

Although it is possible, given the laxity of the regulation, that channels like *Sky News* broadcast fewer ads during the night when audiences are small, which may put their *average* number of commercial minutes per hour within the permitted limits.

45. See blogs.guardian.co.uk/organgrinder/2006/07/itvs_summer_of_doom_1.html - 56k (26 Apr 2007)
46. Miller, T. and Kim, L., "Overview: It Isn't TV, It's the "Real King of the Ring" in *The Essential HBO Reader*, Eds. Gary R. Edgerton and Jeffrey P. Jones. 2008, Lexington: University of Kentucky Press, 217–36.
47. I am indebted to Toby Miller for this observation.
48. Wernick, *Promotional Culture.*
49. See Barwise, T., and Ehrenberg, A., *Television and its Audience.* London: London Business School, 1984.
50. See Miller, T. and Kim, L., *The HBO Reader*, in Edgerton, G and Jones, J.P.(eds.), University of Kentucky Press, 2007.
51. Ouellette, L., "TV Viewing as Good Citizenship? Political Rationality, Enlightened Democracy and PBS", *Cultural Studies* 13 (1), 1999, 62–90.
52. Ibid., 62–90.
53. Ouellette, L. and Lewis, J., "Moving beyond the 'Vast Wasteland': Cultural Policy and Television in the United States", *Television & New Media*, 2(1), 2000 pp. 93–113.

INDEX